About the Authors

Mike Alexander is a Microsoft Certified Application Developer (MCAD) and author of several books on advanced business analysis using Microsoft Access and Excel. He has more than 15 years experience consulting and developing Microsoft Office solutions. Michael has been named a Microsoft MVP for his ongoing contributions to the Excel community. In his spare time he runs a free tutorial site, `www.datapigtechnologies.com`, where he shares basic Access and Excel tips with the Office community.

John Walkenbach is a bestselling Excel author who has published more than 50 books on spread-sheets. He lives amid the saguaros, javelinas, rattlesnakes, bobcats, and gila monsters in southern Arizona — but the critters are mostly scared away by his clawhammer banjo playing. For more information, Google him.

Dedication

This is dedicated to the fans of `DataPigTechnologies.com`...all twelve of you.

Michael Alexander

Excel® Dashboards and Reports

2nd Edition

by Michael Alexander and John Walkenbach

WILEY

Excel® Dashboards and Reports, 2nd Edition

Published by
John Wiley & Sons, Inc.
111 River Street
Hoboken, NJ 07030-5774

www.wiley.com

For general information on our other products and services, please contact our Customer Care Department within the U.S. at 877-762-2974, outside the U.S. at 317-572-3993, or fax 317-572-4002.

For technical support, please visit www.wiley.com/techsupport.

Wiley also publishes its books in a variety of electronic formats. Some material included with standard print versions of this book may not be included in e-books or in print-on-demand. If this book refers to media such as a CD or DVD that is not included in the version you purchased, you may download this material at http://booksupport.wiley.com. For more information about Wiley products, visit www.wiley.com.

Library of Congress Control Number: 2013934910

ISBN 978-1-118-49042-6 (pbk); ISBN 978-1-118-49043-3 (ebk); ISBN 978-1-118-49150-8 (ebk); ISBN 978-1-118-49141-6 (ebk)

Manufactured in the United States of America

10 9 8 7 6 5 4 3

Author's Acknowledgments

My deepest thanks to Katie Mohr and Pat O'Brien, for all the hours of work put into making this book as clear as it can be. Thanks also to the brilliant team of professionals who helped bring this book to fruition. Finally, a special thank you goes to my family for putting up with all the time spent away on this project.

Michael Alexander

Publisher's Acknowledgments

We're proud of this book; please send us your comments at http://dummies.custhelp.com. For other comments, please contact our Customer Care Department within the U.S. at 877-762-2974, outside the U.S. at 317-572-3993, or fax 317-572-4002.

Some of the people who helped bring this book to market include the following:

Acquisitions, Editorial, and Vertical Websites

Sr. Project Editor: Pat O'Brien

Acquisitions Editor: Katie Mohr

Copy Editor: Melba Hoppper

Technical Editor: Doug Steele

Editorial Manager: Kevin Kirschner

Vertical Websites Project Manager:
Laura Moss-Hollister

Editorial Assistant: Annie Sullivan

Sr. Editorial Assistant: Cherie Case

Composition Services

Project Coordinator: Katie Crocker

Layout and Graphics: Jennifer Goldsmith, Christin Swinford, Erin Zeltner

Proofreaders: ConText Editorial Services, Inc., Susan Moritz

Indexer: Ty Koontz

Publishing and Editorial for Technology Dummies

Richard Swadley, Vice President and Executive Group Publisher

Andy Cummings, Vice President and Publisher

Mary Bednarek, Executive Acquisitions Director

Mary C. Corder, Editorial Director

Publishing for Consumer Dummies

Kathleen Nebenhaus, Vice President and Executive Publisher

Composition Services

Debbie Stailey, Director of Composition Services

▶ Contents at a Glance

▶ Table of Contents

Part I: Getting Started with Excel Dashboards

Part II: Introducing Charts into Your Dashboards

Part III: Advanced Dashboarding Concepts

Part IV: Pivot Table Driven Dashboards

Part V: Working with the Outside World

INTRODUCTION

Business intelligence (BI) is what you get when you analyze raw data and turn that information into actionable knowledge. BI can help an organization identify cost-cutting opportunities, uncover new business opportunities, recognize changing business environments, identify data anomalies, and create widely accessible reports.

The BI concept is overtaking corporate executives who are eager to turn impossible amounts of data into useful knowledge. As a result of this trend, software vendors who focus on BI and build dashboards are coming out of the woodwork. Dashboards are ideal mechanisms for delivering this targeted information in a graphical, user-friendly form. New consulting firms touting their BI knowledge are popping up virtually every week. And even the traditional enterprise solution providers like Business Objects and SAP are offering new BI capabilities presented in a dashboard format.

So maybe you've been hit with dashboard fever? Or maybe you're holding this book because someone is asking you to create BI solutions (that is, create a dashboard) in Excel.

Although many IT managers would scoff at the thought of using Excel as a BI tool to create a dashboard, Excel is inherently part of the enterprise-BI-tool portfolio. Whether IT managers are keen to acknowledge it or not, most of the data analysis and reporting done in business today is done by using a spreadsheet program. We see several significant reasons to use Excel as the platform for your dashboards and reports. They are as follows:

> ➤ Familiarity with Excel: If you work in corporate America, you're conversant in the language of Excel. You can send even the most seasoned senior vice-president an Excel-based presentation and trust he'll know what to do with it. With an Excel dashboard, your users spend less time figuring how to use the tool and more time viewing the data.

> ➤ Built-in flexibility: With most enterprise dashboards, the ability to analyze the data outside of the predefined views is either disabled or unavailable. In Excel, features such as pivot tables, drop-down lists, and other interactive controls (such as a check box) don't lock your audience into one view. And because an Excel workbook contains multiple worksheets, the users have space to add their own data analysis as needed.

➤ Rapid development: Using Excel to build your own dashboards can liberate you from assorted resource and time limitations from within an organization. With Excel, you can develop dashboards faster and adapt more quickly to changing business requirements.

➤ Powerful data connectivity and automation capabilities: Excel is not the toy application some IT managers make it out to be. With its own native programming language and its robust object model, Excel can help to automate certain processes and even connect with various data sources. With a few advanced techniques, your dashboard can practically run on its own.

➤ Little to no incremental costs: Not all of us can work for multi-billion dollar companies that can afford enterprise-level reporting solutions. In most companies, funding for new computers and servers is limited, let alone funding for expensive dashboard software packages. For those companies, Excel is frankly the most cost-effective way to deliver key business reporting tools without compromising too deeply on usability and function.

Excel contains so many functions and features that it's difficult to know where to start. Enter your humble authors, spirited into your hands via this book. Here we show you how you can turn Excel into your own personal BI tool. With a few fundamentals and some of the new BI functionality Microsoft has included in this latest version of Excel, you can go from reporting data with simple tables to creating meaningful dashboards sure to wow everyone.

What You Need to Know

The goal of this book is to show you how to leverage Excel functionality to build and manage better presentations. Each chapter in this book provides a comprehensive review of Excel functions and features, and the analytical concepts that will help you create better reporting components — components that can be used for both dashboards and reports. As you move through this book, you'll be able to create increasingly sophisticated components.

After reading this book, you'll be able to:

➤ Analyze large amounts of data and report those results in a meaningful way.

➤ Get better visibility into data from different perspectives.

➤ Add interactive controls to show various views.

➤ Automate repetitive tasks and processes.

➤ Create eye-catching visualizations.

➤ Create impressive dashboards and What-If analyses.

➤ Access external data sources to expand your message.

What You Need to Have

In order to get the most out of this book, it's best that you have certain skills before diving into the topics highlighted in this book. The ideal candidate for this book will have the following:

> ➤ Some experience working with data and familiarity with the basic concepts of data analysis such as working with tables, aggregating data, and performing calculations

> ➤ Experience using Excel with a strong grasp of concepts such as table structures, filtering, sorting, and using formulas

Conventions in This Book

Take a minute to skim this section and become familiar with some of the typographic conventions used throughout this book.

Keyboard conventions

You need to use the keyboard to enter formulas. In addition, you can work with menus and dialog boxes directly from the keyboard — a method you may find easier if your hands are already positioned over the keys.

Formula listings

Formulas usually appear on a separate line in monospace font. For example, we may list the following formula:

```
=VLOOKUP(StockNumber,PriceList,2,False)
```

Excel supports a special type of formula known as an array formula. When you enter an array formula, press Ctrl+Shift+Enter (not just Enter). Excel encloses an array formula in brackets in order to remind you that it's an array formula. When we list an array formula, we include the brackets to make it clear that it is, in fact, an array formula. For example:

```
{=SUM(LEN(A1:A10))}
```

Note

Do not type the brackets for an array formula. Excel puts them in automatically.

Key names

Names of keys on the keyboard appear in normal type, for example Alt, Home, PgDn, and Ctrl. When you need to press two keys simultaneously, the keys are connected with a plus sign: for example, "Press Ctrl+G to display the Go To dialog box."

Functions, procedures, and named ranges

Excel's worksheet functions appear in all uppercase, like so: "Use the SUM function to add the values in column A."

Macro and procedure names appear in normal type: "Execute the InsertTotals procedure." We often use mixed upper- and lowercase letters to make these names easier to read. Named ranges appear in italic: "Select the *InputArea* range."

Unless you're dealing with text inside quotation marks, Excel is not sensitive to case. In other words, both of the following formulas produce the same result:

```
=SUM(A1:A50)
=sum(a1:a50)
```

Excel, however, will convert the characters in the second formula to uppercase.

Mouse conventions

The mouse terminology in this book is all standard fare: "pointing," "clicking," "right-clicking," "dragging," and so on. You know the drill.

What the icons mean

Throughout the book, icons appear to call your attention to points that are particularly important.

New Feature

This icon indicates a feature new to Excel 2013.

Note

This icon tells you that something is important — perhaps a concept that may help you master the task at hand or something fundamental for understanding subsequent material.

Tip

This icon indicates a more efficient way of doing something or a technique that may not be obvious. These icons will often impress your officemates.

On the Web

This icon indicates that an example file is on the companion website:
www.wiley.com/go/exceldr

Caution

We use Caution icons when the operation that we're describing can cause problems if you're not careful.

Cross-Ref

We use the Cross-Reference icon to refer you to other chapters that have more to say on a particular topic.

How This Book Is Organized

The chapters in this book are organized into six parts. Each of these parts includes chapters that build on the previous chapters' instruction. The idea is that as you go through each part, you will be able to build dashboards of increasing complexity until you're an Excel dashboarding guru.

Part I: Getting Started with Excel Dashboards

Part I is all about helping you think about your data in terms of creating effective dashboards and reports. Chapter 1 introduces you to the topics of dashboards and reports, defining some of the basic concepts and outlining key steps to take to prepare for a successful project. Chapter 2 shows you how to design effective data tables. Chapter 3 shows you how you can leverage the sparkline functionality found in Excel 2013. Finally, Chapter 4 rounds out this section with a look at the various techniques that you can use to visualize data without the use of charts or graphs.

Part II: Introducing Charts into Your Dashboards

Part II provides a solid foundation in visualizing data using Excel charts. Chapter 5 starts with the basics, introducing you to Excel's charting engine. Chapters 6 and 7 focus on formatting techniques that enable you to build customized charts that fit your distinct needs. After that, Part II takes you beyond basic chart-building with a look at some advanced business techniques that can help make your dashboards more meaningful. Starting with Chapter 8, we demonstrate how to represent trending across multiple series and distinct time periods. In Chapter 9, we explore how best to use charts to group data into meaningful views. And Chapter 10 demonstrates some of charting techniques that can help you display and measure performance against a target. By the end of this section, you will be able to effectively leverage Excel charts to synthesize your data into meaningful visualizations.

Part III: Advanced Dashboarding Concepts

In Part III, we offer an in-depth look at some of the key dashboarding concepts you can leverage to create a cutting–edge dashboard presentation. Chapter 11 shows you how to build an effective data model that provides the foundation upon which your dashboard or report is built. In this chapter, you discover the impact of poorly organized data and how to set up the source data for the most positive outcome. Chapter 12 illustrates how interactive controls can provide your clients with a simple interface, allowing them to easily navigate through and interact with your dashboard or report. Chapter 13 provides a clear understanding of how you can leverage macros to automate your reporting systems.

Part IV: Pivot Table Driven Dashboards

With Part IV, you find out how pivot tables can enhance your analytical and reporting capabilities, as well as your dashboards. In Chapter 14, we introduce you to pivot tables and explore how this Excel feature can play an integral role in Excel-based presentations. Chapter 15 provides a primer on building pivot charts, giving you a solid understanding of how Excel pivot charts work with pivot tables. Chapter 16 shows you how pivot slicers can add interactive filtering capabilities to your pivot reporting. Finally, Chapter 17 introduces you to the new internal Data Model and Power View features of Excel 2013.

Part V: Working with the Outside World

The theme in Part V is importing information from external data sources. Chapter 18 explores some of the ways to incorporate data that doesn't originate in Excel. In this chapter, you learn how to import data from external sources, such as Microsoft Access and SQL Server, as well as create systems that allow for dynamic refreshing of external data sources. Chapter 19 wraps up this look at Excel dashboards and reports by showing you the various ways to distribute and present your work in a safe and effective way.

About the Companion Website

This book contains many examples, and the workbooks for those examples are available on the companion website that is arranged in directories that correspond to the chapters. You can download example files for this book at the following website:

```
www.wiley.com/go/exceldr
```

The example workbook files on the website aren't compressed (installation isn't required). These files are all Excel 2007–2013 files.

About the Power Utility Pak Offer

Toward the back of the book, you'll find a coupon that you can redeem for a discounted copy of John Walkenbach's award-winning Power Utility Pak — a collection of useful Excel utilities, plus many new worksheet functions. John developed this package using VBA exclusively.

You can also use this coupon to purchase the complete VBA source code for a nominal fee. Studying the code is an excellent way to pick up some useful programming techniques.

You can download a 30-day trial version of the most-recent version of the Power Utility Pak from John's website:

```
http://spreadsheetpage.com
```

If you find it useful, use the coupon to purchase a licensed copy at a discount.

Reach Out

We're always interested in getting feedback on our books. The best way to provide this feedback is via e-mail. Send your comments and suggestions to

```
mha105@yahoo.com
john@j-walk.com
```

Unfortunately, we're not able to reply to specific questions. Posting your question to one of the Excel newsgroups is, by far, the best way to get such assistance.

Also, when you're out surfing the web, don't overlook John's website ("The Spreadsheet Page"). You'll find lots of useful Excel information, including tips and downloads. The URL is

```
http://spreadsheetpage.com
```

Now, without further ado, it's time to turn the page and expand your horizons.

Getting Started with Excel Dashboards

Introducing Dashboards

1

In This Chapter

- Defining dashboards and reports
- Determining user requirements
- Establishing visualization and design principles
- Reviewing your dashboard prior to distribution

Creating a dashboard in Excel is not the same as creating a standard table-driven analysis. It's tempting to jump right in and start building away, but a dashboard requires far more preparation than a typical Excel report. It calls for closer communication with business leaders, stricter data modeling techniques, and the following of certain best practices. It's helpful to be familiar with fundamental dashboard concepts before venturing off into the mechanics of building your own. In this chapter, we discuss basic dashboard concepts and design principles and what it takes to prepare for a dashboarding project.

On the Web

All workbook examples that we list in this book are available on this book's companion website at `www.wiley.com/go/exceldr`.

What Are Dashboards and Reports?

It isn't difficult to use the words *report* and *dashboard* interchangeably. In fact, the line between dashboards and reports frequently gets muddied. We see countless reports that are referred to as dashboards just because they include a few charts. Likewise, we see many examples of what could be considered dashboards but are called reports.

Now this may all seem like semantics to you, but it's helpful to clear the air a bit and understand the core attributes of both dashboards and reports.

Defining reports

Reports are probably the most common way to communicate business intelligence. A *report* can be described as a document that contains data used for viewing and analysis. It can be as simple as a data table (or a database) or as complex as a subtotaled view with interactive drilling.

The key attribute of a report is that it doesn't lead a reader to a predefined conclusion. Although a report can include analysis, aggregations, calculations, and even charts, reports often require the reader to apply his own judgment and analysis to the data.

To clarify this concept, Figure 1-1 shows an example of a report. This report shows National Park visitor statistics by year. Although this data can be useful, this report doesn't steer the reader to any predefined conclusions or in any directions; it simply presents the aggregated data.

	A	B	C	D	E	F
4		**Number of Visitors (thousands)**				
5		2001	2002	2003	2004	2005
6	Great Smoky Mountains NP	9,198	9,316	9,367	9,167	9,192
7	Grand Canyon NP	4,105	4,002	4,125	4,326	4,402
8	Yosemite NP	3,369	3,362	3,379	3,281	3,304
9	Olympic NP	3,416	3,691	3,225	3,074	3,143
10	Yellowstone NP	2,759	2,974	3,019	2,868	2,836
11	Rocky Mountain NP	3,140	2,988	3,067	2,782	2,798
12	Cuyahoga Valley NP	3,123	3,218	2,880	3,306	2,534
13	Zion NP	2,218	2,593	2,459	2,677	2,587
14	Grand Teton NP	2,535	2,613	2,356	2,360	2,463
15	Acadia NP	2,517	2,559	2,431	2,208	2,051
16	Glacier NP	1,681	1,906	1,664	2,034	1,925
17	Hot Springs NP	1,297	1,440	1,561	1,419	1,340
18	Hawaii Volcanoes NP	1,343	1,111	992	1,307	1,661

Figure 1-1: Reports present data for viewing but don't lead readers to predefined conclusions.

Defining dashboards

A *dashboard* is a visual interface that provides at-a-glance views into key measures relevant to a particular objective or business process. A dashboard consists of three key attributes.

➤ Displays data graphically (such as in charts). Provides visualizations that help focus attention on key trends, comparisons, and exceptions.

➤ Displays only data that is relevant to the goal of the dashboard.

➤ Contains predefined conclusions relevant to the goal of the dashboard and relieves the reader from having to perform her own analysis.

Figure 1-2 illustrates a dashboard that uses the same data shown in Figure 1-1. This dashboard displays information about National Park attendance. As you can see, this presentation has all the key attributes that define a dashboard. First, it's a visual display that allows you to quickly recognize the overall trend of the attendance. Second, not all the details of the data are shown in this presentation; only the key pieces of information that support the goal of this dashboard. Finally, by virtue of its objective, this dashboard effectively presents you with analysis and conclusions about the trending of attendance.

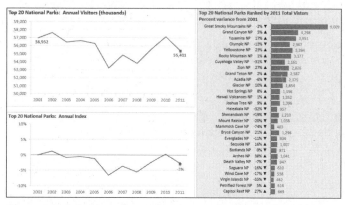

Figure 1-2: A dashboard provides an at-a-glance view into key measures relevant to a particular objective or business process.

As you take in this concept of reports versus dashboards, remember that Excel doesn't provide tools specifically designed for dashboards or reports. The beauty of Excel is that any of its tools can be used to perform virtually any task that you need. For example, you can use the chart, pivot tables, and macros features in a basic report or to play a key role in a dashboard presentation. In this book, we introduce you to the many ways that you can leverage everyday Excel tools to build your own dashboard components.

Establish the User Requirements

Imagine that your objective is to create a dashboard that provides information about monthly service subscriptions. Do you jump to action and slap together whatever comes to mind? Do you take a guess at what information would be useful in a dashboard like this? These questions sound ridiculous, but it happens more that you think. We are constantly called to action but are rarely provided the time to gather the true requirements for the project. Between limited information and false deadlines, the end product often ends up not being used or causing more work than value.

This brings us to one of the key steps in preparing to build a dashboard — collecting user requirements. These user requirements include defining your audience, data sources, performance measures, refresh schedules, and so on.

In the non-IT world of the Excel analyst, user requirements are practically useless because of the hard left and right turns we're asked to make every day. So the gathering of user requirements sometimes seems like a waste of valuable time in the ever-changing business environment.

But it's time to get into the dashboard state of mind. After all, would you rather spend your time upfront gathering user requirements or at the end painstakingly redesigning the dashboard you'll surely come to hate?

Consider how many times you've been asked for an analysis, only to be told, "No. I meant this." Or, "Now that I see it, I realize I need this." As frustrating as that can be for a single analysis, imagine running into this during the creation of a complex dashboard with several data integration processes.

The process of gathering user requirements doesn't have to be an overly complicated or formal one. Here are some simple things you can do to ensure that you have a solid idea of the purpose of the dashboard.

When collecting user requirements for your dashboard, focus on the types of data that you need, the dimensions of data that you require, the data sources that you will use, and so on. This is a good thing; without solid data processes, your dashboards won't be effective or maintainable.

Define the message(s)

When receiving requirements for a new dashboard project, don't be afraid to clarify who exactly is making the initial request and talk to them about what they're really asking for. Discuss the purpose of the dashboard and the triggers that caused them to ask for a dashboard in the first place. You may find, after discussing the matter, that a simple Excel report will meet their needs, foregoing the need for a full-on dashboard.

Establish the audience

If a dashboard is warranted, talk about who the end users will be. Take some time to meet with some of the end users and talk about how they plan to use the dashboard. For example, will the dashboard be used as a performance tool for regional managers or perhaps to share data with external customers? Talking through these fundamentals with the right people will help align your thoughts and avoid missed requirements later.

Define the performance measures

Most dashboards are designed around a set of measures called *Key Performance Indicators (KPIs)*. A KPI is an indicator of the level of performance of a task deemed to be essential to daily operations or processes. The idea around a KPI is that it will reveal performance that is outside the norm, signaling the need for attention and intervention. Although the measures you place into your dashboards may not officially be called KPIs, they undoubtedly serve the same purpose — to draw attention to problem areas.

The topic of creating effective KPIs for your organization is worthy of its own book and outside the scope for this endeavor. For a detailed guide on KPI development strategies, pick up David Parmenter's book, *Key Performance Indicators: Developing, Implementing, and Using Winning KPIs,* published by John Wiley & Sons, Inc. This book provides an excellent step-by-step approach to developing and implementing KPIs.

The measures that you use on a dashboard should support the initial goal of that dashboard. For example, if you create a dashboard that focuses on supply chain processes, it may not make sense to have HR head count data included. It's generally good to avoid *nice-to-know* data in your dashboards simply to fill white space or because the data is available. If the data doesn't support the core goal of the dashboard, leave it out.

Here's another tip. When gathering the measures required for the dashboard, we find that it often helps to write out a sentence to describe the measure needed. For example, instead of simply writing the word "Revenue" into our user requirements, we write what we call a *component question* such as "What is the overall revenue trend for the last two years?" We call it a component question because we will ultimately task a single component, such as a chart or a table, to answer the question. For instance, if the component question is "What is the overall revenue trend for the last two years?" you can imagine a chart component answering that question by showing the two-year revenue trend.

We sometimes take this a step further and actually incorporate the component questions into a mock layout of the dashboard to get a high-level sense of what data the dashboard will require. Figure 1-3 illustrates an example.

Each box in this dashboard layout mockup represents a component on the dashboard and its approximate position. The questions within each box provide a sense of the types of data required to create the measures for the dashboard.

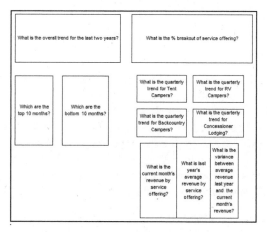

Figure 1-3: Each box in this dashboard layout mockup represents a component and the type of data required to create the measures.

List the required data sources

After you have the list of measures that you need on the dashboard, it's important to take a tally of the available databases or other source systems to determine whether the data required to produce those measures is available.

> ➤ Do you have access to the data sources necessary?
>
> ➤ How often are those data sources updated?
>
> ➤ Who owns and maintains those data sources?
>
> ➤ What are the processes to get the data from those resources?
>
> ➤ Does the data even exist?

You'll need answers to these questions when negotiating development time, refresh intervals, and phasing.

Tip

Conventional wisdom says that the measures on your dashboard should not be governed by the availability of data. Instead, let dashboard KPIs and measures govern the data sources in your organization. Although we agree with the spirit of that statement, we've been involved in too many dashboard projects that have fallen apart because of lack of data. Real-world experience has taught us the difference between the ideal and the ordeal.

If your organizational strategy requires that you collect and measure data that is nonexistent or not available, press pause on the dashboard project and turn your attention to creating a data collection mechanism that will help you to get the data you need.

Define the dimensions and filters

In the context of building a dashboard, a *dimension* is a data category that you use to organize business data. Examples of dimensions are region, market, branch, manager, and employee. When you define a dimension in the user requirements stage, you can determine how the measures should be grouped or distributed. For example, if your dashboard should report data by employee, you will need to ensure that your data collection processes include employee details. As you can imagine, adding a new dimension after the dashboard is built can get complicated, especially when your processes require collecting data across multiple data sources. The bottom line is that locking down the dimensions for a dashboard early in the process will definitely save you headaches.

Along those same lines, you want to know the types of filters that you'll need. *Filters* are mechanisms that allow you to narrow the scope of the data to a single dimension. For example, you can filter by year, employee, or region. Again, if you don't account for a particular filter while establishing your data collection process, you will likely be forced into an unpleasant redesign of both your processes and your dashboard.

Determine the need for drill-down details

Many dashboards provide drill-down features that allow you to click through to the details of a specific measure. You want to get a clear understanding of the types of drill downs your users have in mind.

To most users, a drill-down feature means the ability to get a raw data table supporting the measures shown on the dashboard. Although this isn't always practical or possible, at minimum, you can set expectations and document the request for future dashboard versions. This allows you to plan for any macros, links, or other solutions that you may have to include with your dashboards.

Establish the update schedule

An *update schedule* refers to how often a dashboard is changed to reflect the latest information available. As the one who will build and maintain the dashboard, it's important that you have a say in these schedules. Your customer may not know what it will take to update the dashboard in question. While talking about this schedule, keep in mind the refresh rates of the different data sources you will need to get the measures. You won't be able to refresh your dashboard any faster than your data sources. Also, negotiate enough development time to build macros that will automate redundant and time-consuming updating tasks.

A Quick Look at Dashboard Design Principles

Excel users live in a world of numbers and tables, not visualization and design. Your typical Excel analyst has no background in visual design and is often left to rely on his own visual instincts to design his dashboards. As a result, most Excel-based dashboards have little thought given to effective visual design, often resulting in overly cluttered and ineffective UI.

The good news is that dashboards have been around for a long time, so we have a vast Knowledge Base of prescribed visualization and dashboard design principles. Although many of these principles seem like common sense, these are concepts that Excel users don't think about regularly. Let's break that trend and review a few dashboard design principles that will improve the design of your Excel dashboards.

Note

Many of the concepts in this section come from the work of Stephen Few, visualization expert and author of several books and articles on dashboard design principles. Because this book focuses on the technical aspects of building dashboards in Excel, this section offers a high-level look at dashboard design. If you find yourself captivated by the subject, feel free to visit www.perceptualedge.com **to see Stephen Few's website.**

Rule number 1: Keep it simple

Dashboard design expert Stephen Few has the mantra, "Simplify, Simplify, Simplify." A dashboard that is cluttered with too many measures and too much eye candy can dilute the significant information that you're trying to present. How many times has someone told you that your reports look busy? In essence, they're saying that you have too much on the page or screen, making it hard to see the actual data.

Here are few actions you can take to ensure a simpler and more effective dashboard design.

Don't turn your dashboard into a data mart

Admit it. You include as much information in a report as possible, primarily to avoid being asked for additional information. We all do it. But in the dashboard state of mind, you have to fight the urge to force every piece of data available onto your dashboard.

Overwhelming users with too much data can cause them to lose sight of the primary goal of the dashboard and focus on inconsequential data. The measures used on a dashboard should support the initial purpose of that dashboard. Avoid the urge to fill white space for the sake of symmetry and appearances. Don't include nice-to-know data just because the data is available. If the data doesn't support the core purpose of the dashboard, leave it out.

Forget about the fancy formatting

The key to communicating effectively with your dashboard is to present your data as simply as possible. There's no need to wrap it in eye candy to make it more interesting. It's okay to have a dashboard with little to no color or formatting. You'll find that the lack of fancy formatting only calls attention to the actual data. Focus on the data and not shiny happy graphics.

To help drive this point home, we created the chart shown in Figure 1-4 (formatting and all). Excel makes it easy to achieve these types of effects with its layout and style features. The problem is that these effects subdue the very data we're trying to present. Furthermore, if we include this chart on a page with five to ten other charts with the same formatting, we get a dashboard that's difficult to look at — much less to read.

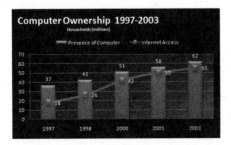

Figure 1-4: Fancy formatting can be overwhelming, overshadowing the very data you're trying to present.

Figure 1-5 shows the same data without the fancy formatting. Not only is the chart easier to read but also you can process the data more effectively from this chart.

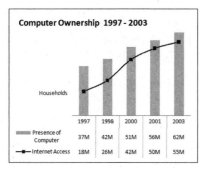

Figure 1-5: Charts should present your data as simply as possible.

Here are some simple tips to keep from overdoing the fancy factor:

➤ Avoid using colors or background fills to organize your dashboards. Colors, in general, should be used sparingly, reserved only for information about key data points. For example, assigning red, yellow, and green to measures traditionally indicates performance level. Coloring sections of your dashboard only distracts your audience from your message.

➤ De-emphasize borders, backgrounds, and other elements that define dashboard areas. Try to use the natural white space between your components to partition your dashboard. If borders are necessary, format them to lighter hues than your data. Light grays are typically ideal for borders. The idea is to indicate sections without distracting from the information displayed.

➤ Excel 2013 makes it easy to apply effects that make everything look shiny, glittery, and generally happy. Although these formatting features make for great marketing tools, they don't do you or your dashboard any favors. Avoid applying fancy effects such as gradients, pattern fills, shadows, glow, soft edges, and other formatting.

➤ Don't try to enhance your dashboard with clip art or pictures. They do nothing to further data presentation, and they often just look tacky.

Skip the unnecessary chart junk

Data visualization pioneer Edward Tufte introduced the notion of data-to-ink ratio. Tufte's basic idea is that a large percentage of the ink on your chart (or on your dashboard) should be dedicated to data. Very little ink should represent what he calls chart junk: borders, gridlines, trend lines, labels, backgrounds, and so on.

Figure 1-6 illustrates the impact that chart junk can have on the ability to effectively communicate your data. Notice how convoluted and cramped the data looks in the top chart.

The bottom chart actually contains the same data. Yet, it more effectively presents the core message that driver registrations in Texas rose from approximately 10.5 million to almost 17 million. This message was diluted in the top chart by excess clutter. So you can see from this simple example how your chart dramatically improves by simply removing elements that don't directly contribute to the core message.

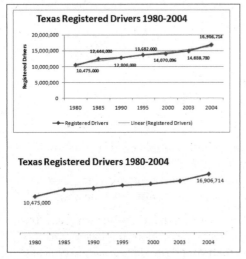

Figure 1-6: Charts with too many chart elements can become convoluted and hard to read. Removing the unnecessary elements clarifies the message.

Here are a few ways to avoid chart junk and ensure that your charts clearly present your data.

➤ **Remove gridlines:** Gridlines (both vertical and horizontal) are almost always unnecessary. The implied reason for gridlines is that they help to visually gauge the value represented by each data point. The truth is, however, people typically gauge the value of a data point by comparing its position to the other data points in the chart. So gridlines become secondary reference points that simply take up ink.

➤ **Remove borders:** You'll find that eliminating borders and frames gives your charts a cleaner look and helps you avoid the dizzying lines you get when placing multiple charts with borders on a single dashboard. Instead of borders, make use of the white space between the charts as implied borders.

➤ **Skip the trend lines:** Seldom does a trend line provide insight that can't be gained with the already plotted data or a simple label. In fact, trend lines often state the obvious and sometimes confuse readers into thinking they are part of another data series. Why place a trend line on a line chart when the line chart is in and of itself a trend line of sorts? Why place a trend line on a bar chart when it's just as easy to look at the tops of the bars? In lieu of trend lines, add a simple label that states what you're trying to say about the overall trend of the data.

➤ **Avoid unnecessary data labels:** Nothing states that you need to show the data label for every value on your chart. It's okay to plot a data point and not display its value. You'll find that your charts have more impact when you show only numbers that are relevant to your message.

➤ **Don't show a legend if you don't have to:** When you're plotting one data series, you don't need to display a space-taking chart legend. Allow your chart title to identify the data that your chart represents.

➤ **Remove any axis that doesn't add value:** The purpose of the X and Y axes are to help a user visually gauge and position the values represented by each data point. However, if the nature and utility of the chart doesn't require a particular axis, remove it. Again, the goal here is not to hack away at your chart. The goal is to include only those chart elements that directly contribute to the core message of your chart.

Limit each dashboard to one viewable page or screen

A dashboard should provide an at-a-glance view into key measures relevant to a particular objective or business process. This implies that all the data is immediately viewable at one time. Although this isn't always the easiest thing to do, it's best to see all the data on one page or screen. You can compare sections more easily, you can process cause and effect relationships more effectively, and you rely less on short-term memory. When a user has to scroll left, right, or down, these benefits are diminished. Furthermore, users tend to believe that when information is placed out of normal view (areas that require scrolling), it is somehow less important.

But what if you can't fit all the data in one viewable area (one page or one screen)? First, review the measures on your dashboard and determine if they really need to be there. Next, format your dashboard to use less space (format fonts, reduce white space, adjust column and row widths). Finally, try adding interactivity to your dashboard, allowing users to dynamically change views to show only those measures that are relevant to them.

 We discuss how to add interactive features in Chapter 12.

Cross-Ref

Use layout and placement to draw focus

As discussed earlier in this chapter, only include measures that support your dashboard's goal. However, just because all measures on your dashboard are significant, they may not always have the same level of importance. In other words, you will frequently want one component of your dashboard to stand out from the others.

Instead of using bright colors or exaggerated sizing differences, you can leverage location and placement to draw focus to the most important components on your dashboard.

Various studies have shown that readers have a natural tendency to focus on particular regions of a document. For example, researchers at the Poynter Institute's Eyetracker III project have found that readers view various regions on a screen in a certain order, paying particular attention to specific regions on the screen. They use the diagram in Figure 1-7 to illustrate what they call *priority zones*. Regions with the number 1 in the diagram seem to have high prominence, attracting the most attention for longer periods of time. Meanwhile number 3 regions seem to have low prominence.

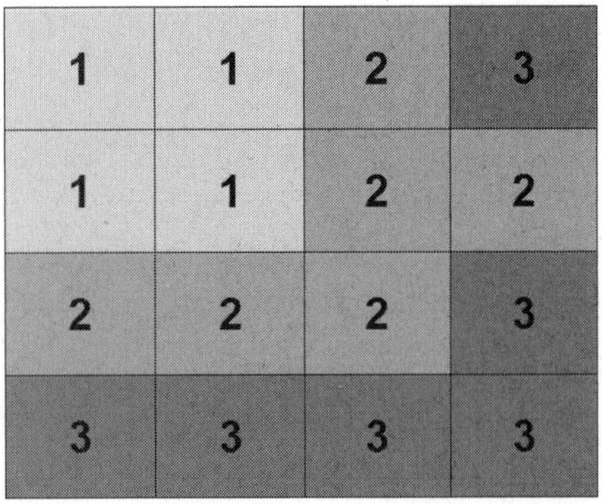

1	1	2	3
1	1	2	2
2	2	2	3
3	3	3	3

Figure 1-7: Studies show that users pay particular attention to the upper left and middle left of a document.

You can leverage these priority zones to promote or demote certain components based on significance. If one of the charts on your dashboard warrants special focus, you can simply place that chart in a region of prominence.

Tip

> Surrounding colors, borders, fonts, and other formatting can affect the viewing patterns of your readers, de-emphasizing a previously high-prominence region.

Format numbers effectively

Undoubtedly, you will use lots of numbers in your dashboards. Some of them will be in charts, whereas others will be in tables. Remember that every piece of information on your dashboard should have a purpose. It's important that you format your numbers effectively so your users can understand the information they represent without confusion or hindrance.

Here are some guidelines to keep in mind when formatting the numbers in your dashboards and reports.

➤ Always use commas to make numbers easier to read. For example, instead of 2345, show 2,345.

➤ Only use decimal places if that level of precision is required. For instance, there is rarely a benefit for showing the decimal places in a dollar amount such as $123.45. Likewise in percentages, use only the minimum number of decimals required to represent the data effectively. For example instead of 43.21%, you may be able to get away with 43%.

➤ Only use the dollar symbol when you need to clarify that you're referring to monetary values. If you have a chart or table that contains all revenue values, and there is a label clearly stating this, you can save room and pixels by leaving out the dollar symbol.

➤ Format very large numbers to thousands or millions place. For instance, instead of displaying 16,906,714, you can format the number to read 17M.

In Chapter 2, you explore how to leverage number formatting tricks to enhance the readability of your dashboards and reports.

Use titles and labels effectively

It's common sense, but people often fail to label items on dashboards effectively. If your customer looks at your dashboard and asks, "What is this telling me?" you likely have labeling issues. Here are a few guidelines for effective labeling in your dashboards and reports.

➤ Always include a timestamp on your dashboard or report. This minimizes confusion when distributing the same dashboard or report in monthly or weekly installments.

➤ Always include some text indicating when the data for the measures was retrieved. In many cases, timing of the data is a critical piece of information for analyzing a measure.

➤ Use descriptive titles for each component. This allows users to clearly identify what they're looking at. Be sure to avoid cryptic titles with lots of acronyms and symbols.

➤ Although it may seem counterintuitive, it's generally good practice to de-emphasize labels by formatting them to lighter hues than your data. Lightly colored labels give your users the information they need without distracting them from the information that's displayed. Ideal colors to use for labels are colors that are commonly found in nature: soft grays, browns, blues, and greens.

Key Questions to Ask Before Distributing Your Dashboard

Before you send out your finished dashboard, it's worth your time to step back and measure it against some of the design principles we discuss in this chapter. Here are some key questions you can use as a checklist before distributing your dashboard.

Does my dashboard present the right information?

Look at the information you're presenting and determine whether it meets the purpose of the dashboard identified during requirements gathering. Don't be timid about clarifying the purpose of the dashboard again with your core users. You want to avoid building the dashboard in a vacuum. Allow a few test users to see iterations as you develop it. This way, communication remains open, and you won't go too far in the wrong direction.

Does everything on my dashboard have a purpose?

Take an honest look at how much information on your dashboard doesn't support its main purpose. In order to keep your dashboard as valuable as possible, you don't want to dilute it with nice-to-know data that's interesting, but not actionable. Remember, if the data doesn't support the core purpose of the dashboard, leave it out. Nothing says you have to fill every bit of white space on the page.

Does my dashboard prominently display the key message?

Every dashboard has one or more key messages. You want to ensure that these messages are prominently displayed. To test whether the key messages in a dashboard are prominent, stand back and squint your eyes while you look at the dashboard. Look away and then look at the dashboard several times. What jumps out at you first? If it's not the key components you want to display, then you'll have to change something. Here are a few actions you can take to ensure that your key components have prominence.

➤ Place the key components of your dashboard in the upper-left or middle-left of the page. As I noted earlier, studies show that these areas attract the most attention for longer periods of time.

➤ De-emphasize borders, backgrounds, and other elements that define dashboard areas. Try to use the natural white space between your components to partition your dashboard. If borders are necessary, format them to lighter hues than your data.

➤ Format labels and other text to lighter hues than your data. Lightly colored labels give your users the information they need without distracting them from the information displayed.

Can I maintain this dashboard?

There's a big difference between updating a dashboard and rebuilding a dashboard. Before you excitedly send out the sweet-looking dashboard you just built, take a moment to think about the maintenance of such a dashboard. You want to think about the frequency of updates and what processes you need to go through each time you update the data. If it's a one-time reporting event, then set that expectation with your users. If you know it will become a recurring report, you'll want to really negotiate development time, refresh intervals, and phasing before agreeing to a time table.

Does my dashboard clearly display its scope and shelf life?

A dashboard should clearly specify its scope and shelf life. That is to say, anyone should be able to look at your dashboard and know the time period it's relevant to and the scope of the information on the dashboard. This comes down to a few simple things you can do to effectively label your dashboards and reports.

➤ Always include a timestamp on your dashboard. This minimizes confusion when distributing the same dashboard or report in monthly or weekly installments.

➤ Always include some text indicating when the data for the measures was retrieved. In many cases, timing of the data is a critical piece of information when analyzing a measure.

➤ Use descriptive titles for each component in your dashboard. Be sure to avoid cryptic titles with lots of acronyms and symbols.

Is my dashboard well documented?

It's important to document your dashboard and the data model behind it. Anyone who has ever inherited an Excel worksheet knows how difficult it can be to translate the various analytical gyrations that go into a report. If you're lucky, the data model will be small enough to piece together in a week or so. If you're not so lucky, you'll have to ditch the entire model and start from scratch. By the way, the Excel data model doesn't even have to be someone else's. I actually went back to a model that I'd built six or so months earlier, only to find that I'd forgotten what I had done. Without documentation, it took me a few days to remember and decipher my own work.

The documentation doesn't even have to be highfalutin' fancy stuff. A few simple things can help in documenting your dashboard.

➤ **Add a Model Map tab to your data model.** The Model Map tab is a separate sheet you can use to summarize the key ranges in the data model and how each range interacts with the reporting components in the final presentation layer.

➤ **Use comments and labels liberally.** It's amazing how a few explanatory comments and labels can help clarify your model even after you've been away from your data model for a long period of time.

➤ **Use colors to identify the ranges in your data model.** Using colors in your data model enables you to quickly look at a range of cells and get a basic indication of what that range does. Each color can represent a range type. For example, yellow could represent staging tables, gray could represent formulas, and purple could represent reference tables.

Cross-Ref

In Chapter 2, we introduce you to data models and building a data model map.

Is my dashboard user-friendly?

Before you distribute your dashboard, you want to ensure that it's user-friendly. It's not difficult to guess what *user-friendly* means.

➤ **Intuitive:** Your dashboard should be intuitive to someone who has never seen it. Test it out on someone and ask her if it makes sense. If you have to start explaining what the dashboard says, something is wrong. Does the dashboard need more labels, less-complicated charts, a better layout, more data, less data? It's a good idea to get feedback from several users.

➤ **Easy to navigate:** If your dashboard is dynamic, allowing for interactivity with macros or pivot tables, then you want to make sure that the navigation works well. Do users have to click several places to get to their data? Is the number of drill-downs appropriate? Does it take too long to switch from one view to another? Again, you'll want to test your dashboard on several users. And be sure to test any interactive dashboard features on several computers other than yours.

➤ **Prints properly:** Nothing is more annoying than printing a dashboard only to find that the person who created the dashboard didn't take the time to ensure that it prints correctly. Be sure you set the print options on your Excel files so that your dashboards print properly.

Is my dashboard accurate?

Nothing kills a dashboard or report faster than the perception that the data in it is inaccurate. It's not within my capabilities to tell you how to determine whether your data is accurate. I can, however, highlight three factors that establish the perception that a dashboard is accurate.

➤ **Consistency with authoritative sources:** It's obvious that if your data doesn't match other reporting sources, you'll have a data credibility issue — especially if those other sources are deemed to be the authoritative sources. Be sure you are aware of the data sources that are considered to be gospel in your organization. If your dashboard contains data associated with an authoritative source, compare your data with that source to ensure consistency.

➤ **Internal consistency:** It's never fun to explain why one part of your dashboard doesn't jibe with other parts of the same dashboard. You want to ensure some level of internal consistency within your dashboard. Be sure comparable components in different areas of your dashboard are consistent with each other. If there is a reason for inconsistency, be sure to clearly notate those reasons. It's amazing how well a simple notation clears up questions about the data.

➤ **Personal experience:** Have you ever seen someone look at a report and say, "That doesn't look right?" They are using what some people call "gut feel" to evaluate the soundness of the data. None of us looks at numbers in a vacuum. When we look at any analysis, we bring with us years of personal knowledge, interaction, and experience. We subconsciously use these experiences in our evaluation of information. When determining the accuracy of your dashboard, take into consideration organizational *anecdotal knowledge*. If possible, show your dashboard to a few content experts in your company.

Table Design Best Practices

In This Chapter

- Table design principles
- Custom number formatting
- Applying custom format colors
- Applying custom format conditions

The Excel table is the number one way information is consolidated and relayed. Look in any Excel report, and you'll find a table of data. Yet the concept of making tables easier to read and more visually appealing escapes most of us.

Even on many highly graphical dashboards, you find key pieces of information (like the top ten sales reps) presented in a table format. But while the visual components of dashboards are treated with overwhelming care and attention, table design rarely goes beyond matching the color scheme of the other visual components of the dashboard.

Maybe the nicely structured rows and columns of a table lull people into believing that the data is presented in the best way possible. Maybe the options of adding color and borders make the table seem nicely packaged. In any case, you can use several design principles to make your Excel table a more effective platform for conveying data points.

In this chapter, you explore how easy it is to apply a handful of table-design best practices. The tips found here will ultimately help you create visually appealing tables that make the data within them easier to consume and comprehend.

On the Web

All workbook examples in this book are available on the companion website for this book at www.wiley.com/go/exceldr.

Table Design Principles

Table design is one of the most underestimated endeavors in Excel reporting. How a table is designed has a direct effect on how well an audience absorbs and interprets the data in that table. Unfortunately, the act of putting a table of data together for consumption is treated trivially by most.

Take, for example, the table illustrated in Figure 2-1. This table is similar to many found in Excel reports. The thick borders, the different colors, and the poorly formatted numbers are all unfortunate trademarks of most tables that come from the average Excel analyst.

Top 10 Domestic Routes by Revenue		Revenue		Margin		Per Passenger	
From	To	Revenue Dollars	Revenue Percent	Margin Dollars	Margin Percent	Revenue per Passenger	Margin per Passenger
Atlanta	New York	$3,602,000	8.09%	$955,000	9%	245	65
Chicago	New York	$4,674,000	10.50%	$336,000	3%	222	16
Columbus (Ohio)	New York	$2,483,000	5.58%	$1,536,000	14%	202	125
New York	Detroit	$12,180,000	27.35%	$2,408,000	23%	177	35
New York	Washington	$6,355,000	14.27%	$1,230,000	12%	186	36
New York	Philadelphia	$3,582,000	8.04%	-$716,000	-7%	125	-25
New York	San Francisco	$3,221,000	7.23%	$1,856,000	18%	590	340
New York	Phoenix	$2,846,000	6.39%	$1,436,000	14%	555	280
New York	Toronto	$2,799,000	6.29%	$1,088,000	10%	450	175
New York	Seattle	$2,792,000	6.27%	$467,000	4%	448	75
Total Domestic routes		$44,534,000		$10,596,000		272	53

Figure 2-1: A poorly designed table.

Throughout this chapter, you'll improve upon this table, applying these four basic design principles.

➤ Use colors sparingly, reserving them only for information about key data points.

➤ De-emphasize borders by using the natural white space between your components to partition your dashboard.

➤ Use effective number formatting to avoid inundating your table with too much ink.

➤ Subdue your labels and headers.

Use colors sparingly

Color is most often used to separate the various sections of a table. The basic idea is that the colors applied to a table suggest the relationships among the rows and columns. The problem is that colors often distract and draw attention away from the important data. In addition, printed tables with dark-colored cells are notoriously difficult to read (especially when printed on black and white printers). They're also hard on the toner budget, if that holds any importance to you.

In general, you should use colors sparingly; reserve them for providing information about key data points. The headers, labels, and natural structure of your table are more than enough to guide your audience. There's no real need to add a layer of color to demark rows and columns.

Figure 2-2 shows a table with the colors removed. As you can see, it's already easier to read.

Top 10 Domestic Routes by Revenue		Revenue		Margin		Per Passenger	
		Revenue Dollars	Revenue Percent	Margin Dollars	Margin Percent	Revenue per Passenger	Margin per Passenger
From	To						
Atlanta	New York	$3,602,000	8.09%	$955,000	9%	245	65
Chicago	New York	$4,674,000	10.50%	$336,000	3%	222	16
Columbus (Ohio)	New York	$2,483,000	5.58%	$1,536,000	14%	202	125
New York	Detroit	$12,180,000	27.35%	$2,408,000	23%	177	35
New York	Washington	$6,355,000	14.27%	$1,230,000	12%	186	36
New York	Philadelphia	$3,582,000	8.04%	-$716,000	-7%	125	-25
New York	San Francisco	$3,221,000	7.23%	$1,856,000	18%	590	340
New York	Phoenix	$2,846,000	6.39%	$1,436,000	14%	555	280
New York	Toronto	$2,799,000	6.29%	$1,088,000	10%	450	175
New York	Seattle	$2,792,000	6.27%	$467,000	4%	448	75
Total Domestic routes		$44,534,000		$10,596,000		272	53

Figure 2-2: Remove unnecessary cell coloring.

To remove color from cells in a table, first highlight the cells, and then go to the Ribbon and select Home➜Theme Colors. From the Theme Colors drop-down menu, select No Fill (see Figure 2-3).

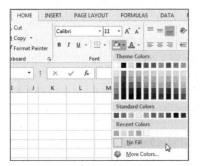

Figure 2-3: Use the No Fill option to clear cell colors.

De-emphasize borders

Believe it or not, borders get in the way of quickly reading the data in a table. This is counterintuitive to the thought that borders help separate data into nicely partitioned sections. The reality is that the borders of a table are the first thing your eyes see when looking at a table. Don't believe it? Try standing back a bit from an Excel table and squint. The borders will pop out at you.

De-emphasize borders and gridlines wherever you can:

➤ Try to use the natural white space between the columns to partition sections.

➤ If borders are necessary, format them to lighter hues than your data.

➤ Light grays are typically ideal for borders. The idea is to indicate sections without distracting from the information displayed.

Figure 2-4 demonstrates these concepts. Notice how the numbers are no longer caged in gridlines. Also, headings now jump out at you with the addition of Single Accounting underlines.

Top 10 Domestic Routes by Revenue

		Revenue		Margin		Per Passenger	
From	To	Revenue Dollars	Revenue Percent	Margin Dollars	Margin Percent	Revenue per Passenger	Margin per Passenger
Atlanta	New York	$3,602,000	8.09%	$955,000	9%	245	65
Chicago	New York	$4,674,000	10.50%	$336,000	3%	222	16
Columbus (Ohio)	New York	$2,483,000	5.58%	$1,536,000	14%	202	125
New York	Detroit	$12,180,000	27.35%	$2,408,000	23%	177	35
New York	Washington	$6,355,000	14.27%	$1,230,000	12%	186	36
New York	Philadelphia	$3,582,000	8.04%	-$716,000	-7%	125	-25
New York	San Francisco	$3,221,000	7.23%	$1,856,000	18%	590	340
New York	Phoenix	$2,846,000	6.39%	$1,436,000	14%	555	280
New York	Toronto	$2,799,000	6.29%	$1,088,000	10%	450	175
New York	Seattle	$2,792,000	6.27%	$467,000	4%	448	75
Total Domestic routes		**$44,534,000**		**$10,596,000**		**272**	**53**

Figure 2-4: Minimize the use of borders and use the Single Accounting underlines to accent the column headers.

Tip

Single Accounting underlines are different from the standard underlines you typically apply by pressing Ctrl+U on the keyboard. Standard underlining draws a line only as far as the text goes. That is to say, if you underline the word YES, you get a line under the three letters. Single Accounting, on the other hand, draws a line across the entire column, regardless of how big or small the word is. This makes for a minimal but apparent visual demarcation that calls out your column headers nicely.

To format your borders, follow these steps:

1. Highlight the cells you're working with, right-click, and select Format Cells.

   The Format Cells dialog box appears.

2. Click the Border tab, shown in Figure 2-5.

3. Select an appropriate line thickness.

   You typically want to select the line with the lightest weight.

4. Select an appropriate color.

   Again, lighter hues are the best option.

5. Use the border buttons to control where your borders are placed.

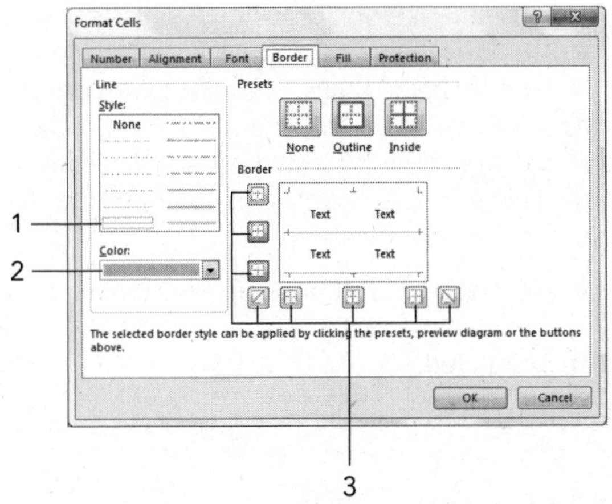

Figure 2-5: Use the Border tab of the Format Cells dialog box to customize your borders.

To apply the Single Accounting underline, follow these steps:

1. Right-click your column headings and select Format Cells.

    The Format Cells dialog box appears.

2. Click the Font tab.

3. Choose the Single Accounting underline, as shown in Figure 2-6.

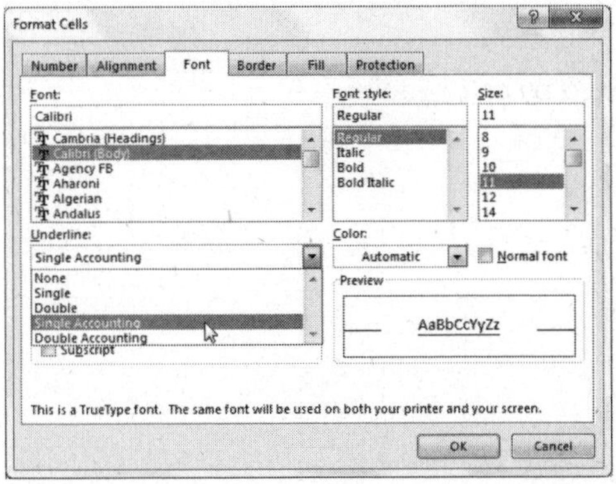

Figure 2-6: Single Accounting underlines effectively call out your column headers.

Use effective number formatting

Every piece of information in your table should have a reason for being there. To clarify, tables often inundate the audience with superfluous ink that doesn't add value to the information. For example, you'll often see tables that show a number like $145.57 when a simple 145 would be relay the data just fine. Why include the extra decimal places that serve only to add to the mass of numbers that your audience will need to plow through?

Here are some guidelines to keep in mind when applying formats to the numbers in your table.

➤ Only use decimal places if that level of precision is required.

➤ In percentages, use only the minimum number of decimals required to represent the data effectively.

➤ Instead of using currency symbols (like $ or £), let your labels clarify that you're referring to monetary values.

➤ Format very large numbers to thousands or millions place.

➤ Right-align numbers so that they're easier to read and compare.

Figure 2-7 shows the table with appropriate number formatting applied. Note the following:

➤ The large revenue and margin dollar amounts are converted to thousands place.

➤ The labels above the numbers now clearly indicate that the numbers are represented in thousands place.

➤ The percentages are truncated to show no decimal places.

➤ The key metric, the Margin % column, is emphasized by color coding.

Top 10 Domestic Routes by Revenue

		Revenue		Margin		Per Passenger	
From	To	Revenue $ (000's)	Revenue %	Margin $ (000's)	Margin %	$ per Passenger	Margin $per Passenger
Atlanta	New York	3,602	8%	955	9%	245	65
Chicago	New York	4,674	10%	336	3%	222	16
Columbus (Ohio)	New York	2,483	6%	1,536	14%	202	125
New York	Detroit	12,180	27%	2,408	23%	177	35
New York	Washington	6,355	14%	1,230	12%	186	36
New York	Philadelphia	3,582	8%	-716	-7%	125	-25
New York	San Francisco	3,221	7%	1,856	18%	590	340
New York	Phoenix	2,846	6%	1,436	14%	555	280
New York	Toronto	2,799	6%	1,088	10%	450	175
New York	Seattle	2,792	6%	467	4%	448	75
Total Domestic routes		**44,534**		**10,596**		**272**	**53**

Figure 2-7: Use number formatting to eliminate clutter in your table and draw attention to key metrics.

Amazingly, all of these improvements were made with simple number formatting. That's right; no formulas were used to convert large numbers to thousands place, no conditional formatting was used to color code the Margin % field, no other peripheral tricks of any kind were used.

Later in this chapter, in the section "Enhancing Reporting with Custom Number Formatting," you explore how to leverage the number-formatting feature to accomplish these improvements.

Subdue your labels and headers

No one will argue that the labels and headers of a table aren't important. On the contrary, they provide your audience with the guidance and structure needed to make sense of the data in a table. However, labels and headers sometimes are overemphasized to the point that they overshadow the data. How many times have you seen bold or oversized font applied to headers? The reality is that your audience will benefit more with the use of subdued labels.

De-emphasizing labels by using lighter hues will actually make a table easier to read and will draw more attention to the data in the table. Lightly colored labels give users the information they need without distracting them from the information being presented.

Tip

Ideal colors for labels are soft grays, light browns, soft blues, and greens.

Font size and alignment also factor into the effective display of tables. Aligning column headers to the same alignment as the numbers beneath them helps reinforce the column structures in your table. Keeping the font size of your labels close to that of the data within the table will help keep eyes focused on the data — not the labels.

Figure 2-8 illustrates how the table looks with subdued headers and labels. Note how the data now becomes the focus of attention, whereas the muted labels work in the background.

Top 10 Domestic Routes by Revenue

From	To	Revenue $ (000's)	Revenue %	Margin $ (000's)	Margin %	$ per Passenger	Margin $ per Passenger
New York	Detroit	12,180	27%	2,408	23%	177	35
New York	Washington	6,355	14%	1,230	12%	186	36
Chicago	New York	4,674	10%	336	3%	222	16
Atlanta	New York	3,602	8%	955	9%	245	65
New York	Philadelphia	3,582	8%	-716	-7%	125	-25
New York	San Francisco	3,221	7%	1,856	18%	590	340
New York	Phoenix	2,846	6%	1,436	14%	555	280
New York	Toronto	2,799	6%	1,088	10%	450	175
New York	Seattle	2,792	6%	467	4%	448	75
Columbus (Ohio)	New York	2,483	6%	1,536	14%	202	125
Total Domestic routes		44,534		10,596		272	53

Figure 2-8: Send your labels and headers to the background by subduing their colors and keeping their font sizes in line with the data.

Tip

Sorting is another key factor in the readability of data. Many tables sort based on labels (alphabetical by route, for example). Sorting the table based on a key data point within the data establishes a pattern that your audience can use to quickly analyze the top and bottom values. In Figure 2-8, note that the data is sorted by the Revenue dollars. This again adds a layer of analysis and provides a quick look at the top and bottom generating routes.

Figure 2-9 shows the table before and after all the improvements are made. It's easy to see how a few design principles can greatly enhance your ability to present table-driven data.

Top 10 Domestic Routes by Revenue

From	To	Revenue		Margin		Per Passenger	
---	---	Revenue Dollars	Revenue Percent	Margin Dollars	Margin Percent	Revenue per Passenger	Margin per Passenger
Atlanta	New York	$3,602,000	8.09%	$955,000	9%	245	65
Chicago	New York	$4,674,000	10.50%	$336,000	3%	222	16
Columbus (Ohio)	New York	$2,483,000	5.58%	$1,536,000	14%	202	125
New York	Detroit	$12,180,000	27.35%	$2,408,000	23%	177	35
New York	Washington	$6,355,000	14.27%	$1,230,000	12%	186	36
New York	Philadelphia	$3,582,000	8.04%	-$716,000	-7%	125	-25
New York	San Francisco	$3,221,000	7.23%	$1,856,000	18%	590	340
New York	Phoenix	$2,846,000	6.39%	$1,436,000	14%	555	280
New York	Toronto	$2,799,000	6.29%	$1,088,000	10%	450	175
New York	Seattle	$2,792,000	6.27%	$467,000	4%	448	75
Total Domestic routes		**$44,534,000**		**$10,596,000**		**272**	**53**

Top 10 Domestic Routes by Revenue

From	To	Revenue		Margin		Per Passenger	
---	---	Revenue $ (000's)	Revenue %	Margin $ (000's)	Margin %	$ per Passenger	Margin $ per Passenger
New York	Detroit	12,180	27%	2,408	23%	177	35
New York	Washington	6,355	14%	1,230	12%	186	36
Chicago	New York	4,674	10%	336	3%	222	16
Atlanta	New York	3,602	8%	955	9%	245	65
New York	Philadelphia	3,582	8%	-716	-7%	125	-25
New York	San Francisco	3,221	7%	1,856	18%	590	340
New York	Phoenix	2,846	6%	1,436	14%	555	280
New York	Toronto	2,799	6%	1,088	10%	450	175
New York	Seattle	2,792	6%	467	4%	448	75
Columbus (Ohio)	New York	2,483	6%	1,536	14%	202	125
Total Domestic routes		*44,534*		*10,596*		*272*	*53*

Figure 2-9: Before and after applying table design principles.

Tip

Although it may seem like a mere matter of taste, font type has a subtle but tangible impact on your tables. Outdated or inappropriate fonts will cause your audience to focus on the fonts rather than the data in your table. Using fonts like Comic Sans may seem cute, but they're rarely appropriate for a report. Older fonts like Times New Roman or Arial can make your reports look old. It may seem strange, but fonts with straight edges and fancy strokes now look old compared to the rounded edges of the more popular fonts being used. This change in font perception is primarily driven by popular online sites, which often use fonts with rounded edges. If possible, consider using modern-looking fonts like Calibri and Segoe UI in your reports and dashboard.

Enhancing Reporting with Custom Number Formatting

You can apply number formatting to cells several ways. Most people utilize the convenient Number commands found on the Home tab. Using these commands, you can quickly apply some default formatting (such as number, percent, and currency) and just be done with it. But a better way is to utilize the Format Cells dialog box, where you can create your own custom number formatting.

Number formatting basics

To apply a custom number format, follow these steps:

1. Right-click on a range of cells and select Format Cells.

   The Format Cells dialog box opens.

2. Go to the Number tab and apply some basic formatting.

   To start, choose a format that makes the most sense for your purposes. In Figure 2-10, the Number format is chosen, with comma separator, no decimal places, and negative numbers wrapped in parentheses.

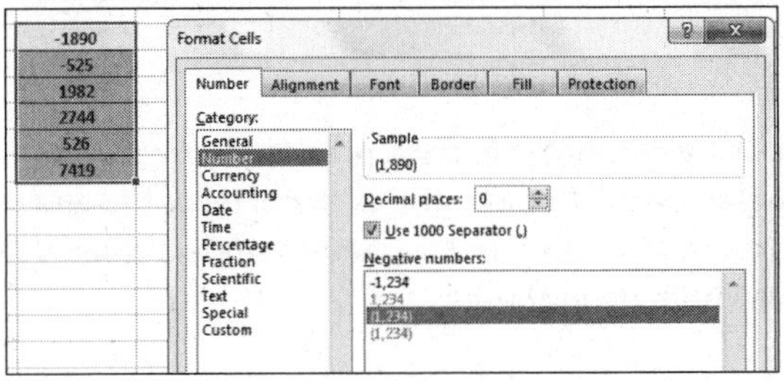

Figure 2-10: Choose a basic format.

3. Click the Custom option, as shown in Figure 2-11.

   Excel takes you to a screen that shows the syntax that makes up the format you selected. The syntax is shown in the Type input box. Here you can edit the syntax to customize the number format.

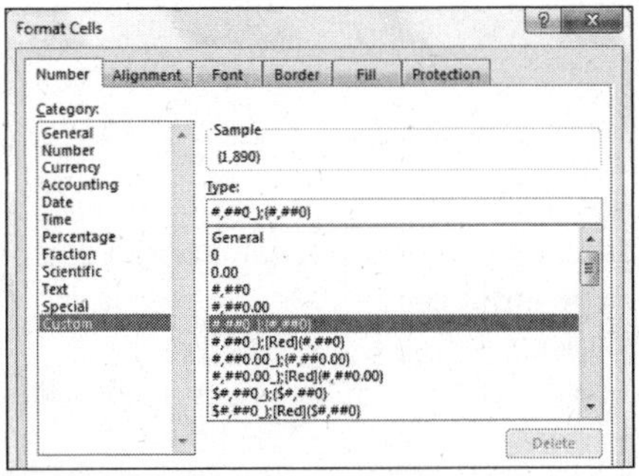

Figure 2-11: The Type input box allows you to customize the syntax for the number format.

In this case, you see

```
#,##0_);(#,##0)
```

The number formatting syntax tells Excel how a number will look in various scenarios. Number formatting syntax consists of different individual number formats separated by semicolons. In this example, you see two different formats:

- The format to the left of the semicolon. By default, any formatting to the left of the first semicolon is applied to positive numbers.

- The format to the right of the semicolon. Any formatting to the right of the first semicolon is applied to negative numbers.

So in this scenario, negative numbers are formatted with parentheses, whereas positive numbers are formatted as a simple number.

```
(1,890)
 1,982
```

Note

Notice that the syntax for the positive formatting in the previous example ends with _). This tells Excel to leave a space the width of a parenthesis character at the end of positive numbers. This syntax ensures that positive and negative numbers align nicely when negative numbers are wrapped within parentheses.

You can edit the syntax in the Type input box so that the numbers are formatted differently. For example, try changing the syntax to:

```
+#,##0;-#,##0
```

When applied, positive numbers will start with the + symbol, and negative numbers will start with a – symbol, like so:

```
+1,200
-15,000
```

This comes in quite handy when formatting percentages. For instance, you can apply a custom percent format by entering the following syntax into the Type input box:

```
+0%;-0%
```

This syntax gives you percentages that look like this:

```
+43%
-54%
```

You can get fancy and wrap your negative percentages with parentheses with this syntax:

```
0%_);(0%)
```

This syntax gives you percentages that look like this:

```
 43%
(54%)
```

Note If you include only one format syntax, meaning you don't add a second formatting option with the use of a semicolon separator, that one format will be applied to all numbers—negative or positive.

Formatting numbers in thousands and millions

Earlier in this chapter, you formatted your revenue numbers to show in thousands. This allowed you to present cleaner numbers and avoid inundating your audience with too much ink. To show your numbers in thousands, follow these steps:

1. Highlight the cells containing your numbers, right-click, and select Format Cells.

   The Format Cells dialog box appears.

2. Click the Custom option.

   The screen shown in Figure 2-12 appears.

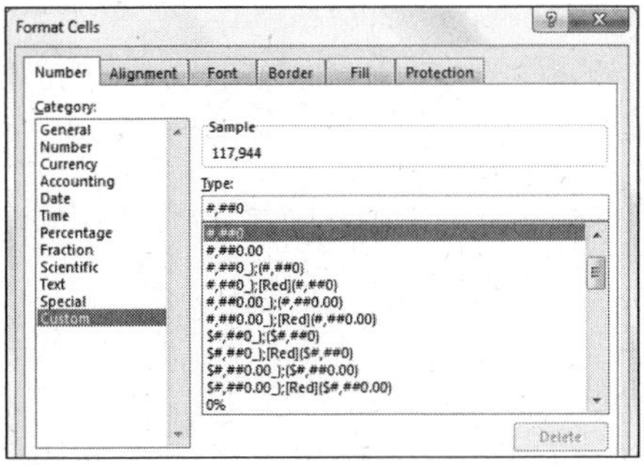

Figure 2-12: Go to the Custom screen of the Format Cells dialog box.

3. In the Type input box, add a comma after the format syntax.

   This syntax cosmetically changes your number to thousands place:

   ```
   #,##0,
   ```

   After confirming your changes, your numbers will automatically show in thousands place.

Here's the beauty of this technique: It doesn't change or truncate your numbers in any way. Excel is simply applying a cosmetic effect to the number. To see what this means, take a look at Figure 2-13.

The selected cell is formatted to show in thousands: You see 118. But when you look in the formula bar, you see the real unformatted number (117943). The 118 you see in the cell is a cosmetically formatted version of the real number shown in the formula bar.

	× ✓ *fx*	117943.605787004		
B	**C**	**D**	**E**	
North	118	380	463	
Northeast	24	803	328	
East	313	780	904	
Southeast	397	466	832	
South	840	118	800	
Southwest	623	977	808	
West	474	79	876	
Northwest	841	102	616	

Figure 2-13: Formatting numbers applies only a cosmetic look. Look in the formula bar to see the real unformatted number.

Note Custom number formatting has obvious advantages over using other techniques to format numbers to thousands. For instance, many beginning analysts convert numbers to thousands by dividing them by 1,000 in a formula. But that changes the integrity of the number dramatically, and it forces you to keep track of and maintain formulas that could cause calculation errors later. Using custom number formatting avoids that by changing only how the number looks, keeping the actual number intact.

If needed, you can even indicate that the number is in thousands by adding a "k" to the number syntax.

```
#,##0,"k"
```

This syntax shows your numbers like this:

```
118k
318k
```

You can use this technique on both positive and negative numbers.

```
#,##0,"k"; (#,##0,"k")
```

After you apply this syntax, your negative numbers will also show in thousands.

```
118k
(318k)
```

Need to show numbers in millions? Easy. Simply edit the Type input box to add two commas to your number format syntax.

```
#,##0.00,, "m"
```

Note the extra decimal places (.00). When converting numbers to millions, it's often useful to show additional precision points, as in:

```
24.65 m
```

Hiding and suppressing zeros

In addition to positive and negative numbers, Excel allows you to provide a format for zeros. You do so by adding another semicolon to your custom number syntax. By default, any format syntax placed after the second semicolon is applied to any number that evaluates to zero.

For example, the following syntax applies a format that shows "n/a" for cells that contain zeros.

```
#,##0_);(#,##0);"n/a"
```

You can also use this syntax to suppress zeros entirely. If you add the second semicolon but don't follow it with any syntax, cells containing zeros will show blank.

```
#,##0_);(#,##0);
```

Again, custom number formatting affects only the cosmetics of the cell. The actual data in the cell is not affected, as demonstrated in Figure 2-14. The selected cell is formatted so that zeros show as n/a, but if you look at the formula bar, you can see the actual unformatted cell contents.

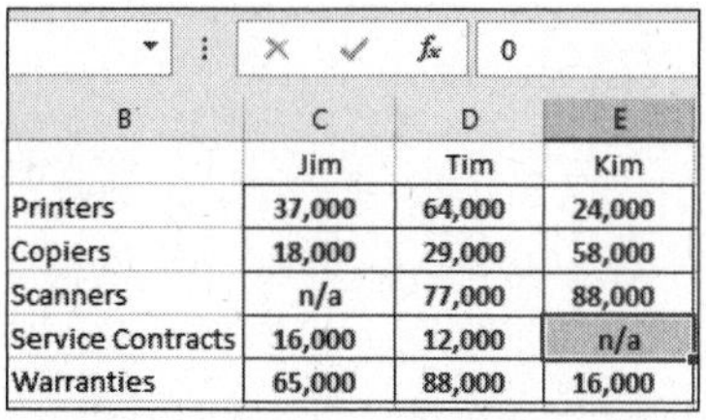

B	C	D	E
	Jim	Tim	Kim
Printers	37,000	64,000	24,000
Copiers	18,000	29,000	58,000
Scanners	n/a	77,000	88,000
Service Contracts	16,000	12,000	n/a
Warranties	65,000	88,000	16,000

Figure 2-14: Custom number formatting that shows zeros as n/a.

Applying custom format colors

Have you ever set the formatting on a cell so that negative numbers show up red? If so, you essentially applied a custom format color. In addition to controlling the look of your numbers with custom number formatting, you can control their color.

In this example, you format the percentages so that positive percentages show blue with a + symbol, whereas negative percentages show red with a – symbol. Again, you enter this syntax in the Type input box shown earlier in Figure 2-12.

```
[Blue]+0%;[Red]-0%
```

To apply a color, just enter the color name wrapped in square brackets [ ].

Now, there are only certain colors you can call out by name. You can call out the eight VB colors by name. These colors make up the first eight colors of the default Excel color palette.

[Black]

[Blue]

[Cyan]

[Green]

[Magenta]

[Red]

[White]

[Yellow]

Caution

Blue and Red are the only colors from the 8 VB colors that are viable in a report or dashboard. The rest of the colors listed are virtually unusable, as they are very unattractive.

Fortunately, the Excel palette comes with 56 colors that you can call up using a color code. Every color has a code: The color code for black is 1, the color code for white is 2, and so on.

You can use color codes in your custom number syntax by replacing the named color with the word COLOR followed by the code.

For example, this syntax formats the percentages so that positive percentages show green with a + symbol, whereas negative percentages show red with a – symbol.

```
[COLOR10]+0%;[COLOR3]-0%
```

So how do you know which color code to use? Well, in the Chapter 2 sample file, you will find a tab called Get Color Codes (see Figure 2-15). The button found on that tab runs a small bit of VBA that extracts the color and color code for you. Simply find the color you deem most appropriate and use the associated code.

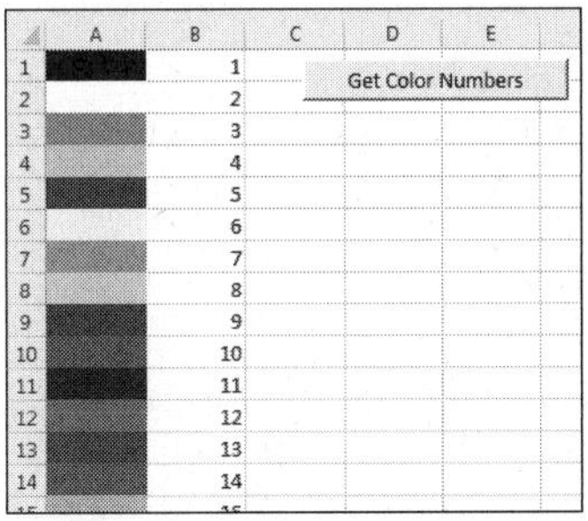

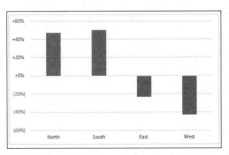

Figure 2-15: Use the Get Color Codes tab in the Chapter 2 Sample file to extract the Excel palette colors and their associated codes.

You may be wondering how using custom number coloring is different from Excel's built-in conditional-formatting feature. In many ways, they're the same. However, you do get a couple of benefits from using custom number coloring rather than conditional formatting.

➤ You don't have to manage separate conditional formatting rules. All the formatting needed is built into the cell.

➤ Every object that uses your custom formatted cell adopts the format automatically. This means your custom formatting can be applied where conditional formatting can't. For example, the chart in Figure 2-16 plots cells that have custom number formatting. Notice how the y axis of the chart faithfully displays the custom number formatting. You couldn't do this with conditional formatting.

Figure 2-16: Custom number formatting is automatically adopted in charts.

Formatting dates and times

Custom number formatting isn't just for numbers. You can also format dates and times. As you can see in Figure 2-17, you use the same dialog box to apply date and time formats using the Type input.

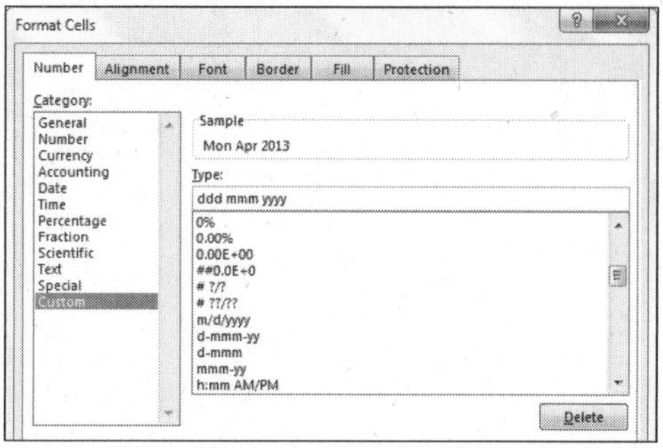

Figure 2-17: You can also format dates and times using the Format Cells dialog box.

Figure 2-17 demonstrates that date and time formatting involves little more than stringing date-specific or time-specific syntax together. The syntax used is fairly intuitive. For example, DDD is the syntax for the three-letter day, mmm is the syntax for the three-letter Month, and yyyy is the syntax for the four-digit year.

There are several variations on the format for days, months, years, hours, and minutes. Take some time and experiment with different combinations of syntax strings.

Table 2-1 lists some common date and time format codes you can use as starter syntax for your reports and dashboards.

Table 2-1: Common Date and Time Format Codes

Format Code	1/31/2013 7:42:53 PM Displays As
m	1
mm	01
mmm	Jan
mmmmm	January
mmmmm	J
dd	31
ddd	Thu
dddd	Thursday
yy	13
yyyy	2013
mmm-yy	Jan-13
dd/mm/yyyy	31/01/2013
dddd mmm yyyy	Thursday Jan 2013

Format Code	1/31/2013 7:42:53 PM Displays As
mm-dd-yyyy h:mm AM/PM	01-31-2013 7:42 PM
h AM/PM	7 PM
h:mm AM/PM	7:42 PM
h:mm:ss AM/PM	7:42:53 PM

Adding conditions to customer number formatting

At this point, you know that Excel's number formatting syntax consists of different individual number formats separated by semicolons. By default, the syntax to the left of the first semicolon is applied to positive numbers, the syntax to the right of the first semicolon is applied to negative numbers, and the syntax to the right of the second semicolon is applied to zeros.

```
Positive Number Format; Negative Number Format; Format for Zeros
```

Interestingly, Excel allows you override this default behavior and repurpose the syntax sections using your own conditions. Conditions are entered in square brackets.

In this syntax example, you apply a blue color to cells containing a number over 500, a red color to cells containing a number less than 500, and n/a to cells containing a number equal to 500.

```
[Blue][>500]#,##0;[Red][<500]#,##0;"n/a"
```

One of the more useful ways to use conditions is to convert numbers to thousands or millions, depending on how big the number is. In this example, numbers equal to or greater than 1,000,000 are formatted as millions, whereas numbers equal to or greater than 1,000 are formatted as thousands.

```
[>=1000000]#,##0.00,,"m";[>=1000]#,##0,"k"
```

Again, the conditions you use must be relatively basic. Even so, conditions give you another avenue to gaining control over the display of the numbers in your dashboards and reports.

Using Excel Sparklines

In This Chapter

- Understanding the Excel 2013 Sparkline feature

- Adding sparklines to a worksheet

- Working with groups of sparklines

- Modifying your sparkline graphics

Sparklines were developed by visualization guru Edward Tufte. Tufte envisioned mini word-sized charts placed in and among the data that they represent. Sparklines enable you to see trends and patterns within your data at a glance using minimal space. Following the sparkline concept, Microsoft then implemented sparklines in Excel worksheets so that you can get visual context for data that doesn't take up a lot of real estate on your dashboard.

This chapter introduces you to sparklines and demonstrates how you can use them to add visualizations to your dashboards and reports.

> **Note**
>
> **Sparklines are available only with Excel 2010 and Excel 2013. If you create a workbook that uses sparklines, and that workbook is opened using a previous version of Excel, the sparkline cells will be empty. If your organization is not fully using Excel 2010 or 2013, you may want to search for alternatives to the built-in Excel sparklines. There are many third-party add-ons that bring sparkline features to earlier versions of Excel. Some of these products support additional sparkline types, and most have many additional customization options. Search the web for** *sparklines excel,* **and you'll find several add-ons to choose from.**

Understanding Sparklines

It's important to understand just how sparklines can enhance your reporting. As I mention in Chapter 2, much of the reporting done in Excel is table-based, where precise numbers are more important than pretty charts. However, in table-based reporting, you often lose the ability to show important aspects of the data such as trends. The number of columns needed to show adequate trend data in a table makes it impractical to do so, and often will do nothing more than render your report unreadable. Sparklines allow you to add extra analysis, such as trends, in a concise visualization within your table without inundating your customers with superfluous numbers.

Take the example in Figure 3-1. The data represents a compact KPI summary designed to be an at-a-glance view of key metrics. Although there is some effort given to comparing various time periods (in columns D, E, and F), the ability to see a full-year trend would be helpful.

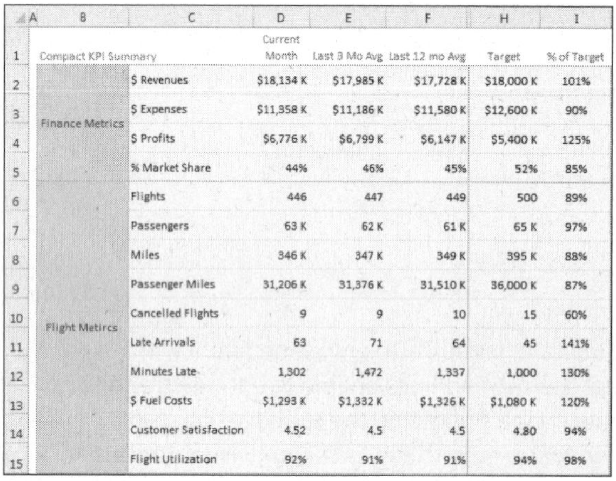

	B	C	D Current Month	E Last 3 Mo Avg	F Last 12 mo Avg	H Target	I % of Target
1	Compact KPI Summary						
2	Finance Metrics	$ Revenues	$18,134 K	$17,985 K	$17,728 K	$18,000 K	101%
3		$ Expenses	$11,358 K	$11,186 K	$11,580 K	$12,600 K	90%
4		$ Profits	$6,776 K	$6,799 K	$6,147 K	$5,400 K	125%
5		% Market Share	44%	46%	45%	52%	85%
6	Flight Metircs	Flights	446	447	449	500	89%
7		Passengers	63 K	62 K	61 K	65 K	97%
8		Miles	346 K	347 K	349 K	395 K	88%
9		Passenger Miles	31,206 K	31,376 K	31,510 K	36,000 K	87%
10		Cancelled Flights	9	9	10	15	60%
11		Late Arrivals	63	71	64	45	141%
12		Minutes Late	1,302	1,472	1,337	1,000	130%
13		$ Fuel Costs	$1,293 K	$1,332 K	$1,326 K	$1,080 K	120%
14		Customer Satisfaction	4.52	4.5	4.5	4.80	94%
15		Flight Utilization	92%	91%	91%	94%	98%

Figure 3-1: Although this KPI Summary is useful, it lacks the ability to show a full-year trend.

Figure 3-2 illustrates the same KPI Summary with Excel sparklines added to visually show the 12-month trend. With the sparklines added, you can see the broader story behind each metric. For example, if you were to look at the Passengers metric based solely on the numbers, it would look like it is merely slightly up from the average. But look at the sparkline, and you see a story of a heroic comeback from a huge hit at the beginning of the year.

It's not about adding flash and pizzazz to your tables. It's about building the most effective message you can in the limited you space you have. Sparklines are another tool you can use to add another dimension to your table-based reports.

Compact KPI Summary			Current Month	Last 3 Mo Avg	Last 12 mo Avg	12 Month Trend	Target	% of Target
		$ Revenues	$18,194 K	$17,985 K	$17,728 K		$18,000 K	101%
		$ Expenses	$11,358 K	$11,186 K	$11,580 K		$12,600 K	90%
	Finance Metrics	$ Profits	$6,776 K	$6,799 K	$6,147 K		$5,400 K	125%
		% Market Share	44%	46%	45%		52%	85%
		Flights	446	447	449		500	89%
		Passengers	63 K	62 K	61 K		65 K	97%
		Miles	346 K	347 K	349 K		395 K	88%
		Passenger Miles	31,206 K	31,376 K	31,510 K		36,000 K	87%
		Cancelled Flights	9	9	10		15	60%
	Flight Metrics	Late Arrivals	63	71	64		45	141%
		Minutes Late	1,302	1,472	1,337		1,000	130%
		$ Fuel Costs	$1,293 K	$1,332 K	$1,326 K		$1,080 K	120%
		Customer Satisfaction	4.52	4.5	4.5		4.80	94%
		Flight Utilization	92%	91%	91%		94%	98%

Figure 3-2: Sparklines allow you to add trending in a compact space, enabling you to see a broader picture for each metric.

Applying Sparklines

Although sparklines look like miniature charts (and can sometimes take the place of a chart), this feature is completely separate from the Excel chart feature (covered in Part II of this book). For example, charts are placed on a worksheet's drawing layer, and a single chart can display several series of data. In contrast, a sparkline is displayed inside a worksheet cell and displays only one series of data.

Excel 2013 supports three types of sparklines: Line, Column, and Win/Loss. Figure 3-3 shows examples of each type of sparkline graphics, displayed in column H. Each sparkline depicts the six data points to the left.

> ➤ **Line:** Similar to a line chart, the line can display with a marker for each data point. The first group in Figure 3-3 shows Line sparklines with markers. A quick glance reveals that with the exception of Fund Number W-91, the funds have been losing value over the six-month period.

> ➤ **Column:** Similar to a column chart, the second group shows the same data with Column sparklines.

> ➤ **Win/Loss:** A binary type chart that displays each data point as a high block or a low block. The third group shows Win/Loss sparklines. Notice that the data is different. Each cell displays the *change* from the previous month. In the sparkline, each data point is depicted as a high block (win) or a low block (loss). In this example, a positive change from the previous month is a win, and a negative change from the previous month is a loss.

Figure 3-3: Three types of sparklines.

Creating Sparklines

Figure 3-4 shows some weather data that you can summarize with sparklines. To create sparkline graphics for the values in these nine rows, follow these steps:

1. Select the data range that you want to summarize. In this example, select B4:M12.

    If you're creating multiple sparklines, select all the data.

Figure 3-4: Data that you want to summarize with sparkline graphics.

2. With the data selected, click the Insert tab on the Ribbon and find the Sparklines group. There you can select any one of the three sparkline types: Line, Column, or Win/Loss. In this case, select the Column option.

    Excel displays the Create Sparklines dialog box, as shown in Figure 3-5.

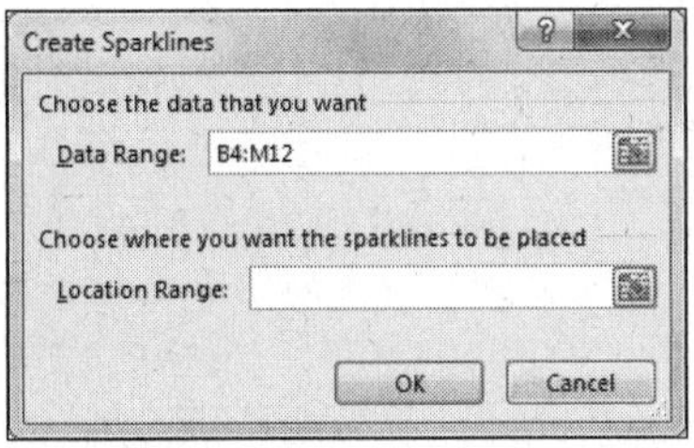

Figure 3-5: Use the Create Sparklines dialog box to specify the data range and the location for the sparkline graphics.

3. Specify the data range and the location for the sparklines. For this example, specify **N4:N12** as the Location Range.

Typically, you put the sparklines next to the data, but that's not required. Most of the time, you'll use an empty range to hold the sparklines. However, Excel doesn't prevent you from inserting sparklines into nonempty cells. The sparkline location that you specify must match the source data in terms of number of rows or number of columns.

4. Click OK.

Excel creates the sparklines graphics of the type you specified (see Figure 3-6).

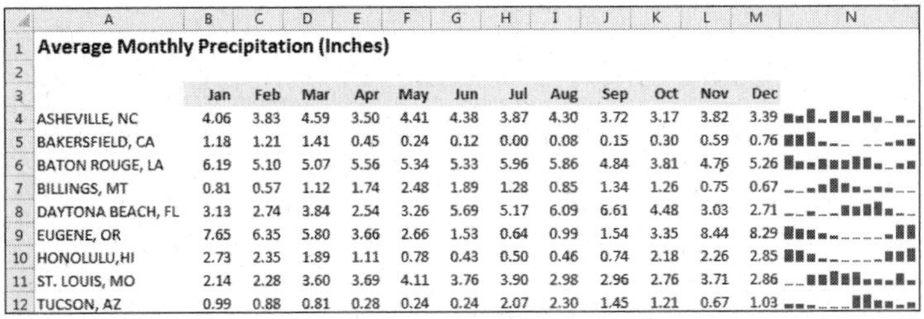

A	Jan	Feb	Mar	Apr	May	Jun	Jul	Aug	Sep	Oct	Nov	Dec	N
1 **Average Monthly Precipitation (Inches)**													
4 ASHEVILLE, NC	4.06	3.83	4.59	3.50	4.41	4.38	3.87	4.30	3.72	3.17	3.82	3.39	
5 BAKERSFIELD, CA	1.18	1.21	1.41	0.45	0.24	0.12	0.00	0.08	0.15	0.30	0.59	0.76	
6 BATON ROUGE, LA	6.19	5.10	5.07	5.56	5.34	5.33	5.96	5.86	4.84	3.81	4.76	5.26	
7 BILLINGS, MT	0.81	0.57	1.12	1.74	2.48	1.89	1.28	0.85	1.34	1.26	0.75	0.67	
8 DAYTONA BEACH, FL	3.13	2.74	3.84	2.54	3.26	5.69	5.17	6.09	6.61	4.48	3.03	2.71	
9 EUGENE, OR	7.65	6.35	5.80	3.66	2.66	1.53	0.64	0.99	1.54	3.35	8.44	8.29	
10 HONOLULU, HI	2.73	2.35	1.89	1.11	0.78	0.43	0.50	0.46	0.74	2.18	2.26	2.85	
11 ST. LOUIS, MO	2.14	2.28	3.60	3.69	4.11	3.76	3.90	2.98	2.96	2.76	3.71	2.86	
12 TUCSON, AZ	0.99	0.88	0.81	0.28	0.24	0.24	2.07	2.30	1.45	1.21	0.67	1.03	

Figure 3-6: Column sparklines summarize the precipitation data for nine cities.

The sparklines are linked to the data, so if you change any of the values in the data range, the sparkline graphic updates.

Tip

Generally, you'll create sparklines on the same sheet that contains the data. If you want to create sparklines on a different sheet, start by activating the sheet where the sparklines will be displayed. Then, in the Create Sparklines dialog box, specify the source data either by pointing or by typing the complete sheet reference (for example, type **Sheet1A1:C12**). The Create Sparklines dialog box lets you specify a different sheet for the Data Range, but not for the Location Range.

▶ Understanding Sparkline Groups

Most of the time, you'll probably create a group of sparklines — one for each row or column of data. A worksheet can hold any number of sparkline groups. Excel remembers each group, and you can work with the group as a single unit. For example, you can select one sparkline in a group and then modify the formatting of all sparklines in the group. When you select one sparkline cell, Excel displays an outline of all the other sparklines in the group.

You can, however, perform some operations on an individual sparkline in a group:

- **Change the sparkline's data source.** Click the sparkline cell and go to the Sparkline Tools tab on the Ribbon. There you can choose Design➜Sparkline➜Edit Data➜Edit Single Sparkline's Data. Excel displays a dialog box that lets you change the data source for the selected sparkline.

- **Delete the sparkline.** Click the sparkline, click the Sparkline Tools tab on the Ribbon, and then select Design➜Group➜Clear➜Clear Selected Sparklines.

Both operations are available from the shortcut menu that appears when you right-click a sparkline cell.

You can also ungroup a set of sparklines. Select any sparkline in the group and then, from the Sparkline Tools tab, select Design➜Group➜Ungroup. After you ungroup a set of sparklines, you can work with each sparkline individually.

Ungrouping sparklines gives you the ability to move, size, and format them separately on your dashboard.

Customizing Sparklines

When you activate a cell that contains a sparkline, Excel displays an outline around all the sparklines in its group. You can then use the commands on the Design tab (select Sparkline Tools➜Design tab) to customize the group of sparklines.

Sizing and merging sparkline cells

When you change the width or height of a cell that contains a sparkline, the sparkline adjusts to fill the new cell size. In addition, you can put a sparkline into merged cells. To merge cells, select at least two cells and choose Home➜Alignment➜Merge & Center.

Figure 3-7 shows the same sparkline, displayed at four sizes resulting from column width, row height, and merged cells.

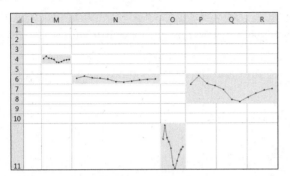

Figure 3-7: A sparkline at various sizes.

Note Generally, the most appropriate aspect ratio for a chart is 2:1, where the chart is about twice as wide as it is tall. Other aspect ratios can distort your visualizations, exaggerating the trend in sparklines that are too tall, and flattening the trend in sparklines that are too wide.

Note If you merge cells, and the merged cells occupy more than one row or one column, Excel won't let you insert a group of sparklines into those merged cells. Rather, you need to insert the sparklines into a normal range (with no merged cells) and then merge the cells.

You can also put a sparkline in nonempty cells, including merged cells. Figure 3-8 shows two sparklines merged with cells containing some text. This gives the appearance of two single cells with both text and graphics.

	A	B	C	D	E F G H I
1		Western	Eastern		
2	Jan	76	76		WESTERN REGION: Following a slow start, sales in the 2nd half picked up considerably, and exceeded expectations.
3	Feb	67	84		
4	Mar	69	79		
5	Apr	71	89		
6	May	87	98		
7	Jun	99	86		
8	Jul	109	83		
9	Aug	143	82		EASTERN REGION: Sales were steady throughout the year, significantly below the levels in the Western Region.
10	Sep	156	87		
11	Oct	178	85		
12	Nov	198	89		
13	Dec	185	81		
14					

Figure 3-8: Sparklines in merged cells (E2:I7 and E9:I14).

Handling hidden or missing data

In some cases, you just want to present the sparkline visualization, without the numbers. One way to do so is to hide the rows or columns that contain the data. Figure 3-9 shows a table with the values displayed, and the same table with the values hidden (by hiding the columns).

By default, if you hide rows or columns that contain data used in a sparkline graphic, the hidden data doesn't appear in the sparkline. In addition, blank cells are displayed as a gap in the graphic.

To change these default settings, go to the Sparkline Tools tab on the Ribbon and select Design→ Sparkline→Edit Data→Hidden & Empty Cells. In the Hidden and Empty Cell Settings dialog box, specify how to handle hidden data and empty cells.

Product Line	Jan	Feb	Mar	Apr	May	Jun	6-Month Trend
Women's shoes	87	92	101	121	89	88	
Men's shoes	67	66	73	59	54	61	
Children's shoes	92	101	114	125	109	111	
Women's hats	76	71	65	73	65	51	
Men's hats	12	15	18	26	13	12	
Children's hats	44	46	48	44	42	41	

Product Line	6-Month Trend
Women's shoes	
Men's shoes	
Children's shoes	
Women's hats	
Men's hats	
Children's hats	

Figure 3-9: Sparklines can use data in hidden rows or columns.

Changing the sparkline type

As mentioned earlier in this chapter, Excel supports three sparkline types: Line, Column, and Win/ Loss. After you create a sparkline or group of sparklines, you can easily change the type by clicking the sparkline and selecting one of the three icons located under Sparkline Tools→Design→Type. If the selected sparkline is part of a group, all sparklines in the group are changed to the new type.

Tip

If you've customized the appearance, when you switch among different sparkline types, Excel remembers your customization settings for each sparkline type.

Changing sparkline colors and line width

After you create a sparkline, changing the color is easy. Simply click the sparkline, go up to the Sparkline Tools tab in the Ribbon, and select Design→Style. There you will find various options to change the color and style of your sparkline.

For Line sparklines, you can also specify the line width. Choose Sparkline Tools→Design→Style→ Sparkline Color→Weight.

Colors used in sparkline graphics are tied to the document theme. If you change the theme (by choosing Page Layout➜Themes➜Themes), the sparkline colors then change to the new theme colors. Be aware that any manual changes you make to color are lost if you change the theme.

Using color to emphasize key data points

Use the commands under Sparkline Tools➜Design➜Show to customize the sparklines to emphasize key aspects of the data. The options in the Show group are as follows:

➤ **High Point:** Apply a different color to the highest data point in the sparkline.

➤ **Low Point:** Apply a different color to the lowest data point in the sparkline.

➤ **Negative Points:** Apply a different color to negative values in the sparkline.

➤ **First Point:** Apply a different color to the first data point in the sparkline.

➤ **Last Point:** Apply a different color to the last data point in the sparkline.

➤ **Markers:** Show data markers in the sparkline. This option is available only for Line sparklines.

You can control the color of the sparkline by using the Marker Color control in the Sparkline Tools➜Design➜Style group. Unfortunately, you cannot change the size of the markers in Line sparklines.

Figure 3-10 shows some Line sparklines with various types of colors added.

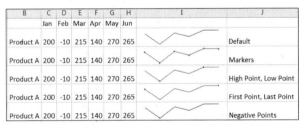

Figure 3-10: Using color to emphasize key data points for Line sparklines.

Adjusting sparkline axis scaling

When you create one or more sparklines, they all use (by default) automatic axis scaling. In other words, Excel determines the minimum and maximum vertical axis values for each sparkline in the group, based on the numeric range of the sparkline data.

The Sparkline Tools➜Design➜Group➜Axis command lets you override this automatic behavior and control the minimum and maximum value for each sparkline, or for a group of sparklines. For even more control, you can use the Custom Value option and specify the minimum and maximum for the sparkline group.

Axis scaling can make a huge difference in the sparklines. Figure 3-11 shows two groups of sparklines. The group at the top uses the default axis settings (Automatic for Each Sparkline). Each sparkline in this group shows the six-month trend for the product, but there is no indication of the magnitude of the values.

The sparkline group at the bottom (which uses the same data), uses the Same for All Sparklines setting for the minimum and maximum axis values. With these settings in effect, the magnitude of the values *across* the products is apparent — but the trend across the months within a product is not apparent.

The axis scaling option you choose depends on what aspect of the data you want to emphasize.

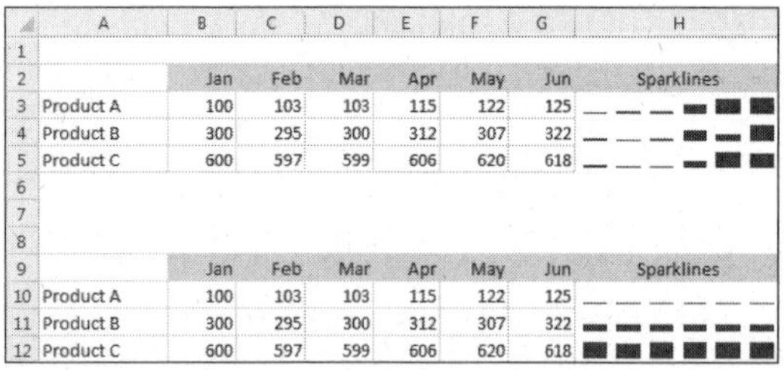

	A	B	C	D	E	F	G	H
1								
2		Jan	Feb	Mar	Apr	May	Jun	Sparklines
3	Product A	100	103	103	115	122	125	
4	Product B	300	295	300	312	307	322	
5	Product C	600	597	599	606	620	618	
6								
7								
8								
9		Jan	Feb	Mar	Apr	May	Jun	Sparklines
10	Product A	100	103	103	115	122	125	
11	Product B	300	295	300	312	307	322	
12	Product C	600	597	599	606	620	618	

Figure 3-11: The bottom group of sparklines shows the effect of using the same axis minimum and maximum values for all sparklines in a group.

Faking a reference line

One useful feature that's missing in the Excel 2013 implementation of sparklines is a reference line. For example, it might be useful to show performance relative to a goal. If the goal is displayed as a reference line in a sparkline, the viewer can quickly see whether the performance for a period exceeded the goal.

One approach is to write formulas that transform the data and then use a sparkline axis as a fake reference line. Figure 3-12 shows an example. Students have a monthly reading goal of 500 pages. The range of data shows the actual pages read, with sparklines in column H. The sparklines show the six-month page data, but it's impossible to tell who exceeded the goal and when they did it.

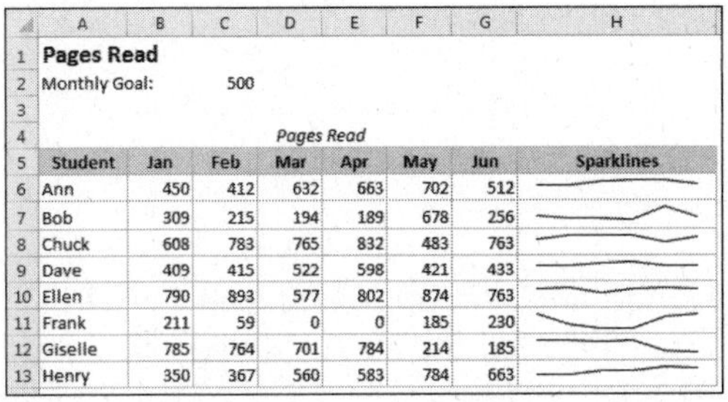

	A	B	C	D	E	F	G	H
1	**Pages Read**							
2	Monthly Goal:		500					
3								
4					Pages Read			
5	Student	Jan	Feb	Mar	Apr	May	Jun	Sparklines
6	Ann	450	412	632	663	702	512	
7	Bob	309	215	194	189	678	256	
8	Chuck	608	783	765	832	483	763	
9	Dave	409	415	522	598	421	433	
10	Ellen	790	893	577	802	874	763	
11	Frank	211	59	0	0	185	230	
12	Giselle	785	764	701	784	214	185	
13	Henry	350	367	560	583	784	663	

Figure 3-12: Sparklines display the number of pages read per month.

The lower set of sparklines in Figure 3-13 shows another approach: Transforming the data so that meeting the goal is expressed as a 1 and failing to meet the goal is expressed as a –1. The following formula (in cell B18) transforms the original data:

```
=IF(B6>$C$2,1,-1)
```

This formula was copied to the other cells in the B18:G25 range.

Using the transformed data, Win/Loss sparklines are used to visualize the results. This approach is better than the original, but it doesn't convey any magnitude differences. For example, you cannot tell whether the student missed the goal by 1 page or by 500 pages.

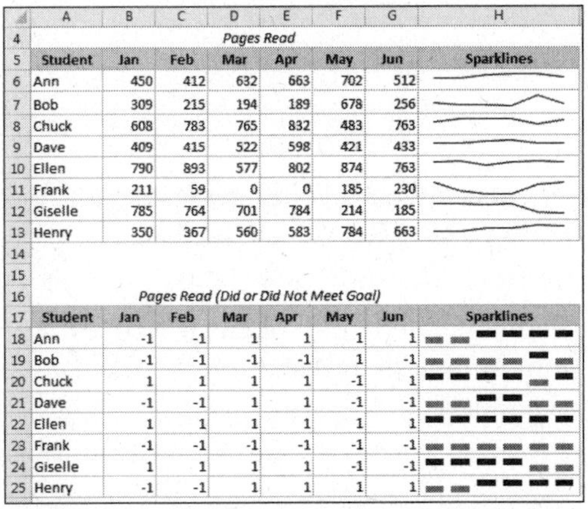

	A	B	C	D	E	F	G	H
4					Pages Read			
5	Student	Jan	Feb	Mar	Apr	May	Jun	Sparklines
6	Ann	450	412	632	663	702	512	
7	Bob	309	215	194	189	678	256	
8	Chuck	608	783	765	832	483	763	
9	Dave	409	415	522	598	421	433	
10	Ellen	790	893	577	802	874	763	
11	Frank	211	59	0	0	185	230	
12	Giselle	785	764	701	784	214	185	
13	Henry	350	367	560	583	784	663	
14								
15								
16				Pages Read (Did or Did Not Meet Goal)				
17	Student	Jan	Feb	Mar	Apr	May	Jun	Sparklines
18	Ann	-1	-1	1	1	1	1	
19	Bob	-1	-1	-1	-1	1	-1	
20	Chuck	1	1	1	1	-1	1	
21	Dave	-1	-1	1	1	-1	-1	
22	Ellen	1	1	1	1	1	1	
23	Frank	-1	-1	-1	-1	-1	-1	
24	Giselle	1	1	1	1	-1	-1	
25	Henry	-1	-1	1	1	1	1	

Figure 3-13: Using Win/Loss sparklines to display goal status.

Figure 3-14 shows a better approach. Here the original data is transformed by subtracting the goal from the pages read. The formula in cell B31 is

```
=B6-C$2
```

This formula was copied to the other cells in the B31:G38 range, and a group of Line sparklines display the resulting values. This group has the Show Axis setting enabled and also uses Negative Point markers so the negative values (failure to meet the goal) clearly stand out.

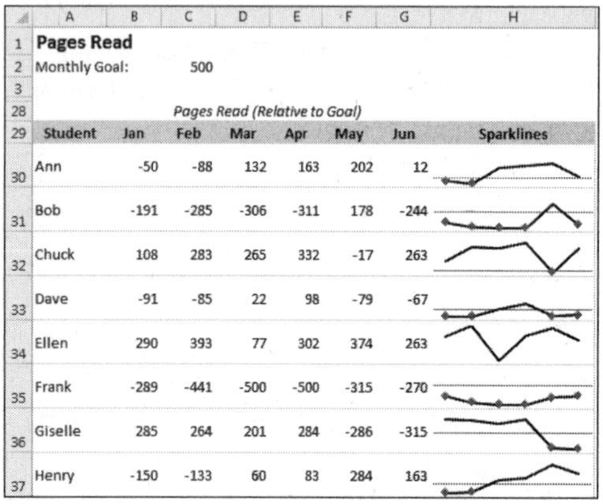

	A	B	C	D	E	F	G	H
1	Pages Read							
2	Monthly Goal:		500					
3								
28			Pages Read (Relative to Goal)					
29	Student	Jan	Feb	Mar	Apr	May	Jun	Sparklines
30	Ann	-50	-88	132	163	202	12	
31	Bob	-191	-285	-306	-311	178	-244	
32	Chuck	108	283	265	332	-17	263	
33	Dave	-91	-85	22	98	-79	-67	
34	Ellen	290	393	77	302	374	263	
35	Frank	-289	-441	-500	-500	-315	-270	
36	Giselle	285	264	201	284	-286	-315	
37	Henry	-150	-133	60	83	284	163	

Figure 3-14: The axis in the sparklines represents the goal.

Specifying a date axis

By default, data displayed in a sparkline is assumed to be at equal intervals. For example, a sparkline may display a daily account balance, sales by month, or profits by year. But what if the data isn't at equal intervals?

Figure 3-15 shows data, by date, along with a sparklines graphic created from column B. Notice that some dates are missing, but the sparkline shows the columns as though the values were spaced at equal intervals.

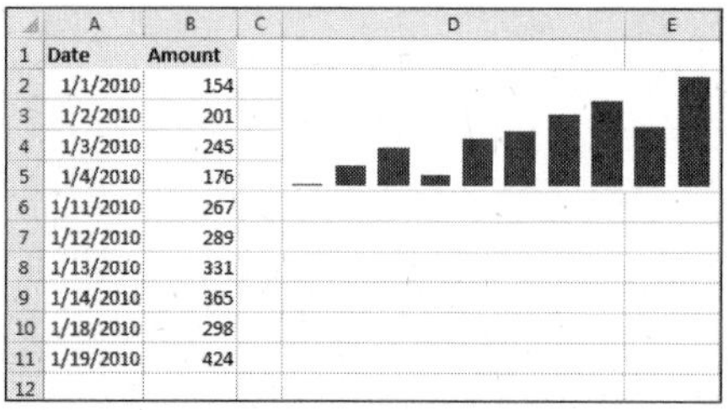

	A	B	C	D	E
1	Date	Amount			
2	1/1/2010	154			
3	1/2/2010	201			
4	1/3/2010	245			
5	1/4/2010	176			
6	1/11/2010	267			
7	1/12/2010	289			
8	1/13/2010	331			
9	1/14/2010	365			
10	1/18/2010	298			
11	1/19/2010	424			
12					

Figure 3-15: The sparkline displays the values as though they're at equal time intervals.

To better depict this type of time-based data, the solution is to specify a date axis. Select the spark-line and choose Sparkline Tools➜Design➜Group➜Axis➜Date Axis Type.

Excel displays a dialog box, asking for the range that contains the corresponding dates. In this example, specify range **A2:A11**.

Click OK, and the sparkline displays gaps for the missing dates (see Figure 3-16).

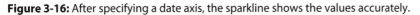

	A	B	C	D	E
1	Date	Amount			
2	1/1/2010	154			
3	1/2/2010	201			
4	1/3/2010	245			
5	1/4/2010	176			
6	1/11/2010	267			
7	1/12/2010	289			
8	1/13/2010	331			
9	1/14/2010	365			
10	1/18/2010	298			
11	1/19/2010	424			
12					

Figure 3-16: After specifying a date axis, the sparkline shows the values accurately.

Auto-updating sparkline ranges

If a sparkline uses data in a normal range of cells, adding new data to the beginning or end of the range does *not* force the sparkline to use the new data. You need to use the Edit Sparklines dialog box to update the data range (choose Sparkline Tools➜Design➜Sparkline➜Edit Data).

But if the sparkline data is in a column within a Table object (created using Insert➜Tables➜Table as described in Chapter 11), the sparkline uses new data that's added to the end of the table.

Figure 3-17 shows an example. The sparkline was created using the data in the Rate column of the table. When you add the new rate for September, the sparkline will automatically update its Data Range.

	A	B	C	D	E
1	End of month interest rates				
2					
3		Month	Rate		
4		Jan	5.20%		
5		Feb	5.02%		
6		Mar	4.97%		
7		Apr	4.99%		
8		May	4.89%		
9		Jun	4.72%		
10		Jul	4.68%		
11		Aug	4.61%		
12					

	A	B	C	D	E
1	End of month interest rates				
2					
3		Month	Rate		
4		Jan	5.20%		
5		Feb	5.02%		
6		Mar	4.97%		
7		Apr	4.99%		
8		May	4.89%		
9		Jun	4.72%		
10		Jul	4.68%		
11		Aug	4.61%		
12		Sep	4.76%		

Figure 3-17: Creating a sparkline from data in a table.

Chartless Visualization Techniques

In This Chapter

- Using conditional formatting
- Leveraging symbols in formulas
- Using the Camera tool

Chartless visualization is less a feature specific to Excel than it is a concept that you can apply to your dashboard presentation. With these types of visualization, you can easily add layers of visualization to your dashboard and take advantage of some common worksheet features that can turn your data into meaningful views.

Enhancing Reports with Conditional Formatting

Conditional formatting applies to the Excel functionality used that dynamically changes the formatting of a value, cell, or range of cells based on a set of conditions you define. Conditional formatting allows you to look at your Excel reports and make split-second determinations on which values are "good" and which are "bad," all based on formatting.

In this section, you discover the world of conditional formatting and find out how to leverage this functionality to enhance your reports and dashboards.

Applying basic conditional formatting

Thanks to the many predefined options offered with Excel 2013, you can apply some basic conditional formatting with a few clicks of the mouse. To get a first taste of what you can do, go the Ribbon, click the Home tab, and choose the Conditional Formatting icon (see Figure 4-1).

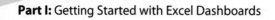

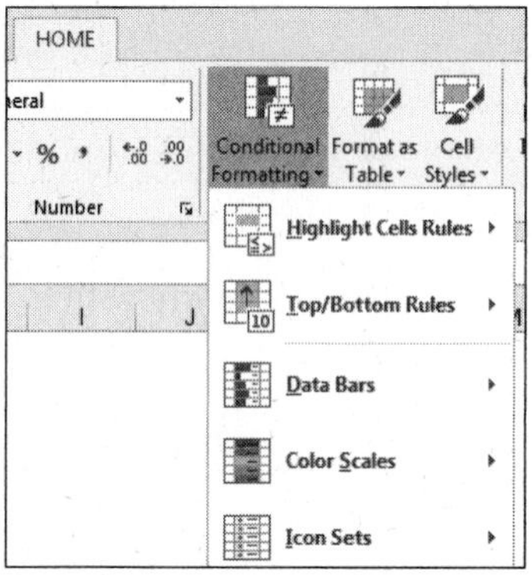

Figure 4-1: Click the Conditional Formatting icon to reveal the predefined options available in Excel 2013.

As you can see, five categories of predefined options are available:

> Highlight Cells Rules
>
> Top/Bottom Rules
>
> Data Bars
>
> Color Scales
>
> Icon Sets

Take a moment now to review what each category enables you to do.

Using Highlight Cells Rules

The formatting options in the Highlight Cells Rules category, shown in Figure 4-2, allow you to highlight those cells whose values meet a specific condition.

Note

These options work very much like an If…Then…Else… statement. That is, if the condition is met, the cell is formatted; if the condition isn't met, the cell isn't touched.

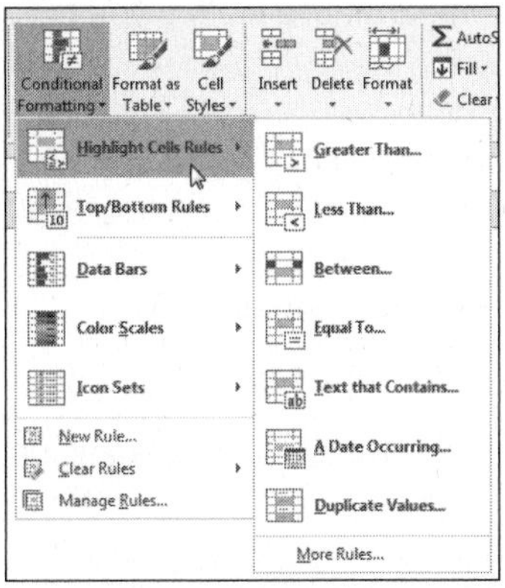

Figure 4-2: The Highlight Cells Rules options apply formats if specific conditions are met.

The options in the Highlight Cells Rules category are pretty self-explanatory:

➤ **Greater Than:** Allows you to conditionally format a cell whose value is greater than a specified amount.

For instance, you can tell Excel to format those cells that contain a value greater than 50.

➤ **Less Than:** Allows you to conditionally format a cell whose value is less than a specified amount.

For instance, you can tell Excel to format those cells that contain a value less than 100.

➤ **Between:** Allows you to conditionally format a cell whose value is between two given amounts.

For example, you can tell Excel to format those cells that contain a value between 50 and 100.

➤ **Text That Contains:** Allows you to conditionally format a cell whose contents contain any form of a given text you specify as a criterion.

For example, you can tell Excel to format the cells that contain the text *North*.

➤ **A Date Occurring:** Allows you to conditionally format a cell whose contents contain a date occurring in a specified period relative to today's date.

For example, Yesterday, Last Week, Last Month, Next Month, Next Week, and so on.

➤ **Duplicate Values:** Allows you to conditionally format both duplicate values and unique values in a given range of cells.

Tip

This rule was designed more for data cleanup than for dashboarding, enabling you to quickly identify duplicates and unique values in your dataset.

Here's a simple example of how to apply one of these options. To highlight all values greater than a certain amount, follow these steps:

1. Select the range of cells to which you need to apply the conditional formatting.

2. In the Highlight Cells Rules category, choose the Greater Than option (see Figure 4-2).

   The Greater Than dialog box opens, as shown in Figure 4-3. The idea here is to define a value that will trigger the conditional formatting. You can either

   - Type the value (400 in this example).

   - Reference a cell that contains the trigger value.

   Also in this dialog box, you can use the drop-down menu to specify the format you want applied.

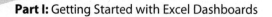

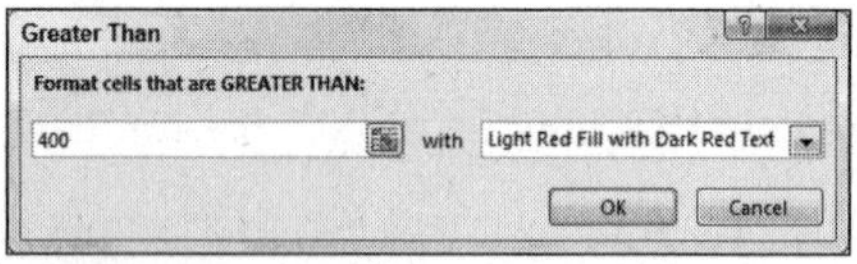

Figure 4-3: Each option has its own dialog box that you can use to define the trigger values and the format for each rule.

3. Click OK.

   You immediately see the formatting rule applied to the selected cells (see Figure 4-4).

	Greater Than 400
Jan	100
Feb	-100
Mar	200
Apr	250
May	-50
Jun	350
Jul	400
Aug	450
Sep	500
Oct	550
Nov	600
Dec	650

Figure 4-4: Cells greater than 400 are formatted.

The benefit of a conditional formatting rule is that Excel automatically reevaluates the rule each time a cell is changed (provided that cell has a conditional formatting rule applied to it). For instance, if you were to change any of the low values to 450, the formatting would automatically change because all of the cells in the dataset have the formatting applied to it.

Applying Top/Bottom Rules

The formatting options in the Top/Bottom Rules category, shown in Figure 4-5, allow you to highlight those cells whose values meet a given threshold.

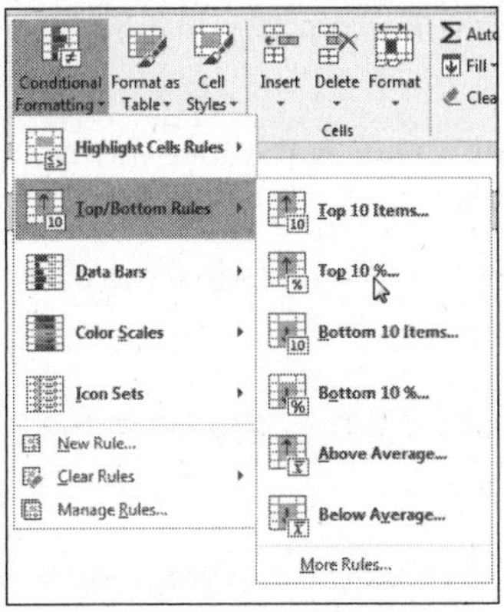

Figure 4-5: The Top/Bottom Rules options apply formats if specific thresholds are met.

As with the Highlight Cells Rules, these options work like If…Then…Else… statements:

➤ If the condition is met, the cell is formatted.

➤ If the condition isn't met, the cell isn't touched.

In the Top/Bottom Options category, you can select a *percentage* or *number* of cells.

> **Tip**
>
> **Some of the names of the options are misleading. Options that are named with *10 Items* can select any number of cells, and options that are named with *10%* can select any percentage.**

You can select from these options:

➤ **Top 10 Items:** Allows you to specify any number of cells to highlight based on individual cell values (not just 10 cells).

For example, you can highlight the cells whose values are the 5 largest numbers of all the cells selected.

➤ **Top 10%:** Allows you to specify any percentage of cells to highlight based on individual cell values (not just 10 percent) option.

For instance, you can highlight the cells whose values make up the top 20 percent of the total values of all the selected cells.

➤ **Bottom 10 Items:** Allows you to specify the number of cells to highlight based on the lowest individual cell values (not just 10 cells).

For example, you can highlight the cells whose values are within the 15 smallest numbers among all the cells selected.

➤ **Bottom 10%:** Allows you to specify any percentage of cells to highlight based on individual cell values (not just 10 percent).

For instance, you can highlight the cells whose values make up the bottom 15 percent of the total values of all the selected cells.

➤ **Above Average:** Allows you to conditionally format each cell whose value is above the average of all cells selected.

➤ **Below Average:** Allows you to conditionally format each cell whose value is below the average of all cells selected.

In this example, you conditionally format all cells whose values are within the top 40 percent of the total values of all cells.

Note

To avoid overlapping different conditional formatting options, before applying a new option, you may want to delete any conditional formatting you've previously applied. To clear the conditional formatting for a given range of cells, select the cells, go to Ribbon, and select Home➜Conditional Formatting. Here you find the Clear Rules selection. Click Clear Rules and select whether you want to clear conditional formatting for the entire sheet or only the selected workbook.

1. Select the range of cells to which you need to apply the conditional formatting.

2. In the Top/Bottom Options category, choose Top 10% (see Figure 4-5).

   The Top 10% dialog box opens, as illustrated in Figure 4-6. Here you define the threshold that that will trigger the conditional formatting.

3. In this example, enter **40**.

   Here you can also use the drop-down menu to specify the format you want to apply.

Top 10%	
Format cells that rank in the TOP:	
40 ⬍ % with	Light Red Fill with Dark Red Text ▾
	OK Cancel

Figure 4-6: Each option has its own dialog box where you can define its trigger values and format.

4. Click OK.

You immediately see the formatting option applied to the selected cells (see Figure 4-7).

	Within Top 40%
Jan	100
Feb	-100
Mar	200
Apr	250
May	-50
Jun	350
Jul	400
Aug	450
Sep	500
Oct	550
Nov	600
Dec	650

Figure 4-7: With conditional formatting, you can easily see that September through December makes up 40 percent of the total value in this dataset.

Creating Data Bars

Data Bars fill each cell you're formatting with mini-bars in varying length, indicating the value in each cell relative to other formatted cells. Excel essentially takes the largest and smallest values in the selected range and calculates the length for each bar.

To apply Data Bars to a range, do the following:

1. Select the target range of cells to which you need to apply the conditional formatting.

2. Click the Home tab and choose Conditional Formatting➜Data Bars.

As you can see in Figure 4-8, you can choose from a menu of Data Bars varying in gradient and color.

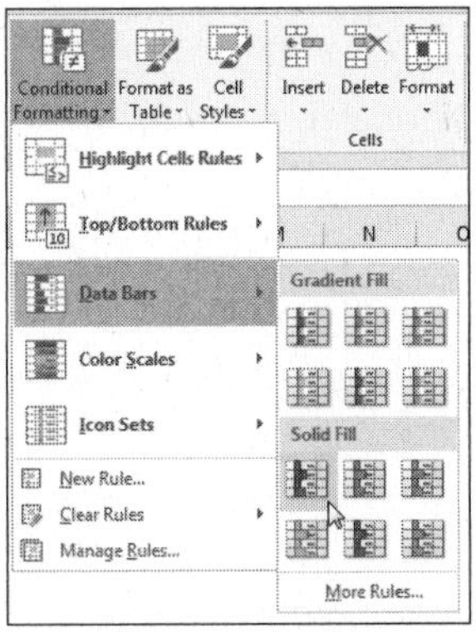

Figure 4-8: Applying Data Bars.

As shown in Figure 4-9, the result is essentially a mini-chart within the cells you selected. Also note that the Data Bars category, by default, accounts for negative numbers nicely by changing the direction of the bar and inverting the color to red.

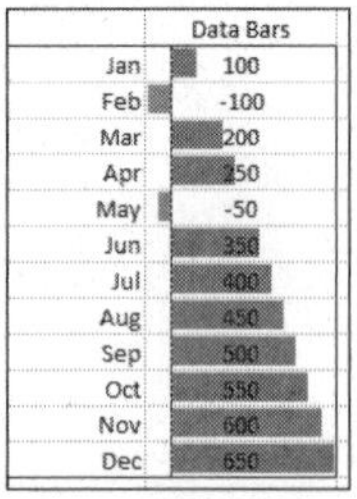

	Data Bars	
Jan		100
Feb		-100
Mar		200
Apr		150
May		-50
Jun		350
Jul		400
Aug		450
Sep		500
Oct		550
Nov		600
Dec		650

Figure 4-9: Conditional formatting with Data Bars.

Note

After you create your Data Bars, it's easy to go back and change their colors. Highlight the range of cells that contain the Data Bars, and then go up to the Home tab and select Conditional Formatting➜Manage Rules. This opens the Rules Manager dialog box that lists all the conditional formatting rules applied to the highlighted range. Here, select your Data Bar rule and click the Edit Rule button. The Edit Formatting Rule dialog box appears, allowing you to change the colors for both positive and negative Data Bars.

Applying Color Scales

Color Scales fill each cell you're formatting with a color, varying in scale based on the value in each cell relative to other formatted cells. Excel essentially takes the largest and smallest values in the selected range and determines the color for each cell.

To apply Color Scales to a range, do the following:

1. Select the target range of cells to which you need to apply the conditional formatting.

2. Click the Home tab and choose Conditional Formatting➜Color Scales.

As you can see in Figure 4-10, you can choose from a menu of Color Scales varying in color.

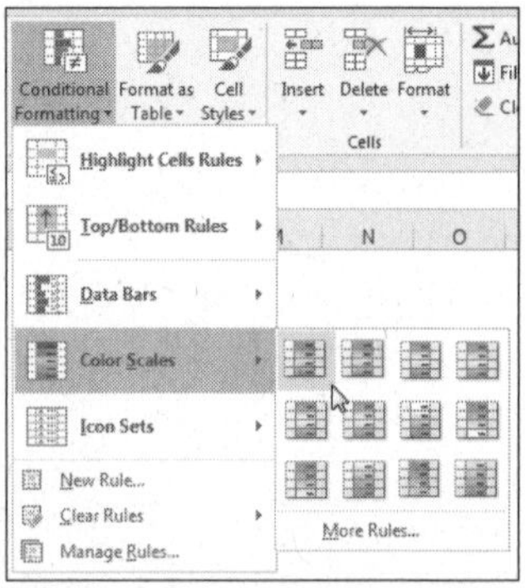

Figure 4-10: Applying Color Scales.

As you can see in Figure 4-11, the result is a kind of heat-map within the cells you selected.

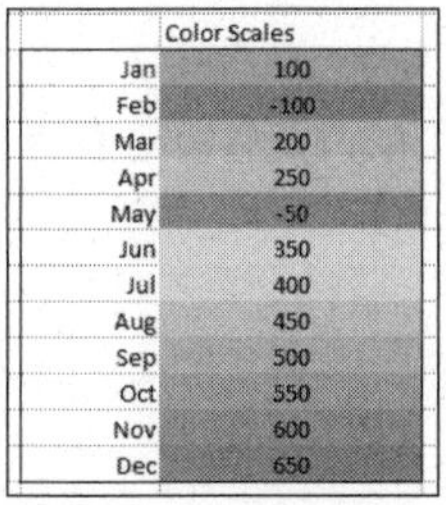

	Color Scales
Jan	100
Feb	-100
Mar	200
Apr	250
May	-50
Jun	350
Jul	400
Aug	450
Sep	500
Oct	550
Nov	600
Dec	650

Figure 4-11: Conditional formatting with Color Scales.

Using icon sets

Icon sets are sets of symbols that are inserted in each cell you're formatting. Excel determines which symbol to use based on the value in each cell relative to other formatted cells.

To apply an icon set to a range, do the following:

1. Select the target range of cells to which you need to apply the conditional formatting.

2. Click the Home tab and choose Conditional Formatting➜Icon Sets.

    As you can see in Figure 4-12, you can choose from a menu of icon sets varying in shape and colors.

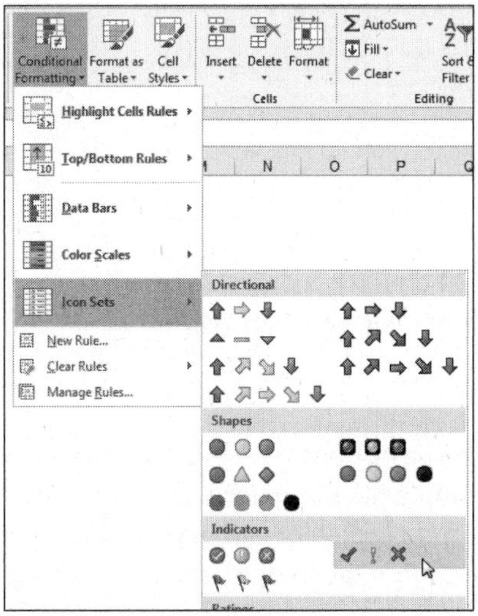

Figure 4-12: Applying icon sets.

Figure 4-13 illustrates how each cell is formatted with a symbol indicating each cell's value based on the other cells.

	Icon Sets	
Jan	✖	100
Feb	✖	-100
Mar	⚡	200
Apr	⚡	250
May	✖	-50
Jun	⚡	350
Jul	⚡	400
Aug	✔	450
Sep	✔	500
Oct	✔	550
Nov	✔	600
Dec	✔	650

Figure 4-13: Conditional formatting with icon sets.

Adding your own formatting rules manually

You don't have to use one of the predefined options offered by Excel. Excel gives you the flexibility to create your own formatting rules manually. Creating your own formatting rule helps you better control how cells are formatted and allows you to do things you can't do with the predefined options.

For example, a useful conditional formatting rule is to tag all above-average values with a Check icon, whereas all below-average values get an X icon, as shown in Figure 4-14.

	A	B		C
1	REGION	MARKET		Sales
2	North	Great Lakes	✖	70,261
3	North	New England	✔	217,858
4	North	New York North	✖	157,774
5	North	New York South	✖	53,670
6	North	North Carolina	✖	124,600
7	North	Ohio	✖	100,512
8	North	Shenandoah Valley	✖	149,742
9	South	Florida	✖	111,606
10	South	Gulf Coast	✔	253,703
11	South	Illinois	✖	129,148
12	South	Indiana	✖	152,471
13	South	Kentucky	✔	224,524
14	South	South Carolina	✔	249,535
15	South	Tennessee	✔	307,490
16	South	Texas	✔	180,167

Figure 4-14: With a custom formatting rule, you can tag the above-average values with a check and the below-average values with an X.

Note

Although the above average and below average options built into Excel allow you to format cell and font attributes, they don't enable the use of icon sets. You can imagine why icon sets will be better on a dashboard than just color variances. Icons and shapes do a much better job at conveying your message, especially when your dashboard is printed in black and white.

To start creating your first custom formatting rule, open the Chapter 4 Samples.xlsx file found in the sample files for this book. With the file open, go to the Create Rule by Hand tab.

1. Select the target range of cells to which you need to apply the conditional formatting and select New Rule as, shown in Figure 4-15.

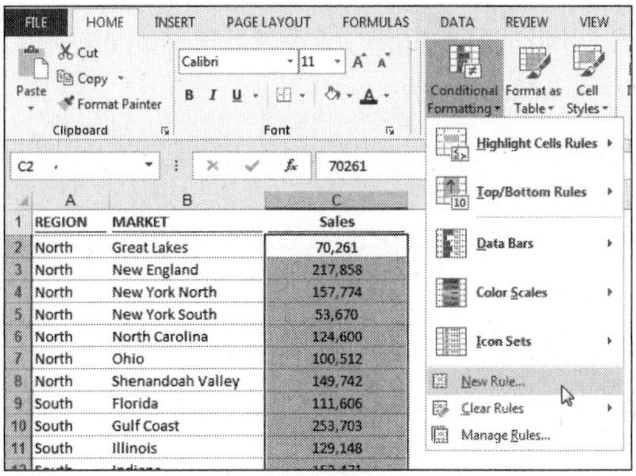

Figure 4-15: Select the target range; then select New Rule.

The New Formatting Rule dialog box opens, as shown in Figure 4-16.

As you can see, some of the rule types at the top of the dialog box are predefined option choices discussed earlier in this chapter:

● **Format All Cells Based on Their Values:** Measures the values in the selected range against each other.

   This selection is handy for finding general anomalies in your dataset.

● **Format Only Cells That Contain:** Applies conditional formatting to those cells that meet specific criteria you define.

   This selection is perfect for comparing values against a defined benchmark.

● **Format Only Top or Bottom Ranked Values:** Applies conditional formatting to those cells that are ranked in the top or bottom nth number or percent of all the values in the range.

● **Format Only Values That Are Above or Below the Average:** Applies conditional formatting to those values that are mathematically above or below the average of all values in the selected range.

● **Format Only Unique or Duplicate Values:** Applies conditional formatting to cells that either contain values that are duplicated within the selected range or contain values are unique (not duplicated) within the selected range.

- **Use a Formula to Determine Which Cells to Format:** Evaluates values based on a formula you specify. If a particular value evaluates to true, then the conditional formatting is applied to that cell.

   This selection is typically used when applying conditions based the results of an advanced formula or mathematical operation.

Tip

You can use Data Bars, Color Scales, and icon sets only with the Format All Cells Based on Their Values rule.

2. Ensure that the Format All Cells Based on Their Values rule is selected; then use the Format Style drop-down menu to switch to icon sets.

3. Click the Icon Style drop-down menu to select your desired icon set.

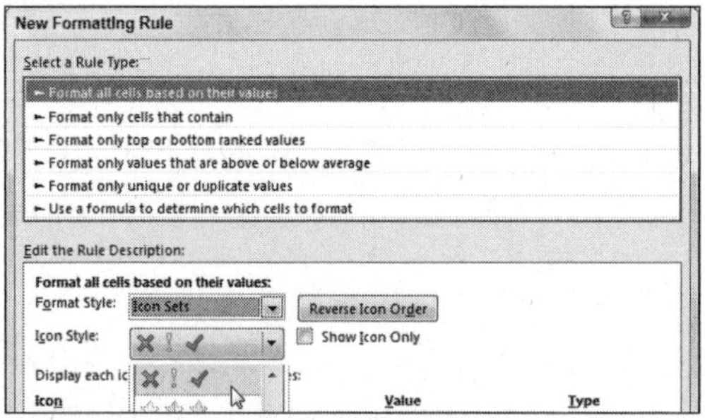

Figure 4-16: Select the Format All Cells Based on Their Values rule; then use the Format Style drop-down menu to switch to icon sets.

4. In the Type drop-down boxes, change both types to Formula.

5. In each Value box, enter **=Average($C$2:$C$22)**.

   This tells Excel that the value in each cell must be greater than the average of the entire dataset in order to get the Check icon.

   At this point, your dialog box will look similar to the one in Figure 4-17.

6. Click OK to apply your conditional formatting.

It's worth taking some time to understand how this conditional formatting rule works. Excel will assess every cell in your target range to see if its contents match the logic in each Value box in order (top box first):

➤ If a cell contains a number or text that evaluates true to the first Value box, the first icon is applied, and Excel moves on to the next cell in your range.

➤ If not, Excel continues down each Value box until one of them evaluates to true.

➤ If the cell being assessed doesn't fit any of the logic placed in the Value boxes, Excel automatically tags that cell with the last icon.

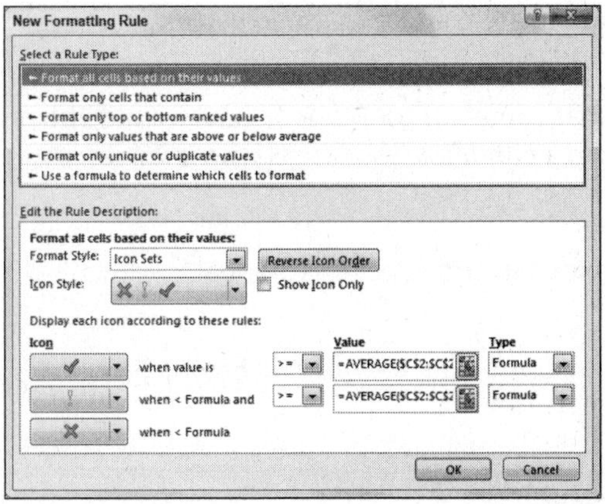

Figure 4-17: Change the Type drop-down box to Formula and enter the appropriate formulas in the Value boxes.

In this example, you want your cells to get a Check icon only if the value of that cell is greater than (or equal to) the average of the total values. Otherwise, you want Excel to skip right to the X icon and apply the X.

Show only one icon

In many cases, you may not need to show all icons when applying the icon set. In fact, showing too many icons at one time may only serve to obstruct the data you're trying to convey in your dashboard.

In the last example, you applied Check icons to values above the average for the range, whereas all below-average values were formatted with the X icon (see Figure 4-18). However, in the real world, you often need to bring attention only to the below-average values. This way, your eyes aren't inundated with superfluous icons.

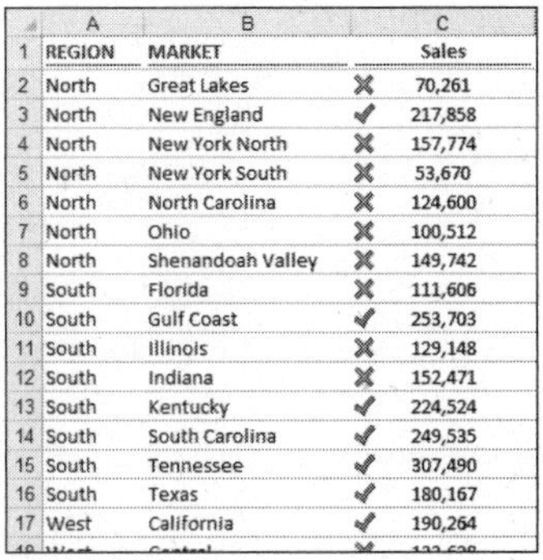

	A	B		C
1	REGION	MARKET		Sales
2	North	Great Lakes	✗	70,261
3	North	New England	✓	217,858
4	North	New York North	✗	157,774
5	North	New York South	✗	53,670
6	North	North Carolina	✗	124,600
7	North	Ohio	✗	100,512
8	North	Shenandoah Valley	✗	149,742
9	South	Florida	✗	111,606
10	South	Gulf Coast	✓	253,703
11	South	Illinois	✗	129,148
12	South	Indiana	✗	152,471
13	South	Kentucky	✓	224,524
14	South	South Carolina	✓	249,535
15	South	Tennessee	✓	307,490
16	South	Texas	✓	180,167
17	West	California	✓	190,264

Figure 4-18: Too many icons can hide the items you want to draw attention to.

Excel provides a clever mechanism to allow you to stop evaluating and formatting values if a condition is true.

In this example, you remove the Check icons. The cells that contain those icons all have values above the average for the range. Therefore, you first need to add a condition for all cells whose values are above average.

1. Select the target range of cells; then click the Home tab and select Conditional Formatting➜Manage Rules.

   The Conditional Formatting Rules Manager dialog box opens, as shown in Figure 4-19.

2. Click the New Rule button to start a new rule.

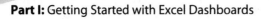

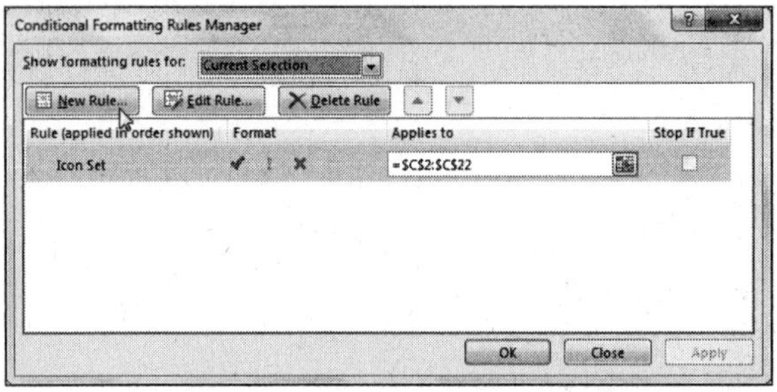

Figure 4-19: Open the Conditional Formatting Rules Manager and select New Rule.

3. Click the rule type Format Only Cells That Contain. Then configure the rule so that the format applies to cell values greater than the average (see Figure 4-20).

4. Click OK without changing any of the formatting options.

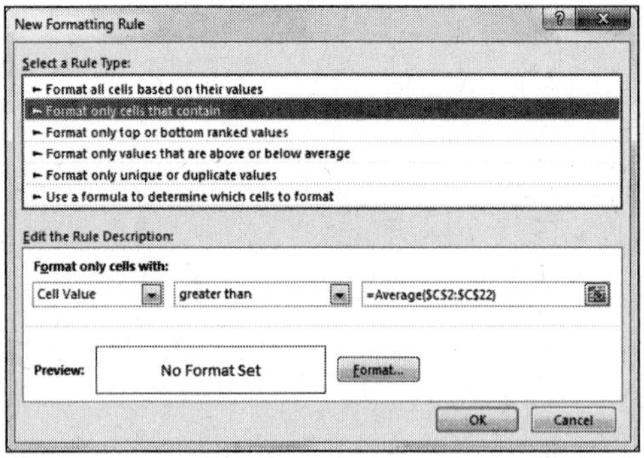

Figure 4-20: This new rule applies to any cell value that you don't want formatted.

5. Back in the Conditional Formatting Rules Manager, place a check in the Stop If True check box, as demonstrated in Figure 4-21.

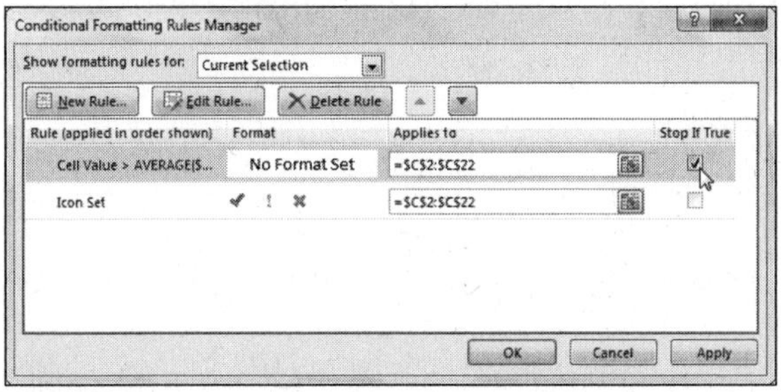

Figure 4-21: Click Stop If True to tell Excel to stop evaluating those cells that meet the first condition.

6. Click OK to apply your changes.

As you can see in Figure 4-22, only the X icons are now shown. Again, this allows your audience to focus on the exceptions, rather than determining which icons are good and bad.

	A	B	C	
1	REGION	MARKET		Sales
2	North	Great Lakes	✖	70,261
3	North	New England		217,858
4	North	New York North	✖	157,774
5	North	New York South	✖	53,670
6	North	North Carolina	✖	124,600
7	North	Ohio	✖	100,512
8	North	Shenandoah Valley	✖	149,742
9	South	Florida	✖	111,606
10	South	Gulf Coast		253,703
11	South	Illinois	✖	129,148
12	South	Indiana	✖	152,471
13	South	Kentucky		224,524
14	South	South Carolina		249,535
15	South	Tennessee		307,490
16	South	Texas		180,167
17	West	California		190,264

Figure 4-22: This table is now formatted to show only one icon.

Show Data Bars and icons outside of cells

Although Data Bars and icon sets give you a snazzy way of adding visualizations to your dashboards, you don't have a lot of say in where they appear within your cell. Take a look at Figure 4-23 to see what I mean.

The Data Bars are, by default, placed directly inside each cell, almost obfuscating the data. From a dashboarding perspective, this is less than ideal for two reasons:

➤ The numbers can get lost in the colors of the Data Bars, making them difficult to read — especially when printed in black and white.

➤ It's difficult to see the ends of each bar.

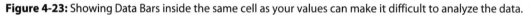

Figure 4-23: Showing Data Bars inside the same cell as your values can make it difficult to analyze the data.

The answer to this issue is to show the Data Bars outside the cell that contains the value. Here's how:

1. To the right of each cell, enter a formula that references the cell that contains your data value.

   For example, if your data is in B2, go to cell C2 and enter =B2.

2. Apply the Data Bar conditional formatting to the formulas you just created.

3. Select the formatted range of cells; then click the Home tab and select Conditional Formatting➔Manage Rules.

   The Conditional Formatting Rules Manager dialog box opens.

4. Click the Edit Rule button.

5. Place a check in the Show Bar Only option, as demonstrated in Figure 4-24.

6. Click OK to apply your change.

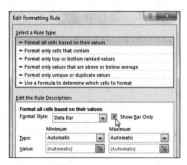

Figure 4-24: Edit the formatting rule to show only the Data Bars, not the data.

The reward for your efforts is a view that is cleaner and much better suited for reporting in a dashboard environment. Figure 4-25 illustrates the improvement gained with this technique.

	A	B	C
1	MARKET	Sales	
2	Great Lakes	70,261	
3	New England	217,858	
4	New York North	157,774	
5	New York South	53,670	
6	Ohio	100,512	
7	Shenandoah Valley	149,742	
8	South Carolina	249,535	
9	Florida	111,606	
10	Gulf Coast	253,703	
11	Illinois	129,148	
12	Indiana	152,471	
13	Kentucky	224,524	
14	North Carolina	124,600	
15	Tennessee	307,490	

Figure 4-25: Data Bars cleanly placed next to the data values.

Using the same technique, you can separate icon sets from the data, allowing you to position the icons where they best suit your dashboard.

Representing trends with icon sets

In a dashboard environment, there may not always be enough space available to add a chart that shows trending. In these cases, icon sets are an ideal replacement, enabling you to visually represent the overall trending without taking up a lot of space. Figure 4-26 illustrates this with a table that provides a nice visual element, allowing for an at-a-glance view of which markets are up, down, and flat over the previous month.

In your situations, you will want to do the same type of thing. The key is to create a formula that gives you a variance or trending of some sort.

	A	B	C	D	E
1	REGION	MARKET	Previous Month	Current Month	Variance
2	North	Great Lakes	70,261	72,505	3.2%
3	North	New England	217,858	283,324	30.0%
4	North	New York North	157,774	148,790	-5.7%
5	North	New York South	53,670	68,009	26.7%
6	North	Ohio	100,512	98,308	-2.2%
7	North	Shenandoah Valley	149,742	200,076	33.6%
8	South	South Carolina	249,535	229,473	-8.0%
9	South	Florida	111,606	136,104	22.0%
10	South	Gulf Coast	253,703	245,881	-3.1%
11	South	Illinois	129,148	131,538	1.9%
12	South	Indiana	152,471	151,699	-0.5%
13	South	Kentucky	224,524	225,461	0.4%
14	North	North Carolina	124,600	130,791	5.0%
15	South	Tennessee	307,490	268,010	-12.8%

Figure 4-26: Conditional Formatting icon sets enable trending visualizations.

To achieve this type of view, follow these steps:

1. Select the target range of cells to which you need to apply the conditional formatting.

   In this case, the target range will be the cells that hold your variance formulas.

2. Click the Home tab and choose Conditional Formatting➔Icon Set; then choose the most appropriate icons for your situation.

In this example, the set with three arrows works (see Figure 4-27).

- The up arrow indicates an upward trend.
- A down arrow indicates a downward trend.
- A right-pointing arrow indicates a flat trend.

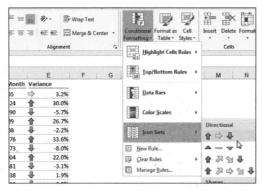

Figure 4-27: Your newly applied conditional formatting allows for a quick view of performance.

In most cases, you will want to adjust the thresholds that define what up, down, and flat mean. Imagine that you need any variance above 3% to be tagged with an up arrow, any variance below –3% to be tagged with a down arrow and all others to show flat.

3. Select the target range of cells; then click the Home tab and select Conditional Formatting➔Manage Rules.

The Conditional Formatting Rules Manager dialog box opens.

4. Click the Edit Rule button.

The Edit Formatting Rule dialog box opens.

5. Adjust the properties, as shown in Figure 4-28.

6. Click OK to apply your changes.

Tip

In Figure 4-28, notice that the Type property for the formatting rule is set to Number even though the data you're working with (the variance) is in percentages. You'll find that working with the Number setting gives you more control and predictability when setting thresholds.

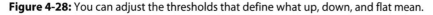

Figure 4-28: You can adjust the thresholds that define what up, down, and flat mean.

Using Symbols to Enhance Reporting

Symbols are essentially tiny graphics, not unlike those you see when you use the Wingdings, Webdings, or the other fancy fonts. However, symbols are not really fonts. They're Unicode characters. *Unicode characters* are a set of industry-standard text elements designed to provide a reliable character set that remains viable on any platform regardless of international font differences.

One example of a commonly used symbol is the Copyright symbol (©). This symbol is a Unicode character. You can use this symbol on a Chinese, Turkish, French, and American PC, and it will be available reliably with no international differences.

In terms of Excel presentations, Unicode characters (or symbols) can be used in places where conditional formatting cannot. For instance, in the chart labels that you see in Figure 4-29, notice that the x-axis shows some trending arrows that allow an extra layer of analysis. This couldn't be done with conditional formatting.

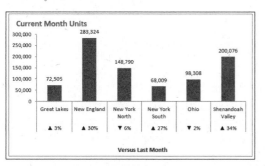

Figure 4-29: Use symbols to add an extra layer of analysis to charts.

Now, take some time to review the steps that led to the chart in Figure 4-29.

Start with the data shown in Figure 4-30. Note a cell (C1 in this case) is designated to hold any symbols you're going to use. This cell isn't really all that important. It's just a holding cell for the symbols you will insert.

	A	B	C	D
1		Symbols>>		
2				
3		vs. Prior Month	Market	Current Month
4		3%	Great Lakes	72,505
5		30%	New England	283,324
6		-6%	New York North	148,790
7		27%	New York South	68,009
8		-2%	Ohio	98,308
9		34%	Shenandoah Valley	200,076
10				

Figure 4-30: The starting data with a holding cell for your symbols.

Follow these steps to integrate symbols into your visualization:

1. Click in C1 and then select the Symbol command on the Insert tab.

   The Symbol dialog box opens, as shown in Figure 4-31.

2. Find and select your desired symbols, clicking the Insert button for each symbol.

   Then follow these steps:

   a. Select the DOWN symbol; then click Insert.

   b. Click the UP symbol; then click insert.

3. Close the dialog box when you're done.

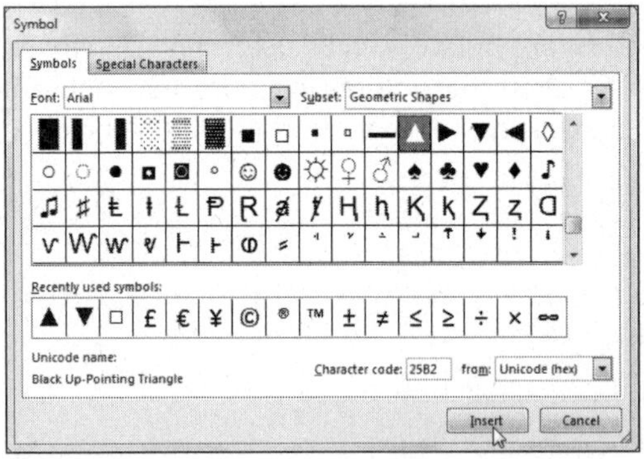

Figure 4-31: Use the Symbol dialog box to insert the desired symbols into your holding cell.

At this point, you have the UP and DOWN symbols in cell C1 (see Figure 4-32).

4. Click in the cell, go to the Formula bar, and copy the two symbols (highlight them and press Ctrl+C on your keyboard).

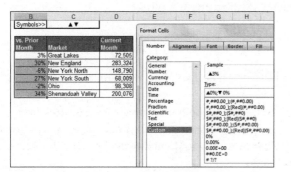

Figure 4-32: Copy the newly inserted symbols to the Clipboard.

5. Go to your data table, right-click on the percentages and then select Format Cells.

    The Format Cells dialog box appears.

6. Create a new custom format by pasting the UP and DOWN symbols into the appropriate syntax parts (see Figure 4-33).

    In this case, any positive percent will be preceded with the UP symbol, whereas any negative percent will be preceded with the DOWN symbol.

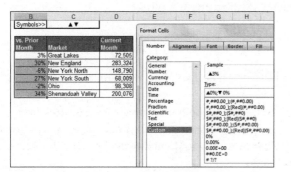

Figure 4-33: Create a custom number format using the symbols.

Cross-Ref

Not familiar with custom number formatting? Feel free to visit Chapter 2 where we cover the ins and outs of custom number formatting in detail.

7. Click OK, and you will see that the symbols are now a part of your number formatting.

    Figure 4-34 illustrates what your percentages will look like. Changing any number from positive to negative (or vice versa) will automatically apply the appropriate symbol.

	A	B	C	D
1		Symbols>>	▲▼	
2				
3		vs. Prior Month	Market	Current Month
4		▲3%	Great Lakes	72,505
5		▲30%	New England	283,324
6		▼ 6%	New York North	148,790
7		▲27%	New York South	68,009
8		▼ 2%	Ohio	98,308
9		▲34%	Shenandoah Valley	200,076

Figure 4-34: Your symbols are now part of your number formatting.

Because charts automatically adopt number formatting, a chart created from this data will show the symbols as part of the labels. Simply use this data as the source for the chart.

This is just one way to use symbols in your reporting. Using this basic technique, you can use inserted symbols to add visual appeal to tables, pivot tables, formulas, or other objects you can think of.

Using Excel's Camera Tool

Excel's Camera tool enables you to take a live picture of a range of cells that updates dynamically while the data in that range updates. If you haven't heard of this tool, don't feel too badly. Microsoft has hidden this nifty tool in the last few versions of Excel by not including it on the Ribbon. However, it's actually quite useful for those of us building dashboards and reports.

Finding the Camera tool

Before you can use the Camera tool, you have to find it and add it to your Quick Access toolbar.

Tip

The Quick Access toolbar is a customizable toolbar on which you can store frequently used commands so that they're always accessible with just one click. You can add commands to the Quick Access toolbar by dragging them directly from the Ribbon or by going through the Customize menu.

Follow these steps to add the Camera tool to the Quick Access toolbar:

1. Click the File tab and then click the Options button.

   The Excel Options dialog box opens.

2. Click the Quick Access Toolbar button.
3. In the Choose Commands From drop-down menu, select Commands Not in the Ribbon.
4. Scroll down the alphabetical list of commands (see Figure 4-35) and find Camera; double-click to add it to the Quick Access toolbar.
5. Click OK.

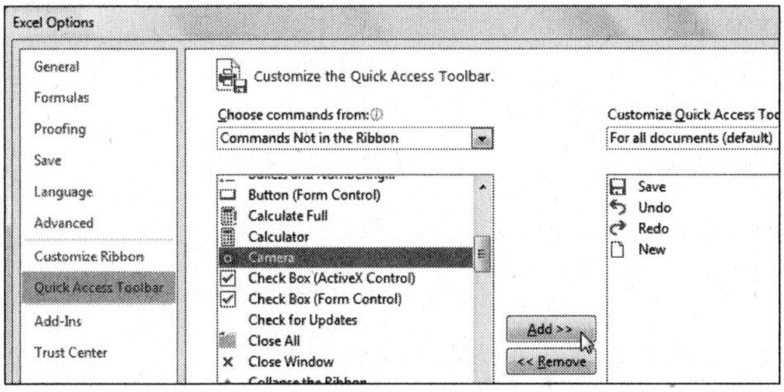

Figure 4-35: Add the Camera tool to the Quick Access toolbar.

After you take these steps, you see the Camera tool in your Quick Access toolbar, as shown in Figure 4-36.

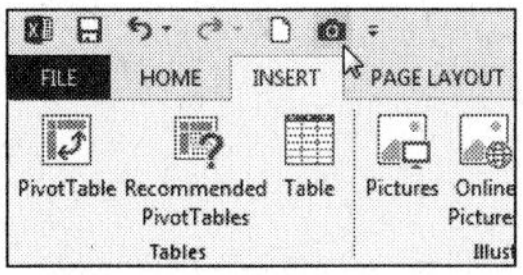

Figure 4-36: Not surprisingly, the icon for the Camera tool looks like a camera.

Using the Camera tool

To use the Camera tool, you simply highlight a range of cells to capture everything in that range in a live picture. The cool thing about the Camera tool is that you're not limited to showing a single cell's value like you are with a linked text box. Also, because the picture is live, all updates made to the source range automatically change the picture.

In Figure 4-37, you see some simple numbers and a chart based on those numbers. The goal here is to create a live picture of the range that holds both the numbers and the chart.

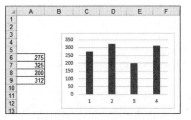

Figure 4-37: Enter some simple numbers in a range and create a basic chart from those numbers.

Take a moment to walk through this basic demonstration of the Camera tool.

1. Highlight the range that contains the information you want to capture.

   In this scenario, B3:F13 is selected to capture the area with the chart.

2. Select the Camera tool icon in the Quick Access toolbar.

   You added the Camera tool to the Quick Access toolbar in the preceding section.

3. Click the worksheet in the location where you want to place the picture.

   Excel immediately creates a live picture of the entire range, as shown in Figure 4-38.

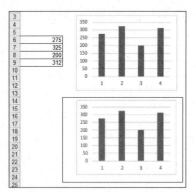

Figure 4-38: A live picture is created via the Camera tool.

Changing any number in the original range automatically causes the picture to update.

Tip

By default, the picture that's created has a border around it. To remove the border, right-click the picture and select Format Picture. This opens the Format Picture dialog box. On the Colors and Lines tab, you see a Line Color drop-down menu. Here you can select No Color, thereby removing the border. On a similar note, to get a picture without gridlines, simply remove the gridlines from the source range.

▶ Creating a live picture without the Camera tool

Did you know you can create a live picture without actually using the Camera tool? That's right. Excel 2013 made it relatively easy to manually mimic the Camera tool's functionality.

1. Select the target range and copy it.
2. On the Ribbon, click the Home tab and then click the drop-down control under the Paste command.
3. In the Other Paste Options group, select the Linked Picture icon.

Of course, the advantage of using the Camera tool is that you can do the same thing with two clicks.

Enhancing a dashboard with the Camera tool

Here are a few ways to go beyond the basics and use the Camera tool to enhance your dashboards and reports.

- Consolidate varied ranges from different sources into one print area.
- Rotate objects to simplify your work.
- Create small charts.

Consolidating disparate ranges into one print area

Sometimes a data model gets so complex that it's difficult to keep all the final data in one printable area. This often forces the printing of multiple pages that are inconsistent in layout and size. Given that dashboards are most effective when contained in a compact area that can be printed in a page or two, complex data models prove to be problematic when it comes to layout and design.

When you create pictures with the Camera tool, you can resize and move the pictures around freely. This gives you the freedom to test different layouts without needing to work on column widths, hidden rows, or other such nonsense. In short, you can create and manage multiple analyses on different tabs and then bring all your presentation pieces together in a nicely formatted presentation layer; see Figure 4-39.

REGION	MARKET	Previous Month	Current Month	Variance
North	Great Lakes	70,261	72,505	3.2%
North	New England	217,858	283,324	30.0%
North	New York North	157,774	148,790	-5.7%
North	New York South	53,670	68,009	26.7%
North	Ohio	100,512	98,308	-2.2%
North	Shenandoah Valley	149,742	200,076	33.6%
South	South Carolina	249,535	229,473	-8.0%
South	Florida	111,606	136,104	22.0%
South	Gulf Coast	253,703	245,881	-3.1%
South	Illinois	129,148	131,538	1.9%
South	Indiana	152,471	151,699	-0.5%
South	Kentucky	224,524	225,461	0.4%
North	North Carolina	124,600	130,791	5.0%
South	Tennessee	307,490	268,010	-12.8%

REGION	MARKET	Last Month Sales
North	Great Lakes	70,261
North	New England	217,858
North	New York North	157,774
North	New York South	53,670
North	North Carolina	124,600
North	Ohio	100,512
North	Shenandoah Valley	149,742
South	Florida	111,606
South	Gulf Coast	253,703
South	Illinois	129,148
South	Indiana	152,471
South	Kentucky	224,524
South	South Carolina	249,535
South	Tennessee	307,490
South	Texas	180,167
West	California	190,264
West	Central	133,628
West	Colorado	134,039
West	North West	120,143
West	Southwest	248,098
West	Topeka	222,389

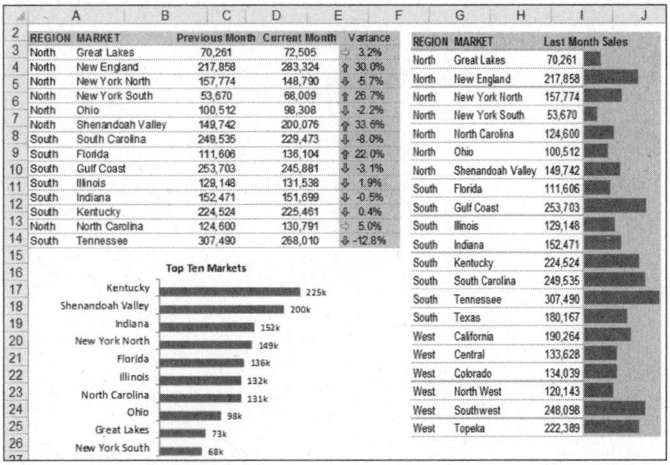

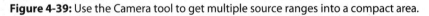

Figure 4-39: Use the Camera tool to get multiple source ranges into a compact area.

Rotating objects to save time

Again, because the Camera tool outputs pictures, you can rotate the pictures in situations where placing the copied range on its side can help save time. A great example is a chart. Certain charts are relatively easy to create in a vertical orientation but extremely difficult to create in a horizontal orientation.

Figure 4-40 shows a vertical bullet graph (on the left). Whereas creating a horizontal bullet graph involves lots of intricate steps with multiple chart types, this graph is relatively easy to create in this vertical format.

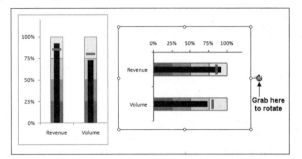

Figure 4-40: Use the rotation handle to rotate your live pictures to a horizontal orientation, as seen here on the right.

The Camera tool to the rescue! When the live picture of the chart is created, all you have to do is change the alignment of the chart labels and then rotate the picture using the rotate handle to create a horizontal version.

Introducing Charts into Your Dashboards

Chapter 5

Excel Charting for the Uninitiated

In This Chapter

- What is a chart?
- How Excel handles charts
- Embedded charts versus chart sheets
- The parts of a chart
- The basic steps for creating a chart
- Working with charts

No other tool is more synonymous with dashboards and reports than the chart. Charts offer a visual representation of numeric values and at-a-glance views that allow you to specify relationships between data values, point out differences, and observe business trends. Few mechanisms allow you to absorb data faster than a chart, which can be a key component in your dashboard.

When most people think of a spreadsheet product such as Excel, they think of crunching rows and columns of numbers. However, Excel is no slouch when it comes to presenting data visually, in the form of a chart. In this chapter, we present an overview of Excel's charting ability and show you how to create and customize your own charts using Excel.

What Is a Chart?

We start with the basics. A *chart* is a visual representation of numeric values. Charts (also known as *graphs*) have been an integral part of spreadsheets since the early days of Lotus 1-2-3. Charts generated by early spreadsheet products were extremely crude by today's standards, but over the years, their quality and flexibility improved significantly. You'll find that Excel provides you with the tools to create a wide variety of highly customizable charts that can help you effectively communicate your message.

Displaying data in a well-conceived chart can make your numbers more understandable. Because a chart presents a picture, charts are particularly useful for summarizing a series of numbers and their interrelationships. Making a chart can often help you spot trends and patterns that might otherwise go unnoticed.

Figure 5-1 shows a worksheet that contains a simple column chart that depicts a company's sales volume by month. Viewing the chart makes it very apparent that sales were off in the summer months (June through August), but they increased steadily during the final four months of the year. You could, of course, arrive at this same conclusion simply by studying the numbers. But viewing the chart makes the point much more quickly.

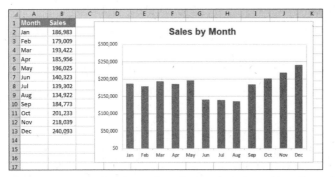

Figure 5-1: A simple column chart depicts the sales volume for each month.

A column chart is just one of many different types of charts that you can create with Excel. By the way, creating this chart is simple: Select the data in A1:B13 and press Alt+F1.

On the Web

All the charts pictured in this chapter are available at www.wiley.com/go/exceldr **in a workbook file named** Chapter 5 Samples.xlsx.

How Excel Handles Charts

Before you can create a chart, you must have some numbers — sometimes known as *data*. The data, of course, is stored in the cells in a worksheet. Normally, the data that is used by a chart resides in a single worksheet, but that's not a strict requirement. A chart can use data that's stored in any number of worksheets, and the worksheets can even be in different workbooks. The decision to use data from one sheet or multiple sheets really depends on your data model, the nature of your data sources, and the interactivity you want to give your dashboard.

A chart is essentially an "object" that Excel creates upon request. This object consists of one or more *data series*, displayed graphically. The appearance of the data series depends on the selected *chart type*. For example, if you create a line chart that uses two data series, the chart contains two lines, and each line represents one data series.

> ➤ The data for each series is stored in a separate row or column.

> ➤ Each point on the line is determined by the value in a single cell and is represented by a marker.

> You can distinguish the lines by their thickness, line style, color, and data markers.

Figure 5-2 shows a line chart that plots two data series across a nine-year period. The series are identified by using different data markers (squares versus circles), shown in the *legend* at the bottom of the chart. The lines also use different colors, which is not apparent in the grayscale figure.

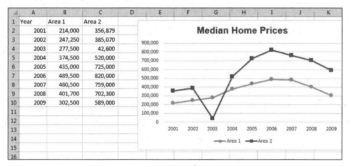

Figure 5-2: This line chart displays two data series.

A key point to keep in mind is that charts are dynamic. In other words, a chart series is linked to the data in your worksheet. If the data changes, the chart is updated automatically to reflect those changes so your dashboard can show the most current information.

After you create a chart, you can always change its type and formatting, add new data series to it, or change an existing data series so that it uses data in a different range.

Charts can reside in either of two locations in a workbook:

> ➤ On a worksheet (an embedded chart)

> ➤ On a separate chart sheet

Embedded charts

An *embedded chart* basically floats on top of a worksheet, on the worksheet's drawing layer. The charts shown previously in this chapter are both embedded charts.

As with other drawing objects (such as a text box or a shape), you can move an embedded chart, resize it, change its proportions, adjust its borders, and add effects such as a shadow. Using embedded charts enables you to view the chart next to the data that it uses. Or you can place several embedded charts together so that they print on a single page.

As we discuss in Chapter 11, you ideally place your charts in the presentation layer, presenting the relevant charts in a single viewable area that fit on one page or a single screen.

When you create a chart, it always starts off as an embedded chart. The exception to this rule is when you select a range of data and press F11 to create a default chart. Such a chart is created on a chart sheet.

To make changes to the actual chart in an embedded chart object, you must click the chart to *activate* it. When a chart is activated, Excel displays the two Chart Tools context tabs, Design and Format, as shown in Figure 5-3. To access these commands, choose Chart Tools➜Design and Chart Tools➜ Format, respectively.

In addition, when clicking a chart, you'll see several buttons next to the chart. These are helper buttons that provide an easy way to customize the various properties of the chart. These include

> Chart Elements
>
> Chart Style
>
> Chart Filter

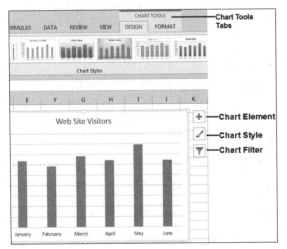

Figure 5-3: Activating a chart displays additional tabs on the Excel Ribbon and helper buttons next to the chart.

Chart sheets

You can move an embedded chart to its own chart sheet so that you can view it by clicking a sheet tab (covered later in this chapter in the "Moving and resizing a chart" section). When you move a chart to a chart sheet, the chart occupies the entire sheet. If you plan to print a chart on a page by itself, using a chart sheet is often your better choice. If you have many charts to create, you may want to put each one on a separate chart sheet to avoid cluttering your worksheet. This technique also makes locating a particular chart easier because you can change the names of the chart sheets' tabs to provide a description of the chart that it contains. Although chart sheets are not typically used in traditional dashboards, they can come in handy when producing reports that will be viewed in a multi-tab workbook.

Figure 5-4 shows a chart on a chart sheet. When a chart sheet is activated, Excel displays the Chart Tools context tabs, as described in the previous section.

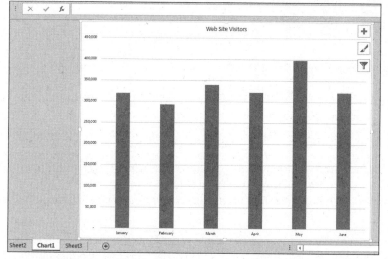

Figure 5-4: A chart on a chart sheet.

Parts of a Chart

A chart is made up of many different elements, and all of these elements are optional. Yes, you can create a chart that contains no chart elements — an empty chart. It's not very useful, but Excel allows it.

Refer to the chart in Figure 5-5 as you read the following description of the chart's elements.

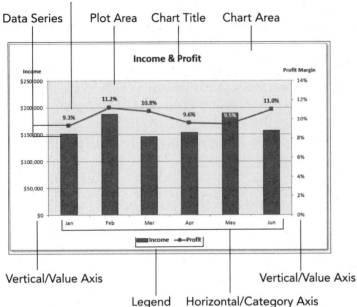

Figure 5-5: Parts of a chart.

This particular chart is a combination chart that displays both columns and a line. The chart has two data series: Income and Profit Margin. Income is plotted as vertical columns, and the Profit Margin is plotted as a line with square markers. Each bar (or marker on the line) represents a single *data point* (the value in a cell).

The chart has a horizontal axis, known as the *category axis*. This axis represents the category for each data point (January, February, and so on). This axis doesn't have a label because the category units are obvious.

Notice that this chart has two vertical axes. These are known as *value axes,* and each one has a different scale. The axis on the left is for the column series (Income), and the axis on the right is for the line series (Profit Margin).

The value axes also display scale values. The axis on the left displays scale values from 0 to 250,000, in major unit increments of 50,000. The value axis on the right uses a different scale: 0 percent to 14 percent, in increments of 2 percent. For a value axis, you can command the minimum and maximum values, as well as the increment value.

A chart with two value axes is appropriate because the two data series vary dramatically in scale. If the Profit Margin data were to be plotted using the left axis, the line would not even be visible.

If a chart has more than one data series, you'll usually need a way to identify the data series or data points. A *legend,* for example, is often used to identify the various series in a chart. In this example, the legend appears at the bottom of the chart. Some charts also display *data labels* to identify specific data points. The example chart displays data labels for the Profit Margin series, but not for the Income series. In addition, most charts (including the example chart) contain a chart title and additional labels to identify the axes or categories.

The example chart also contains horizontal *gridlines* (which correspond to the values on the left axis). Gridlines are basically extensions of the value axis scale, which makes it easier for the viewer to determine the magnitude of the data points.

In addition, all charts have a *chart area* (the entire background area of the chart) and a *plot area* (the part that shows the actual chart, including the plotted data, the axes, and the axis labels).

Charts can have additional parts or fewer parts, depending on the chart type. For example, a pie chart (see Figure 5-6) has "slices" and no axes. A 5-D chart may have walls and a floor (see Figure 5-7).

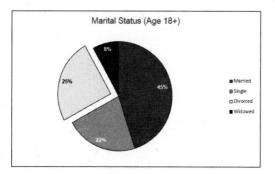

Figure 5-6: A pie chart.

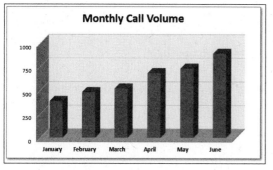

Figure 5-7: A 3-D column chart.

Several other types of items can be added to a chart. For example, you can add a trend line or display error bars.

Like everything else in Excel, charts do have limitations. Table 5-1 lists the limitations of Excel charts.

Table 5-1: Chart Limitations

Item	Limitation
Charts in a worksheet	Limited by available memory
Worksheets referred to by a chart	255
Data series in a chart	255
Data points in a data series	32,000
Data points in a data series (3D charts)	4,000
Total data points in a chart	256,000

Most users never find these limitations to be a problem. However, one item that frequently does cause problems is the limit on the length of the SERIES formula. Each argument is limited to 255 characters, and in some situations, that's simply not enough characters. See Chapter 6 for more information about SERIES formulas.

Basic Steps for Creating a Chart

Creating a chart is relatively easy. The following sections describe how to create and then customize a basic chart in Excel 2013 to best communicate your business goals.

Creating the chart

Follow these steps to create a chart using the data in Figure 5-8:

1. Select the data that you want to use in the chart.

   Make sure that you select the column headers, if the data has them.

   Tip
   If you select a single cell within a range of data, Excel uses the entire data range for the chart.

	A	B	C
1		Projected	Actual
2	Jan	2,000	1,895
3	Feb	2,500	2,643
4	Mar	3,500	3,648
5			

Figure 5-8: This data would make a good chart.

2. Click the Insert tab and then in the Charts group, click a Chart icon.

   The icon expands into a gallery list that shows subtypes (see Figure 5-9).

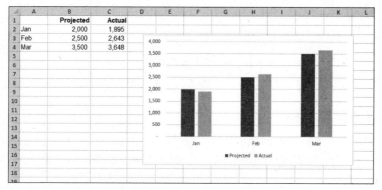

Figure 5-9: The icons in the Insert➔Charts group expand to show a gallery of chart subtypes.

3. Click a Chart subtype, and Excel creates the chart of the specified type.

   Figure 5-10 shows a column chart created from the data.

Figure 5-10: A column chart with two data series.

Tip

To quickly create a default chart, select the data and press Alt+F1 to create an embedded chart, or press F11 to create a chart on a chart sheet.

Switching the row and column orientation

When Excel creates a chart, it uses an algorithm to determine whether the data is arranged in columns or in rows. Most of the time, Excel guesses correctly, but if it creates the chart using the wrong orientation, you can quickly change the orientation by selecting the chart and choosing Chart Tools➞Design➞Data➞Switch Row/Column. This command is a toggle, so if changing the data orientation doesn't improve the chart, just choose the command again (or click the Undo button found on the Quick Access toolbar).

The orientation of the data has a drastic effect on the look (and, perhaps, understandability) of your chart. Figure 5-11 shows the column chart in Figure 5-10 after changing the orientation. Notice that the chart now has three data series, one for each month. If the goal of your dashboard is to compare actual values to projected values for each month, this version of the chart is much more difficult to interpret because the relevant columns are not adjacent.

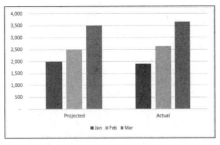

Figure 5-11: The column chart, after swapping the row/column orientation.

Changing the chart type

After you create a chart, you can easily change the chart type. Although a column chart may work well for a particular data set, there's no harm in checking out other chart types. You can choose Chart Tools➞Design➞Type➞Change Chart Type to display the Change Chart Type dialog box and experiment with other chart types. Figure 5-12 shows the Change Chart Type dialog box.

In the Change Chart Type dialog box, the main categories are listed on the left, and the subtypes are shown as icons. Select an icon and click OK, and Excel displays the chart using the new chart type. If you don't like the result, click the Undo button.

Tip

If the chart is an embedded chart, you can also change a chart's type by using the icons in the Insert➞Charts group. In fact, this method is more efficient because it doesn't involve a dialog box.

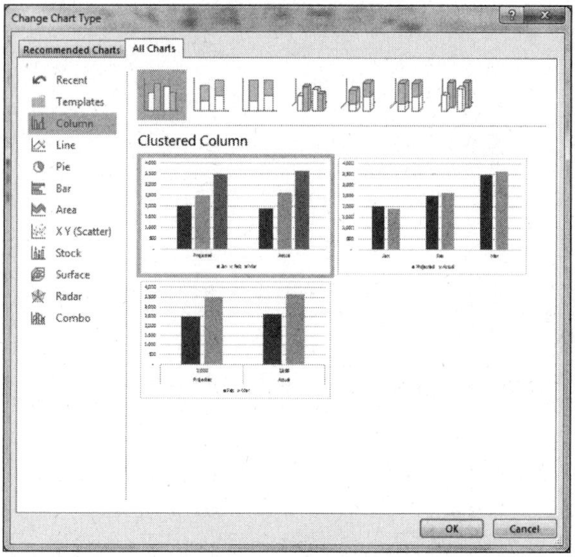

Figure 5-12: The Change Chart Type dialog box.

Applying chart styles

Each chart type has a number of prebuilt styles that you can apply with a single mouse click. A style contains additional chart elements, such as a title, data labels, and axes. This step is optional, but one of the prebuilt designs might be just what you're looking for. Even if the style isn't exactly what you want, it may be close enough that you need to make only a few adjustments.

To apply a style, select the chart and use the Chart Tools➜Design➜Chart Styles gallery. Figure 5-13 shows how a column chart looks using various styles.

Applying a chart style

The Chart Tools➜Design➜Chart Styles gallery contains quite a few styles that you can apply to your chart. The styles consist of various color choices and some special effects. Again, this step is optional.

> **Tip**
> The styles displayed in the gallery depend on the workbook's theme. When you choose Page Layout➜Themes to apply a different theme, you see a new selection of chart styles designed for the selected theme.

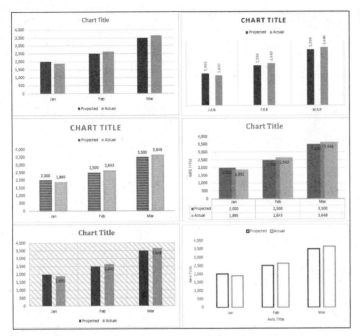

Figure 5-13: One-click design variations of a column chart.

Adding and deleting chart elements

In some cases, applying a chart layout (as described previously) gives you a chart with all the elements you need. Most of the time, however, you need to add or remove some chart elements and fine-tune the layout. You do so using the Chart Elements button next to the chart command.

For example, to give a chart a title, choose the Chart Elements button and place a check next to Chart Title (see Figure 5-14).

As you can see in Figure 5-14, you add all kinds of chart elements, such as axis titles, data labels, gridlines, and trend lines.

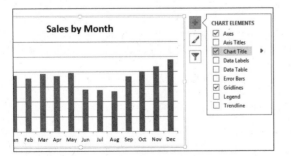

Figure 5-14: Use the Chart Elements button to add or remove various chart elements.

Moving and deleting chart elements

Some of the elements within a chart can be moved. The movable chart elements include the plot area, titles, the legend, and data labels. To move a chart element, click it to select it. Then drag its border.

The easiest way to delete a chart element is to select it and then press Delete. Note that if you delete a chart element and later decide that you want to add it back, all previous formatting will be lost, and you'll need to reapply the formatting.

A few chart elements consist of multiple objects. For example, the data labels element consists of one label for each data point. To move or delete one data label, click once to select the entire element and then click a second time to select the specific data label. You can then move or delete the single data label.

Formatting chart elements

Many users are content to stick with the predefined chart layouts and chart styles. For more precise customizations, Excel allows you to work with individual chart elements and apply additional formatting.

Every element in a chart can be formatted and customized in many ways. Many users are content with charts that are created using the steps described earlier in this chapter. But because you're reading this book, you probably want to find out how to customize charts for maximum impact.

Cross-Ref

For more detailed information about formatting and customizing your chart, see Chapter 6.

Excel provides two ways to format and customize individual chart elements. Both of the following methods require that you select the chart element first:

➤ Use the Ribbon commands on the Chart Tools➜Format tab.

➤ Press Ctrl+1 to display the Format dialog box that's specific to the selected chart element.

If you use Excel 2013, you can also double-click a chart element to display the Format dialog box for the element.

Note

The Ribbon commands contain only a subset of the formatting options. For maximum command, use the Format dialog box.

For example, assume that you want to change the color of the columns for one of the series in the chart. Click any column in the series (which selects the entire series). Then choose Chart Tools➜Format➜Shape Styles➜Shape Fill and select a color from the list that appears. To change the properties of the outline around the columns, use the Chart Tools➜Format➜Shape Styles➜Shape Outline command. To change the effects used in the columns (for example, add a shadow), use the Chart Tools➜Format➜Shape Styles➜Shape Effects command.

Alternatively, you can select a series in the chart, press Ctrl+1, and use the Format Data Series dialog box shown in Figure 5-15. Note that this is a tabbed dialog box. Click the icons along the top of the dialog box to view additional commands. It's also a persistent dialog box, so you can click another element in the chart. In other words, you don't have to close the dialog box to see the changes you specify.

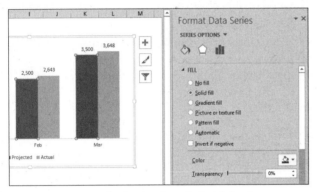

Figure 5-15: Using the Format Data Series dialog box.

Working with Charts

As you develop your charts in Excel, you will find the need to move your charts around, resize your charts, duplicate your charts, etc. The following section covers some of the common actions you will inevitably have to perform when working with charts.

Note

Before you can work with a chart, you must activate it. To activate an embedded chart, click an element in the chart. Doing so activates the chart and also selects the element that you click. To activate a chart on a chart sheet, just click its sheet tab.

Moving and resizing a chart

If your chart is an embedded chart, you can freely move and resize it with your mouse. Click the chart's border and then drag the border to move the chart. Drag any of the handles to resize the chart. The *handles* consist of dots that appear on the chart's corners and edges when you click the chart's border. When the mouse pointer turns into a double arrow, click and drag to resize the chart.

When a chart is selected, you can use the Chart Tools➜Format➜Size commands to adjust the height and width of the chart. Use the spinners or type the dimensions directly into the Height and Width commands. Oddly, Excel doesn't provide similar commands to specify the top and left positions of the chart.

To move an embedded chart, just click its border at any location except one of the eight resizing handles. Then drag the chart to its new location. You also can use standard cut-and-paste techniques to move an embedded chart. Select the chart and choose Home➜Clipboard➜Cut (or press Ctrl+X). Then activate a cell near the desired location and choose Home➜Clipboard➜Paste (or press Ctrl+V). The new location can be in a different worksheet or even in a different workbook. If you paste the chart to a different workbook, it will be linked to the data in the original workbook. Another way to move a chart to a different location is to choose Chart Tools➜Design➜Location➜Move Chart. This command displays the Move Chart dialog box, which lets you specify a new sheet for the chart (either a chart sheet or a worksheet).

Converting an embedded chart to a chart sheet

When you create a chart using the icons in the Insert➜Charts group, the result is always an embedded chart. If you prefer that your chart be located on a chart sheet, you can easily move it.

To convert an embedded chart to a chart on a chart sheet, select the chart and choose Chart➜Tools➜ Design➜Location➜Move Chart to display the Move Chart dialog box shown in Figure 5-16. Select the New Sheet option and (optionally) provide a different name for the chart sheet.

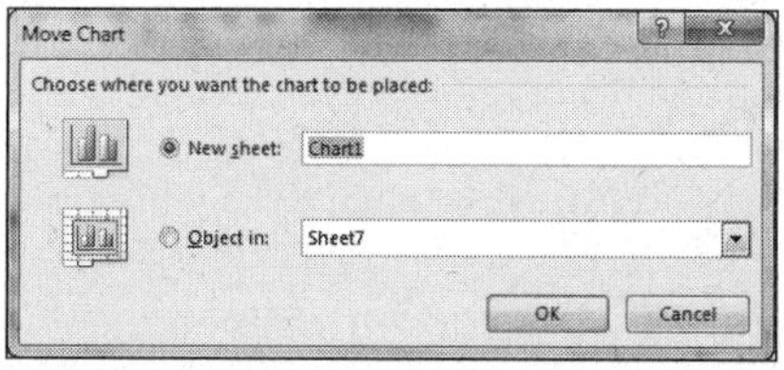

Figure 5-16: Use the Move Chart dialog box to move an embedded chart to a chart sheet (or vice versa).

To convert a chart on a chart sheet to an embedded chart, activate the chart sheet and then choose Chart➜Tools➜Design➜Location➜Move Chart to display the Move Chart dialog box. Select the Object In option and specify the sheet by using the drop-down command.

Copying a chart

To make an exact copy of an embedded chart, select the chart and choose Home➜Clipboard➜Copy (or press Ctrl+C). Then activate a cell near the desired location and choose Home➜Clipboard➜Paste (or press Ctrl+V). The new location can be in a different worksheet or even in a different workbook. If you paste the chart to a different workbook, it will be linked to the data in the original workbook.

To copy a chart on a chart sheet, press Ctrl while you click and drag the sheet tab to the left or right. After you let go of the mouse, you will have a copy of the chart sheet.

Deleting a chart

To delete an embedded chart, click the chart (this selects the chart as an object). Then press Delete. With the Ctrl key pressed, you can select multiple charts and then delete them all with a single press of the Delete key.

To delete a chart sheet, right-click its sheet tab and choose Delete from the shortcut menu. To delete multiple chart sheets, select them by pressing Ctrl while you click the sheet tabs.

Copying a chart's formatting

If you create a nicely formatted chart and realize that you need to create several more charts that have the same formatting, you have these three choices:

➤ Make a copy of the original chart and then change the data used in the copied chart. One way to change the data used in a chart is to choose the Chart Tools➜Design➜Data➜Select Data command and make the changes in the Select Data Source dialog box.

➤ Create the other charts, but don't apply any formatting. Then activate the original chart and press Ctrl+C. Select one of the other charts and choose Home➜Clipboard➜Paste➜Paste Special. In the Paste Special dialog box, click the Formats option and then click OK. Repeat for each additional chart.

➤ Create a chart template and then use the template as the basis for the new charts. Or you can apply the new template to existing charts.

Renaming a chart

When you activate an embedded chart, its name appears in the Name box (located to the left of the Formula bar). To change the name of an embedded chart, just type the new name into the Name box and press Enter.

Why rename a chart? If a worksheet has many charts, you may prefer to activate a particular chart by name. Just type the chart's name in the Name box and press Enter. It's much easier to remember a chart named Monthly Sales as opposed to a chart named Chart 9.

Note When you rename a chart, Excel allows you to use a name that already exists for another chart. Normally, it doesn't matter if multiple charts have the same name, but it can cause problems if you use VBA macros that select a chart by name.

Printing charts

Printing embedded charts is nothing special; you print them the same way that you print a worksheet. As long as you include the embedded chart in the range that you want to print, Excel prints the chart as it appears on-screen. When printing a sheet that contains embedded charts, it's a good idea to preview first (or use Page Layout view) to ensure that your charts don't span multiple pages. If you create the chart on a chart sheet, Excel always prints the chart on a page by itself.

Tip

If you select an embedded chart and choose File➔Print, Excel prints the chart on a page by itself (as though it were a chart sheet) and does *not* print the worksheet.

If you don't want a particular embedded chart to appear on your printout, select the background area of the chart (the chart area), right-click, and choose Format. In the Format Chart Area dialog box, click the Properties tab and deselect the Print Object check box (see Figure 5-17).

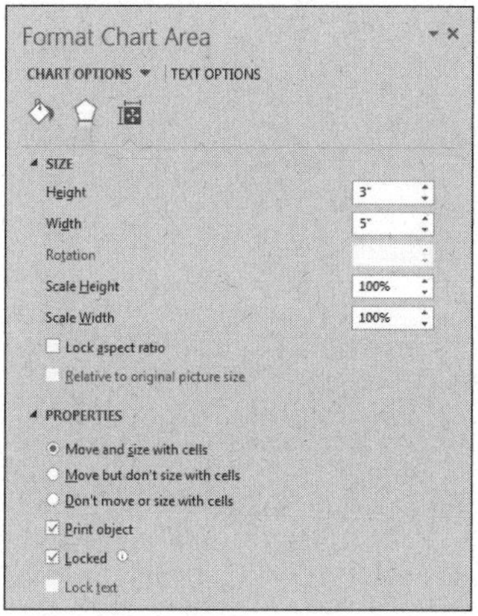

Figure 5-17: Specifying that a chart should not be printed with the worksheet.

Working with Chart Series

In This Chapter

- Adding and removing series from a chart
- Finding various ways to change the data used in a chart
- Using noncontiguous ranges for a chart
- Charting data from different worksheets or workbooks
- Dealing with missing data
- Controlling a data series by hiding data
- Unlinking a chart from its data
- Using secondary axes

Every chart consists of at least one series, and the data used in that series is (normally) stored in a worksheet. This chapter provides an in-depth discussion of data series for charts and presents lots of tips to help you select and modify the data used in your charts.

On the Web
All workbook examples in this book are available on the companion website for this book at `www.wiley.com/go/exceldr`.

Specifying the Data for Your Chart

When you create a chart, you almost always start by selecting the worksheet data to be plotted. Normally, you select the numeric data as well as the category labels and series names, if they exist.

When creating a chart, a key consideration is the orientation of your data: by rows or by columns. In other words, is the data for each series in a single row or in a single column?

Excel attempts to guess the data orientation by applying a simple rule: If the data rows outnumber the data columns, each series is assumed to occupy a column. If the number of data columns is greater than or equal to the number of data rows, each series is assumed to occupy a row. In other words, Excel always defaults to a chart that has more category labels than series.

After you create the chart, it's a simple matter to override Excel's orientation guess. Just activate the chart and choose Chart Tools➜Design➜Data➜Switch Row/Column.

Your choice of orientation determines how many series the chart has, and it affects the appearance and (possibly) the legibility of your chart. Figure 6-1 shows two charts that use the same data. The chart on the left displays three series, arranged in columns. The chart on the right shows four series, arranged in rows.

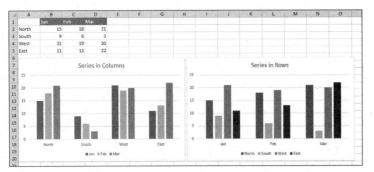

Figure 6-1: Your choice of data orientation (by row or by column) determines the number of series in the chart.

In many situations, you may find it necessary to modify the ranges used by a chart. Specifically, you may want to do the following:

➤ Add a new series to the chart.

➤ Delete a series from the chart.

➤ Extend the range used by a series (show more data).

➤ Contract the range used by a series (show less data).

➤ Add or modify the series names.

All these topics are covered in the following sections.

Note

Chart types vary in the number of series that they can use. All charts are limited to a maximum of 255 series. Other charts require a minimum number of series. For example, a high-low-close stock chart requires three series. A pie chart can use only one series.

Dealing with numeric category labels

It's not uncommon to have category labels that consist of numbers. For example, you may create a chart that shows sales by year, and the years are numeric values. If your category labels include a heading, Excel will (incorrectly) interpret the category labels as a data series and use generic category labels that consist of integers (1, 2, 3, and so on). The following figure shows an example.

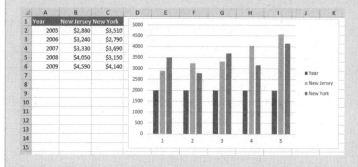

You can, of course, choose Chart Tools➞Design➞Data➞Select Data and use the Select Data Source dialog box to fix the chart. But a more efficient solution is to make a simple change before you create the chart: Remove the header text above the category labels! The following figure shows the chart that was created when the heading was removed from the category label column.

Adding a New Series to a Chart

Excel provides four ways to add a new series to an existing chart:

➤ Copy the range and then paste the data into the chart.

➤ Use the Select Data Source dialog box.

➤ Select the chart and extend the blue highlighting rectangle to include the new series.

➤ Activate the chart, click in the Formula bar, and manually type a SERIES formula.

These techniques are described in the following sections.

Note Attempting to add a new series to a pie chart has no apparent effect because a pie chart can have only one series. The series, however, is added to the chart but isn't displayed. If you select a different chart type for the chart, the added series is then visible.

Adding a new series by copying a range

One way to add a new series to a chart is to perform a standard copy/paste operation. Follow these steps:

1. Select the range that contains the data to be added (including the series name).

2. Choose Home➡Clipboard➡Copy (or press Ctrl+C).

3. Click the chart to activate it.

4. Choose Home➡Clipboard➡Paste (or press Ctrl+V).

Note If the series you are trying to copy and paste into your chart has a series name that is a number (for example, a year like 2009) Excel will try to plot that series name as an actual value to the chart. In these cases, you can use the Paste Special feature to avoid this problem. Read on to find out how.

For more control when adding data to a chart, choose Home➡Clipboard➡Paste➡Paste Special in Step 4. This command displays the Paste Special dialog box. Figure 6-2 shows a new series (using data in row 5) being added to a line chart.

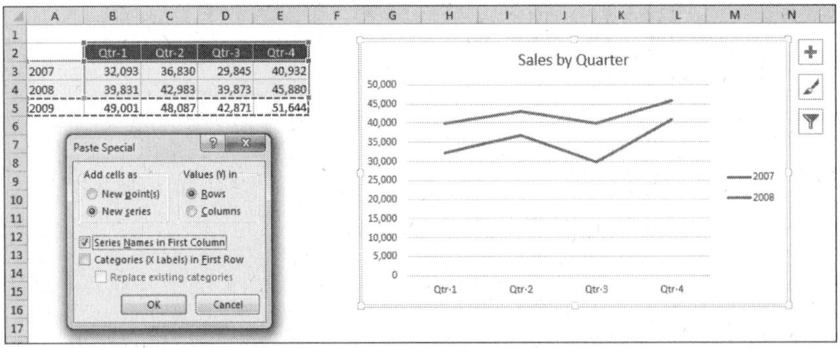

Figure 6-2: Using the Paste Special dialog box to add a series to a chart.

Following are some pointers to keep in mind when you add a new series using the Paste Special dialog box:

➤ Make sure that the New Series option is selected.

➤ Excel will guess at the data orientation, but you should verify that the Rows or Columns option is guessed correctly.

➤ If the range you copied included a cell with the series name, ensure that the Series Names in First Row/Column option is selected.

➤ If the first column of your range selection included category labels, make sure that the Categories (X Labels) in First Column/Row check box is selected.

➤ If you want to replace the existing category labels, select the Replace Existing Categories check box.

Adding a new series by extending the range highlight

When you select a series in a chart, Excel displays an outline around the data used by that series. When you select something other than a series in a chart, Excel displays an outline around the entire data range used by the chart — but only if the data is in a contiguous range of cells.

If you need to add a new series to a chart (and the new series is contiguous with the existing chart's data), you can just drag the blue range highlight to add the new series. Start by selecting any chart element *except* a series. Excel highlights the range with a blue outline. Drag a corner of the blue outline to include the new data, and Excel creates a new series in the chart.

Adding a new series using the Select Data Source dialog box

The Select Data Source dialog box provides another way to add a new series to a chart, as follows:

1. Click the chart to activate it.

2. Choose Chart Tools➜Design➜Data➜Select Data to display the Select Data Source dialog box.

3. Click the Add button to display the Edit Series dialog box.

4. Use the range selector controls to specify the cell for the Series Name (optional) and Series Values (see Figure 6-3).

5. Click OK to close the Edit Series dialog box and return to the Select Data Source dialog box.

6. Click OK to close the Select Data Source dialog box or click the Add button to add another series to the chart.

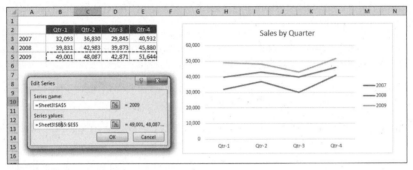

Figure 6-3: Using the Edit Series dialog box to add a series to a chart.

Note

The configuration of the Edit Series dialog box varies, depending on the chart type. For example, if the chart is a scatter chart, the Edit Series dialog box displays range selectors for the Series Name, the Series X Values, and the Series Y Values. If the chart is a bubble chart, the dialog box displays an additional range selector for the Series Bubble Size.

Adding a new series by typing a new SERIES formula

Excel provides yet another way to add a new series: Type a new SERIES formula. Follow these steps:

1. Click the chart to activate it.

2. Click the Formula bar.

3. Type the new SERIES formula and press Enter.

This method is certainly not the most efficient way to add a new series to a chart. It requires that you understand how the SERIES formula works, and (as you might expect) it can be rather error-prone. Note, however, that you don't need to type the SERIES formula from scratch. You can copy an existing SERIES formula, paste it into the Formula bar, and then edit the SERIES formula to create a new series.

Cross-Ref

For more information about the SERIES formula, see the "SERIES formula syntax" sidebar, later in this chapter.

Deleting a Chart Series

The easiest way to delete a series from a chart is to select the series and press Delete.

Note

Deleting the only series in a chart does not delete the chart. Rather, it gives you an empty chart. If you'd like to delete this empty chart, just press Delete a second time.

You can also use the Select Data Source dialog box to delete a series. Choose Chart Tools→Design→Data→Select Data to display this dialog box. Then select the series from the list and click the Remove button.

Modifying the Data Range for a Chart Series

After you've created a chart, you may want to modify the data ranges used by the chart. For example, you may need to expand the range to include new data. Or you might need to substitute an entirely different range. Excel offers a number of ways to perform these operations:

➤ Drag the range highlights.

➤ Use the Select Data Source dialog box.

➤ Edit the SERIES formula.

Each of these techniques is described in the following sections.

Tip

If you create your chart from data in a table (created by choosing Insert→Tables→Table), the chart will adjust automatically if you add new data to the table.

Using range highlighting to change series data

When you select a series in a chart, Excel highlights the worksheet ranges used in that series. This range highlighting consists of a colored outline around each range used by the series. Figure 6-4 shows an example in which the chart series (Region 1) is selected. Excel highlights the following ranges:

➤ C2 (the series name)

➤ B3:B8 (the category labels)

➤ C3:C8 (the values)

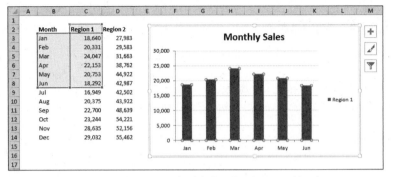

Figure 6-4: Selecting a chart series highlights the data used by the series.

Each of the highlighted ranges contains a small handle at each corner. You can perform two operations with the highlighted data:

➤ **Expand or contract the data range.** Click one of the handles and drag it to expand the outlined range (specify more data) or contract the data range (specify less data). When you move your cursor over a handle, the mouse pointer changes to a double arrow.

➤ **Specify an entirely different data range.** Click one of the borders of the highlight and then drag it to highlight a different range. When you move the cursor over a border, the mouse pointer changes to a four-way arrow.

Figure 6-5 shows the chart after the data range has been changed. In this case, the highlight around cell C2 was dragged to cell D2, and the highlight around C3:C8 was dragged to D3:D8 and then expanded to include D3:D14. Notice that the range for the category labels (B3:B8) wasn't modified — and the missing labels aren't shown in the chart. To finish the job, that range needs to be expanded to B3:B14.

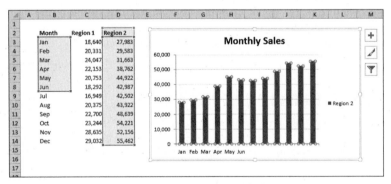

Figure 6-5: The chart's data range has been modified.

Modifying chart source data by using the range highlights is probably the simplest method. Note, however, that this technique works only with embedded charts (not with chart sheets). In addition, it doesn't work when the chart's data is in a worksheet other than the sheet that contains the embedded chart.

Note

A surface chart is a special case. You cannot select an individual series in a surface chart. But when you select the plot area of a surface chart, Excel highlights all the data used in the chart. You can then use the range highlighting to change the ranges used in the chart.

Using the Select Data Source dialog box to change series data

Another method of modifying a series data range is to use the Select Data Source dialog box. Select your chart and then choose Chart Tools→Design→Data@>Select Data. Figure 6-6 shows the Select Data Source dialog box.

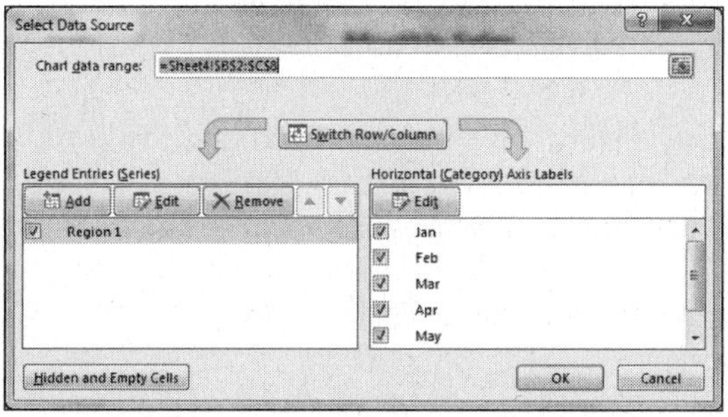

Figure 6-6: The Select Data Source dialog box.

Notice that the Select Data Source dialog box has three parts:

➤ The top part of the dialog box shows the entire data range used by the chart. You can change this range by selecting new data.

➤ The lower-left part displays a list of each series. Select a series and click the Edit button to display the Edit Series dialog box to change the data used by a single series.

➤ The lower-right part displays the category axis labels. Click the Edit button to display the Axis Labels dialog box to change the range used as the axis labels.

Note

The Edit Series dialog box can vary somewhat, depending on the chart type. The Edit Series dialog box for a bubble chart, for example, has four range selector controls: Series Name, Series X Values, Series Y Values, and Series Bubble Size.

Editing the SERIES formula to change series data

Every chart series has its own SERIES formula. When you select a data series in a chart, its SERIES formula appears in the Formula bar. In Figure 6-7, for example, you can see one of two SERIES formulas in the Formula bar for a chart that displays two data series.

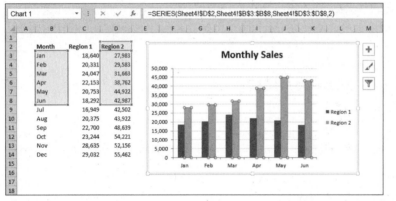

Figure 6-7: The SERIES formula for the selected data series appears in the Formula bar.

Although a SERIES formula is displayed in the Formula bar, it isn't a "real" formula. In other words, you can't put this formula into a cell, and you can't use worksheet functions within the SERIES formula. You can, however, edit the arguments in the SERIES formula to change the ranges used by the series. To edit the SERIES formula, just click in the Formula bar and use standard editing techniques. Refer to the sidebar, "SERIES formula syntax," to find out about the various arguments for a SERIES formula.

Note   When you modify a series data range using either of the techniques discussed previously in this section, the SERIES formula is also modified. In fact, those techniques are simply easy ways of editing the SERIES formula.

Following is an example of a SERIES formula:

```
=SERIES(Sheet4!$D$2,Sheet4!$B$3:$B$8,Sheet4!$D$3:$D$8,2)
```

This SERIES formula does the following:

➤ Specifies that cell D2 (on Sheet4) contains the series name.

➤ Specifies that the category labels are in B3:B8 on Sheet4.

➤ Specifies that the data values are in D3:D8, also on Sheet4.

➤ Specifies that the series will be plotted second on the chart (the final argument is 2).

▶ SERIES formula syntax

A SERIES formula has the following syntax:

```
=SERIES(series_name, category_labels, values, order, sizes)
```

The arguments you can use in the SERIES formula include the following:

- **series_name:** (Optional) A reference to the cell that contains the series name used in the legend. If the chart has only one series, the name argument is used as the title. This argument can also consist of text in quotation marks. If omitted, Excel creates a default series name (for example, Series 1).

- **category_labels:** (Optional) A reference to the range that contains the labels for the category axis. If omitted, Excel uses consecutive integers beginning with 1. For scatter charts, this argument specifies the x values. A noncontiguous range reference is also valid. (The ranges' addresses are separated by a comma and enclosed in parentheses.) The argument may also consist of an array of comma-separated values (or text in quotation marks) enclosed in braces.

- **values:** (Required) A reference to the range that contains the values for the series. For scatter charts, this argument specifies the y values. A noncontiguous range reference is also valid. (The ranges' addresses are separated by a comma and enclosed in parentheses.) The argument may also consist of an array of comma-separated values enclosed in braces.

- **order:** (Required) An integer that specifies the plotting order of the series. This argument is relevant only if the chart has more than one series. Using a reference to a cell is not allowed.

- **sizes:** (Only for bubble charts) A reference to the range that contains the values for the size of the bubbles in a bubble chart. A noncontiguous range reference is also valid. (The ranges' addresses are separated by a comma and enclosed in parentheses.) The argument may also consist of an array of values enclosed in braces.

Notice that range references in a SERIES formula always include the worksheet name, and the range references are always absolute references. An absolute reference, as you may know, uses a dollar sign before the row and column part of the reference. If you edit a SERIES formula and remove the sheet name or make the cell references relative, Excel will override these changes.

Understanding Series Names

Every chart series has a name, which is displayed in the chart's legend. If you don't explicitly provide a name for a series, it will have a default name, such as Series1, Series2, and so on.

The easiest way to name a series is to do so when you create the chart. Typically, a series name is contained in a cell adjacent to the series data. For example, if your data is arranged in columns, the column headers usually contain the series names. If you select the series names along with the chart data, those names will be applied automatically.

Figure 6-8 shows a chart with three series. The series names, which are stored in B3:D3, are Main, N. County, and Westside. The SERIES formula for the first data series is as follows:

```
=SERIES(Sheet1!$B$3,Sheet1!$A$4:$A$9,Sheet1!$B$4:$B$9,1)
```

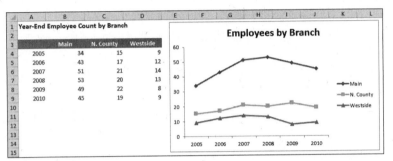

Figure 6-8: The series names are picked up from the worksheet.

Note that the first argument for this SERIES formula is a reference to the cell that contains the series name.

Changing a series name

The series name is the text that appears in a chart's legend. In some cases, you may prefer the chart to display a name other than the text that's in the worksheet. To change the name of a series, follow these steps:

1. Activate the chart.

2. Choose Chart Tools→Design→Data→Select Data to display the Select Data Source dialog box.

3. In the Select Data Source dialog box, select the series that you want to modify, and click the Edit button to display the Edit Series dialog box.

4. Type the new name in the Series Name box.

Normally, the Series Name box contains a cell reference. But you can override this and enter any text.

Note

If you go back to a series that you've already renamed, you'll find that Excel has converted your text into a formula — an equal sign, followed by the text you entered (the new series name), within quotation marks.

Figure 6-9 shows the previous chart, after changing the series names. The first argument in each of the SERIES formulas no longer displays a cell reference. It now contains the literal text. For example, the SERIES formula for the first series is as follows:

```
=SERIES("Branch 1",'Figure 6-9'!$A$4:$A$9,'Figure 6-9'!$B$4:$B$9,1)
```

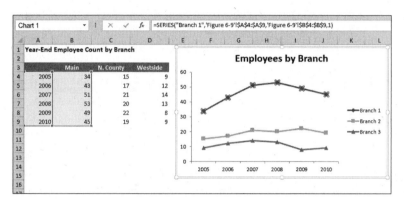

Figure 6-9: The series names have been changed; the new names are shown in the legend.

You can also change the name of a series by editing the SERIES formula directly. Select the series, click inside the Formula bar, and replace the first argument with your text (make sure that the text is enclosed within quotation marks).

Deleting a series name

To delete a series name, use the Edit Series dialog box as described previously. Highlight the range reference (or text) in the Series Name box and press Delete.

Alternatively, you can edit the SERIES formula and remove the first argument. Here's an example of a SERIES formula for a series with no specified name (it will use the default name):

```
=SERIES(,Sheet2!$A$2:$A$6,Sheet2!$B$2:$B$6,1)
```

Note

When you remove the first argument in a SERIES formula, make sure that you do not delete the comma that follows the first argument. The comma is required as a place-holder to indicate the missing argument.

To create a series with no name, use a set of empty quotation marks for the first argument in the SERIES formula. A series with no name still appears in the chart's legend, but no text is displayed.

Adjusting the Series Plot Order

Every chart series has a plot order parameter. A chart's legend usually displays the series' names in the order in which they're plotted. I say *usually,* because you do find exceptions. For example, consider a combination chart that displays a column series and a line series. Changing the series order doesn't change the order in which the series are listed in the legend.

To change the plot order of a chart's data series, use the Select Data Source dialog box. In the lower-left list, the series are listed in the order in which they're plotted. Select a series and then use the up- or down-arrow buttons to adjust its position in the list — which also changes the plot order of the series.

Alternatively, you can edit the SERIES formulas — specifically, the fourth parameter in the SERIES formulas. See the "SERIES formula syntax" sidebar, earlier in this chapter, for more information about SERIES formulas.

For some charts, the plot order is not important. For others, however, you may want to change the order in which the series are plotted. Figure 6-10 shows a stacked column chart generated from the data in A2:E6. Notice that the columns are stacked, beginning with the first data series (Region 1) on the bottom. You may prefer to stack the columns in the order in which the data appears. To do so, you need to change the plot order.

	Qtr-1	Qtr-2	Qtr-3	Qtr-4
Region 1	32,093	36,830	29,845	40,932
Region 2	39,831	42,983	39,873	45,880
Region 3	49,001	48,087	42,871	51,644
Region 4	25,093	21,882	15,092	14,110

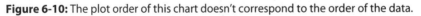

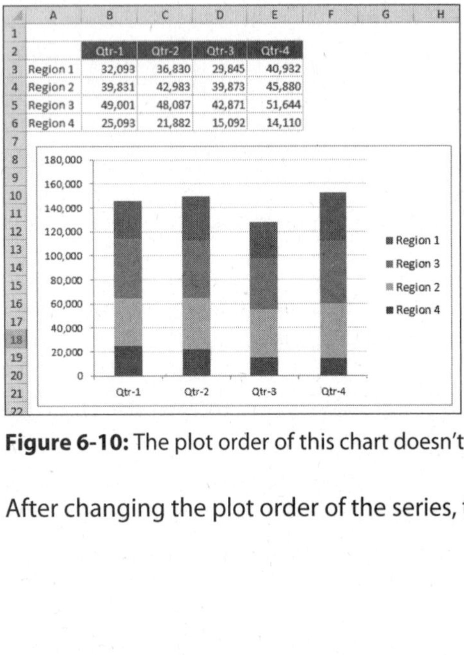

Figure 6-10: The plot order of this chart doesn't correspond to the order of the data.

After changing the plot order of the series, the chart now appears as in Figure 6-11.

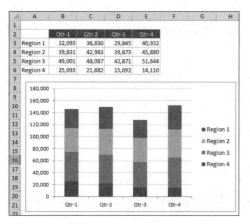

Figure 6-11: After changing the plot order, the stacked columns correspond to the order of the data.

Charting a Noncontiguous Range

Most of the time, a chart series consists of a contiguous range of cells. But Excel does allow you to plot data that isn't in a contiguous range. Figure 6-12 shows an example of a noncontiguous series. This chart displays monthly data for the first and fourth quarters. The data in this single series is contained in rows 2:4 and 11:13. Notice that the category labels display Jan, Feb, Mar, Oct, Nov, and Dec.

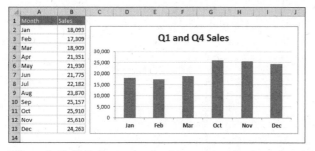

Figure 6-12: This chart uses data in a noncontiguous range.

The SERIES formula for this series is as follows:

```
=SERIES('Figure 6-12'!$B$1,('Figure 6-12'!$A$2:$A$4,'Figure
   6-12'!$A$11:$A$13),('Figure 6-12'!$B$2:$B$4,'Figure 6-12'!$B$11:$B$13),1)
```

The first argument is omitted, so Excel uses the default series name. The second argument specifies six cells in column A as the category labels. The third argument specifies six corresponding cells in column B as the data values. Note that the range arguments for the noncontiguous ranges are displayed in parentheses, and each subrange is separated by a comma.

Note

When a series uses a noncontiguous range of cells, Excel doesn't display the range highlights when the series is selected. Therefore, the only way to modify the series is to use the Select Data Source dialog box or to edit the SERIES formula manually.

Using Series on Different Sheets

Typically, data to be used on a chart resides on a single sheet. Excel, however, does allow a chart to use data from any number of worksheets, and the worksheets don't need to be in the same workbook.

Normally, you select all the data for a chart before you create the chart. But if your chart uses data from different worksheets, you need to create an empty chart and then add the series (see the section "Adding a New Series to a Chart," earlier in this chapter).

Figure 6-13 shows a chart that uses data from two other worksheets. Each of the three worksheets is shown in a separate window.

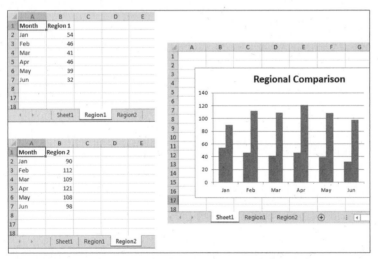

Figure 6-13: This chart uses data from different worksheets.

The SERIES formulas for this chart are as follows:

```
=SERIES(Region1!$B$1,Region1!$A$2:$A$7,Region1!$B$2:$B$7,1)
=SERIES(Region2!$B$1,Region1!$A$2:$A$7,Region2!$B$2:$B$7,2)
```

Tip

Another way to handle data in different worksheets is to create a summary range in a single worksheet. This summary range consists of simple formulas that refer to the data in other sheets. Then you can create a chart from the summary range.

Handling Missing Data

Sometimes, data that you use in a chart may lack one or more data points. Excel offers the following ways to handle the missing data:

➤ Ignore the missing data. Plotted data series will have a gap.

➤ Treat the missing data as zero values.

➤ Interpolate the missing data (for line and scatter charts only).

For some reason, Excel makes these options rather difficult to locate. The Ribbon doesn't contain these options, and you don't specify these options in the Format Data Series dialog box. Rather, you must follow these steps:

1. Select your chart.

2. Choose Chart Tools➜Design➜Data➜Select Data to display the Select Data Source dialog box.

3. In the Select Data Source dialog box, click the Hidden and Empty Cells button. Excel displays the dialog box shown in Figure 6-14.

4. Choose the appropriate option and click OK.

Figure 6-14: Use the Hidden and Empty Cell Settings dialog box to specify how to handle missing data.

The setting that you choose applies only to the active chart and applies to all series in the chart. In other words, you can't specify a different missing data option for different series in the same chart. In addition, not all chart types support all missing data options.

Figure 6-15 shows three charts that depict the three missing data options. The chart shows temperature readings at one-hour intervals, and four data points are missing. The "correct" missing data option depends on the message that you want to convey. In the top chart, the missing data is obvious because of the gaps in the line. In the middle chart, the missing data is shown as zero — which is clearly misleading. In the bottom chart, the missing data is interpolated. Because of the time-based and relatively smooth nature of the data, interpolating the missing data may be an appropriate choice.

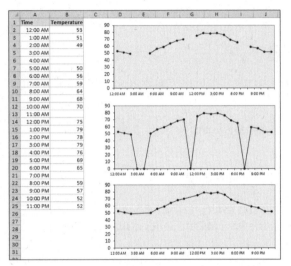

Figure 6-15: These three charts depict the three ways to present missing data in a chart.

Tip

For line charts, you can force Excel to interpolate missing values by placing =NA() in the empty cells. Those cell values will be interpolated, regardless of the missing data option that is in effect for the chart. For other charts, =NA() is interpreted as zero.

Controlling a Data Series by Hiding Data

By default, Excel doesn't plot data that is in a hidden row or column. You can sometimes use this to your advantage because it's an easy way to control what data appears in the chart.

Figure 6-16 shows a line chart that plots 365 days of data stored in a table (created by choosing Insert➜Tables➜Table). Figure 6-17 shows the same chart after I applied a filter to the table. The filter hides all rows except those in which the month is September.

In some cases, when you're working with outlines or filtered tables (both of which use hidden rows), you may not like the idea that hidden data is removed from your chart. To override this, activate the chart and choose Chart Tools➜Design➜Data➜Select Data to display the Select Data Source dialog box. Click the Hidden and Empty Cells button and select the Show Data in Hidden Rows and Columns check box.

Figure 6-16: A line chart that uses data in a table.

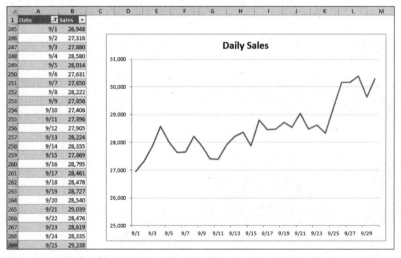

Figure 6-17: After filtering the table, the chart shows only data for September.

Unlinking a Chart Series from Its Data Range

Typically, an Excel chart uses data stored in a range. Change the data in the range, and the chart updates automatically. In some cases, you may want to "unlink" the chart from its data ranges and produce a *static* chart — a chart that never changes. For example, if you plot data generated by various what-if scenarios, you may want to save a chart that represents some baseline so that you can compare it to other scenarios. You can create such a chart in the following ways:

➤ Convert the chart to a picture.

➤ Convert the range references to arrays.

Converting a chart to a picture

To convert a chart to a static picture, follow these steps:

1. Create the chart as usual and make any necessary modifications.

2. Click the chart to activate it.

3. Choose Home➡Clipboard➡Copy (or press Ctrl+C).

4. Click in any cell to deselect the chart.

5. Choose Home➡Clipboard➡Paste➡Picture.

The result is a picture of the original chart. This picture can be edited as a picture, but not as a chart. In other words, you can no longer modify properties such as chart type, data labels, and so on.

When you select such a picture, you see Excel's Picture Tools➡Format tab. Figure 6-18 shows a few examples of built-in formatting options applied to a picture of a chart.

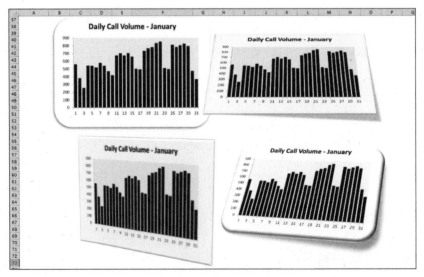

Figure 6-18: After converting a chart to a picture, you can apply various types of formatting to the picture.

Converting a range reference to arrays

The other way to unlink a chart from its data is to convert the SERIES formula range references to arrays. Figure 6-19 shows an example of a pie chart that doesn't use data stored in a worksheet. Rather, the chart's data is stored directly in the SERIES formula, which is as follows:

```
=SERIES(,{"Work","Sleep","Drive","Eat","Other"},{9,7,2.5,3,2.5},1)
```

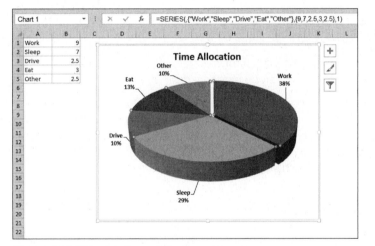

Figure 6-19: This chart is not linked to a data range.

The first argument, the series name, is omitted. The second argument consists of an array of five text strings. Notice that each array element appears within quotation marks and is separated by a comma. The array is enclosed in braces. The chart's data is stored as another array (the third argument).

This chart was originally created by using data stored in a range. Then the SERIES formula was delinked from the range, and the original data was deleted. The result is a chart that doesn't rely on data stored in a range.

Follow these steps to convert the range references in a SERIES formula to arrays:

1. Create the chart as usual.

2. Click the chart series.

   The SERIES formula appears in the Formula bar.

3. Click inside the Formula bar.

4. Press F9.

5. Press Enter, and the range references are converted to arrays.

Repeat this procedure for each series in the chart. This method of unlinking a chart series (as opposed to creating a picture) enables you to continue to edit the chart and apply formatting. Note that you can also convert just a single argument to an array. Highlight the argument in the SERIES formula and press F9.

 Note

Excel imposes a 1,024-character limit to the length of a SERIES formula, so this technique doesn't work if a chart series contains a large number of values or category labels.

Working with Multiple Axes

An *axis* is a chart element that contains category or value information for a series. A chart can use zero, two, three, or four axes, and any or all of them can be hidden if desired.

Pie charts and doughnut charts have no axes. Common chart types, such as a standard column or line chart, use a single category axis and a single value axis. If your chart has at least two series — and it's not a 3-D chart — you can create a secondary value axis. Each series is associated with either the primary or the secondary value axis. Why use two value axes? Two value axes are most often used when the data being plotted in a series varies drastically in scale from the data in another series.

Creating a secondary value axis

Figure 6-20 shows a line chart with two data series: Income and Profit Margin. Compared to the Income values, the Profit Margin numbers (represented by squares) are so small that they barely show up on the chart. This is a good candidate for a secondary value axis.

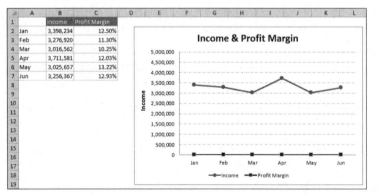

Figure 6-20: The values in the Profit Margin series are so small that they aren't visible in the chart.

To add a secondary value axis, follow these steps:

1. Select the Profit Margin series on the chart.

2. Press Ctrl+1 to display the Format Data Series dialog box.

3. In the Format Data Series dialog box, click the Series Options tab.

4. Choose the Secondary Axis option.

A new value axis is added to the right side of the chart, and the Profit Margin series uses that value axis. Figure 6-21 shows the dual-axis chart.

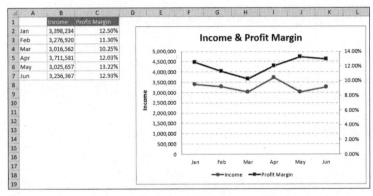

Figure 6-21: Using a secondary value axis for the Profit Margin series.

Creating a chart with four axes

Very few situations warrant a chart with four axes. The problem, of course, is that using four axes almost always causes the chart to be difficult to understand. An exception is scatter charts. Figure 6-22 shows a scatter chart that has two series, and the series vary quite a bit in magnitude on both dimensions. If the objective is to compare the shape of the lines, this chart doesn't do a very good job because most of the chart consists of white space. Using four axes might solve the problem.

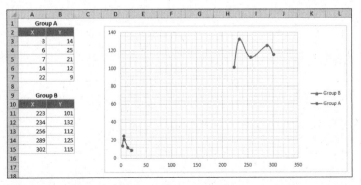

Figure 6-22: The two series vary in magnitude.

Follow these steps to add two new value axes for this scatter chart:

1. Select the Group B series.

2. Press Ctrl+1 to display the Format Data Series dialog box.

3. In the Format Data Series dialog box, click the Series Options tab.

4. Choose the Secondary Axis option.

    At this point, each of the series has its own *y*-value axis (one on the left, one on the right), but they share a common *x*-value axis.

5. Choose Chart Tools→Layout→Axes→Secondary Horizontal Axis→Show Default Axis.

    Note that this Ribbon command is available only if you've assigned a series to the secondary axis.

Figure 6-23 shows the result. The Group B series uses the left and bottom axes, and the Group A series uses the right and top axes. The chart also has four axis titles to clarify the axes for each group. If necessary, the scales for each axis can be adjusted separately.

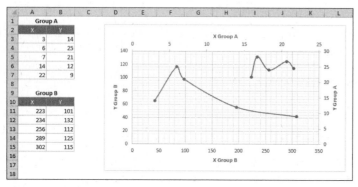

Figure 6-23: This chart uses four value axes.

Formatting and Customizing Charts

In This Chapter

- Getting an overview of chart formatting

- Formatting fill and borders

- Formatting chart background elements

- Working with chart titles

- Working with legends, data labels, gridlines, and data tables

- Understanding chart axes

- Formatting 3-D charts

If you create a chart for your own use, spending a lot of time on formatting and customizing the chart may not be worth the effort. But if you want to create the most effective chart possible, or if you need to create a chart for presentation purposes, you will want to take advantage of the additional customization techniques available in Excel.

This chapter discusses the ins and outs of formatting and customizing your charts. It's easy to become overwhelmed with all the chart customization options. However, the more you work with charts, the easier it becomes. Even advanced users tend to experiment a great deal with chart customization, and they rely heavily on trial and error — a technique that's highly recommend.

Chart Formatting Overview

Customizing a chart involves changing the appearance of its elements, as well as possibly adding new elements to it or removing elements from it. These changes can be purely cosmetic (such as changing colors or modifying line widths) or quite substantial (such as changing the axis scales).

Before you can customize a chart, you must activate it. To activate an embedded chart, click any-where within the chart. To deactivate an embedded chart, just click anywhere in the worksheet or press Esc (once or twice, depending on which chart element is currently selected). To activate a chart on a chart sheet, click its sheet tab.

Tip

If you press Ctrl while you activate an embedded chart, the chart is selected as an object. In fact, you can select multiple charts using this technique. When a group of charts is selected, you can move and resize them all at once. In addition, the tools in the Drawing Tools➜Format➜Arrange group are available. For example, you can align the selected charts vertically or horizontally.

Selecting chart elements

Modifying a chart is similar to everything else you do in Excel: First you make a selection (in this case, select a chart element); then you issue a command to do something with the selection.

You can select only one chart element at a time. For example, if you want to change the font for two axis labels, you must work on each label separately. The exceptions to the single-selection rule are elements that consist of multiple parts, such as gridlines. Selecting one gridline selects them all.

Excel provides three ways to select a particular chart element:

> ➤ Use the mouse

> ➤ Use the keyboard

> ➤ Use the Chart Elements drop-down list

These selection methods are described in the following sections.

Selecting with the mouse

To select a chart element with your mouse, just click the element.

Tip

To ensure that you've selected the chart element that you intended to select, check the name that's displayed in the Chart Elements dropdown found on the far left of the Chart Tools➜Format tab. The Chart Elements dropdown displays the name of the selected chart element, and you can also use this control to select a particular element. See the "Selecting with the Chart Elements dropdown" section later in this chapter.

When you move the cursor over a selected chart, a small "chart tip" displays the name of the chart element under the mouse pointer. When the mouse pointer is over a data point, the chart tip also displays the series, category, and value of the data point. If you find these chart tips annoying, you can turn them off in the Advanced tab in the Excel Options dialog box. In the Chart section, you'll find two check boxes: Show Chart Element Names on Hover, and Show Data Point Values on Hover.

Some chart elements (such as a chart series, a legend, and data labels) consist of multiple items. For example, a chart series is made up of individual data points. To select a single data point, you need to click twice: First click the series to select it; then click the specific element within the series (for example, a column or a line chart marker). Selecting an individual element enables you to apply formatting only to a particular data point in a series. This might be useful if you'd like one marker in a line chart to stand out from the others.

Note

If you find that some chart elements are difficult to select with the mouse, you're not alone. If you rely on the mouse for selecting a chart element, it may take several clicks before the desired element is actually selected. And in some cases, selecting a particular element with the mouse is almost impossible. Fortunately, Excel provides other ways to select a chart element, and it's worth your while to be familiar with them.

Selecting with the keyboard

When a chart is active, you can use the up- and down-arrow keys on your keyboard to cycle among the chart's elements. Again, keep your eye on the Chart Elements control to verify which element is selected.

When a chart series is selected, use the left- and right-arrow keys to select an individual data point within the series. Similarly, when a set of data labels is selected, you can select a specific data label by using the left- or right-arrow key. And when a legend is selected, you can select individual elements within the legend by using the left- or right-arrow keys.

Selecting with the Chart Elements dropdown

As noted earlier, the Chart Elements drop-down list (found on the far left of the Chart Tools➜Format tab) displays the name of the selected chart element. This control contains a drop-down list of all chart elements (excluding shapes and text boxes), so you can also use it to select a particular chart element.

The Chart Elements drop-down list lets you select a particular chart element from the active chart (see Figure 7-1). This drop-down list lists only the top-level elements in the chart. To select an individual data point within a series, for example, you need to select the series and then use one of the other techniques to select the desired data point.

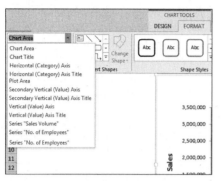

Figure 7-1: Use the Chart Elements drop-down list to select an element on a chart.

Note When a single data point is selected, the Chart Elements control *will* display the name of the selected element, even though it's not actually available for selection in the drop-down list.

Common chart elements

Table 4-1 contains a list of the various chart elements that you may encounter. Note that the actual chart elements that are present in a particular chart depend on the chart type and on the customizations that you've performed on the chart.

Table 4-1 Chart Elements

Part	Description
Category Axis	The axis that represents the chart's categories.
Category Axis Title	The title for the category axis.
Chart Area	The chart's background.
Chart Title	The chart's title.
Data Label	A data label for a point in a series. The name is preceded by the series and the point. Example: Series 1 Point 1 Data Label.
Data Labels	Data labels for a series. The name is preceded by the series. Example: Series 1 Data Labels.
Data Table	The chart's data table.
Display Units Label	The units label for an axis.
Up/Down Bars	Vertical bars in a line chart or stock market chart.
Drop Lines	Lines that extend from each data point downward to the axis (line and area charts only).
Error Bars	Error bars for a series. The name is preceded by the series. Example: Series 1 Error Bars.

Part	Description
Floor	The floor of a 3-D chart.
Gridlines	A chart can have major and minor gridlines for each axis. The element is named using the axis and the type of gridlines. Example: Primary Vertical Axis Major Gridlines.
High-Low Lines	Vertical lines in a line chart or stock market chart.
Legend	The chart's legend.
Legend Entry	One of the text entries inside a legend.
Plot Area	The chart's plot area — the actual chart, without the legend.
Point	A point in a data series. The name is preceded by the series name. Example: Series 1 Point 2.
Secondary Category Axis	The second axis that represents the chart's categories.
Secondary Category Axis Title	The title for the secondary category axis.
Secondary Value Axis	The second axis that represents the chart's values.
Secondary Value Axis Title	The title for the secondary value axis.
Series	A data series.
Series Axis	The axis that represents the chart's series (3-D charts only).
Series Lines	A line that connects a series in a stacked column or stacked bar chart.
Trendline	A trend line for a data series.
Trendline Equation	The equation for a trend line.
Value Axis	The axis that represents the chart's values. There also may be a Secondary Value Axis.
Value Axis Title	The title for the value axis.
Walls	The walls of a 3-D chart only (except 3-D pie charts).

UI choices for formatting

When a chart element is selected, you have some choices as to which UI method you can use to format the element:

➤ The Ribbon

➤ The mini toolbar

➤ The Format dialog box

Formatting by using the Ribbon

The controls in the Chart Tools➜Format tab are used to change the appearance of the selected chart element. For example, if you would like to change the color of a series in a column chart, one approach is to use one of the predefined styles in the Chart➜Tools➜Format➜Shape Styles group.

For a bit more control, follow these steps:

1. Click the series to select it.

2. Choose Chart Tools➔Format➔Shape Styles➔Shape Fill, and select a color.

3. Choose Chart Tools➔Format➔Shape Styles➔Shape Outline, and select a color for the outline of the columns.

   You can also modify the outline width and the type of dashes (if any).

4. Choose Chart Tools➔Format➔Shape Styles➔Shape Effects, and add one or more effects to the series.

Note that you can modify the Shape Fill, Shape Outline, and Shape Effects for almost every element in a chart.

Here's one way to change the formatting of a chart's title so that the text is white on a black background:

1. Click the chart title to select it.

2. Choose Chart Tools➔Format➔Shape Styles➔Shape Fill, and select black.

3. Choose Chart Tools➔Format➔WordArt Styles➔Text Fill, and select white.

Notice that some of the controls in the Home➔Font and Home➔Alignment groups are also available when a chart element is selected. An alternate way of changing a chart's title to white on black is as follows:

1. Click the chart title to select it.

2. Choose Home➔Font➔Fill Color, and select black.

3. Choose Home➔Font➔Font Color, and select white.

Note

The Ribbon commands do not contain all possible formatting options for chart elements. In fact, the Ribbon controls contain only a small subset of the chart formatting commands. For optimal control, you need to use the Format dialog box (discussed later in this chapter).

Formatting by using the Mini Toolbar

When you right-click a chart element, Excel displays its shortcut menu, with the Mini Toolbar on top. Figure 7-2 shows the Mini Toolbar that appears when you right-click a chart title. Use the Mini Toolbar to make formatting changes to the selected element. Note that the Mini Toolbar also works if you've selected only some of the characters in the chart element. In such a case, the text formatting applies only to the selected characters.

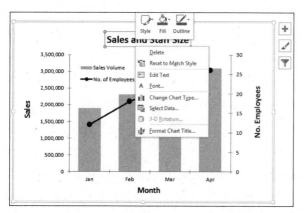

Figure 7-2: You can use the Mini Toolbar to format chart elements.

A few of the common keystroke combinations also work when a chart element that contains text is selected — specifically: Ctrl+B (bold), Ctrl+I (italic), and Ctrl+U (underline).

Formatting by using the Format dialog box

For complete control over text element formatting, use the Format dialog box. Each chart element has a unique Format dialog box, and the dialog box has several tabs.

You can access the Format dialog box by using either of the following methods:

➤ Select the chart element and press Ctrl+1.

➤ Right-click the chart element and choose Format *xxxx* from the shortcut menu (where *xxxx* is the chart element's name).

In addition, some of the Ribbon controls contain a menu item that, when clicked, opens the Format dialog box and displays a specific tab. For example, when you choose Chart Tools➜Format➜Shape Outline➜Weight, one of the options is More Lines. Click this option, and Excel displays the Format dialog box with the Border Styles tab selected. This tab enables you to specify formatting that's not available on the Ribbon.

Figure 7-3 shows an example of a Format dialog box. Specifically, the figure shows the Legend Options tab of the Format Legend dialog box. As noted, each chart element has a different Format dialog box, which shows options that are relevant to the chart element.

Note

The Format dialog box is a stay-on-top dialog box. In other words, you can keep this dialog box open while you're working on a chart. It's not necessary to close the dialog box to see the changes on the chart. In some cases, however, you need to activate a different control in the dialog box to see the changes you've specified. Usually, pressing Tab will move to the next control in the dialog box and force Excel to update the chart.

Figure 7-3: Each chart element has its own Format dialog box. This dialog box controls formatting for the chart's legend.

Adjusting Fills and Borders: General Procedures

Many of the Format dialog boxes for chart elements include a tab named Fill as well as other tabs that deal with border formatting. These tabs are used to change the interior and border of the selected element.

About the Fill tab

Figure 7-4 shows the Fill tab in the Format Chart Area dialog box when the Solid Fill option is selected. The controls on this tab change, depending on which option is selected.

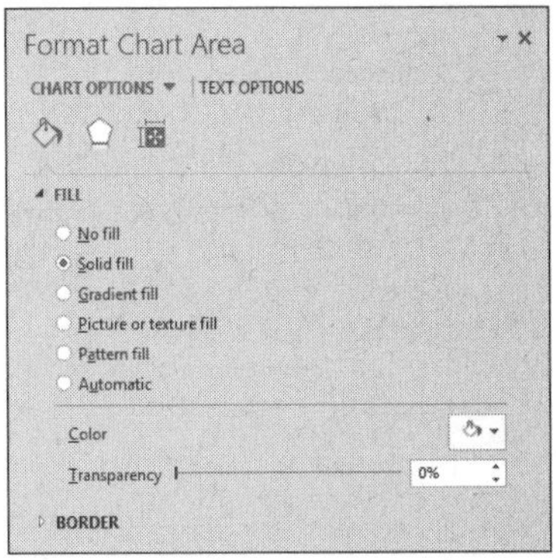

Figure 7-4: The Fill tab of the Format Chart Area dialog box.

Although the Fill tabs of the various Format dialog boxes are similar, they are not identical. Depending on the chart element, the dialog box may have additional options that are relevant for the selected item.

Not all chart elements can be filled. For example, the Format Major Gridlines dialog box does not have a Fill tab because filling a line makes no sense. You can, however, change the gridline formatting by using the tabs that *are* displayed.

The main Fill tab options are as follows:

> ➤ **No Fill:** Makes the chart element transparent.

> ➤ **Solid Fill:** Displays a color selector so that you can choose a single color. You can also specify the transparency level for the color.

> ➤ **Gradient Fill:** Displays several additional controls that allow you to select a preset gradient or construct your own gradient. A gradient consists of from two to ten colors that are blended together in various ways. You have literally millions of possibilities.

> ➤ **Picture or Texture Fill:** Enables you to select from 24 built-in textures, choose an image file, or use clip art for the fill. This feature can often be useful in applying special effects to a data series. See the section "Formatting Chart Series," later in this chapter.

> ➤ **Pattern Fill:** Lets you specify a two-color pattern. This option is not available in Excel 2007.

> ➤ **Automatic:** Sets the fill to the default color. All chart elements start out with Automatic fill.

As a general rule, it's best to use these fill options sparingly. Using too much fill formatting can subdue your data, hindering the chart's ability to communicate the data. For example, Figure 7-5 shows a very ugly chart with various types of fill formatting applied. The column data series uses clip art, in the form of stacked monkeys. The plot area uses a texture, the chart area uses a gradient fill, and the axis labels use a solid black fill.

Figure 7-5: Using too many fill types can quickly lead to ugly charts that are difficult to read.

Formatting borders

A *border* is the line around an object. Excel offers four general choices for formatting a border:

> ➤ **No Line:** The chart element has no line.

> ➤ **Solid Line:** The chart element has a solid line. You can specify the color, the transparency, and a variety of other settings.

> ➤ **Gradient Line:** The chart element has a line that consists of a color gradient.

> ➤ **Automatic:** The default setting. Excel decides the border settings automatically.

Figure 7-6 shows the Border Styles tab of the Format Chart Area dialog box. If you explore this dialog box, you'll soon discover that a border can have a huge number of variations. Keep in mind that all settings are not available for all chart elements. For example, the Arrow Settings are disabled when a chart element that can't display an arrow is selected.

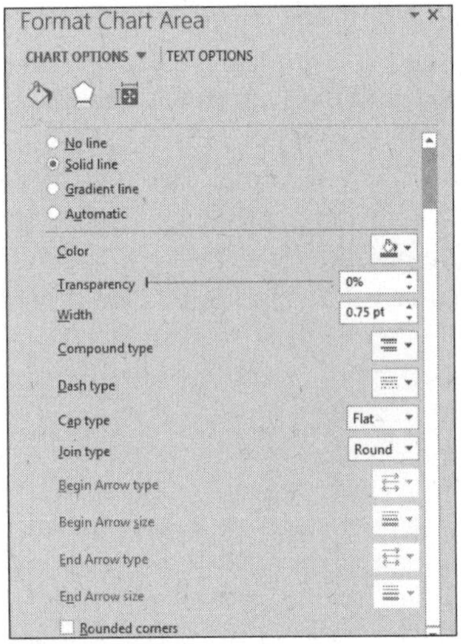

Figure 7-6: Some of the settings available for a chart element border.

Formatting Chart Background Elements

Every chart has two key components that play a role in the chart's overall appearance:

> ➤ **The chart area:** The background area of the chart object

> ➤ **The plot area:** The area (within the chart area) that contains the actual chart

The default colors of the chart area and the plot area depend on which chart style you choose from the Chart Tools➜Design➜Chart Styles gallery.

Working with the chart area

The *chart area* is an object that contains all other elements on the chart. You can think of it as a chart's master background. The chart area is always the same size as the chart object (the chart's container).

Tip

When the chart area is selected, you can adjust the font for all the chart elements that display text. In other words, if you want to make all text in a chart 12 point, select the chart area and then apply the font formatting.

In some cases, you may want to make the chart area transparent so that the underlying worksheet shows through. Figure 7-7 shows a column chart with a transparent chart area. You can accomplish this by setting the chart area's fill to No Fill, or set it to a Solid Fill and make it 100% transparent.

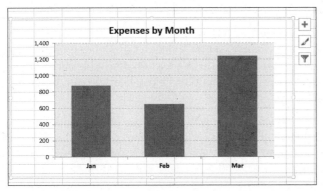

Figure 7-7: The chart area for this chart is transparent. The plot area, however, contains a fill color.

Working with the plot area

The plot area is the part of the chart that contains the actual chart. The plot area contains all chart elements except the chart title and the legend.

Although the plot area consists of elements such as axes and axis labels, when you change the fill of the plot area, these "outside" elements are not affected.

Tip

If you set the Fill option to No Fill, the plot area will be transparent. Therefore, the color and patterns applied to the chart area will show through. You can also set the plot area to a solid color and adjust the Transparency setting so that the chart area shows through partially.

In some situations, you may want to insert an image into the plot area. To do so, use the Fill tab of the Format Plot Area dialog box, and choose the Picture or Texture Fill option. The image can come from a file, the Clipboard, or clip art. Figure 7-8 shows a column chart that uses a graphic in the plot area. In addition, the column series is partially transparent.

Figure 7-8: The plot area for this chart uses a graphic image.

To reposition the plot area within the chart area, select the plot area and then drag a border to move it. To change the size of the plot area, drag one of the corner "handles." If you like, you can expand the plot area so that it fills the entire chart area.

You'll find that different chart types vary in how they respond to changes in the plot area dimensions. For example, you cannot change the relative dimensions of the plot area of a pie chart or a radar chart (it's always square). But with other chart types, you can change the aspect ratio of the plot area by changing either the height or the width.

Copying chart formatting

You created a killer chart and spent hours customizing it. Now you need to create another one just like it. What are your options? You have several choices:

- **Copy the formatting.** Create a standard chart with the default formatting. Then select your original chart and press Ctrl+C. Click your new chart and choose Home➜Clipboard➜ Paste➜Paste Special. In the Paste Special dialog box, select Formats.

- **Copy the chart; change the data sources.** Select the original chart and press Ctrl+C. Then, activate any cell and press Ctrl+V. This creates an exact copy of your chart. Activate a series in the new chart and drag the range highlights to the new ranges (and repeat for each series). Or, you can choose Chart Tools➜Design➜Data➜Select Data to display the Select Data Source dialog box.

- **Create a chart template.** Select your chart and then choose Chart Tools➜Design➜Type➜ Save as Template. In the Save Chart Template dialog box, provide a descriptive filename. When you create your next chart, choose Insert➜Charts➜Other Charts➜All Chart Types, and select the Templates tab. Then, specify the template you created.

Also, be aware that the size of the plot area can be changed automatically when you adjust other elements of your chart. For example, if you add a legend or title to a chart, the size of the plot area may be reduced to accommodate the legend.

Tip

Remember to think of the purpose and utility of your chart before adding images to the plot area. Images may be appropriate for charts used as marketing or sales tools where visual components and eye candy help attract attention. Although in an analytical environment where the data is the primary product of your chart, there is no be a need to dress up your data with superfluous images.

Formatting Chart Series

Making a few simple formatting changes to a chart series can make a huge difference in the readability of your chart. When you create a chart, Excel uses its default colors and marker styles for the series. In many cases, you'll want to modify these colors or marker styles for clarity (basic formatting). In other cases, you may want to make some drastic changes for impact.

You can apply formatting to the entire series or to a single data point within the series — for example, make one column a different color to draw attention to it.

On the Web

This workbook, named `Chapter 7 Samples.xlsx`, **is available at** www.wiley.com/go/exceldr **with the other example files for this book.**

Basic series formatting

Basic series formatting is very straightforward: Just select the data series on your chart and use the tools in the Chart Tools➜Format➜Shape Styles group to make changes. For more control, press Ctrl+1 and use the Format Data Series dialog box.

Using pictures and graphics for series formatting

You can add a picture to several chart elements, including data markers on line charts and series fills for column, bar, area, bubble, and filled radar charts. Figure 7-9 shows a column chart that uses a clip art image of a car. The picture was added using the Fill tab of the Format Data Series dialog box (select the Picture or Texture Fill option; then click the Clip Art button to select the image). In addition, the original image is sized so that each car represents approximately 20 units.

Figure 7-10 shows another example. The data markers in this line chart display a shape that was inserted in the worksheet and then copied to the Clipboard. Select the line series and press Ctrl+V to paste the shape.

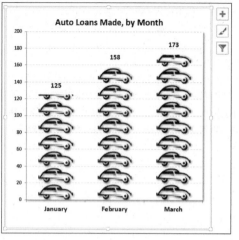

Figure 7-9: This column chart uses a clip art image.

You can also use the Marker Fill tab of the Format Data Series dialog box to specify Picture or Texture Fill. However, the result is very different. If you use the Clipboard button to paste the copied shape, the pasted image will fill the existing marker (not replace it). You'll probably need to increase the marker size, and also hide the marker borders.

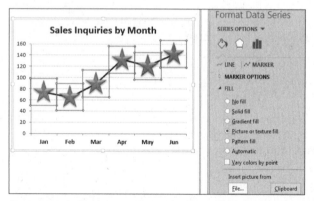

Figure 7-10: The data markers use a shape that was copied to the Clipboard.

Tip

Again, the purpose and utility of your chart should dictate whether pictures and graphics are appropriate. Charts for sales presentations, for example, can benefit from pictures and graphics given that visual enhancements can increase the possibility of prospective buyers paying attention to you. But in boardroom presentations where data is king, images will just get in the way. Think of it as selecting the right outfit for the right occasion. You wouldn't give a serious a speech in a Roman general's uniform. How well will you get your point across when your audience is thinking, "What's the deal with Tiberius"?

Additional series options

Chart series offer a number of additional options. These options are located in the Series Options tab of the Format Data Series dialog box. The set of options varies, depending on the chart type of the series. In most cases, the options are self-explanatory. But, if you are unsure about a particular series option, try it! If the result isn't satisfactory, change the setting to its original value or press Ctrl+Z to undo the change.

Figure 7-11 shows an example of modifying series settings. The chart uses a Series Overlap of 50% and a Gap Width of 28%.

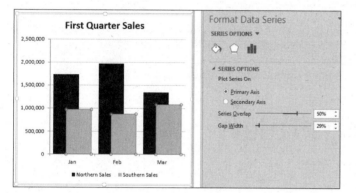

Figure 7-11: A column chart, after adjusting the Series Overlap and Gap Width settings

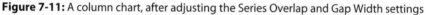

▶ About those fancy effects

Excel 2007 introduced several new formatting options, which are known as *effects*. Access these effects by choosing Chart Tools➜Format➜Shape Styles➜Shape Effects. For more options, use the Format dialog box. Note that not all effects work with all chart elements.

Following is a general description of the effect types:

- **Shadow:** Adds a highly customizable shadow to the selected chart element. Choose from a number of preset shadows, or create your own using the Shadow tab of the Format dialog box. Shadows, when used tastefully, can improve the appearance of a chart by adding depth.

- **Glow:** Adds a color glow around the element. Charts are rarely improved by adding a glow to any element.

- **Soft Edges:** Makes the edges of the element softer. Extreme settings make the element appear to be out of focus, become smaller, or even disappear.

- **Bevel:** Adds a 3-D bevel look to the element. This effect is highly customizable, and you can use it to create a frame for your chart (see the accompanying figure).

- **3-D Rotation:** This effect does not work with any chart elements.

continued

continued

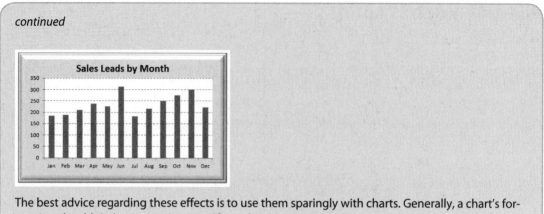

The best advice regarding these effects is to use them sparingly with charts. Generally, a chart's formatting shouldn't draw attention away from the point you're trying to make with the chart.

Working with Chart Titles

A chart can have as many as five different titles:

➤ Chart title

➤ Category axis title

➤ Value axis title

➤ Secondary category axis title

➤ Secondary value axis title

The number of titles depends on the chart type. For example, a pie chart supports only a chart title because it has no axes. Figure 7-12 shows a chart that contains four titles: the chart title, the horizontal category axis title, the vertical value axis title, and the secondary vertical axis title.

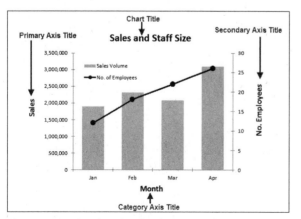

Figure 7-12: This chart has four titles.

Adding titles to a chart

To add a chart title to a chart, activate the chart and click the Chart Elements button next to the chart. This will expand a menu of chart elements you can add to your chart. Place a check next to Chart Title.

To add axis titles to a chart, simply place a check next to the Axis Titles option. Keep in mind that the options include only those that are appropriate for the chart. For example, if the chart doesn't have a secondary value axis, you don't have an option to add a title to the nonexistent axis.

Note

Contrary to what you might expect, you cannot resize a chart title. When you select a title, it displays the characteristic border and handles — but the handles cannot be dragged to change the size of the object. The only way to change the size is to change the size of the font used in the title. For more control over a chart's title, you can use a text box instead of an official title.

Changing title text

When you add a title to a chart, Excel inserts generic text to help you identify the title. To edit the text used in a chart title, click the title once to select it; then click a second time inside the text area. If the title has a vertical orientation, things get a bit tricky because you need to use the up- and down-arrow keys rather than the left- and right- arrow keys.

Tip

For lengthy titles, Excel handles the line breaks automatically. To force a line break in the title, press Enter. To add a line break within existing title text, press Ctrl+Shift+Enter.

Formatting title text

Unfortunately, Excel does not provide a "one-stop" place to change all aspects of a chart title. The Format Chart Title dialog box provides options for changing the fill, border, shadows, 3-D format, and alignment. If you want to change anything related to the font, you need to use the Ribbon (or right-click and use the mini toolbar). Yet another option is to right-click the chart element and choose Font from the shortcut menu. This displays the Font dialog box, with options that aren't available elsewhere. For example, the Font dialog box lets you control the character spacing of the text.

Most of the font changes you make will use the tools in the Home➡Font group. You may be tempted to use the controls in the Chart Tools➡Format➡WordArt Styles group, but these controls are primarily for special effects.

Tip

You can easily modify the formatting for individual characters within a title. Select the title, highlight the characters that you want to modify, and apply the formatting. The formatting changes you make will affect only the selected characters.

Linking title text to a cell

When you create a chart, you might like to have some of the chart's text elements linked to cells. That way, when you change the text in the cell, the corresponding chart element updates. And, of course, you can even link chart text elements to cells that contain a formula. For example, you might link the chart title to a cell that contains a formula that returns the current date.

You can create a link to a cell for the chart title or any of the axis titles. Follow these steps:

1. Select the chart element that will contain the cell link. Make sure that the text element itself is selected (don't select text within the element).

2. Click the Formula bar.

3. Type an equal sign (=).

4. Click the cell that will be linked to the chart element.

5. Press Enter.

Figure 7-13 shows a chart that has links for the following elements: chart title, the vertical axis title, and the horizontal axis title.

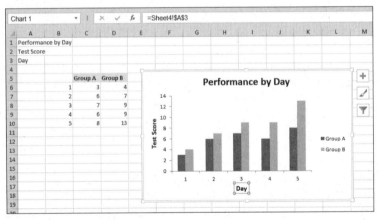

Figure 7-13: The titles in this chart are linked to cells.

▶ Adding free-floating text to a chart

Text in a chart is not limited to titles. In fact, you can add free-floating text anywhere you want by inserting a text box into the chart. To do so, follow these steps:

1. Select the chart.

2. Choose Insert➜Text Box.

3. Click and drag within the chart to create the text box.

4. Start typing the text.

You can click and drag the text box to change its size or location. And when the text box is selected, you can access the formatting tools using the controls on the Drawing Tools➔Format tab.

The accompanying figure shows a chart with a text box that contains quite a bit of formatted text. The chart's plot area was reduced in size to accommodate the text box.

There's nothing special about a text box. A text box is actually a rectangular shape object that contains text. You can change it to a different shape, if you like. Select the text box and choose Drawing Tools➔ Format➔ Insert Shapes➔ Edit Shape ➔Change Shape, and select a shape from the list. The Format Shape dialog box gives you lots of options for changing the look of the text box.

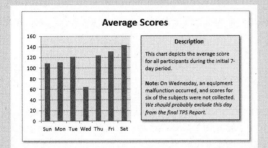

If you would like to link the text box to a cell, follow these steps:

1. Select the text box.

2. Click the Formula bar.

3. Type an equal sign (=).

4. Click the cell that will be linked to the chart element.

After you create the link, the text box will always display the contents of the cell it's linked to.

Some people prefer to use a text box in place of a chart's title because a text box provides much more control over formatting. When a text box is selected, its Format Shape dialog box provides several additional options, compared to the Format Chart Title dialog box.

Working with a Chart's Legend

A chart legend identifies the series in the chart and consists of text and keys. A *key* is a small graphic image that corresponds to the appearance of the corresponding chart series. The text displayed in a legend corresponds to the series names. The order of the items within a legend varies, depending on the chart type.

Adding or removing a legend

To add a legend to a chart, activate the chart and click the Chart Elements button next the chart. This will expand a menu of chart elements you can add to your chart. Place a check next to Legend.

The quickest way to remove a legend is to select it and press Delete.

Moving or resizing a legend

To move a legend, click it and drag it to the desired location. Alternatively, you can activate the chart, click the Chart Elements button next the chart, and then click the arrow next to the Legend option to choose any one of the predefined positions listed (Right, Top, Left, or Bottom). If you move a legend from its default position, you may want to change the size of the plot area to fill in the gap left by the legend. Just select the plot area and drag a border to make it the desired size.

To change the size of a legend, select it and drag any of its corners. Excel will adjust the legend automatically and may display it in multiple columns.

Formatting a legend

You can select an individual legend entry within a legend and format it separately. For example, you may want to make the text bold to draw attention to a particular data series. To select an element in the legend, first select the legend and then click the desired entry.

You can't change the formatting of individual characters in a legend entry. For example, if you'd like the legend to display a superscript or subscript character, you're out of luck.

When a single legend entry is selected, you can use the Format Legend Entry dialog box to format the entry. When a legend entry is selected, and you apply any type of formatting except text formatting, the formatting affects the legend key and the corresponding series. In other words, the appearance of the legend key will *always* correspond to the data series.

Note

You can't use the Chart Elements drop-down list to select a legend entry. You must either click the item or select the legend itself, and then press the right-arrow key until the desired element is selected.

Changing the legend text

The legend text corresponds to the names of the series on the chart. If you didn't include series names when you originally selected the cells to create the chart, Excel displays a default series name (Series 1, Series 2, and so on) in the legend.

To add series names, choose Chart Tools➜Design➜Select Data to display the Select Data Source dialog box. Select the series name and click the Edit button. In the Edit Series dialog box, type the series name or enter a cell reference that contains the series name. Repeat for each series that needs naming. Alternatively, you can edit the SERIES formula, as described in Chapter 5.

Deleting a legend entry

For some charts, you may prefer that one or more of the data series not appear in the legend. To delete a legend entry, just select it and press Delete. The legend entry will be deleted, but the data series will remain intact.

If you've deleted one or more legend entries, you can restore the legend to its original state by deleting the entire legend and then adding it back.

Identifying series without using a legend

Legends are appropriate for charts that have at least two series. But even then, all charts do not require a legend. You may prefer to identify relevant data using other methods, such as a data label, a text box, or a shape with text. Figure 7-14 shows a chart in which the data series are identified by using text in shapes, which were added to the chart using Insert➜Illustrations➜Shapes.

Figure 7-14: This chart uses shapes as an alternative to a legend.

Working with Chart Axes

As you know, charts vary in the number of axes that they use. Pie and doughnut charts have no axes. All 2-D charts have at least two axes, and they can have three (if you use a secondary value or category axis) or four (if you use a secondary category axis and a secondary value axis). Three-dimensional charts have three axes — the "depth" axis is known as the series axis.

Excel provides you with a great deal of control over the look of chart axes. To modify any aspect of an axis, access its Format Axis dialog box. The dialog box varies, depending on which type of axis is selected.

On the Web

This workbook, named `axes.xlsx`**, is available at** `www.wiley.com/go/exceldr` **with the other example files for this book.**

All aspects of axis formatting are covered in the sections that follow.

Value axis versus category axis

Before getting into the details of formatting, it's important to understand the difference between a category axis and a value axis. A category axis displays arbitrary text, whereas a value axis displays numerical intervals. Figure 7-15 shows a simple column chart with two series. The horizontal category axis displays labels that represent the categories. The vertical value axis, on the other hand, is a value axis which has a numerical scale.

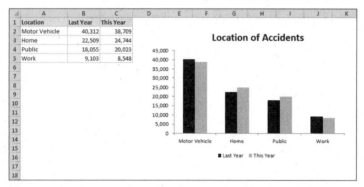

Figure 7-15: The category axis displays arbitrary labels, whereas the value axis displays a numerical scale.

In this example, the category labels happen to be text. Alternatively, the categories *could* be numbers. Figure 7-16 shows the same chart after replacing the category labels with numbers. Even though the chart becomes meaningless, it should be clear that the category axis does not display a true numeric scale. The numbers displayed are completely arbitrary, and the chart itself was not affected by changing these labels.

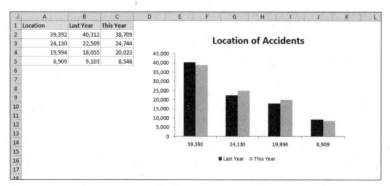

Figure 7-16: The category labels have been replaced with numbers — but the numbers do not function as numbers.

Two of Excel's chart types are different from the other chart types in one important respect. Scatter charts and bubble charts use *two* value axes. For these chart types, both axes represent numeric scales.

Figure 7-17 shows two charts (a scatter chart and a line chart) that use the same data. The data shows world population estimates for various years. Note that the interval between the years in column A is not consistent.

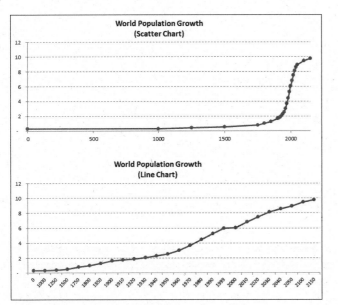

Figure 7-17: These charts plot the same data but present very different pictures.

The scatter chart, which uses two value axes, plots the years as numeric values. The line chart, on the other hand, uses a (non-numeric) category axis, and it assumes that the categories (the years) are equally spaced. This, of course, is not a valid assumption, and the line chart presents a very inaccurate picture of the population growth: It appears to be linear, but it's definitely not.

For more information about time-based axes, refer to the "Using time-scale axes" section later in this chapter.

Cross-Ref

Value axis scales

The numerical range of a value axis represents the axis's scale. By default, Excel automatically scales each value axis. It determines the minimum and maximum scale values for the axis, based on the numeric range of the data. Excel also automatically calculates a major unit and a minor unit for each axis scale. These settings determine how many intervals (or tick marks) are displayed on the axis and determine how many gridlines are displayed. In addition, the value at which the axis crosses the category axis is also calculated automatically.

You can, of course, override this automatic behavior and specify your own minimum, maximum, major unit, minor unit, and cross-over for any value axis. You set these specifications by right-clicking on the axis and selecting Format Axis. This will activate the Format Axis dialog box shown in Figure 7-18. Use the settings under Axis Options to customize the axis as needed.

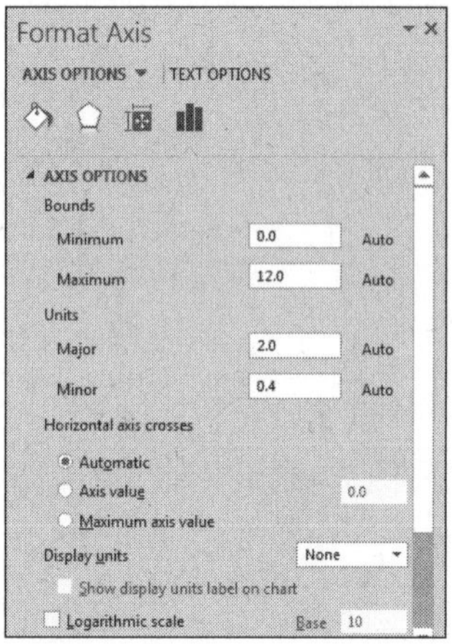

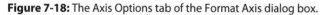

Figure 7-18: The Axis Options tab of the Format Axis dialog box.

Note

A category axis does not have a scale because it displays arbitrary category names. For a category axis, the Axis Options tab of the Format Axis dialog box displays a number of other options that determine the appearance and layout of the axis.

Adjusting the scale of a value axis can dramatically affect the chart's appearance. Manipulating the scale, in some cases, can present a false picture of the data. Figure 7-19 shows two line charts that depict the same data. The top chart uses Excel's default axis scale values, which extend from 8,000 to 9,200. In the bottom chart, the Minimum scale value was set to 0, and the Maximum scale value was set to 10,000. A casual viewer might draw two very different conclusions from these charts. The top chart makes the differences in the data seem more prominent. The lower chart gives the impression that not much change has occurred over time.

The actual scale that you use depends on the situation. There are no hard-and-fast rules regarding setting scale values, except that you shouldn't misrepresent data by manipulating the chart to prove a point that doesn't exist. In addition, most agree that the value axis of a bar or column chart should always start at zero (and even Excel follows that rule).

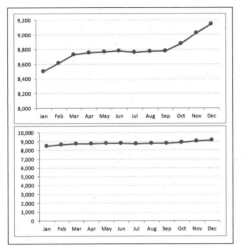

Figure 7-19: These two charts show the same data, but they use different value axis scales.

If you're preparing several charts that use similarly scaled data, keeping the scales constant across all charts facilitates comparisons across charts. The charts in Figure 7-20 show the distribution of responses for two survey questions. For the top chart, the value axis scale ranges from 0% to 50%. For the bottom chart, the value axis scale extends from 0% to 35%. Because the same scale was not used on the value axes, however, comparing the responses across survey items is difficult.

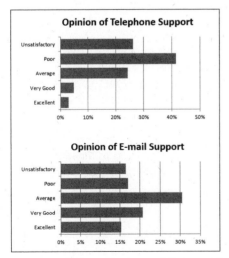

Figure 7-20: These charts use different scales on the value axis, making a comparison between the two difficult.

Another option in the Format Axis dialog box is Values in Reverse Order. The top chart in Figure 7-21 uses default axis settings. The bottom chart uses the Values in Reverse Order option, which reverses the scale's direction. Notice that the category axis is at the top. If you would prefer that it remain at the bottom of the chart, select the Maximum Axis Value option for the Horizontal Axis Crosses setting.

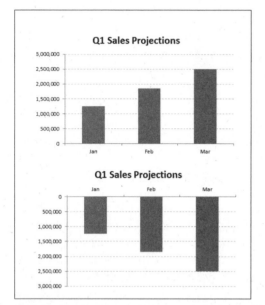

Figure 7-21: The bottom chart uses the Values in Reverse Order option.

If the values to be plotted cover a very large range, you may want to use a logarithmic scale for the value axis. A log scale is most often used for scientific applications. Figure 7-22 shows two charts. The top chart uses a standard scale, and the bottom chart uses a logarithmic scale. Note that the base is 10, so each scale value in the chart is 10 times greater than the one below it. Increasing the base unit to 100 would result in a scale in which each tick mark value is 100 times greater than the one below.

If your chart uses very large numbers, you may want to change the Display Units settings. Figure 7-23 shows a chart that uses very large numbers. The lower chart uses the Display Units as Millions setting, with the option to Show Display Units Label on Chart. Excel inserted the label "Millions," which was edited to display as "Millions of Miles."

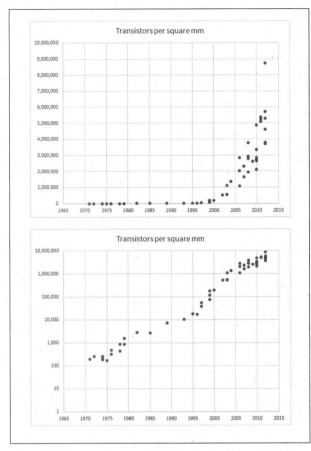

Figure 7-22: These charts display the same data, but the lower chart uses a logarithmic scale.

Tip

Another way to change the number display is to use a custom number format for the axis values. For example, to display the values in millions, click the Number tab of the Format Axis dialog box, select the Custom category, and then enter this format code:

```
#,##0,,
```

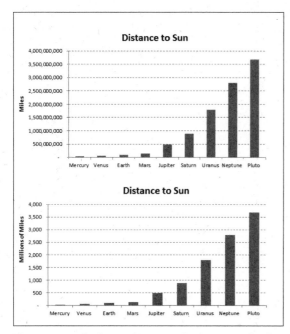

Figure 7-23: The lower chart uses display units of millions.

An axis also has tick marks — the short lines that depict the scale units and are perpendicular to the axis. In the Axis Options dialog box, you can select the type of tick mark for the major units and the minor units. The options are as follows:

➤ None: No tick marks

➤ Inside: Tick marks on the inside of the axis only

➤ Outside: Tick marks on the outside of the axis only

➤ Cross: Tick marks on both sides of the axis

You can also control the position of the tick mark labels. The options are as follows:

➤ None: No labels.

➤ Low: For a horizontal axis, labels appear at the bottom of the plot area; for a vertical axis, labels appear to the left of the plot area.

➤ High: For a horizontal axis, labels appear at the top of the plot area; for a vertical axis, labels appear to the right of the plot area.

➤ Next to axis: Labels appear next to the axis (the default setting).

Note

Major tick marks are the axis tick marks that normally have labels next to them. Minor tick marks are between the major tick marks.

When you combine these settings with the Axis Crosses At option, you have a great deal of flexibility, as shown in Figure 7-24. These charts all display the same data, but the axes are formatted differently.

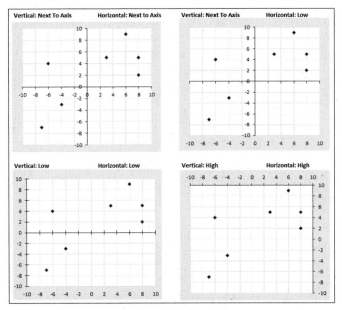

Figure 7-24: Various ways to display axis labels and crossing points.

Using time-scale axes

When you create a chart, Excel attempts to determine whether your category axis contains date or time values. If so, it creates a time-series chart. Figure 7-25 shows a simple example. Column A contains dates, and column B contains the values plotted on the column chart. The data consists of values for only ten dates, yet Excel created the chart with 31 intervals on the category axis. It recognized that the category axis values were dates, and created an equal-interval scale.

If you would like to override Excel's decision to use a time-based category axis, you need to access the Axis Options tab of the Format Axis dialog box. There, you'll discover that the default category axis option is Automatically Select Based on Data. Change this option to Text Axis, and the chart will resemble Figure 7-26. On this chart, the dates are treated as arbitrary text labels.

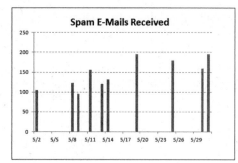

Figure 7-25: Excel recognizes the dates and creates a time-based category axis.

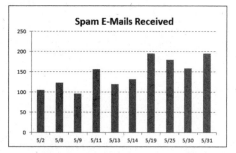

Figure 7-26: The previous chart, using a standard category axis.

 A time-scale axis option is available only for the category axis (not the value axis).

Note

When a category axis uses dates, the Axis Options tab of the Format Axis dialog box lets you specify the Base Unit, the Major Unit, and the Minor Unit — each in terms of days, months, or years.

If you need a time-scale axis for smaller units (such as hours), you need to use a scatter chart. That's because a date-scale axis treats all values as integers. Therefore, every time value is plotted as midnight of that day. Figure 7-27 shows a scatter chart that plots scheduled versus actual arrival times for flights. Note that both of the value axes display times, in one-hour increments.

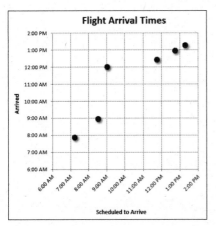

Figure 7-27: This scatter chart displays times on both value axes.

Unfortunately, Excel does not allow you to specify time values on the Axis Options tab of the Format Axis dialog box. If you want to override the default minimum, maximum, or major unit values, you must manually convert the time value to a decimal value.

This chart uses the following scale values:

➤ Minimum axis scale value: .25 (6:00 am)

➤ Maximum axis scale value: .58333 (2:00 pm)

➤ Major unit: .041666 (1:00:00)

To convert a time value to a decimal number, enter the time value into a cell. Then apply General number formatting to the cell. Time values are expressed as a percentage of a 24-hour day. For example, 12:00 noon is 0.50.

Creating a multiline category axis

Most of the time, the labels on a category axis consist of data from a single column or row. You can, however, create multiline category labels, as shown in Figure 7-28. This chart uses the text in columns A:C for the category axis labels.

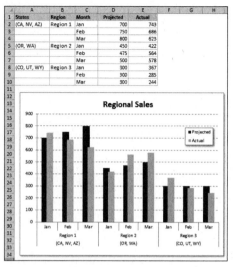

Figure 7-28: The category axis contains labels from three columns.

When this chart was created, range A1:E10 was selected. Excel determined automatically that the first three columns would be used for the category axis labels.

> **This type of data layout is common when you work with pivot table, and pivot charts often use multiline category axes.**

Note

Removing axes

To remove an axis is to select it and then press Delete.

Figure 7-29 shows three charts with no axes displayed. Using data labels makes the value axis superfluous, and it is assumed that the reader understands what the horizontal axis represents.

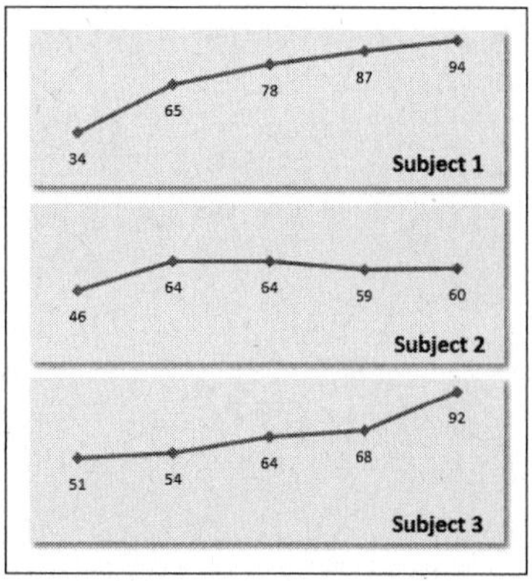

Figure 7-29: Three line charts with no axes.

Axis number formats

A value axis, by default, displays its values using the same number format that's used by the chart's data. You can provide a different number format, if you like, by using the Number tab of the Format Axis dialog box. Changing the number format for a category axis that displays text will have no effect.

Don't forget about custom number formats. Figure 7-30 shows a chart that uses the following custom number format for the value axis:

```
General " mph"
```

This number format causes the text *mph* to be appended to each value.

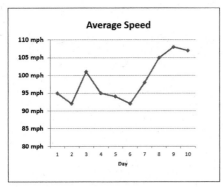

Figure 7-30: The value axis uses a custom number format to provide units for the values.

Working with Gridlines

Gridlines can help the viewer determine the values represented by the series on the chart. Gridlines are optional, and you have quite a bit of control over the appearance of gridlines. Gridlines simply extend the tick marks on the axes. The tick marks are determined by the major unit and minor unit specified for the axis.

 Gridlines are applicable to all chart types except pie charts and doughnut charts.

Note

Some charts look better with gridlines; others appear more cluttered. It's up to you to decide whether gridlines can enhance your chart. Sometimes, horizontal gridlines alone are enough, although scatter charts often benefit from both horizontal and vertical gridlines. In many cases, gridlines will be less overpowering if you make them dashed lines with a gray color.

Adding or removing gridlines

To add or remove gridlines, activate the chart and click the Chart Elements button next the chart. This will expand a menu of chart elements you can add to your chart. Place a check next to Gridlines to add gridlines. Remove the check to remove gridlines.

Each axis has two sets of gridlines: major and minor. Major units are the ones that display a label. Minor units are those in between the labels. If you're working with a chart that has a secondary category axis, a secondary value axis, or a series axis (for a 3-D chart), the dialog box has additional options for three sets of gridlines.

A more direct way to remove a set of gridlines is to select the gridlines and press Delete.

Note

> If a chart uses a secondary axis, you can specify either or both value axes to display gridlines. As you might expect, displaying two sets of gridlines in the same direction can be confusing and result in additional clutter.

To modify the properties of a set of gridlines, select one gridline in the set (which selects all in the set) and access the Format Gridlines dialog box. Or, use the controls in the Chart Tools➜Format➜ Shape Styles group.

Note

> You can't apply different formatting to individual gridlines within a set of gridlines. All gridlines in a set are always formatted identically.

Working with Data Labels

For some charts, you may want to identify the individual data points in a series by displaying data labels.

Adding or removing data labels

To add data labels, activate the chart and click the Chart Elements button next the chart. This will expand a menu of chart elements you can add to your chart. Place a check next to Data Labels.

To remove data labels from a particular series, select the data labels and press Delete. To remove a single data label, click the individual label once to select the series data labels; then click the individual label again. This will ensure that only the targeted label is selected. At this point, you can press Delete.

Note

> If an entire chart series is selected, data labels will be added to the selected series. If a single point is selected, a data label will be applied to only to the selected point. If a chart element other than a series (or single point) is selected, Excel adds data labels to all series in the chart.

Editing data labels

After adding data labels to a series, you can apply formatting to the labels by right-clicking on the labels and selecting Format Data Labels. This will activate the Format Data Labels dialog box. To specify the contents of the data labels, use the Label Options tab of the Format Data Labels dialog box. Figure 7-31 shows this dialog box for a pie chart.

Note When you click a data label, the labels for the entire series are selected. If you click a second time (on a single label), only that data label is selected. In other words, Excel lets you format all data labels at once or format just a single data label.

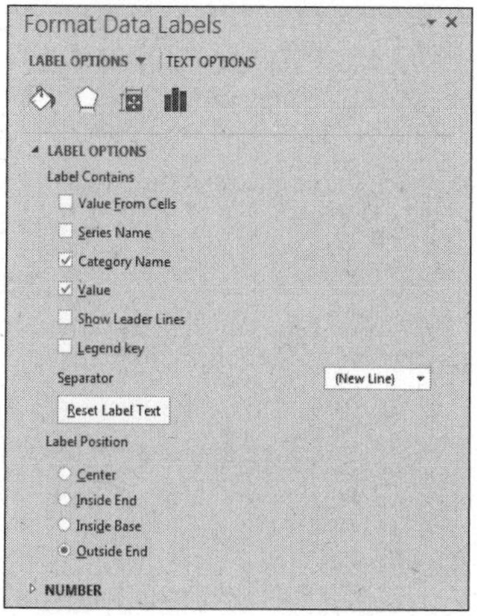

Figure 7-31: Options for displaying data labels.

The types of information that can be displayed in data labels are as follows:

➤ The series name

➤ The category name

➤ The numeric value

➤ The value as a percentage of the sum of the values in the series (for pie charts and doughnut charts only)

➤ The bubble size (for bubble charts only)

Other options are as follows. Keep in mind that not all options are available for all chart types.

➤ Show Leader Lines: If selected, Excel displays a line that connects the data label with the chart series data point.

➤ Label Position: Specifies the location of the data labels, relative to each data point.

➤ Include Legend Key in Label: If selected, each data label displays its legend key image next to it.

➤ Separator: If you specify multiple contents for the data labels, this control enables you to specify the character that separates the elements (a comma, a semicolon, a period, a space, or a line break).

The Format Data Labels dialog box also lets you specify a variety of other formatting options for your data labels.

The column chart in Figure 7-32 contains data labels that display category names and their values. These labels are positioned to appear on the Outside End. These data labels use the New Line separator option, so the value appears on a separate line. Because the category name is included in the data labels, the horizontal category axis labels aren't necessary.

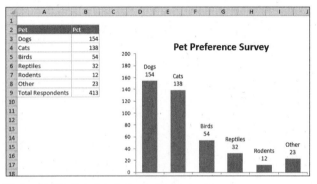

Figure 7-32: Data labels in a column chart.

Note The data labels display the values for each data point. For this particular chart, it would be preferable to display the value as a percentage of the total. Unfortunately, the Percent option is available only for a pie or doughnut chart. The alternative is to calculate the percentages using formulas and then plot the percentage data rather than the actual value data.

Figure 7-33 shows a line chart in which the data labels are positioned on top of the (large) markers. The data labels were positioned using the Center option.

Figure 7-33: Positioning data labels on series markers.

Note

To make your markers large, right-click on any of the markers in your series and select Format Data Series. This will activate the Format Data Series dialog box. Click on the Fill & Line icon (the paint bucket) and choose Marker➜Maker Options. Adjust the Size property to make your markers as big as you need them to be.

To override a particular data label with other text, select the label and enter the new text. To select an individual data label, click once to select all the data labels; then click the specific data label to select it.

To link a selected data label to a cell, follow these steps:

1. Click in the Formula bar.
2. Type an equal sign (=).
3. Click the cell that contains the text.
4. Press Enter.

After adding data labels, you'll often find that the data labels aren't positioned optimally. For example, one or more of the labels may be obscured by another data point or a gridline. If you select an individual label, you can drag the label to a better location.

Problems and limitations with data labels

As you work with data labels, you will probably discover that Excel's Data Labels feature leaves a bit to be desired. For example, it would be nice to be able to specify a range of text to be used for the data labels. This would be particularly useful in scatter charts in which you want to identify each data point with a particular text item. Figure 7-34 shows a scatter chart. If you would like to apply data labels to identify the student for each data point, you're out of luck.

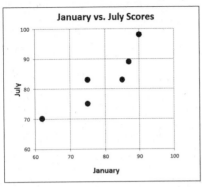

Figure 7-34: Excel provides no direct way to add descriptive data labels to the data points.

Despite what must amount to thousands of requests, Microsoft still has not added this feature to Excel! You need to add data labels and then manually edit each label.

Note A few utility add-ins are available, which allow you to specify an arbitrary range of text to be used for data labels. One such product is Power Utility Pak, available from John Walkenbach's website (`http://spreadsheetpage.com`).

As you work with data labels, you'll find that this feature works best for series that contain a relatively small number of data points. The chart in Figure 7-35, for example, contains 24 data points. You can't display all the data labels on this chart and keep the chart legible.

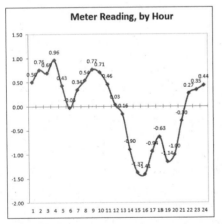

Figure 7-35: Data labels don't work well for this chart.

One option is to delete some of the individual data labels. For example, you might want to delete all the data labels except those at the high and low points of the series. Deleting only certain data labels is, however, a manual process. To delete an individual data label, select it and press Delete. Using gridlines provides another way to let the reader discern the values for the data points. Yet another alternative is to use a data table, which is described in the next section.

Working with a Chart Data Table

There may be situations where it's valuable to show all the data values along with the plotted data points. However, you've adding data labels can inundate your audience with a bevy of numbers that muddle the chart.

Instead of using data labels, you can attach a *Data Table* to your Excel chart. A data table allows you to see the data values for each plotted data point, beneath the chart, showing the data without overcrowding the chart itself. Figure 7-36 shows a chart that includes a data table.

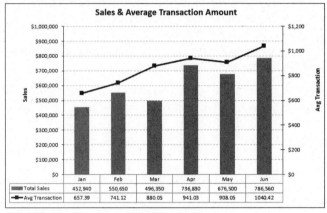

Figure 7-36: This chart includes a data table.

This workbook, named `data table.xlsx`, **is available at** `www.wiley.com/go/ exceldr` **with the example files for this book.**

Note

Adding and removing a data table

To add or remove data tables, activate the chart and click the Chart Elements button next the chart. This will expand a menu of chart elements you can add to your chart. Place a check next to Data Table to add a data table. Remove the check to remove the data table.

Problems and limitations with data tables

One problem with data tables, as noted previously, is that this feature is available for only a few chart types. Formatting options for a data table are relatively limited. Data table formatting changes are made in the Format Data Table dialog box.

The Fill tab is a bit misleading because it does not actually allow you to change the fill color for the data table. Rather, you are limited to formatting the background of the text and numbers in the data table.

Unfortunately, you cannot apply different font formatting to individual cells or rows within the data table. You also can't change the number formatting. The numbers displayed in a data table always use the same number formatting as the source data.

When you add a data table to a chart, the data table essentially replaces the axis labels on the horizontal axis. The first row of the data table contains these labels, so losing them isn't a major problem. However, you will not be able to apply separate formatting to the axis labels — they will have the same formatting as the other parts of the data table.

Note

An exception to the behavior described in the preceding paragraph occurs with bar charts and charts with a time-scale category axis. For these types of charts, the data table is positioned below the chart and does not replace any axis labels.

Another potential problem with data tables occurs when they are used with embedded charts. If you resize the chart to make it smaller, the data table may not show all the data.

Using a data table is probably best suited for charts on chart sheets. If you need to show the data used in an embedded chart, you can do so using data in cells, which provides you with much more flexibility in terms of formatting.

Components That Show Trending

One of the most common concepts used in dashboards and reports is the concept of trending. A *trend* is a measure of variance over some defined interval — typically time periods, like days, months, or years.

The reason trending is so popular is that it provides a rational expectation of what might happen in the future. If we know this book has sold 5,000 copies a month over the last 12 months, we have reason to believe that sales next month will be around 5,000 copies. In short, trending tells you where you've been and where you might be going.

In this chapter, you explore basic trending concepts and some of the advanced dashboard techniques you can use to take your trending components beyond simple line charts.

Trending Dos and Don'ts

Building trending components for your dashboards has some dos and don'ts. This section helps you avoid some common trending *faux pas*.

Using chart types appropriate for trending

It would be nice if you could definitively say which chart type you should use when building trending components. But the truth is that no chart type is the silver bullet for all situations. For effective trending, you need to understand which chart types are most effective in different trending scenarios.

Using line charts

Line charts are the kings of trending. In business presentations, a line chart almost always indicates movement across time. Even in areas not related to business, the concept of lines is used to indicate time — consider timelines, family lines, bloodlines, and so on. The benefit of using a line chart for trending is that it's instantly recognized as a trending component, avoiding any delay in information processing.

Line charts are especially effective in presenting trends with many data points — as the top chart in the Figure 8-1 shows. You can also use a line chart to present trends for more than one time period, as shown in the bottom chart in Figure 8-1.

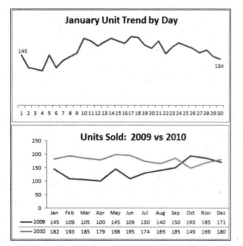

Figure 8-1: Line charts are the chart of choice when you need to show trending over time.

Using area charts

An *area chart* is essentially a line chart that's been filled in. So, technically, area charts are appropriate for trending. They're particularly good at highlighting trends over a long time span. For example, the chart in Figure 8-2 spans more than 120 days of data.

Using combination charts

If you're trending one series of time, a line chart is absolutely the way to go. However, if you're comparing two or more time periods on the same chart, combination charts may bring out the comparisons better.

Figure 8-2: You can use area charts to trend over a long time span.

Figure 8-3 demonstrates how a *combination chart* can more easily call attention to the exact months when 2010 sales fell below 2009. A combination of line and column charts is a very effective way to show the difference in units sold between two time periods. We show you how to create this type of chart later in this chapter.

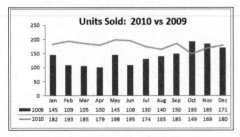

Figure 8-3: Using columns and lines emphasizes the trending differences between two time periods.

Starting the vertical scale at zero

The vertical axis on trending charts should almost always start at zero. The reason we say *almost* is because you may have trending data that contains negative values or fractions. In those situations, it's generally best to keep Excel's default scaling. However, in situations where there are only non-negative integers, ensure that your vertical axis starts at zero.

The reason is that the vertical scale of a chart can have a significant impact on the representation of a trend. For instance, the two charts shown in Figure 8-4 contain the same data. The only difference is that in the top chart, we did nothing to fix the vertical scale assigned by Excel (it starts at 96), but in the bottom chart, we fixed the scale to start at zero.

Now, you may think the top chart is more accurate because it shows the ups and downs of the trend. However, if you look at the numbers closely, you see that the units represented went from 100 to 107 in 12 months. That's not exactly a material change, and it certainly doesn't warrant such a dramatic chart. Actually, the trend is relatively flat, yet the top chart makes it look as though the trend is way up.

The bottom chart more accurately reflects the true nature of the trend. We achieved this effect by locking the Minimum value on the vertical axis to zero.

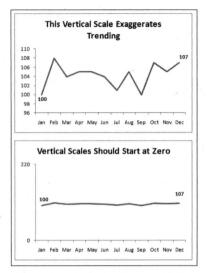

Figure 8-4: Vertical scales should always start at zero.

To adjust the scale of your vertical axis, follow these simple steps:

1. Right-click the vertical axis and choose Format Axis.

   The Format Axis dialog box appears. (See Figure 8-5.)

2. In the Format Axis dialog box, expand the Axis Options section and set the Minimum value to 0.

3. (Optional) You can set the Major Unit value to half the Maximum value in your data.

   This ensures that your trend line is placed in the middle of your chart.

4. Click the Close button (the x) to apply your changes.

Figure 8-5: Always set the Minimum value of your vertical axis to zero.

Tip   Some of you would argue that the bottom chart shown in Figure 8-4 hides the small-scale trending that may be important. That is, a seven unit difference may be very significant in some businesses. Well, if that's true, why use a chart at all? If each unit has such an impact on the analysis, why use a broad-sweep representation like a chart? A table with conditional formatting will do a better job at highlighting small-scale changes than any chart can.

Leveraging Excel's logarithmic scale

In some situations, your trending may start with very small numbers and end with very large numbers. In these cases, you end up with charts that don't accurately represent the true trend. Take Figure 8-6, for instance. In this figure, you see the unit trending for both 2009 and 2010. As you can see in the source data, 2009 started with a modest 50 units. As the months progressed, the monthly unit count increased to 11,100 units through December 2010. Because the two years are on such different scales, it's difficult to discern a comparative trending for the two years together.

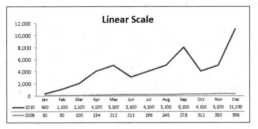

Figure 8-6: A standard linear scale doesn't allow for accurate trending in this chart.

The solution is to use a logarithmic scale instead of a standard linear scale.

Without going into high school math, a logarithmic scale allows your axis to jump from 1 to 10, to 100 to 1,000, and so on without changing the spacing between axis points. In other words, the distance between 1 and 10 is the same as the distance between 100 and 1,000.

Figure 8-7 shows the same chart as the one in Figure 8-6, but in a logarithmic scale. Notice that the trending for both years is now clear and accurately represented.

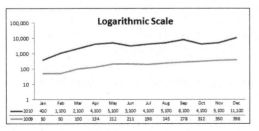
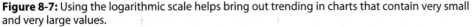

Figure 8-7: Using the logarithmic scale helps bring out trending in charts that contain very small and very large values.

To change the vertical axis of a chart to logarithmic scaling, follow these steps:

1. Right-click the vertical axis and choose Format Axis. The Format Axis dialog box appears.

2. Expand the Axis Options section and place a check next to Logarithmic scale, as shown in Figure 8-8.

Figure 8-8: Setting the vertical axis to Logarithmic scale.

Logarithmic scales work only with positive numbers.

Note

Applying creative label management

As trivial as it may sound, labeling can be one of the sticking points to creating effective trending components. Trending charts tend to hold lots of data points, whose category axis labels take up lots of room. Inundating users with a gaggle of data labels can definitely distract from the main message of the chart. In this section, you find a few tips to help manage the labels in your trending components.

Abbreviating instead of changing alignment

Month names look and feel very long when you have to place them in a chart — especially when that chart must fit on a dashboard. However, the solution isn't to change their alignment, as shown in Figure 8-9. Words that are placed on their sides inherently cause a reader to stop for a moment and read the labels. This isn't ideal when you want them to think about your data and not spend time reading with their heads tilted.

Although it's not always possible, the first option is always to keep your labels normally aligned. So instead of jumping right to the alignment option to squeeze them in, try abbreviating the month names. As you can see in Figure 8-9, even using the first letter of the month name is appropriate.

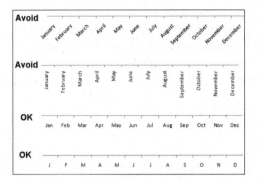

Figure 8-9: Choose to abbreviate category names instead of changing alignment.

Implying labels to reduce clutter

When you're listing the same months over the course of multiple years, you may be able to imply the labels for months instead of labeling each and every one of them.

Take Figure 8-10, for example. In this figure, you see a chart that shows trending through two years. There are so many data points that the labels are forced to be vertically aligned. To reduce clutter, as you can see, only certain months are explicitly labeled. The others are implied by a dot. To achieve this effect, you can simply replace the label in the original source data with a dot (or whatever character you like).

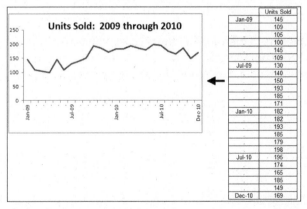

Figure 8-10: To save real estate on your dashboard, try labeling only certain data points.

Going vertical when you have too many data points for horizontal

Trending data by day is common, but it does prove to be painful if the trending extends to 30 days or more. In these scenarios, it becomes difficult to keep the chart to a reasonable size and even more difficult to effectively label it.

One solution is to show the trending vertically using a bar chart. (See Figure 8-11.) With a bar chart, you have room to label the data points and keep the chart to a reasonable size. This isn't something to aspire to, however. Trending vertically isn't as intuitive and may not convey your information in a very readable form. Nevertheless, this solution can prove to be just the workaround you need when the horizontal view proves to be impractical.

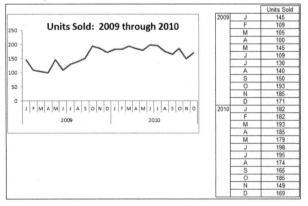

Figure 8-11: A bar chart can prove to be effective when trending days extending to 30 or more data points.

Nesting labels for clarity

Often, the data you're trying to chart has multiple time dimensions. In these cases, you can call out these dimensions by nesting your labels. Figure 8-12 demonstrates how including a year column next to the month labels clearly partitions each year's data. You simply include the year column when identifying the data source for your chart.

		Units Sold
2009	J	145
	F	109
	M	105
	A	100
	M	145
	J	109
	J	130
	A	140
	S	150
	O	193
	N	185
	D	171
2010	J	182
	F	182
	M	193
	A	185
	M	179
	J	198
	J	195
	A	174
	S	165
	O	185
	N	149
	D	169

Figure 8-12: Excel is smart enough to recognize and plot multiple layers of labels.

Comparative Trending

Although the name is fancy, *comparative trending* is a simple concept. You chart two or more data series on the same chart so that the trends from those series can be visually compared. In this section, you walk through a few techniques that allow you to build components that present comparative trending.

Creating side-by-side time comparisons

Figure 8-13 shows a chart that presents a side-by-side time comparison of three time periods. With this technique, you can show different time periods in different colors without breaking the continuity of the overall trending.

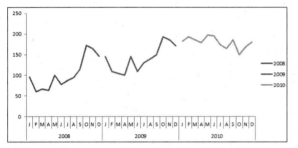

Figure 8-13: You can show trends for different time periods side by side.

1. To create this type of chart, structure your source data similar to the structure shown in Figure 8-14.

   Note that instead of placing all the data into one column, you're staggering the data into respective years. This tells the chart to create three separate lines (allowing for the three colors).

2. Select the entire table and create a line chart.

   This creates the chart shown in Figure 8-13.

3. If you want to get a bit fancy, click the chart to select it and then right-click. Select Change Chart Type from the context menu that opens.

4. When the Change Chart Type dialog box opens, select Stacked Column Chart.

   As you can see in Figure 8-15, your chart now shows the trending for each year in columns.

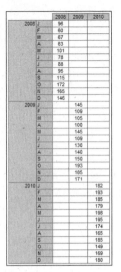

		2008	2009	2010
2008	J	96		
	F	60		
	M	67		
	A	63		
	M	101		
	J	78		
	J	88		
	A	95		
	S	115		
	O	172		
	N	165		
	D	146		
2009	J		145	
	F		109	
	M		105	
	A		100	
	M		145	
	J		109	
	J		130	
	A		140	
	S		150	
	O		193	
	N		185	
	D		171	
2010	J			182
	F			193
	M			185
	A			179
	M			198
	J			195
	J			174
	A			165
	S			185
	O			149
	N			169
	D			180

Figure 8-14: The source data needed to display side-by-side trends.

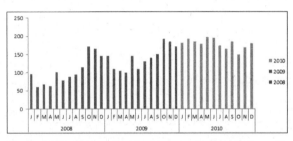

Figure 8-15: Change the chart type to Stacked Column Chart to present columns instead of lines.

Would you like a space in between the years? Adding a space in the source data (between each 12-month sequence) adds a space in the chart. (See Figure 8-16.)

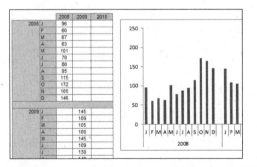

Figure 8-16: If you want to separate each year with a space, simply add a space into the source data.

Creating stacked time comparisons

The stacked time comparison places two series on top of each other instead of side-by-side. Although this approach removes the benefit of having an unbroken overall trending, you get the benefit of an at-a-glance comparison within a compact space. Figure 8-17 illustrates a common stacked time comparison.

Figure 8-17: A stacked time comparison allows you to view and compare two years of data in a compact space.

1. Create a new structure and add data to it like the one shown in Figure 8-18.

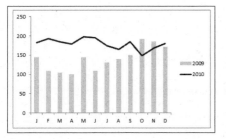

Figure 8-18: Start with a structure containing the data for two time periods.

2. Highlight the entire structure and create a column chart.

3. Select and right-click any of the bars for the 2010 data series and then choose Change Series Chart Type.

4. When the Change Chart Type dialog box opens, select the Line type.

Tip

This technique works well with two time series. You generally want to avoid stacking any more than that. Stacking more than two series often muddies the view and causes users to constantly reference the legend to keep track of the series they're evaluating.

Trending with a secondary axis

In some trending components, you'll have series that trend two very different units of measure. For instance, in Figure 8-19, you have a table that shows a trend for People Count and a trend for % of Labor Cost.

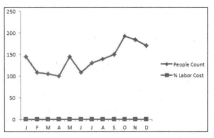

	A	B	C
1		People Count	% Labor Cost
2	J	145	20%
3	F	109	21%
4	M	105	23%
5	A	100	23%
6	M	145	24%
7	J	109	25%
8	J	130	24%
9	A	140	25%
10	S	150	24%
11	O	193	26%
12	N	185	28%
13	D	171	29%

Figure 8-19: You often need to trend two very different units of measure, such as counts and percentages.

These are two very different units of measure that, when charted, produce the unimpressive chart you see in Figure 8-20. Because Excel builds the vertical axis to accommodate the largest number, the percentage of labor cost trending gets lost at the bottom of the chart. Even a logarithmic scale doesn't help in this scenario.

Figure 8-20: The trending for percentage of labor cost gets lost at the bottom of the chart.

Because the default vertical axis (or *primary* axis) doesn't work for both series, the solution is to create another axis to accommodate the series that doesn't fit into the primary axis. This other axis is the *secondary* axis.

To place a data series on the secondary axis, follow these steps:

1. Right-click the data series and select Format Data Series.

    The Format Data Series dialog box appears (see Figure 8-21).

2. In the Format Data Series dialog box, expand the Series Options section and then select the Secondary Axis radio button.

Figure 8-21: Placing a data series on the secondary axis.

Figure 8-22 illustrates the newly added axis to the right of the chart. Any data series on the secondary axis has its vertical axis labels shown on the right.

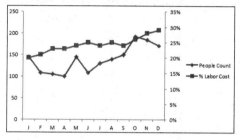
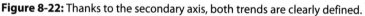

Figure 8-22: Thanks to the secondary axis, both trends are clearly defined.

Again, changing the chart type of any one of the data series can help in comparing the two trends. In Figure 8-23, the chart type for the People Count trend has been changed to a column. Now you can easily see that although the number of people went down in November and December, the percentage of labor cost continues to rise.

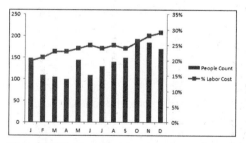
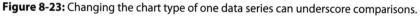

Figure 8-23: Changing the chart type of one data series can underscore comparisons.

Tip

Technically, it doesn't matter which data series you place on the secondary axis. A general rule is to place the problem data series on the secondary axis. In this scenario, because the data series for percentage of labor cost seems to be the problem, we place that series on the secondary axis.

Emphasizing Periods of Time

Some of your trending components may contain certain periods where a special event occurred, causing an anomaly in the trending pattern. For instance, you may have an unusually large spike or dip in the trend caused by some occurrence in your organization. Or maybe you need to mix actual data with forecasts in your charting component. In such cases, it could be helpful to emphasize specific periods in your trending with special formatting.

Formatting specific periods

Imagine you just created the chart component illustrated in Figure 8-24, and you want to explain the spike in October. You could, of course, use a footnote somewhere, but that would force your audience to look for an explanation elsewhere on your dashboard. Calling attention to an anomaly directly on the chart helps give your audience context without the need to look away from the chart.

Figure 8-24: The spike in October warrants emphasis.

A simple solution is to format the data point for October to display in a different color and then add a simple text box that explains the spike.

To format a single data point:

1. Click the data point once.

   This places dots on all the data points in the series.

2. Click the data point again to ensure Excel knows you're formatting only that one data point.

   The dots disappear from all but the target data point.

3. Right-click and select Format Data Point.

   The Format Data Point dialog box opens, as shown in Figure 8-25. The idea is to adjust the formatting properties of the data point as you see fit.

Note

The dialog box shown in Figure 8-25 is for a column chart. Different chart types have different options in the Format Data Point dialog box. Nevertheless, the idea remains the same in that you can adjust the properties in the Format Data Point dialog box to change the formatting of a single data point.

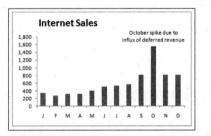

Figure 8-25: The Format Data Point dialog box gives you formatting options for a single data point.

After changing the fill color of the October data point and adding a text box with some context, the chart nicely explains the spike. (See Figure 8-26.)

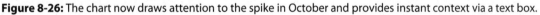

Figure 8-26: The chart now draws attention to the spike in October and provides instant context via a text box.

Note

> To add a text box to a chart, click the Insert tab on the Ribbon and select the Text Box icon. Then click inside the chart to create an empty text box, which you can fill with your words.

Using dividers to mark significant events

Every now and then a particular event shifts the entire paradigm of your data permanently. A good example is a price increase. The trend shown in Figure 8-27 has been permanently affected by a price increase implemented in October. As you can see, a dividing line (along with some labeling) provides a distinct marker for the price increase, effectively separating the old trend from the new.

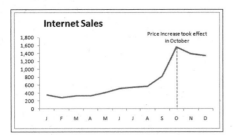

Figure 8-27: Use a simple line to mark particular events along a trend.

Although there are lots of fancy ways to create this effect, you will rarely need to get any fancier than manually drawing a line yourself. To draw a dividing line inside a chart, take the following steps:

1. Click the chart to select it.

2. Select the Insert tab on the Ribbon and click the Shapes drop-down command.

3. Select the line shape, go to your chart, and draw the line where you want it.

4. Right-click your newly drawn line and select Format Shape.

5. Use the Format Shape dialog box to format your line's color, thickness, and style.

Representing forecasts in your trending components

It's common to be asked to show both actual data and forecast as a single trending component. When you do show the two together, you want to ensure that your audience can clearly distinguish where actual data ends and where forecasting begins. Take a look at Figure 8-28.

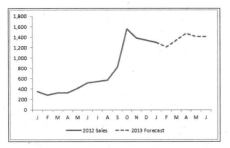
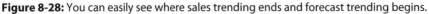

Figure 8-28: You can easily see where sales trending ends and forecast trending begins.

The best way to achieve this effect is to start with a data structure similar to the one shown in Figure 8-29. As you can see, sales and forecasts are in separate columns so that when charted, you get two distinct data series. Also note that the value in cell B14 is actually a formula referencing C14. This value serves to ensure a continuous trend line (with no gaps) when the two data series are charted together.

	A	B	C
1		2012 Sales	2013 Forecast
2	J	355	
3	F	284	
4	M	327	
5	A	326	
6	M	408	
7	J	514	
8	J	541	
9	A	571	
10	S	815	
11	O	1,553	
12	N	1,385	
13	D	1,341	
14	J	1,297	1,297
15	F		1,212
16	M		1,341
17	A		1,469
18	M		1,405
19	J		1,405
20			
21			
22			
23	=C14		

Figure 8-29: Start with a table that places your actual data and your forecasts in separate columns.

When you have the appropriately structured dataset, you can create a line chart. At this point, you can apply special formatting to the 2013 forecast data series. Follow these steps:

1. Click the data series that represents the 2013 forecast.

   This places dots on all the data points in the series.

2. Right-click and select Format Data Series.

   This opens the Format Data Series dialog box. When the Format Data Series dialog box opens, you can adjust the properties to format the series color, thickness, and style.

Other Trending Techniques

In this section, you explore a few techniques that go beyond the basic concepts covered so far.

Avoiding overload with directional trending

Do you work with a manager who is crazy for data? Are you getting headaches from trying to squeeze three years of monthly data into a single chart? Although it's understandable to want to see a three-year trend, placing too much information on a single chart can make for a convoluted trending component that tells you almost nothing.

When you're faced with the need to display impossible amounts of data, step back and think about the true purpose of the analysis. When your manager asks for a three-year sales trend by month, what's he really looking for? It could be that he's really asking whether current monthly sales are declining when compared to historical data. Do you really need to show each and every month or can you show the directional trend?

A *directional* trend is one that uses simple analysis to imply a relative direction of performance. The key attribute of a directional trend is that the data used is often a set of calculated values as opposed to actual data values. For instance, instead of charting each month's sales for a single year, you could chart the average sales for Q1, Q2, Q3, and Q4. With such a chart, you get a directional idea of monthly sales, without the need to look into detailed data.

Take a look at Figure 8-30, which shows two charts. The bottom chart trends each year's monthly data in a single trending component. You can see how difficult it is to discern much from this chart. It looks like monthly sales are dropping in all three years. The top chart shows the same data in a directional trend, showing average sales for key time periods. The trend really jumps at you, showing that sales have flattened out after healthy growth in 2011 and 2012.

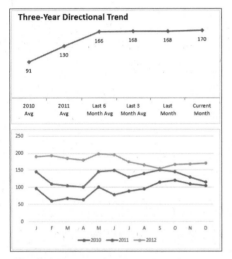

Figure 8-30: Directional trending (bottom) can help you reveal trends that may be hidden in more complex charts.

Smoothing data

Certain lines of business lend themselves to wide fluctuations in data from month to month. For instance, a consulting practice may go months without a steady revenue stream before a big contract comes along and spikes the sales figures for a few months. Some call these ups and downs *seasonality* or *business cycles*.

Whatever you call them, wild fluctuations in data can prevent you from effectively analyzing and presenting trends. Figure 8-31 demonstrates how highly volatile data can conceal underlying trends.

This is where the concept of smoothing comes in. *Smoothing* does just what it sounds like — it forces the range between the highest and lowest values in a dataset to smooth to a predictable range without disturbing the proportions of the dataset.

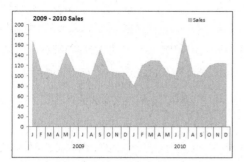

Figure 8-31: The volatile nature of this data makes it difficult to seek the underlying trend.

You can use lots of different techniques to smooth a dataset. Take a moment to walk through two of the easier ways to apply smoothing.

Smoothing with Excel's moving average functionality

Excel has a built-in smoothing mechanism in the form of a moving average trend line. That is, a trend line that calculates and plots the moving average at each data point. A moving average is a statistical operation that is used to track daily, weekly, or monthly patterns. A typical moving average starts calculating the average of a fixed number of data points; then with each new day's (or week's or month's) numbers, the oldest number is dropped, and the newest number is included in the average. This calculation is repeated over the entire dataset, creating a trend that represents the average at specific points in time.

Figure 8-32 illustrates how Excel's moving average trend line can help smooth volatile data, highlighting a predictable range.

In this example, a four-month moving average is applied.

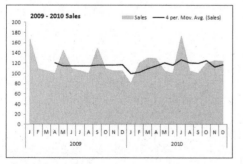

Figure 8-32: A four–month moving average trend line is added to smooth the volatile nature of the original data.

To add a moving average trend line, follow these steps:

1. Right-click the data series that represents the volatile data and then select Add Trendline.

2. In the Format Trendline dialog box that opens (see Figure 8-33), select Moving Average and then specify the number of periods.

   In this case, Excel will average a four–month moving trend line.

Figure 8-33: Applying a four–month moving average trend line.

Creating your own smoothing calculation

As an alternative to Excel's built-in trend lines, you can create your own smoothing calculation and simply include it as a data series in your chart. In Figure 8-34, a calculated column (appropriately called smoothing) provides the data points needed to create a smoothed data series.

	A	B	C	D	E
1				Sales	Smoothing
2		2009	J	167	
3			F	109	=AVERAGE($D$2:D3)
4			M	105	127
5			A	100	120
6			M	145	125
7			J	109	123
8			J	105	120
9			A	100	118
10			S	150	121
11			O	109	120
12			N	105	119
13			D	105	117
14		2010	J	80	115

Figure 8-34: A calculated smoothing column feeds a new series to your chart.

In this example, the second row of the smoothing column contains a simple average formula that averages the first data point and the second data point. Note that the reference to the first data point (cell D2) is locked as an absolute value with dollar ($) signs. This ensures that when this formula is copied down, the range grows to include all previous data points.

Once the formula is copied down to fill the entire smoothing column, it can simply be included in the data source for the chart. Figure 8-35 illustrates the smoothed data plotted as a line chart.

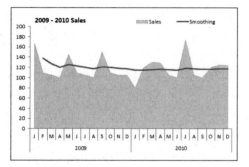

Figure 8-35: Plotting the smoothed data reveals the underlying trend.

Components That Group Data

In This Chapter

- Showing top and bottom views
- Tracking progress using histograms
- Emphasizing top values in charts

It's often helpful to organize your data into logical groups. Grouping allows you to focus on manageable sets of information that have key attributes. For example, instead of looking at all customers in one giant view, you can analyze customers who buy only one product. This allows you to focus attention and resources on those customers who have the potential to buy more products. The benefit is that you can more easily pick out groups that fall outside the norm for your business.

In this chapter, you focus on how you can organize groups of data using dashboard components.

Listing Top and Bottom Values

When you look at the list of Fortune 500 companies, you often look for the top 20 companies. Then perhaps you look at who eked out at the bottom 20 slots. It's unlikely that you check to see which company came in at number 251. It's not necessarily because you don't care about number 251; it's just that you can't spend the time or energy to process all 500 companies. So you process the top and bottom of the list.

This is the same concept behind creating top and bottom displays. Your audience has only a certain amount of time and resources to dedicate to solving any issues you can emphasize in your dashboard. Showing them the top and bottom values in your data can help them pinpoint where and how they can have the most impact with the time and resources they do have.

Organizing source data

The top and bottom displays you create can be as simple as source data that you incorporate into your dashboard. Typically placed to the right of a dashboard, this data can emphasize details a manager may use to take action on a metric. For example, the simple dashboard in Figure 9-1 shows sales information with top and bottom sales reps.

Figure 9-1: Top and bottom displays that emphasize certain metrics.

To get a little fancier, you can supplement your top and bottom displays with some ranking information, some in-cell bar charts, or some conditional formatting (see Figure 9-2).

You can create the in-cell bar charts with the Data Bars conditional formatting function, covered in Chapter 4. The arrows are also simple conditional formatting rules that are evaluated against the variance in current and last months' ranks.

Top 10 Sales Reps	Sales	Rank	Last Month	vs Last Month
HIRNANDIZ, EDUARDO	$137,707	1	1	➡ 0
WATTS, GREER	$111,682	2	3	⬆ 1
SLECIM, ROBERT	$106,299	3	5	⬆ 2
MCCILLEIGH, JEFFREY	$102,240	4	2	⬇ -2
BICKIR, WILLIAM	$83,526	5	3	⬇ -2
GALL, JASON	$78,824	6	12	⬆ 6
PHALLAPS, JAMES	$77,452	7	7	➡ 0
KIMPIRT, RONALD	$76,790	8	9	⬆ 1
SIN, THOEUNG	$76,685	9	8	⬇ -1
IDWERDS, MICHAEL	$76,532	10	4	⬇ -6

Bottom 10 Sales Reps	Sales	Rank	Last Month	vs Last Month
NEBLE, JASON	$5,547	244	244	➡ 0
CELIMAN, WILLIAM	$9,779	243	241	⬇ -2
KRIZILL, ADAM	$11,454	242	235	⬇ -7
MIDANA, FRANK	$15,044	241	221	⬇ -20
GRANGIR, DAVID	$16,129	240	240	➡ 0
DALLEARE, ANDRE	$16,265	239	239	➡ 0
HICKLIBIRRY, JERRY	$16,870	238	225	⬇ -13
VAN HUILE, KENNETH	$18,821	237	242	⬆ 5
RACHERDSEN, KENNETH	$19,675	236	237	⬆ 1
STIGALL, DAVID	$20,092	235	243	⬆ 8

Figure 9-2: You can use some conditional formatting to add visual components to your top and bottom displays.

Using pivot tables to get top and bottom views

A pivot table is an amazing tool that can help you create interactive reporting. If you're new to pivot tables, fear not. You learn about them in detail in Part IV of this book. For now, take a moment to go through an example of how pivot tables can help you build interactive top and bottom displays.

On the Web

You can open the `Chapter 9 Samples.xlsx` **file, found on this book's companion website at** `www.wiley.com/go/exceldr` **to follow along.**

Follow these steps to display a Top filter with a pivot table:

1. Start with a pivot table that shows the data you want to display with your top and bottom views.

   In this case, the pivot table shows Sales Rep and Sales_Amount (see Figure 9-3).

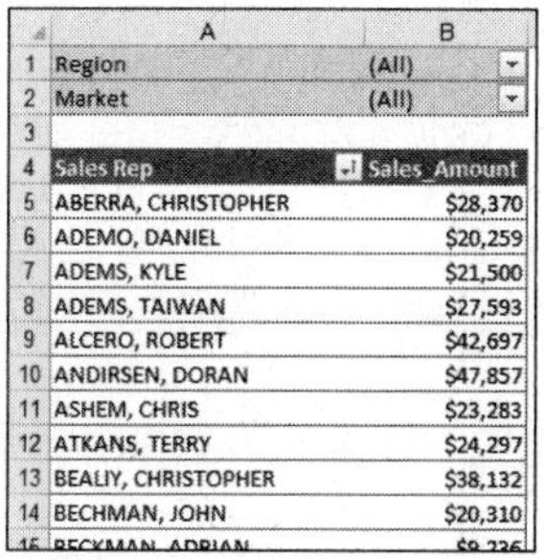

Figure 9-3: Start with a pivot table that contains the data you want to filter.

2. Right-click on the field you want to use to determine the top values. In this example, you use the Sales Rep field. Choose Filter➜Top 10 (see Figure 9-4).

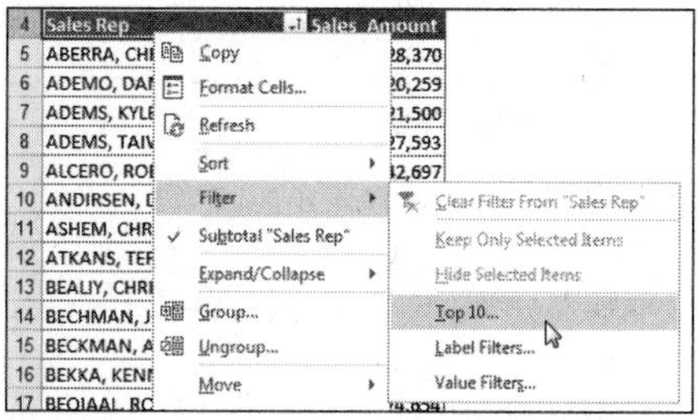

Figure 9-4: Select the Top 10 filter option.

The Top 10 Filter (Sales Rep) dialog box appears (see Figure 9-5).

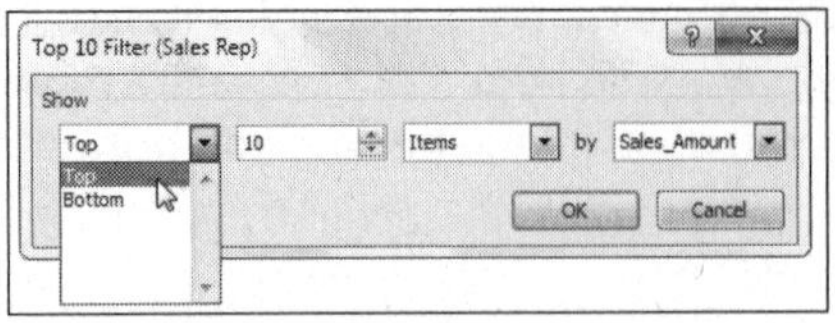

Figure 9-5: Specify the filter you want to apply.

3. In the Top 10 Filter (Sales Rep) dialog box, define the view you're looking for. In this example, you want the Top 10 Items (Sales Reps) as defined by the Sales_Amount field.
4. Click OK to apply the filter.

   At this point, your pivot table is filtered to show you the top ten sales reps for the selected Region and Market. You can change the Market filter to Charlotte and get the top ten sales reps for Charlotte only (see Figure 9-6).
5. To view the bottom ten Sales Rep list, copy the entire pivot table and paste it next to the existing one.
6. Repeat Steps 2–4 in the newly copied pivot table, except this time choose to filter on the *bottom* ten items as defined by the Sales_Amount field.

If all went well, you now have two pivot tables similar to Figure 9-7: one that shows the top ten sales reps and one that shows the bottom ten. You can link back to these two pivot tables in the analysis layer of your data model using formulas. This way, when you update the data, your top and bottom values display the new information.

	A	B
1	Region	(All)
2	Market	CHARLOTTE
3		
4	Sales Rep	Sales_Amount
5	MCCILLEIGH, JEFFREY	$98,090
6	CERDWILL, TIMOTHY	$54,883
7	BRADFERD, JAMES	$49,435
8	DIDLIY, CHARLES	$47,220
9	SWANGIR, ADAM	$46,608
10	SKILTEN, JAMES	$43,569
11	PIORSEN, HEYWARD	$41,005
12	CRIOMIR, TIMOTHY	$34,169
13	PERSENS, GREGORY	$33,026
14	BIOCH, RONALD	$30,168
15	Grand Total	$478,172

Figure 9-6: You can interactively filter your pivot table report to instantly show the top ten sales reps for any Region and Market.

	A	B	C	D	E
1	Region	(All) ▾		Region	(All) ▾
2	Market	CHARLOTTE .▼		Market	CHARLOTTE .▼
3					
4	Sales Rep ▾	Sales_Amount		Sales Rep ▾	Sales_Amount
5	MCCILLEIGH, JEFFREY	$98,090		MEERE, TERRY	$27,149
6	CERDWILL, TIMOTHY	$54,883		BRAGHT, THOMAS	$25,005
7	BRADFERD, JAMES	$49,435		CRAVIY, ANTHONY	$22,761
8	DIDLIY, CHARLES	$47,220		WALLAEMS, SHAUN	$15,477
9	SWANGIR, ADAM	$46,608		HERVIY, CHRISTOPHER	$15,260
10	SKILTEN, JAMES	$43,569		HELT, CHRISTOPHER	$15,147
11	PIORSEN, HEYWARD	$41,005		REBIRTS, ADAMS	$13,237
12	CRIOMIR, TIMOTHY	$34,169		BECKMAN, ADRIAN	$9,236
13	PERSENS, GREGORY	$33,026		GERRUIS, ROBERT	$7,786
14	BIOCH, RONALD	$30,168		MEERE, RUSSELL	$6,635
15	Grand Total	$478,172		Grand Total	$157,693

Figure 9-7: You now have two pivot tables that show top and bottom displays.

Note

If there's a tie for any rank in the top or bottom values, Excel shows you all the tied records. This means that you may get more than the number you filtered for. If you filtered for the top 10 sales reps and there's a tie for the number 5 rank, Excel shows you 11 sales reps (both reps ranked at number 5 will be shown).

Using Histograms to Track Relationships and Frequency

A *histogram* is essentially a graph that plots frequency distribution. A *frequency distribution* shows how often an event or category of data occurs. With a histogram, you can visually see the general distribution of a certain attribute.

Take a look at the histogram shown in Figure 9-8. This histogram represents the distribution of units sold in one month among your sales reps. As you can see, most reps sell somewhere between 5 and 25 units per month. As a manager, you want the hump in the chart to move to the right — more people selling a higher number of units per month. So you set a goal to have a majority of your sales reps sell between 15 and 25 units within the next 3 months. With this histogram, you can visually track the progress toward that goal.

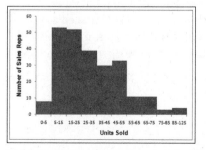

Figure 9-8: A histogram showing the distribution of units sold per month among your sales force.

This chapter discusses how to create a histogram using formulas and pivot tables. The techniques covered here fit nicely in data models where you separate data, analysis, and presentation information. In addition, these techniques allow for a level of automation and interactivity that comes in handy when updating dashboards each month.

Cross-Ref

We discuss how to develop a data model in Chapter 11.

Adding formulas to group data

First, you need a table that contains your raw data. The raw data ideally consists of records that represent unique counts for the data you want to group. For instance, the raw data table in Figure 9-9 contains unique sales reps and the number of units each has sold. Follow these steps to create a formula-driven histogram:

1. Before you create your histogram, you need to create a bin table (see Figure 9-9).

   The bin table dictates the grouping parameters that are used to break your raw data into the frequency groups. The bin table tells Excel to cluster all sales reps selling fewer than 5 units into the first frequency group, any sales reps selling 5 to 14 units in the second frequency group, and so on.

	A	B	C	D
1	Raw Data			
2	Sales Rep	Units Sold		Bins
3	ERSINEILT, MIKE	5		0
4	HANKSEN, COLE	5		5
5	LYNN, THEODORE	5		15
6	MATTANGLY, JOHN	5		25
7	NEBLE, JASON	5		35
8	SEREILT, LUC	5		45
9	SHEW, DONALD	5		55
10	WINTLAND, ROBERT	5		65
11	BLANCHIT, DANNY	6		75
12	BLEKE JR, SAMUEL	6		85
13	ETEVAC, ROBERT	6		125
14	KNEIP, ANTHONY	6		

Figure 9-9: Start with your raw data table and a bin table.

Tip

You can freely set your own grouping parameters when you build your bin table. However, it's generally a good idea to keep your parameters as equally spaced as possible. We typically end our bin tables with the largest number in our dataset. This allows us to have clean groupings that end in a finite number — not in an open-ended *greater than* designation.

2. Create a new column that holds the FREQUENCY formulas. Name the new column Frequency Formulas, as seen in Figure 9-10.

   Excel's FREQUENCY function counts how often values occur within the ranges you specify in a bin table.

3. Select a number of cells equal to the cells in your bin table.

4. Type the FREQUENCY formula you see in Figure 9-10 and then press Ctrl+Shift+Enter on your keyboard.

Note The FREQUENCY function does have a quirk that often confuses first-time users. The FREQUENCY function is an *array formula* — that is, it's a formula that returns many values at one time. In order for this formula to work properly, you have to press Ctrl+Shift+Enter after typing the formula. If you just press the Enter key, you won't get the results you need.

	A	B	C	D	E
1	Raw Data				
2	Sales Rep	Units Sold		Bins	Frequency Formulas
3	ERSINEILT, MIKE	5		0	=FREQUENCY(B3:B246,D3:D13)
4	HANKSEN, COLE	5		5	
5	LYNN, THEODORE	5		15	
6	MATTANGLY, JOHN	5		25	
7	NEBLE, JASON	5		35	
8	SEREILT, LUC	5		45	
9	SHEW, DONALD	5		55	
10	WINTLAND, ROBERT	5		65	
11	BLANCHIT, DANNY	6		75	
12	BLEKE JR, SAMUEL	6		85	
13	ETEVAC, ROBERT	6		125	

Figure 9-10: Type the FREQUENCY formula you see here; be sure to hold down the Ctrl+Shift+Enter keys on your keyboard.

At this point, you should have a table that shows the number of sales reps that fall into each of your bins. You could chart this table, but the data labels would come out wonky. For the best results, build a simple chart feeder table that creates appropriate labels for each bin, which you do as follows:

1. Create a new table that feeds the charts a bit more cleanly (see Figure 9-11). Use a simple formula that concatenates Bins into appropriate labels. Use another formula to bring in the results of your FREQUENCY calculations.

   In Figure 9-11, we made the formulas in the first record of the chart feeder table visible. These formulas are essentially copied down to create a table appropriate for charting.

2. Use your newly created chart feeder table to plot the data into a column chart.

   Figure 9-12 illustrates the resulting chart. You can certainly use the initial column chart as your histogram.

   If you like your histograms to have spaces between the data points, you're done. If you like the continuous blocked look you get with no gaps between the data points, follow the next few steps.

3. Right-click any of the columns in the chart and choose Format Data Series.

   The Format Data Series dialog box appears.

4. Adjust the Gap Width property to 0% (see Figure 9-13).

C	D	E		F	G	H
1					Chart Feeder	
2	Bins	Frequency Formulas			Units Sold	Count of Sales Reps
3	0	0			=D3& "-" &D4	=E4
4	5	8			5-15	53
5	15	53			15-25	52
6	25	52			25-35	39
7	35	39			35-45	30
8	45	30			45-55	33
9	55	33			55-65	11
10	65	11			65-75	11
11	75	11			75-85	3
12	85	3			85-125	4
13	125	4				

Figure 9-11: Build a simple chart feeder table that creates appropriate labels for each bin.

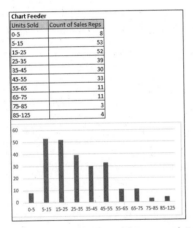

Chart Feeder	
Units Sold	Count of Sales Reps
0-5	8
5-15	53
15-25	52
25-35	39
35-45	30
45-55	33
55-65	11
65-75	11
75-85	3
85-125	4

Figure 9-12: Plot your histogram data into a column chart.

Format Data Series

SERIES OPTIONS ▾

◢ SERIES OPTIONS

Plot Series On

• Primary Axis
○ Secondary Axis

Series Overlap   -27%

Gap Width   0%

Figure 9-13: To eliminate the spaces between columns, set the Gap Width to 0%.

Adding a cumulative percent

A nice feature to add to your histograms is a cumulative percent series. With a cumulative percent series, you can show the percent distribution of the data points to the left of the point of interest.

Figure 9-14 shows an example of a cumulative percent series. At each data point in the histogram, the cumulative percent series tells you the percent of the population that fills all the bins up to that point. For instance, you can see that 25% of the sales reps denoted sold 15 units or fewer. In other words, 75% of the sales reps sold more than 15 units.

Take another look at the chart in Figure 9-14 and find the point where you see 75% on the cumulative series. At 75%, look at the label for that Bin range (you see 35–45). The 75% mark tells you that 75% of sales reps sold between 0 and 45 units. This means that only 25% of sales reps sold more than 45 units.

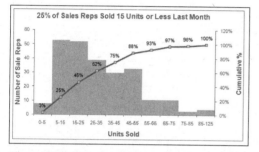

Figure 9-14: The cumulative percent series shows the percent of the population that fills all the bins up to each point in the histogram.

To create a cumulative percent series for your histogram, follow these steps:

1. After you perform Steps 1 through 5 to create a histogram (outlined earlier in this chapter), add a column to your chart feeder that calculates the percent of total sales reps for the first bin (see Figure 9-15).

   Note the dollar symbols ($) used in the formula to lock the references while you copy the formula down.

Chart Feeder		
Units Sold	Count of Sales Reps	Cumulative %
0-5	8	=SUM($H$3:H3)/SUM($H$3:$H$12)
5-15	53	
15-25	52	
25-35	39	
35-45	30	
45-55	33	
55-65	11	
65-75	11	
75-85	3	
85-125	4	

Figure 9-15: In a new column, create a formula that calculates the percent of total sales reps for the first bin.

2. Copy the formula down for all the bins in the table.

3. Use the chart feeder table to plot the data into a line chart.

   As you can see in Figure 9-16, the resulting chart needs some additional formatting.

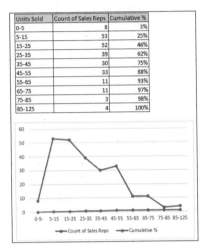

Units Sold	Count of Sales Reps	Cumulative %
0-5	8	3%
5-15	53	25%
15-25	52	46%
25-35	39	62%
35-45	30	75%
45-55	33	88%
55-65	11	93%
65-75	11	97%
75-85	3	98%
85-125	4	100%

Figure 9-16: Your initial chart will need some formatting to make it look like a histogram.

4. Right-click the series that makes up your histogram (Count of Sales Rep), select Change Chart Type, and then change the chart type to a column chart.

5. Right-click any of the columns in the chart and choose Format Data Series.

6. Adjust the Gap Width property to 0% (refer to Figure 9-13).

7. Right-click Cumulative Percent series and choose Format Data Series.

8. In the Format Data Series dialog box, change the Plot Series On option to Secondary Axis.

9. Right-click Cumulative Percent series and choose Add Data Labels.

At this point, your base chart is complete. It should look similar to the one shown at the beginning of this section in Figure 9-14. When you get to this point, you can adjust the colors, labels, and other formatting.

Using a pivot table to create a histogram

Did you know you can use a pivot table as the source for a histogram? That's right. With a little-known trick, you can create a histogram that is as interactive as a pivot chart!

As in the formula-driven histogram, the first step in creating a histogram with a pivot table is to create a frequency distribution.

Cross-Ref **If you're new to pivot tables, rest easy. In Part IV of this book, we cover the ins and outs of pivot tables. This section allows you to get a preview of the types of advanced analysis you can accomplish with pivot tables.**

1. Create a pivot table and plot the data values in the row area (not the data area). As you can see in Figure 9-17, the SumOfSales Amount field is placed in the ROWS area. Place the Sales Rep field in the VALUES area as a Count.

	A	B	C D E F G
1	Region	(All) ▼	**PivotTable Fields** ▼ ×
2	Market	(All) ▼	
3			Choose fields to add to report: ⚙ ▼
4	SumOfSales_Amount ▼	Count of Sales Rep	☑ **Region**
5	$5,502.48	1	☑ **Market**
6	$5,504.14	1	☑ **Sales Rep**
7	$5,506.13	1	☐ Hire_Date
8	$5,518.49	1	☐ Business_Segment
9	$5,521.70	1	☐ Product_Description
10	$5,529.18	1	☑ **SumOfSales_Amount**
11	$5,534.25	2	MORE TABLES...
12	$5,543.33	1	
13	$5,547.04	1	Drag fields between areas below:
14	$5,554.74	1	▼ FILTERS ▥ COLUMNS
15	$5,558.18	1	Region ▼
16	$5,566.79	1	Market ▼
17	$5,586.85	1	
18	$5,600.05	1	▥ ROWS Σ VALUES
19	$5,625.18	1	SumOfSales_Amount ▼ Count of Sales Rep ▼
20	$5,636.53	1	
21	$5,642.06	1	

Figure 9-17: Place your data values in the ROWS area and the Sales Rep field in the VALUES area as a Count.

2. Right-click any value in the ROWS area and choose Group.

The Grouping dialog box appears (see Figure 9-18).

Grouping	? ×
Auto	
☐ Starting at:	5000
☐ Ending at:	100000
By:	1000
OK	Cancel

Figure 9-18: The Grouping dialog box.

3. In the dialog box, set the start and end values and then set the intervals.

This essentially creates your frequency distribution. In Figure 9-18, the distribution is set to start at 5,000 and to create groups in increments of 1,000 until it ends at 100,000.

4. Click OK to confirm your settings.

   The pivot table calculates the number of sales reps for each defined increment, just as in a frequency distribution. (See Figure 9-19.) You can now leverage this result to create a histogram!

	A	B
1	Region	(All)
2	Market	(All)
3		
4	SumOfSales_Amount	Count of Sales Rep
5	5000-6000	69
6	6000-7000	78
7	7000-8000	58
8	8000-9000	66
9	9000-10000	41
10	10000-11000	45
11	11000-12000	39
12	12000-13000	33
13	13000-14000	25
14	14000-15000	25
15	15000-16000	22

Figure 9-19: The result of grouping the values in the Row area is a frequency distribution that can be charted into a histogram.

The obvious benefit to this technique is that after you have a frequency distribution and a histogram, you can interactively filter the data based on other dimensions, like Region and Market. For instance, you can see the histogram for the Canada market and then quickly switch to see the histogram for the California market.

Tip

Note that you can't add cumulative percentages to a histogram based on a pivot table.

Emphasizing Top Values in Charts

Sometimes a chart is indeed the best way to display a set of data, but you still want to call attention to the top values in that chart. In these cases, you can use a technique that *actually* highlights the top values in your charts. That is to say, you can use Excel to figure out which values in your data series are in the top *n*th value and then apply special formatting to them. Figure 9-20 illustrates an example where the top five quarters are highlighted and given a label.

The secret to this technique lies in Excel's obscure LARGE function. The LARGE function returns the *n*th largest number from a dataset. In other words, you tell it where to look and the number rank you want.

To find the largest number in the dataset, you enter the formula LARGE(Data_Range, 1). To find the fifth largest number in the dataset, you use LARGE(Data_Range, 5). Figure 9-21 illustrates how the LARGE function works.

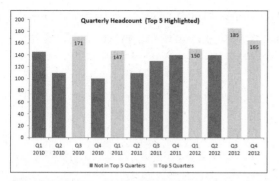

Figure 9-20: This chart highlights the top five quarters with different font and labeling.

	B	C	D	E
1		People Count		
2	J	145		
3	F	109		
4	M	171		
5	A	100		
6	M	147		
7	J	109		
8	J	130		
9	A	140		
10	S	150		
11	O	140		
12	N	185		
13	D	165		
14				
15	Largest Value	185	←	=LARGE(C2:C13,1)
16				
17	5th Largest Value	147	←	=LARGE(C2:C13,5)

Figure 9-21: Using the LARGE function returns the *n*th largest number from a dataset.

The idea is fairly simple. In order to identify the top five values in a dataset, you first need to identify the fifth largest number (LARGE function to the rescue) and then test each value in the dataset to see if it's bigger than the fifth largest number. Here's what you do:

1. Build a chart feeder that consists of formulas that link back to your raw data. The feeder should have two columns: one to hold data that isn't in the top five and one to hold data that is in the top five (see Figure 9-22).

2. In the first row of the chart feeder, enter the formulas shown in Figure 9-22.

   The formula for the first column (F4) checks to see if the value in cell C4 is less than the number returned by the LARGE formula (the fifth largest value). If it is, the value in cell C4 is returned. Otherwise, NA is used. The formula for the second column works in the same way, except the IF statement is reversed: If the value in cell C4 is greater than or equal to the number returned by the LARGE formula, then the value is returned; otherwise NA is used.

3. Copy the formulas down to fill the table.

4. Use the chart feeder table to plot the data into a stacked column chart.

    You immediately see a chart that displays two data series: one for data points not in the top five and one for data points in the top five (see Figure 9-23).

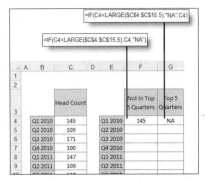

Figure 9-22: Build a new chart feeder that consists of formulas that plot values into one of two columns.

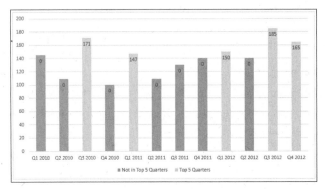

Figure 9-23: After adding data labels to the top five data series and doing a bit of formatting, your chart should look similar to the one shown here.

Notice in Figure 9-23 that the chart shows some rogue zeros. You can fix the chart so that the zeros don't display by performing the next few steps.

5. Right-click any of the data labels for the top five series and choose Format Data Labels.

6. In the Format Data Labels dialog box, expand the Numbers section and select Custom in the Category list.

7. Enter #,##0;; as the custom number format, as shown in Figure 9-24.

8. Click the Add button and then click Close.

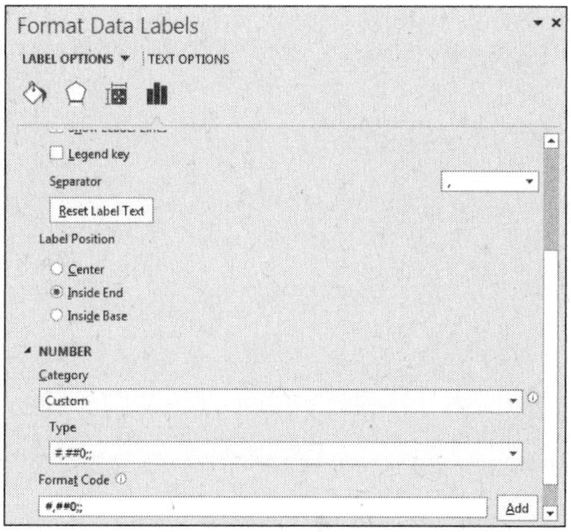

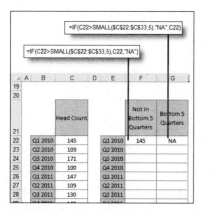

Figure 9-24: Entering #,##0;; as the custom format for a data label renders all zeros in that data series hidden.

When you go back to your chart, you see that the rogue zeros are now hidden and your chart is ready for colors, labels, and other formatting you want to apply.

You can apply the same technique to highlight the bottom five values in your data set. The only difference is that instead of using the LARGE function, you use the SMALL function. Whereas the LARGE function returns the largest nth value from a range, the SMALL function returns the smallest nth value.

Figure 9-25 illustrates the formulas you use to apply the same technique outlined here for the bottom five values.

Figure 9-25: Use the SMALL function to highlight the bottom values in a chart.

The formula for the first column (F4) checks to see if the value in cell C22 is greater than the number returned by the SMALL formula (the fifth smallest value). If it is, the value in cell C22 is returned. Otherwise, NA is used. The formula for the second column works in the same way, except the IF statement is reversed: If the value in cell C22 is greater than the number returned by the SMALL formula, then NA is used; otherwise, the value is returned.

Components That Show Performance Against a Target

In This Chapter

- Using variance to compare performance with a target
- Displaying performance against organizational trends
- Creating a thermometer-style chart
- Creating a bullet graph
- Showing performance against a target range

No matter what business or industry you talk about, you can always point to some sort of target to measure data against. That target could be anything from a certain amount of revenue to the number of boxes shipped or phone calls made. The business world is full of targets and goals. Your job is to find effective ways to represent performance against those targets.

What is performance against a target? Imagine that your goal is to break the land speed record (currently 763 miles per hour). Your target speed is 771 miles per hour. After you jump into your car and go as fast as you can, you will have a final speed of some number. That number is considered to be your performance against the target.

In this chapter, we discuss some new and interesting ways to create components that show performance against a target.

Showing Performance with Variances

The standard way of displaying performance against a target is to plot the target and then plot the performance. This is usually done with a line chart or a combination chart, such as the one shown in Figure 10-1.

Figure 10-1: A typical chart showing performance against a target.

Although this chart allows you to visually pick the points where performance exceeded or fell below targets, it gives you a rather one-dimensional view and provides minimal information. Even if this chart offered labels that showed the actual percent of sales revenue versus target, you'd still get only a mildly informative view.

A more impactful and informative way of displaying performance against a target is to plot the variances between the target and the performance. Figure 10-2 shows the same performance data you see in Figure 10-1, but includes the variances (sales revenue minus target). This way, you not only see where performance exceeded or fell below targets but also you get an extra layer of information showing the dollar impact of each rise and fall.

Figure 10-2: Consider using variances to plot performance against a target.

Showing Performance Against Organizational Trends

The target you use to measure performance doesn't necessarily have to be set by management or organizational policy. In fact, some of the things you measure may never have a target or goal set for them. In situations where you don't have a target to measure against, it's often helpful to measure performance against some organizational statistic.

For example, the component in Figure 10-3 measures the sales performance for each division against the median sales for all the divisions. You can see that divisions 1, 3, and 6 fall well below the median for the group.

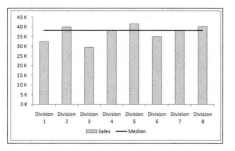

Figure 10-3: Measuring data when there's no target for a measure.

Here's how you create a median line similar to the one you see in Figure 10-3:

1. Start a new column next to your data and type the simple MEDIAN formula, as shown in Figure 10-4.

   Note that this formula can be any mathematical or statistical operation that works for the data you're representing. Just ensure that the values returned are the same for the entire column. This gives you a straight line.

	A	B	C
1		Sales	Median
2	Division 1	32,526	=MEDIAN($B$2:$B$9)
3	Division 2	39,939	
4	Division 3	29,542	
5	Division 4	38,312	
6	Division 5	41,595	
7	Division 6	35,089	
8	Division 7	38,270	
9	Division 8	40,022	
10			

Figure 10-4: Start a new column and enter a formula.

2. Copy the formula down to fill the table.

   Again, all the numbers in the newly created column should be the same.

3. Plot the table into a column chart.

4. Right-click the Median data series and choose Change Series Chart Type.

5. Change the chart type to a line chart.

Using a Thermometer-Style Chart

A thermometer-style chart offers a unique way to view performance against a goal. As the name implies, the data points shown in this type of chart resemble a thermometer. Each performance value and its corresponding target are stacked on top of one another, giving an appearance similar to that of mercury rising in a thermometer. In Figure 10-5, you see an example of a thermometer-style chart.

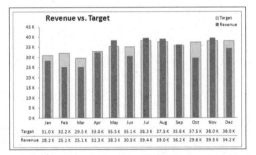

Figure 10-5: Thermometer-style charts offer a unique way to show performance against a goal.

To create this type of chart, follow these steps:

1. Starting with a table that contains revenue and target data, plot the data into a new column chart.

2. Right-click the Revenue data series and choose Format Data Series.

3. In the Format Data Series dialog box, select the Secondary Axis.

4. Go back to your chart and delete the new vertical axis that was added; it's the vertical axis to the right of the chart.

5. Right-click the Target series and choose Format Data Series.

6. In the dialog box, adjust the Gap Width property so that the Target series is slightly wider than the Revenue series — between 45% and 55% is typically fine.

Using a Bullet Graph

A *bullet* graph is a type of column/bar graph developed by visualization expert Stephen Few to serve as a replacement for dashboard gauges and meters. He developed bullet graphs to allow for the clear display of multiple layers of information without occupying a lot of space on a dashboard. A bullet graph, as seen in Figure 10-6, contains a single performance measure (such as YTD [year-to-date] revenue); compares that measure to a target; and displays it in the context of qualitative ranges, such as Poor, Fair, Good, and Very Good.

Figure 10-6: Bullet graphs display multiple perspectives in an incredibly compact space.

Figure 10-7 breaks down the three main parts of a bullet graph. The *performance bar* represents the performance measure. The *target marker* represents the comparative measure. And the *background fills* represent the qualitative range.

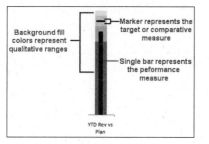

Figure 10-7: The parts of a bullet graph.

Creating a bullet graph

Creating a bullet graph in Excel involves quite a few steps, but it isn't necessarily difficult. Follow these steps to create your first bullet graph:

1. Start with a data table that gives you all the data points you need to create the three main parts of the bullet graph.

   Figure 10-8 illustrates what that data table looks like. The first four values in the data set (Poor, Fair, Good, and Very Good) make up the qualitative range. You don't have to have four values — you can have as many or as few as you need. In this scenario, you want the qualitative range to span from 0 to 100%. Therefore, the percentages (75%, 15%, 10%, and 5%) must add up to 100%. Again, this can be adjusted to suit your needs. The fifth value in Figure 10-8 (Value) creates the performance bar. The sixth value (Target) makes the target marker.

	A	B
1		YTD Rev vs Plan
2	Poor	70%
3	Fair	15%
4	Good	10%
5	VeryGood	5%
6	Value	80%
7	Target	90%
8		

Figure 10-8: Start with data that contains the main data points of the bullet graph.

2. Select the entire table and plot the data on a stacked column chart.

   The chart that's created is initially plotted in the wrong direction.

3. To fix the direction, click the chart and select the Switch Row/Column button, as shown in Figure 10-9.

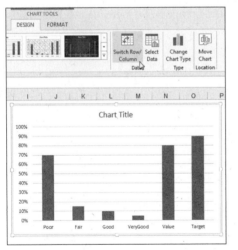

Figure 10-9: Switch the orientation of the chart to read from columns.

4. Right-click the Target series and choose Change Series Chart Type. Use the Change Chart Type dialog box to change the Target series to a Stacked Line with Markers and to place it on the secondary axis (see Figure 10-10). After you confirm your change, the Target series will show on the chart as a single dot.

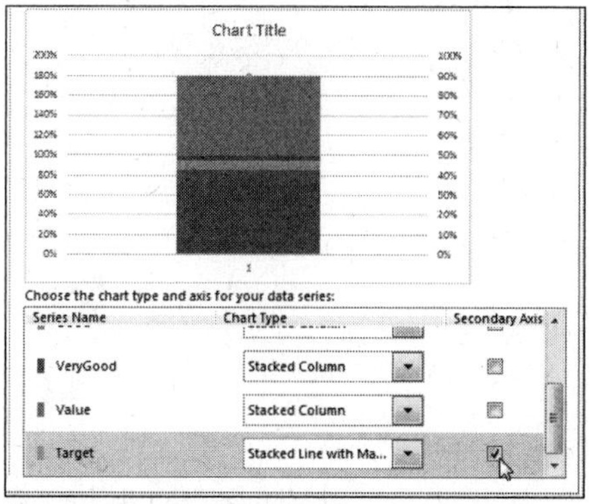

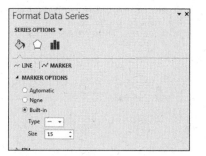

Figure 10-10: Use the Change Chart Type dialog box to change the Target series to a Stacked Line with Markers and place it on the secondary axis.

5. Right-click the Target series again and choose Format Data Series to open that dialog box. Click the Marker option and adjust the marker to look like a dash, as shown in Figure 10-11.

Figure 10-11: Adjust the marker to a dash.

6. Still in the Format Data Series dialog box, click the Fill & Line icon (the paint bucket). Expand the Fill section and Solid Fill property to set the color of the marker to a noticeable color like red.

7. Still in the Format Data Series dialog box, expand the Border section and set the Border to No Line.

8. Go back to your chart and delete the new secondary axis that was added to the right of your chart (see Figure 10-12).

    This is an important step to ensure that the scale of the chart is correct for all data points.

Figure 10-12: Be sure to delete the newly created secondary vertical axis.

9. Right-click the Value series and choose Format Data Series.

10. In the Format Data Series dialog box, click Secondary Axis.

11. Still in the Format Data Series dialog box under Series Options, adjust the Gap Width property so that the Value series is slightly narrower than the other columns in the chart — between 205% and 225% is typically okay.

12. Still in the Format Data Series dialog box, click the Fill icon (the paint bucket), expand the Fill section, and then select the Solid fill option to set the color of the Value series to black.

13. All that's left to do is change the color for each qualitative range to incrementally lighter hues.

At this point, your bullet graph is essentially done! You can apply whatever minor formatting adjustments to size and shape the chart to make it look the way you want. Figure 10-13 shows the newly created bullet graph formatted with a legend and horizontal labels.

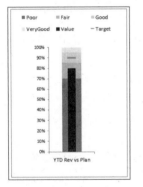

Figure 10-13: Your formatted bullet graph.

Adding data to your bullet graph

After you've built your chart for the first performance measure, you can use the same chart for any additional measures. Take a look at Figure 10-14.

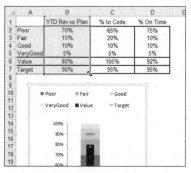

Figure 10-14: To add more data to your chart, manually expand the chart's data source range.

As you can see in Figure 10-14, you've already created this bullet graph with the first performance measure. Imagine that you add two more measures and want to graph those. Here's how to do so:

1. Click the chart so that the blue outline appears around the original source data.

2. Hover your mouse over the blue dot in the lower-right corner of the blue box.

   Your cursor turns into an arrow, as seen in Figure 10-14.

3. Click and drag the blue dot to the last column in your expanded data set.

Figure 10-15 illustrates how the new data points are added without one ounce of extra work!

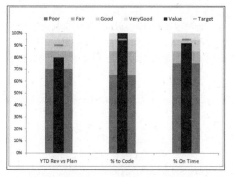

Figure 10-15: Expanding the data source automatically creates new bullet graphs.

Final thoughts on formatting bullet graphs

Before wrapping up this introduction to bullet graphs, we discuss two final thoughts on formatting:

➤ Creating qualitative bands

➤ Creating horizontal bullet graphs

Creating qualitative bands

First, if the qualitative ranges are the same for all the performance measures in your bullet graphs, you can format the qualitative range series to have no gaps between them. For instance, Figure 10-16 shows a set of bullet graphs where the qualitative ranges have been set to 0 Gap Width. This creates the clever effect of qualitative bands.

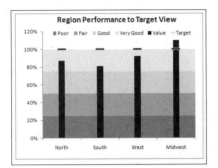

Figure 10-16: Try setting gap widths to zero to create clean-looking qualitative bands.

1. Right-click any one of the qualitative series and choose Format Data Series.

2. In the Format Series dialog box, adjust the Gap Width property to 0%.

Creating horizontal bullet graphs

If you're waiting for the section about horizontal bullet graphs, there's good and bad news. The bad news is that creating a horizontal bullet graph from scratch in Excel is a much more complex endeavor than creating a vertical bullet graph — one that doesn't warrant the time and effort it takes to create it.

The good news is that there is a clever way to get a horizontal bullet graph from a vertical one — and in three steps, no less. Here's how you do it:

1. Create a vertical bullet graph.

    Refer to the earlier section "Creating a bullet graph" for more on that topic.

2. Change the alignment for the axis and other labels on the bullet graph so that they're rotated 270 degrees (see Figure 10-17).

3. Use Excel's Camera tool to take a picture of the bullet graph.

    After you have a picture, you can rotate it to be horizontal. Figure 10-18 illustrates a horizontal bullet graph.

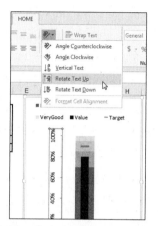

Figure 10-17: Rotate all labels so that they're on their sides.

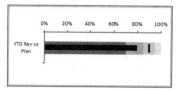

Figure 10-18: A horizontal bullet graph.

The nifty thing about this trick is that because the picture is taken with the Camera tool, the picture automatically updates when the source table changes.

Never heard of the Camera tool? Check out Chapter 4 for a detailed look at benefits of the Camera tool.

Tip

Showing Performance Against a Target Range

In some businesses, a target isn't one value — it's a range of values. That is to say, the goal is to stay within a defined target range. Imagine you manage a small business selling boxes of meat. Part of your job is to keep your inventory stocked between 25 and 35 boxes in a month. If you have too many boxes of meat, the meat will go bad. If you have too few boxes, you'll lose money.

To track how well you do at keeping your inventory of meat between 25 and 35 boxes, you need a performance component that displays on-hand boxes against a target range. Figure 10-19 illustrates a component you can build to track performance against a target range. The gray band represents the target range you must stay within each month. The line represents the trend of on-hand meat.

Figure 10-19: You can create a component that plots performance against a target range.

Obviously, the trick to this type of component is to set up the band that represents the target range. Here's how you do it:

1. Set up a *limit table* where you can define and adjust the upper and lower limits of your target range.

    Cells B2 and B3 in Figure 10-20 serve as the place to define the limits for the range.

2. Build a chart feeder that's used to plot the data points for the target range.

    This feeder consists of the formulas revealed in cells B8 and B9 in Figure 10-20.

    The idea is to copy these formulas across all the data.

    The values you see for Feb, Mar, and Apr are the results of these formulas.

3. Add a row for the actual performance values (see Figure 10-21).

    These data points create the performance trend line.

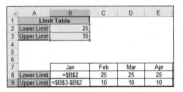

	A	B	C	D	E
1		Limit Table			
2	Lower Limit	25			
3	Upper Limit	35			
4					
5					
6					
7		Jan	Feb	Mar	Apr
8	Lower Limit	=$B$2	25	25	25
9	Upper Limit	=$B$3-$B$2	10	10	10

Figure 10-20: Create a chart feeder that contains formulas that define the data points for the target range.

	A	B	C	D	E	F
1		Limit Table				
2	Lower Limit	25				
3	Upper Limit	35				
4						
5						
6						
7		Jan	Feb	Mar	Apr	May
8	Lower Limit	25	25	25	25	25
9	Upper Limit	10	10	10	10	10
10	Values	33	27	23	28	26

Figure 10-21: Add a row for the performance values.

4. Select the entire chart feeder table and plot the data on a stacked column chart.

5. Right-click the Values series and choose Change Series Chart Type. Use the Change Chart Type dialog box to change the Values series to a Line and to place it on the secondary axis (see Figure 10-22). After confirming your change, the Values series will show on the chart as a line.

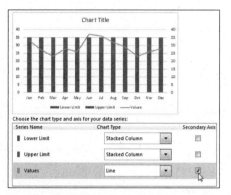

Figure 10-22: Use the Change Chart Type dialog box to change the Values series to a Line chart and place it on the secondary axis.

6. Go back to your chart and delete the new vertical axis that was added; it's the vertical axis to the right of the chart.

7. Right-click the Lower Limit data series and choose Format Data Series.

8. In the Format Data Series dialog box, click the Fill icon. Choose the No Fill option under Fill and the No Line option under Border (see Figure 10-23).

Figure 10-23: Format the Lower Limit series so that it's hidden.

9. Right-click the Upper Limit series and select Format Data Series.

10. In the Format Series dialog box, adjust the Gap Width property to 0%.

That's it. All that's left to do is apply the minor adjustments to colors, labels, and other formatting.

Advanced Dashboarding Concepts

Developing Your Data Model

In This Chapter

- Setting up the data, analysis, and presentation layers
- Applying data model best practices
- Leveraging Excel functions to deliver data
- Using Excel tables that expand with data

A *data model* provides the foundation upon which your dashboard or report is built. When you collect and analyze data, you're essentially building a data model that feeds your presentation. In this chapter, we discuss how to build and manage an efficient data model. Although you'll discover how to build cool dashboard components in later chapters, they won't do you any good if you can't construct an effective data model. On that note, let's get started.

Building a Data Model

Building an effective data model isn't as complicated as you may think. The problem is that most people spend little time thinking about the data model that supports a final presentation. If they think about it at all, they usually start by imagining a mock-up of the finished dashboard and work backward from there.

So try thinking a bit about the end-to-end process. Where does the source data reside? How should that data be organized? What calculations do you need to perform? How will those results be fed to the dashboard? How will the dashboard be updated?

Obviously, the answers to these questions are situation-specific. But here is a good place to start.

Separating the data, analysis, and presentation layers

One of the key concepts of a data model is the organization of data into three layers: data, analysis, and presentation. The basic idea is that you don't want your data to become too tied into any one particular way of presenting that data.

For example, think about a business invoice. The financial data on that invoice is not the true source of that data. It's merely a presentation of the actual data that's stored in some database. That data can then be organized and presented to you in many ways: in charts, in tables, on dashboards, or even on websites. This sounds obvious, but Excel users often fuse the data, analysis, and presentation layers together into one final project.

The best approach is to create three layers in your data model. You can think of these layers as three different worksheets in an Excel workbook. Sometimes this also is a good way to organize your data model. One sheet holds the raw data that feeds your report, one sheet serves as a staging area where the calculations are performed, and one serves as the final presentation. Figure 11-1 illustrates the three layers of an effective data model.

Tip

You don't necessarily have to place your data, analysis, and presentation layers on different worksheets. In small data models, you may find it easier to place your data in one area of a worksheet while building your staging tables in another area of the same worksheet.

Why even bother with the three-tiered data model? Imagine that you have only the table in Figure 11-2. Hard-coded tables, such as this one, are common. This table is a combination of data, calculations, and presentation. Not only does this table tie you to a specific analysis but also there's little to no transparency into the content of the analysis. Also, what happens when you need to report by quarters or when another dimension of analysis is needed? Do you import a table that consists of more columns and rows? How does that affect your data model?

Taking the easy route and avoiding the extra work of separating the data, analysis, and presentation layers can lead to more problems later. Take a moment to review each layer and the role it plays in building out your dashboard model.

The data layer

As you can see in Figure 11-1, the data layer consists of the raw data that feeds your dashboard. The data in the data layer is typically used "as is" from whatever source you derived it from. That is to say, you perform no analysis in the data layer.

DATA

	A	B	C	D	E	F	G
1	**SalesPeriod**	**Sales Amount**	**UnitPrice**				
2	Jan	$6,120	$2,040				
3	Jan	$4,050	$2,025				
4	Jan	$6,075	$2,025				
5	Jan	$46	$6				
6	Jan	$2,040	$2,040				
7	Jan	$6,075	$2,025				
8	Jan	$6,120	$2,040				
9	Jan	$4,080	$2,040				
10	Jan	$4,050	$2,025				
11	Jan	$4,080	$2,040				
60918	Dec	$61	$20				
60919	Dec	$8,160	$2,040				
60920	Dec	$1,445	$723				
60921							

‹ › **Data** | Analysis | Presentation | Report Style | Flat File | ...

ANALYSIS

	A	B	C	D	E	F	G
1	**This Table Feeds the Revenue Trend Chart**						
2		Jan	Feb	Mar	Apr	May	Jun
3	Sales (millions)	3.69 M	6.99 M	5.77 M	4.96 M	8.48 M	4.71 M	7.4
4	% Distribution	5%	9%	7%	6%	10%	6%
5							
6							
7							
8							
9							
10							
11							
12							
13							
14							
15							

‹ › Data | **Analysis** | Presentation | Report Style | Flat File | ...

PRESENTATION

	A	B	C	D	E	F	G
1							
2	10 M						
3	9 M				12%		
4	8 M			10%		10%	
5	7 M				9%		11%
6	6 M	9%					9%
7	5 M	7%	6%		6%		
8	4 M					6%	
9	3 M	5%					
10	2 M						
11	1 M						
12	0 M	Jan Feb Mar Apr May Jun Jul Aug Sep Oct Nov Dec					
13	Sales (millions)	3.69 6.99 5.77 4.96 8.48 4.71 7.48 9.48 8.20 4.94 8.88 7.42					
14	% Distribution	5% 9% 7% 6% 10% 6% 9% 12% 10% 6% 11% 9%					
15							

‹ › Data | Analysis | **Presentation** | Report Style | Flat File | ...

Figure 11-1: An effective data model separates data, analysis, and presentation layers.

	A	B	C	D	E	F	G	H	I
1									
2			Jan	Feb	Mar	Apr	May	Jun	Jul
3		Sales	3.69 M	6.99 M	5.77 M	4.96 M	8.48 M	4.71 M	7.48 M
4		% Distribution	5%	9%	7%	6%	10%	6%	9%

Figure 11-2: Avoid using hard-coded tables that fuse data, analysis, and presentation.

However, you'll find that not all data makes for effective data modeling. For example, the data shown in Figure 11-3 would make it impractical to apply any analysis outside what's already there. For instance, how would you calculate and present the average of all bike sales? How would you calculate a list of the top ten best performing markets?

	A	B	C	D	E	F	G
1							
2		Europe				North America	
3	**France**				**Canada**		
4	Segment	Sales Amount	Unit Price		Segment	Sales Amount	Unit Price
5	Accessories	$48,942	$7,045		Accessories	$119,303	$22,381
6	Bikes	$3,597,879	$991,098		Bikes	$11,714,700	$3,908,691
7	Clothing	$129,508	$23,912		Clothing	$383,022	$72,524
8	Components	$871,125	$293,854		Components	$2,246,255	$865,410
9							
10	**Germany**				**Northeast**		
11	Segment	Sales Amount	Unit Price		Segment	Sales Amount	Unit Price
12	Accessories	$35,681	$5,798		Accessories	$51,246	$9,666
13	Bikes	$1,602,487	$545,175		Bikes	$5,690,285	$1,992,517
14	Clothing	$75,593	$12,474		Clothing	$163,442	$30,969
15	Components	$337,787	$138,513		Components	$1,051,702	$442,598
16							
17	**United Kingdom**				**Northwest**		
18	Segment	Sales Amount	Unit Price		Segment	Sales Amount	Unit Price
19	Accessories	$43,180	$7,419		Accessories	$53,308	$11,417
20	Bikes	$3,435,134	$1,094,354		Bikes	$10,484,495	$3,182,041
21	Clothing	$120,225	$21,981		Clothing	$201,052	$40,055
22	Components	$712,588	$253,458		Components	$1,784,207	$695,876

Figure 11-3: Not all data can be a good source for your data layer.

With this setup, you're forced into very manual processes that are difficult to maintain month after month. Any analysis outside the high-level ones already in the report is basic at best — even with fancy formulas. Furthermore, what happens when you're required to show bike sales by month? When your data model requires analysis with data that isn't in the worksheet report, you're forced to search for other data.

Ideally, you want your data layer to come in one of two forms:

➤ **Flat data tables:** Data repositories are organized by row and column. Each row corresponds to a set of data elements, or a *record*. Each column is a field. A *field* corresponds to a unique data element in a record. Figure 11-4 contains the same data as the data shown in Figure 11-3, but is in flat data table format. Flat tables lend themselves nicely to data modeling in Excel because they can be detailed enough to hold the data that you need and still be conducive to a wide array of simple formulas and calculations in your analysis layer — SUM, AVERAGE, VLOOKUP, and SUMIF, just to name a few. Later in this chapter, we discuss functions that come in handy in a data model.

	A	B	C	D	E	F
1	Region	Market	Business Segment	Jan Sales Amount	Feb Sales Amount	Mar Sales Amount
2	Europe	France	Accessories	2,628	8,015	3,895
3	Europe	France	Bikes	26,588	524,445	136,773
4	Europe	France	Clothing	6,075	17,172	6,043
5	Europe	France	Components	20,485	179,279	54,262
6	Europe	Germany	Accessories	2,769	6,638	2,615
7	Europe	Germany	Bikes	136,161	196,125	94,840
8	Europe	Germany	Clothing	7,150	12,374	7,159
9	Europe	Germany	Components	46,885	56,611	29,216
10	Europe	United Kingdom	Accessories	4,205	2,579	5,745
11	Europe	United Kingdom	Bikes	111,830	175,522	364,844
12	Europe	United Kingdom	Clothing	7,888	6,763	12,884
13	Europe	United Kingdom	Components	31,331	39,005	124,030
14	North America	Canada	Accessories	3,500	12,350	9,768

Figure 11-4: A flat data table.

➤ **Tabular data set:** Ideal for pivot-table-driven data models. Figure 11-5 illustrates a tabular data set. Note that the primary difference between a tabular data set, as shown in Figure 11-5, and a flat data file is that the column labels don't double as actual data. For instance, in Figure 11-4, the month identifiers are integrated into the column labels. In Figure 11-5, the Sales Period column contains the month identifier. This subtle difference in structure is what makes tabular data sets optimal data sources for pivot tables. This structure ensures that key pivot table functions, such as sorting and grouping, work the way they should.

	A	B	C	D	E
1	Region	Market	Business Segment	Sales Period	Sales Amount
2	Europe	France	Accessories	Jan	1,706
3	Europe	France	Accessories	Feb	3,767
4	Europe	France	Accessories	Mar	1,219
5	Europe	France	Accessories	Apr	3,091
6	Europe	France	Accessories	May	7,057
7	Europe	France	Accessories	Jul	5,930
8	Europe	France	Accessories	Aug	9,628
9	Europe	France	Accessories	Sep	4,279
10	Europe	France	Accessories	Oct	2,504
11	Europe	France	Accessories	Nov	7,493
12	Europe	France	Accessories	Dec	2,268
13	Europe	France	Bikes	Jan	64,895
14	Europe	France	Bikes	Feb	510,102
15	Europe	France	Bikes	Mar	128,806
16	Europe	France	Bikes	Apr	81,301
17	Europe	France	Bikes	May	510,504

Figure 11-5: A tabular data set.

The analysis layer

The *analysis layer* consists primarily of formulas that analyze and pull data from the data layer into formatted tables (commonly referred to as *staging tables*). These staging tables ultimately feed the reporting components in your presentation layer. In short, the sheet that contains the analysis layer becomes the staging area where data is summarized and shaped to feed the reporting components.

This setup offers a couple of benefits:

➤ You can easily update the entire data model simply by replacing the raw data with updated data. The formulas in the analysis tab then continue to work with the latest data.

➤ You can create any added analyses easily by using different combinations of formulas on the analysis tab. If you need data that doesn't exist in the data layer, you can add a column to the end of the raw data without disturbing the analysis or presentation layers.

The presentation layer

The presentation layer is your storefront. It contains all the charts, visualizations, and dashboard components that you want your audience to see. The presentation layer is the most flexible because you can choose a plethora of tools, graphics, and charts to create the theme and style of your dashboard. Also, because the presentation layer feeds from the analysis layer, the data needed for each component is always consistent in content and format.

Data Model Best Practices

One of Excel's most attractive features is its flexibility. You can construct an intricate system of calculations, linked cells, and formatted summaries that work together to create your final presentation. But creating a successful dashboard requires more than just slapping data onto a worksheet. A poorly designed data model can lead to hours of excess work maintaining and updating your presentation. On the other hand, an effective data model enables you to easily repeat monthly update processes without damaging your dashboards or your sanity.

In this section, we discuss some data modeling best practices that help you start on the right foot with your dashboard projects.

Avoid storing excess data

In Chapter 1, you may have read that measures used on a dashboard should absolutely support the initial purpose of that dashboard. The same concept applies to the back-end data model. You should import only data that's necessary to fulfill the purpose of your dashboard or report.

In an effort to have as much data as possible at their fingertips, many Excel users bring into their worksheets every piece of data they can get their hands on. You can spot these people by the 40MB files they send through e-mail. You've seen these worksheets — two tabs that contain presentation and then six hidden tabs that contain thousands of lines of data (most of which isn't used). They essentially build a database in their worksheet.

What's wrong with utilizing as much data as possible? Well, here are a few issues:

➤ **Excess data increases the number of formulas.** If you're bringing in all raw data, you have to aggregate that data in Excel. This inevitably causes you to exponentially increase the number of formulas you have to employ and maintain. Remember your data model is a vehicle for presenting analyses, not processing raw data. The data that works best in the presentation layer is what's already been aggregated and summarized into useful views that can be navigated and fed to dashboard components. Importing data that's already been aggregated as much as possible is far better. For example, if you need to report on Revenue by Region and Month, there's no need to import sales transactions into your data model. Instead, use an aggregated table consisting of Region, Month, and Sum of Revenue.

➤ **Excess data degrades the performance of your presentation layer.** In other words, because your dashboard is fed by your data model, you need to maintain the model behind the scenes (likely in hidden tabs) when distributing the dashboard. Besides the fact that it causes the file size to be unwieldy, including too much data in your data model can actually degrade the performance of your dashboard. Why? When you open an Excel file, the entire file is loaded into memory (or *RAM*) to ensure quick data processing and access. The drawback to this behavior is that Excel requires a great deal of RAM to process even the smallest change in your worksheet. You may have noticed that when you try to perform an action on a large formula-intensive data, Excel is slow to respond, giving you a Calculating indicator in the status bar. The larger your data is, the less efficient the data crunching in Excel is.

➤ **Excess data limits the scalability of your data model.** Imagine that you're working in a small company and you're using monthly transactions in your data model. Each month holds 80,000 lines of data. As time goes on, you build a robust process complete with all the formulas, pivot tables, and macros you need to analyze the data that's stored in your neatly maintained tab. Now what happens after one year? Do you start a new tab? How do you analyze two data on two different tabs as one entity? Are your formulas still good? Do you have to write new macros?

You can avoid such issues by importing only aggregated and summarized data that's useful to the core purpose of your dashboard.

Use tabs to document and organize your data model

Wanting to keep your data model limited to one worksheet tab is natural. In our opinion, keeping track of one tab is much simpler than using different tabs. However, limiting your data model to one tab has its drawbacks, including the following:

➤ **Limits the quality of your analysis.** Because only so much text can fit on a tab, using one tab imposes real-estate restrictions that can limit your analyses. Consider adding tabs to your data model to provide additional data and analysis that may not fit on just one tab.

➤ **Makes for a confusing data model.** When working with a large quantity of data, you need plenty of staging tables to aggregate and shape the raw data so that it can be fed to your dashboard components. If you use only one tab, you're forced to position these staging tables below or to the right of your data. Although this may provide all the elements needed to feed your presentation layer, a good deal of scrolling is necessary to view all the elements positioned in a wide range of areas. This makes the data model difficult to understand and maintain. Use separate tabs to hold your staging tables, particularly in data models that contain large quantities of data that take a lot of real estate.

➤ **Limits the amount of documentation you can include.** You'll find that your data models easily become a complex system of intertwining links among components, input ranges, output ranges, and formulas. Sure, it all makes sense while you're building your data model, but try coming back to it after a few months. You'll find that you've forgotten what each data range does and how each range interacts with the final presentation layer. To avoid this problem, consider adding a data model map tab to your data model. The map tab essentially summarizes the key ranges in the data model and allows you to document how each range interacts with the dashboard components in the final presentation layer. As you can see in Figure 11-6, the data model map is nothing fancy; just a table that lists some key information about each range in the model.

Tab	Range	Purpose	Linked Component/s
Analysis 1	A2:A11	Provides the data source for the trend graph component.	United States trend 1
Analysis 2	A3:A11	Data source for the List Box component.	List Box 1
Analysis 2	C1	Output range for the selected item in the List Box component.	Conditional trend icon
Analysis 2	D1:R1	Vlookup formulas that reference cell C1. This range also serves as the source data for the Combination Chart component.	Combination Chart 1
Data	C4:R48	Main data set for this data model.	

Figure 11-6: A data model map provides documentation that outlines how your data model works.

You can include any information you think appropriate in your data model map. The idea is to give yourself a handy reference that guides you through the elements in your data model.

Test your data model before building presentation components

This best practice is simple. Make sure that your data model does what it's supposed to do before building dashboard components on top of it. In that vein, here are a few things to watch for:

➤ **Test your formulas to be sure that they're working properly.** Make sure your formulas don't produce errors and that each formula outputs expected results.

➤ **Double-check your main data to be sure that it's complete.** Check that your data table has not truncated when transferring to Excel. Also, be sure that each column of data you need is present with appropriate data labels.

➤ **Make sure all numeric formatting is appropriate.** Be sure that the formatting of your data is appropriate for the field. For example, check to see that dates are formatted as dates, currency values are formatted properly, and that the correct number of decimal places is displayed where needed.

The obvious goal here is to eliminate easily avoidable errors that may cause complications later.

▶ Speaking of documenting your data model . . .

Another way to document the logic in your data model is to use comments and labels liberally. It's amazing how a few explanatory comments and labels can help clarify your worksheets. The general idea here is that the logic in your model should be clear to you even after you've been away from your data model for a long period of time.

Also, consider using colors to identify the ranges in your data model. Using colors in your data model enables you to quickly look at a range of cells and get a basic indication of what that range does. The general concept behind this best practice is that each color represents a range type. For example, you could use yellow to represent staging tables used to feed the charts and the tables in your presentation layer. You could use gray to represent formulas that aren't to be altered or touched, or purple to represent reference tables used for lookups and drop-down lists.

You can use any color you want; it's up to you to give these colors meaning. The important thing is that you have a visual distinction between the various ranges being used in your data model. If you use different colors, it's important to fully document what each color means.

Excel Functions for Your Data Model

As we discussed, the optimal data model for any dashboard separates data, analysis, and presentation into three distinct layers. Although all three layers are important, the analysis layer is where the real art comes into play. The fundamental task of the analysis layer is to extract information from the data layer for use in the staging tables that feed your charts, tables, and other dashboard components. To do this effectively, you need to use formulas that serve as data delivery mechanisms — formulas that deliver data to a destination range.

You see, the information you need lives in your data layer (typically, a table containing aggregated data). *Data delivery* formulas are designed to get that data and deliver it to the analysis layer so it can be analyzed and shaped. The cool thing is that after you've set up your data delivery formulas, your analysis layer automatically updates each time your data layer is refreshed.

Now, take a look at a few Excel functions that work particularly well in data delivery formulas. As you go through the examples here, you'll start to see how these concepts come together.

Understanding lookup tables

In the following sections, you'll see frequent use of the term lookup table. A *lookup table* is essentially a range of data that holds information in a structure that can be used to extract the needed data points. In the context of these examples, you can assume the lookup table will be the data layer.

A lookup table can come in several forms:

➤ **One column or row:** You may have a list of manager names in a single column. That list can be used as a lookup table to find a manager based on his name or his position number within the column.

➤ **Range with multiple data columns:** You may have a table with product numbers and prices. You can use a list table as a lookup to find a specific price based on its corresponding product number. In this scenario, you need a formula that performs lookup on the product number to get the appropriate price.

➤ **A position array:** In some cases, you need to look up a value solely based on a particular position within an array of values. For instance, you may need to find the revenue amount for the 14th week in a year. If you have every value for each week in the year listed in order, you can extract the revenue amount for the 14th value in the list.

The VLOOKUP function

The VLOOKUP function finds a specific value in the first column of a lookup table and returns the corresponding value in a specified table column. The lookup table is arranged vertically. In Figure 11-7, the table on the top shows sales by month and product number. The table on the bottom translates those product numbers to actual product names. The VLOOKUP function connects the appropriate product name to each respective product number.

Month	Product Number	Sales	Product Name	
Feb	5	$ 396	Pinapples	#VLOOKUP(C3,$D$16:$E$22,2,FALSE)
Feb	2	$ 388	Oranges	#VLOOKUP(C4,$D$16:$E$22,2,FALSE)
Feb	1	$ 377	Apples	#VLOOKUP(C5,$D$16:$E$22,2,FALSE)
Feb	3	$ 204	Bananas	#VLOOKUP(C6,$D$16:$E$22,2,FALSE)
Feb	4	$ 200	Pears	#VLOOKUP(C7,$D$16:$E$22,2,FALSE)
Feb	6	$ 161	Mangos	#VLOOKUP(C8,$D$16:$E$22,2,FALSE)
Jan	3	$ 489	Bananas	#VLOOKUP(C9,$D$16:$E$22,2,FALSE)
Jan	6	$ 465	Mangos	#VLOOKUP(C10,$D$16:$E$22,2,FALSE)
Jan	1	$ 382	Apples	#VLOOKUP(C11,$D$16:$E$22,2,FALSE)
Jan	2	$ 285	Oranges	#VLOOKUP(C12,$D$16:$E$22,2,FALSE)
Jan	4	$ 200	Pears	#VLOOKUP(C13,$D$16:$E$22,2,FALSE)
Jan	5	$ 113	Pinapples	#VLOOKUP(C14,$D$16:$E$22,2,FALSE)

Product Number	Product Name
1	Apples
2	Oranges
3	Bananas
4	Pears
5	Pinapples
6	Mangos

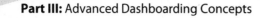

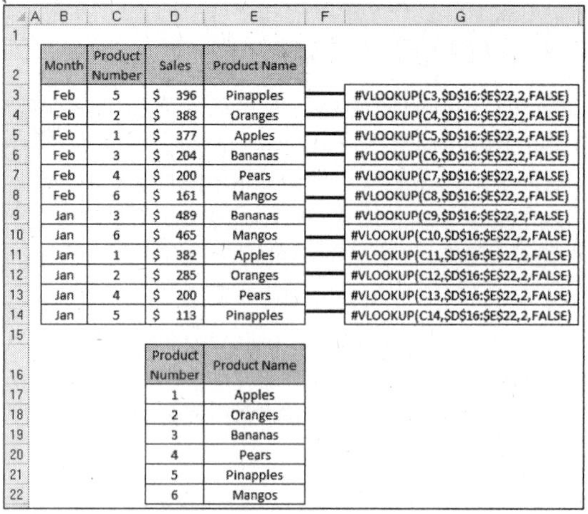

Figure 11-7: The VLOOKUP function finds the appropriate product name for each product number.

VLOOKUP basics

To see how the VLOOKUP function works, take a moment to review the basic syntax. A VLOOKUP function requires four arguments:

```
VLOOKUP(lookup_value,table_array,col_index_num,range_lookup)
```

- **lookup_value:** The value that you want to look up in the first column of the lookup table. In Figure 11-7, the lookup_value is the product number. Therefore, the first argument for all the formulas shown in Figure 11-7 references column C.
- **table_array:** The range that contains the lookup table. In Figure 11-7, that range is D16:E22. Please note that for the VLOOKUP function to work, the leftmost column of the table must be the matching value. For example, if you're matching product numbers, product numbers must be in the first column of the lookup table. Also, the reference that you use for this argument is an absolute reference. This means that the column and row references are prefixed with dollar ($) signs — as in $G$2:$H$8. This ensures that the references don't shift while you copy the formulas down or across.
- **col_index_num:** The column number from within the lookup table that contains the matching value. In Figure 11-7, the second (column E) contains the product name, so the formula uses the number 2. If the product name column were the fourth column in the lookup table, the number 4 would be used.
- **range_lookup: Optional.** You can specify whether you're looking for an exact match for your value or an approximate match. If an exact match is needed, type **FALSE** for this argument. If the closest match will do, type **TRUE** or leave the argument blank.

Adding VLOOKUP formulas to a data model

Using a few VLOOKUP formulas and a simple drop-down list, you can create a data model that not only delivers data to the appropriate staging table but also allows you to dynamically change data views based on a selection you make. Figure 11-8 illustrates the setup.

On the Web

To see this effect in action, go to www.wiley.com/go/exceldr **to get the** Chapter 11 Samples.xlsx **workbook. Open that workbook to see the VLOOKUP1 tab.**

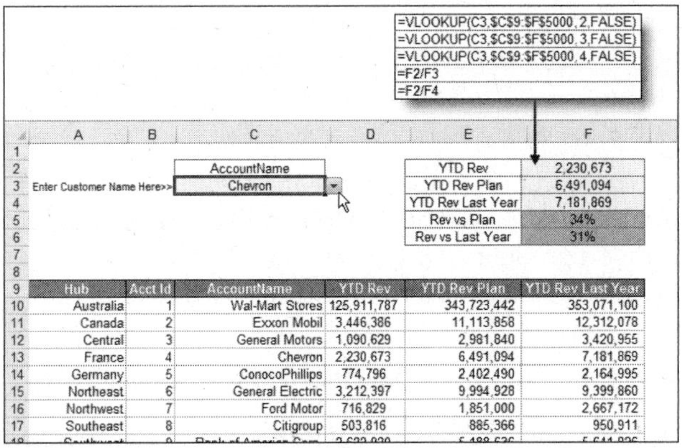

Figure 11-8: Using the VLOOKUP function to extract data and change data views.

The data layer in Figure 11-8 resides in the range A9:F209. The analysis layer displays in range E2:F6. The data layer consists of all the formulas that extract the appropriate data. As you can see, if you select Chevron in cell C3, the VLOOKUP formula extracts the data for Chevron from the data layer.

Note

You may notice that the VLOOKUP formulas in Figure 11-8 specify a table_array argument of $C$9:$F$5000. So the lookup table that the formulas point to stretches from C9 to F5000. That may seem strange because the table ends at F209. Why would you force your VLOOKUP formulas to look at a range far past the end of the data table?

Remember that the idea behind separating the data layer and the analysis layer is that your analysis layer can automatically update when you update your data. So when you get new data next month, you can simply replace the data layer in the model without having to rework your analysis layer. Allowing for more rows than necessary in your VLOOKUP formulas ensures that if your data layer grows, records won't fall outside the lookup range of the formulas.

Later in this chapter (in the "Working with Excel Tables" section), we show you how to automatically keep up with growing data tables by using the Excel table feature.

Using drop-down lists

In the example illustrated in Figure 11-8, the data model allows you to select customer names (that is, the AccountName field) from a drop-down list when you click cell C3. The customer name serves as the lookup value for the VLOOKUP formulas. Changing the customer name extracts a new set of data from the data layer. This allows you to quickly switch from one customer to another without having to remember and type the customer name.

Now, as cool as this seems, the reasons for this setup aren't all cosmetic. There are practical reasons for adding drop-down lists to your data models.

Many of your models consist of multiple analysis layers. Although each analysis layer is different, the layers often need to revolve around a shared dimension, such as the same customer name, the market, or the region. For instance, when you have a data model that reports on Financials, Labor Statistics, and Operational Volumes, you want to ensure that when the model is reporting Financials for the South region, the Labor Statistics are for the South region as well.

An effective way to ensure that this happens is to force your formulas to use the same dimension references. If cell C3 is where you switch customers, every analysis that is customer-dependent should reference cell C3. Drop-down lists allow you to have a predefined list of valid variables located in a single cell. With a drop-down list, you can easily switch dimensions while building and testing multiple analysis layers.

Adding a drop-down list is a relatively easy thing to do with Excel's Data Validation functionality. To add a drop-down list:

1. Click the Data tab on the Ribbon.

2. Click the Data Validation button.

3. In the Data Validation dialog box, click the Settings tab (see Figure 11-9).

4. In the Allow drop-down list, select List.

5. In the Source box, specify the range of cells that contain your predefined selection list.

6. Click OK.

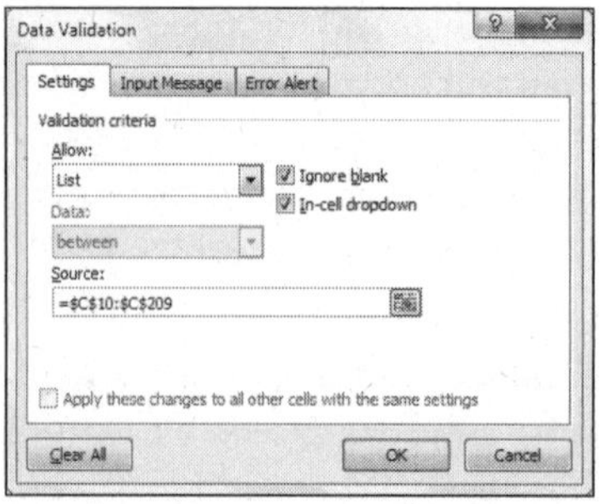

Figure 11-9: You can use data validation to create a predefined list of valid variables for your data model.

The HLookup function

The HLOOKUP function is the less popular cousin of the VLOOKUP function. The H in HLOOKUP stands for horizontal. Because Excel data is typically vertically oriented, most situations require a vertical lookup (or VLOOKUP). However, some data structures are horizontally oriented, requiring a horizontal lookup; thus the HLOOKUP function comes in handy. The HLOOKUP searches a lookup table to find a single value from a row of data where the column label matches a given criterion.

HLOOKUP basics

Figure 11-10 demonstrates a typical scenario where HLOOKUP formulas are used. The table in C3 requires quarter-end numbers (March and June) for 2012. The HLOOKUP formulas use the column labels to find the correct month columns and then locate the 2012 data by moving down the appropriate number of rows. In this case, 2012 data is in row 4, so the number 4 is used in the formulas.

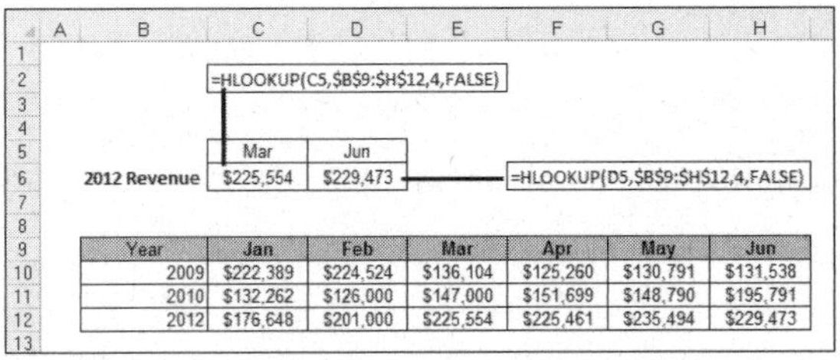

=HLOOKUP(C5,$B$9:$H$12,4,FALSE)

	Mar	Jun
2012 Revenue	$225,554	$229,473

=HLOOKUP(D5,$B$9:$H$12,4,FALSE)

Year	Jan	Feb	Mar	Apr	May	Jun
2009	$222,389	$224,524	$136,104	$125,260	$130,791	$131,538
2010	$132,262	$126,000	$147,000	$151,699	$148,790	$195,791
2012	$176,648	$201,000	$225,554	$225,461	$235,494	$229,473

Figure 11-10: HLOOKUP formulas help find March and June numbers from the lookup table.

To get your mind around how this works, take a look at the basic syntax of the HLOOKUP function.

```
HLOOKUP(lookup_value,table_array,row_index_num,range_lookup)
```

- **lookup_value:** The value that you want to look up. In most cases, these values are column names. In the example in Figure 11-10, the column labels are being referenced for the lookup_value. This points the HLOOKUP function to the appropriate column in the lookup table.
- **table_array:** The range that contains the lookup table. In Figure 11-10, that range is B9:H12. Like the VLOOKUP examples earlier in this chapter, the references used for this argument are absolute, which means the column and row references are prefixed with dollar ($) signs — as in $B$7:$H$10. This ensures that the reference doesn't shift while you copy the formula down or across.
- **row_index_num:** The row number that contains the value that you're looking for. In the example in Figure 11-10, the 2012 data is located in row 4 of the lookup table. Therefore, the formulas use the number 4.
- **range_lookup:** You can specify whether you're looking for an exact match or an approximate match. If an exact match is needed, enter **FALSE** for this argument. If the closest match will do, enter **TRUE** or leave the argument blank.

Applying HLOOKUP formulas to a data model

HLOOKUPs are especially handy for shaping data into structures appropriate for charting or other types of reporting. A simple example is demonstrated in Figure 11-11. With HLOOKUPs, the data shown in the raw data table at the bottom of the figure is reoriented in a staging table at the top. When the raw data is changed or refreshed, the staging table captures the changes.

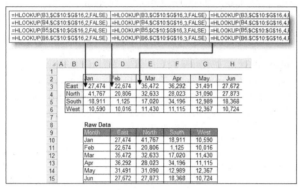

Figure 11-11: In this example, HLOOKUP formulas pull and reshape data without disturbing the raw data table.

The SUMPRODUCT function

The SUMPRODUCT function is actually listed under the math and trigonometry category of Excel functions. Because the primary purpose of SUMPRODUCT is to calculate the sum product, most people don't know you can actually use it to look up values. In fact, you can use this versatile function quite effectively in most data models.

SUMPRODUCT basics

The SUMPRODUCT function is designed to multiply values from two or more ranges of data and then add the results together to return the sum of the products. Take a look at Figure 11-12 to see a typical scenario where the SUMPRODUCT is useful.

In Figure 11-12, you see a common analysis where you need the total sales for the years 2012 and 2011. As you can see, to get the total sales for each year, you first have to multiply Price by the number of Units to get the total for each Region. Then you have to sum those results to get the total sales for each year.

With the SUMPRODUCT function, you can perform the two-step analysis with just one formula. Figure 11-13 shows the same analysis with SUMPRODUCT formulas. Instead of using 11 formulas, you can accomplish the same analysis with just three!

Year	Region	Price	Units			
2012	North	$40	751	$30,040		=D3*E3
2012	South	$35	483	$16,905		=D4*E4
2012	East	$32	789	$25,248		=D5*E5
2012	West	$41	932	$38,212		=D6*E6
2011	North	$40	877	$35,080		=D7*E7
2011	South	$35	162	$5,670		=D8*E8
2011	East	$32	258	$8,256		=D9*E9
2011	West	$41	517	$21,197		=D10*E10
		2012 total	$110,405			=SUM(F3:F6)
		2011 total	$70,203			=SUM(F7:F10)
		Variance	$40,202			=F12-F13

Figure 11-12: Without the SUMPRODUCT, getting the total sales for each year involves a two-step process: First multiply price and units and then sum the results.

Year	Region	Price	Units		
2012	North	$40	751		
2012	South	$35	483		
2012	East	$32	789		
2012	West	$41	932		
2011	North	$40	877		
2011	South	$35	162		
2011	East	$32	258		
2011	West	$41	517		
2007 total	$110,405		=SUMPRODUCT(D3:D6,E3:E6)		
2006 total	$70,203		=SUMPRODUCT(D7:D10, E7:E10)		
Variance	$40,202		=E12-E13		

Figure 11-13: The SUMPRODUCT function allows you to perform the same analysis with just three formulas instead of 11.

The syntax of the SUMPRODUCT function is fairly simple:

```
SUMPRODUCT(array1,array2, ...)
```

The array argument represents a range of data. You can use anywhere from two to 255 arrays in a SUMPRODUCT formula. The arrays are multiplied together and then added. The only hard-and-fast rule you have to remember is that all the arrays must have the same number of values. That is to say, you can't use the SUMPRODUCT if range X has 10 values and Range Y has 11 values. Otherwise, you get the #VALUE! error.

A twist on the SUMPRODUCT function

The interesting thing about the SUMPRODUCT function is that you can use it to filter out values. Take a look at Figure 11-14 to see what I mean.

The formula in cell E12 is pulling the sum of total units for just the North region. Meanwhile, cell E13 is pulling the units logged for the North region in the year 2011.

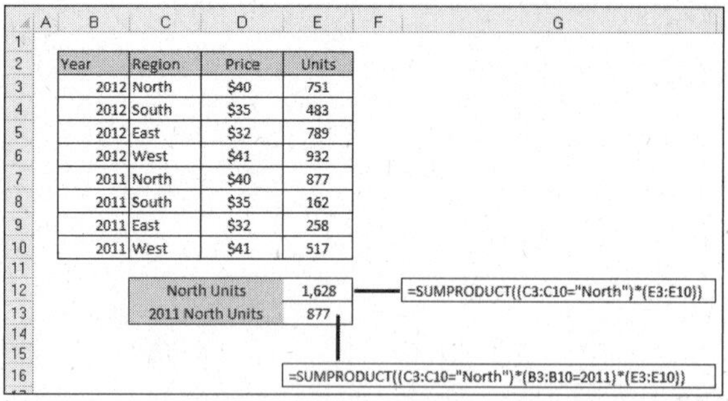

Figure 11-14: You can use the SUMPRODUCT function to filter data based on criteria.

To understand how this works, take a look at the formula in cell E12 shown in Figure 11-14. That formula reads SUMPRODUCT((C3:C10="North")*(E3:E10)).

In Excel, TRUE evaluates to 1 and FALSE evaluates to 0. Every value in Column C that equals "North" evaluates to TRUE or 1. Where the value is not "North", it evaluates to FALSE or 0. The part of the formula that reads (C3:C10="North") enumerates through each value in the range C3:C10, assigning a 1 or 0 to each value. Then internally, the SUMPRODUCT formula translates to

```
(1*E3)+(0*E4)+(0*E5)+(0*E6)+(1*E7)+(0*E8)+(0*E9)+(0*E10).
```

This gives you the answer of 1628 because this next formula equals 1628.

```
(1*751)+(0*483)+(0*789)+(0*932)+(1*877)+(0*162)+(0*258)+(0*517)
```

Applying SUMPRODUCT formulas to a data model

As always in Excel, you don't have to hard-code the criteria in your formulas. Instead of explicitly using "North" in the SUMPRODUCT formula, you can reference a cell that contains the filter value. You can imagine that cell A3 contains the word "North", in which case, you can use (C3:C10=A3) instead of (C3:C10="North"). This way, you can dynamically change your filter criteria, and your formula keeps up.

Figure 11-15 demonstrates how you can use this concept to pull data into a staging table based on multiple criteria. Note that each of the SUMPRODUCT formulas shown here references cells B3 and C3 to filter on Account and Product Line. Again, you can add data validation drop-down lists to cells B3 and C3, allowing you to easily change criteria.

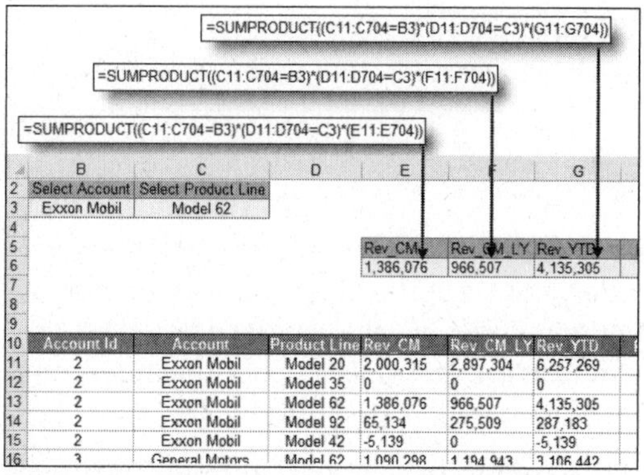

Figure 11-15: You can use the SUMPRODUCT function to pull summarized numbers from the data layer into staging tables.

The Choose function

The CHOOSE function returns a value from a specified list of values based on a specified position number. For instance, if you enter the formulas CHOOSE(3,"Red", "Yellow", "Green", "Blue") into a cell, Excel returns Green because Green is the third item in the list of values. The formula CHOOSE(1,"Red", "Yellow", "Green", "Blue") returns Red. Although this may not look useful on the surface, the CHOOSE function can enhance your data models dramatically.

CHOOSE basics

Figure 11-16 illustrates how CHOOSE formulas can help pinpoint and extract numbers from a range of cells. Note that instead of using hard-coded values, like Red, Green, and so on, you can use cell references to list the choices.

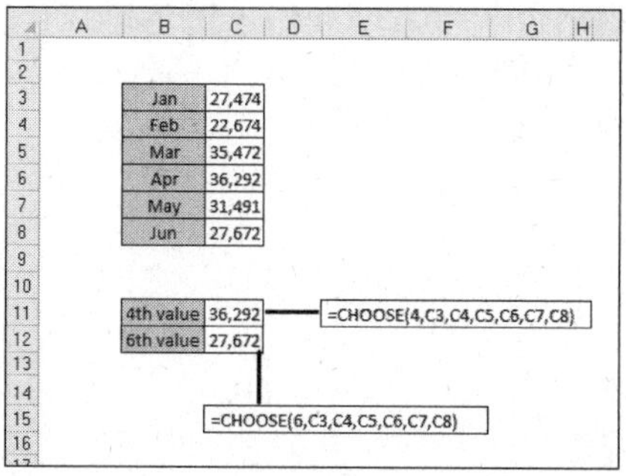

Figure 11-16: The CHOOSE function allows you to find values from a defined set of choices.

Take a moment to review the basic syntax of the CHOOSE function:

```
CHOOSE(index_num,value1,value2,...)
```

> ➤ **index_num:** Allows you to specify the position number of the chosen value in the list of values. If the third value in the list is needed, the Index_num is 3. The Index_num argument must be an integer between one and the maximum number of values in the defined list of values. That is to say, if there are ten choices defined in the CHOOSE formula, the Index_num argument can't be more than ten.

> ➤ **value:** Represents a choice in the defined list of choices for that CHOOSE formula. The value arguments can be hard-coded values, cell references, defined names, formulas, or functions. Starting in Excel 2007, you can have up to 255 choices listed in your CHOOSE functions. In Excel 2003, you were limited to 29 value arguments.

Applying CHOOSE formulas to a data model

The CHOOSE function is especially valuable in data models where there are multiple layers of data that need to be brought together. Figure 11-17 illustrates an example where CHOOSE formulas help pull data together.

In this example, you have two data tables: one for Revenues and one for Net Income. Each contains numbers for separate regions. The idea is to create a staging table that pulls data from both tables so that the data corresponds to a selected region.

To understand what's going on, focus on the formula in cell F3 shown in Figure 11-17. The formula is CHOOSE($C$2,F7,F8,F9,F10). The index_num argument is actually a cell reference that looks at the value in cell C2, which happens to be the number 2. As you can see, cell C2 is actually a VLOOKUP formula that pulls the appropriate index number for the selected region. The list of defined choices in the CHOOSE formula is essentially the cell references that make up the revenue values for each region: F7, F8, F9, and F10. So the formula in cell F3 translates to CHOOSE(2, 27474, 41767, 18911, 10590). The answer is 41,767.

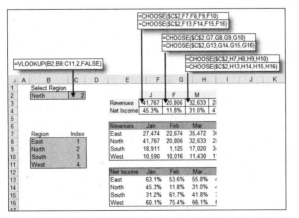

Figure 11-17: The CHOOSE formulas ensure that the appropriate data is synchronously pulled from multiple data feeds.

Working with Excel Tables

One of the challenges you can encounter when building a data model is a data table that expands over time. That is to say, as you add new data, the number of records increases. Take a look at Figure 11-18. In this figure, you see a simple table that serves as the source for the bar chart. Notice that the table lists data for January through June.

Imagine that next month, this table expands to include July data. You'll have to manually update your chart to include July data. Now imagine that you have this same issue across your data model, with multiple data tables that link to multiple staging tables and dashboard components. You can see that keeping up with changes each month would be an extremely painful task.

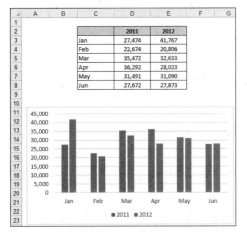

Figure 11-18: This table has the potential to grow every month.

To solve this issue, you can use Excel's table feature (you can tell they spent all night coming up with that name). The table feature allows you to convert a range of data into a defined table that's treated independently of other rows and columns on the worksheet. After a range is converted to a table, Excel views the individual cells in the table as a single object that has the functionality a normal data range doesn't have.

For instance, Excel tables offer the following features:

➤ Drop-down lists in the Header row that allow you to filter and sort data in each column easily

➤ A Total row feature with various aggregate functions

➤ Ability to apply distinct formatting to the table independent of the rest of the worksheet

➤ Ability to automatically expand in dimensions to accommodate new data (key for data modeling purposes)

Tip

The table feature did exist in Excel 2003 under a different name. In Excel 2003, this feature was the List feature (found in Excel's Data menu). The benefit of this fact is that Excel tables are fully compatible with Excel 2003!

Converting a range to an Excel table

To convert a range of data to an Excel table, follow these steps:

1. Highlight the range of cells that contain the data you want to include in your Excel table.

2. On the Insert tab of the Ribbon, click the Table button.

   The Create Table dialog box opens, as shown in Figure 11-19.

3. In the Create Table dialog box, verify the range for the table and specify whether the first row of the selected range is a Header row.

4. Click OK.

Figure 11-19: Converting a range of data to an Excel table.

After the conversion takes place, notice a few small changes. Excel put drop-down lists in each Header row, the rows in your table now have alternate shading, and any header that didn't have a value has been named by Excel.

You can use Excel tables as the source for charts, pivot tables, list boxes, or anything else for which you normally use a data range. In Figure 11-20, a bar chart has been linked to the Excel table.

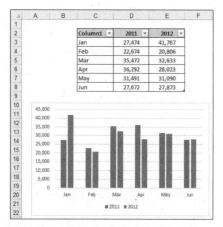

Figure 11-20: Excel tables can be used as source data for charts, pivot tables, named ranges, and so on.

Here's the impressive bit. When data is added to the table, Excel automatically expands the range of the table and incorporates the new range into any linked object. That's just a fancy way of saying that any chart or pivot table tied to an Excel table automatically captures new data without manual intervention.

For example, if I add July and August data to the end of the Excel table, the chart automatically updates to capture the new data. In Figure 11-21, I added July with no data and August with data to show you that the chart captures any new records and automatically plots the data given.

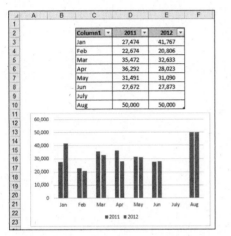

Figure 11-21: An Excel table automatically expands when new data is added.

Take a moment to think about what Excel tables mean to a data model. Pivot tables never have to be reconfigured, charts automatically capture new data, and ranges automatically keep up with changes.

Converting an Excel table back to a range

If you want to convert an Excel table back to a normal range, you can follow these steps:

1. Place your cursor in any cell inside the Excel table and select the Table Tools Design tab in the Ribbon.

2. Choose the Convert to Range command, as shown in Figure 11-22.

3. When asked if you're sure (via a message box), click Yes.

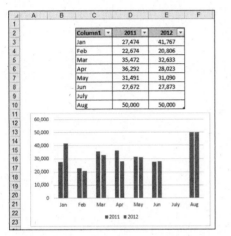

Figure 11-22: To remove Excel table functionality, convert the table back to a range.

Any object you have connected to the range (pivot tables, charts, and so on) will continue to work. However, they will no longer dynamically update as you add or remove data from the range.

Adding Interactive Controls to Your Dashboard

In This Chapter

- Introducing Form controls
- Using a button control
- Using a check box control to toggle a chart series
- Using an option button to filter your views
- Using a combo box to control multiple pivot tables
- Using a list box to control multiple charts

Today, business professionals increasingly want to be empowered to switch from one view of data to another with a simple list of choices. For those who build dashboards and reports, this empowerment comes with a whole new set of issues. The overarching question is — how do you handle a user who wants to see multiple views for multiple regions or markets?

Fortunately, Excel offers a handful of tools that enable you to add interactivity into your presentations. With these tools and a bit of creative data modeling, you can accomplish these goals with relative ease. In this chapter, we discuss how to incorporate various controls (such as buttons, check boxes, and scroll bars) into your dashboards and reports, and present you with several solutions that you can implement.

Getting Started with Form Controls

Excel offers a set of controls called *Form controls,* designed specifically for adding UI elements directly onto a worksheet. After you place a Form control on a worksheet, you can then configure it to perform a specific task. Later in the chapter, we demonstrate how to apply the most useful controls to a presentation.

Finding Form controls

You can find Excel's Form controls on the Developer tab, which is initially hidden in Excel 2010. To enable the Developer tab, follow these steps:

1. Go to the Ribbon and select the File tab.

2. To open the Excel Options dialog box, click the Options button.

3. Click the Customize Ribbon button.

   In the list box on the right, you'll see all the available tabs.

4. Select the check box next to the Developer tab (see Figure 12-1).

5. Click OK.

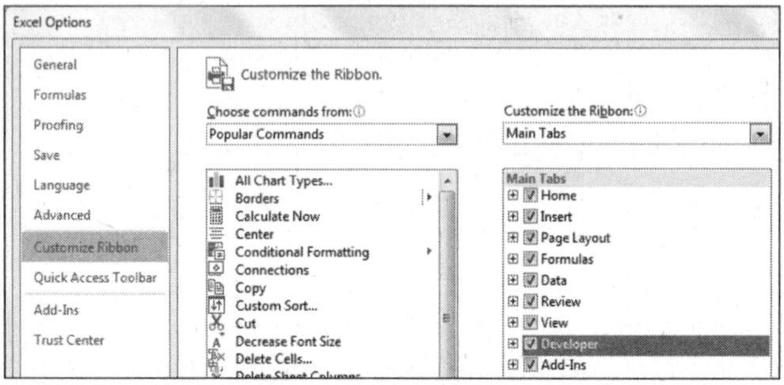

Figure 12-1: Enabling the Developer tab.

Now, select the Developer tab and choose the Insert command, as shown in Figure 12-2. Here you find two sets of controls: Form controls and ActiveX controls. Form controls are designed specifically for use on a spreadsheet, whereas ActiveX Controls are typically used on Excel UserForms. Because Form controls need less overhead and can be configured far easier than their ActiveX counterparts, you generally want to use Form controls.

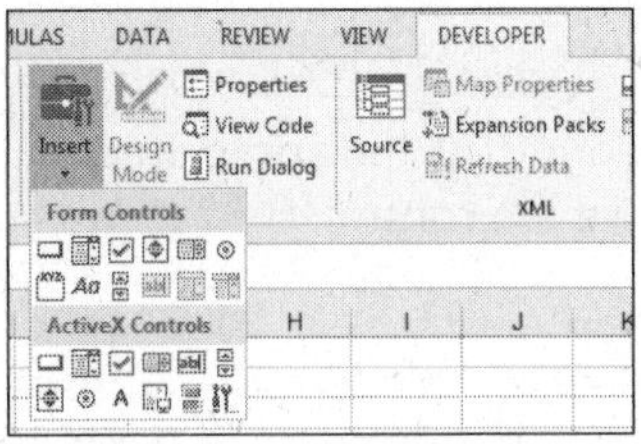

Figure 12-2: Form controls and ActiveX controls.

Here are the nine Form controls that you can add directly to a worksheet (see Figure 12-3). They are as follows:

➤ **Button:** Executes an assigned macro when a user clicks the button.

➤ **Combo Box:** Gives a user an expandable list of options from which to choose.

➤ **Check Box:** Provides a mechanism for a select/deselect scenario. When selected, it returns a value of True. Otherwise, it returns False.

➤ **Spin Button:** Enables a user to easily increment or decrement a value by clicking the up and down arrows.

➤ **List Box:** Gives a user a list of options from which to choose.

➤ **Option Button:** Enables a user to toggle through two or more options one at a time. Selecting one option automatically deselects the others.

➤ **Scroll Bar:** Enables a user to scroll to a value or position using a sliding scale that can be moved by clicking and dragging the mouse.

➤ **Label:** Allows you to add text labels to your worksheet. You can also assign a macro to the label, effectively using it as a button of sorts.

➤ **Group Box:** Typically used for cosmetic purposes, this control serves as a container for groups of other controls.

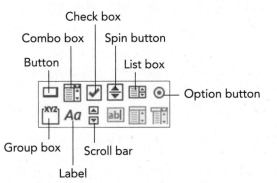

Figure 12-3: Nine Form controls labeled so that you can add to your worksheet.

Adding a control to a worksheet

To add a control to a worksheet, simply click the control that you require and click the approximate location that you want to place the control. You can easily move and resize the control later just as you would a chart or shape.

After you add a control, you want to configure it to define its look, behavior, and utility. Each control has its own set of configuration options that allows you to customize it for your purposes. To get to these options, right-click the control and select Format Control. This opens the Format Control dialog box (illustrated in Figure 12-4) with all the configuration options for that control.

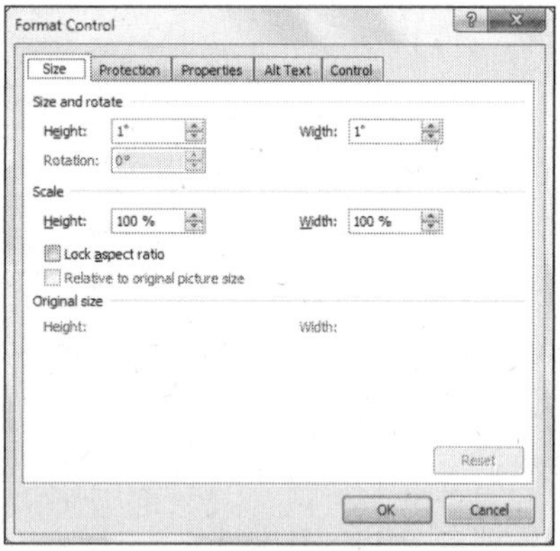

Figure 12-4: Right-click and select Format Control to open a dialog box with the configuration options.

Each control has its own set of tabs that allows you to customize everything from formatting, to security, to configuration arguments. You'll see different tabs based on which control you're using, but most Form controls have the Control tab. The Control tab is where the meat of the configuration lies. Here, you find the variables and settings that need to be defined in order for the control to function.

Note
The button and label controls don't have the Control tab. They have no need for one. The button simply fires whichever macro you assign it. As for the Label, it's not designed to run macro events.

Throughout the rest of the chapter, you walk through a few exercises that demonstrate how to use the most useful controls in a reporting environment. At the end of this chapter, you'll have a solid understanding of Form controls and how they can enhance your dashboards and reports.

Using the Button Control

The button control gives your audience a clear and easy way to execute the macros you've recorded. To insert and configure a button control, follow these steps:

1. Select Insert drop-down list under the Developer tab.

2. Select the button Form control.

3. Click the location in your spreadsheet where you want to place your button.

   The Assign Macro dialog box appears and asks you to assign a macro to this button (see Figure 12-5).

4. Edit the text shown on the button by right-clicking the button, highlighting the existing text, and then overwriting it with your own.

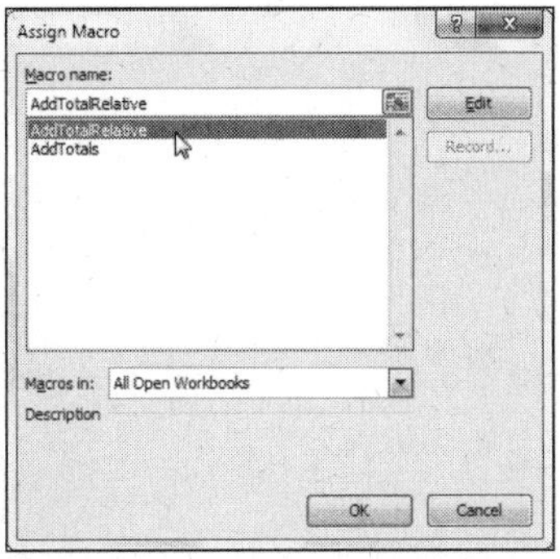

Figure 12-5: Assign a macro to the newly added button.

Tip

To assign a different macro to the button, simply right-click and select Assign Macro to reactivate the Assign Macro dialog box, as shown in Figure 12-5.

Using the Check Box Control

The check box control provides a mechanism for selecting/deselecting options. When a check box is selected, it returns a value of True. When it isn't selected, False is returned. To add and configure a check box control, follow these steps:

1. Select the Insert drop-down list under the Developer tab.

2. Select the check box Form control.

3. Click the location in your spreadsheet where you want to place your check box.

4. After you drop the check box control onto your spreadsheet, right-click the control and select Format Control.

5. Click the Control tab to see the configuration options, as shown in Figure 12-6.

6. Select the state in which the check box should open.

   The default selection (Unchecked) typically works for most scenarios, so you rarely have to update this selection.

7. In the Cell Link box, enter the cell to which you want the check box to output its value.

   By default, a check box control outputs either True or False, depending on whether it's checked. Notice in Figure 12-6 that this particular check box outputs to cell A5.

8. (Optional) You can check the 3-D property if you want the control to have a 3-D appearance.

9. Click OK to apply your changes.

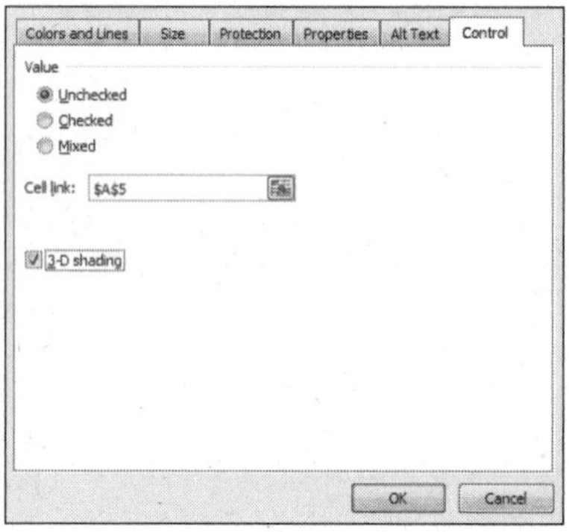

Figure 12-6: Formatting the check box control.

Tip

To rename the check box control, right-click the control, select Edit Text, and then over-write the existing text with your own.

As Figure 12-7 illustrates, the check box outputs its value to the specified cell. If the check box is selected, a value of True is output. If the check box isn't selected, a value of False is output.

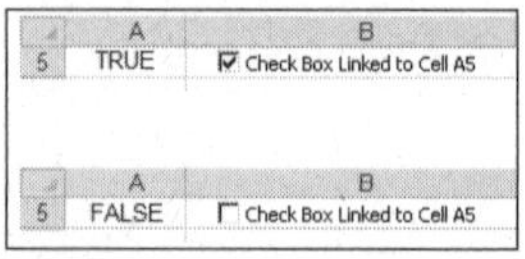

Figure 12-7: The two states of the check box.

If you're having a hard time figuring out how this could be useful, take a stab at this next exercise, which illustrates how you can use a check box to toggle a chart series on and off.

Check box example: Toggling a chart series on and off

Figure 12-8 shows the same chart twice. Notice that the top chart contains only one series, with a check box offering to Show 2011 Trend data. The bottom chart shows the same chart with the check box selected. The on/off nature of the check box control is ideal for interactivity that calls for a visible/not visible state.

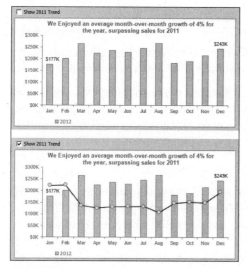

Figure 12-8: A check box can help create the disappearing data series effect.

On the Web

To download the `Chapter 12 Samples.xlsx` **file, go to the book's companion website at** `www.wiley.com/go/exceldr`.

You start with the raw data (in Chapter 12 Sample File.xlsx) that contains both 2011 and 2012 data (see Figure 12-9). In the first column is a cell where the check box control will output its value (cell A12, in this example). This cell will contain either True or False.

	A	B	C	D	E	F	G
10			Raw Data				
11	Toggle for 2011 Data		Jan	Feb	Mar	Apr	May
12	TRUE	2011	$222,389	$224,524	$136,104	$125,260	$130,791
13		2012	$176,648	$201,000	$265,720	$225,461	$235,494
14							

Figure 12-9: Start with raw data and a cell where a check box control can output its value.

Next, you create the analysis layer (staging table) that consists of all formulas, as shown in Figure 12-10. The idea is that the chart actually reads from this data, not the raw data. This way, you can control what the chart sees.

	A	B	C	D	E	
4						
5			Jan	Feb	Mar	
6		2011	=IF($A12=TRUE,C12,NA())	=IF($A12=TRUE,D12,NA())	=IF($A12=TRUE,E12,NA())	=I
7		2012	=C13	=D13	=E13	=F
8						
9						
10			Raw Data			
11	Toggle for 2011 Data		Jan	Feb	Mar	
12	TRUE	2011	$222,389	$224,524	$136,104	$1
13		2012	$176,648	$201,000	$265,720	$2
14						

Figure 12-10: Create a staging table that will feed the chart. The values of this data are all formulas.

As you can see in Figure 12-10, the formulas for the 2012 row simply reference the cells in the raw data for each respective month. You do that because you want the 2012 data to show at all times.

For the 2011 row, you test the value of cell A12 (the cell that contains the output from the check box). If A12 reads True, you reference the respective 2011 cell in the raw data. If A12 doesn't read True, the formula uses Excel's NA() function to return an #N/A error. Excel charts can't read a cell with the #N/A error. Therefore, they simply don't show the data series for any cell that contains #N/A. This is ideal when you don't want a data series to be shown at all.

Tip Notice that the formula shown in Figure 12-10 uses an absolute reference with cell A12. That is, the reference to cell A12 in the formula is prefixed with a $ sign ($A12). This ensures that the column references in the formulas don't shift when they're copied across.

Figure 12-11 illustrates the two scenarios in action in the staging tables. In the scenario shown at the bottom of Figure 12-11, cell A12 is True, so the staging table actually brings in 2011 data. In the scenario shown at the top of Figure 12-11, cell A12 is False, so the staging table returns #N/A for 2011.

	A	B	C	D	E	F	G
4							
5			Jan	Feb	Mar	Apr	May
6		2011	#N/A	#N/A	#N/A	#N/A	#N/A
7		2012	$176,648	$201,000	$265,720	$225,461	$235,494
8							
9							
10			Raw Data				
11	Toggle for 2011 Data		Jan	Feb	Mar	Apr	May
12	FALSE	2011	$222,389	$224,524	$136,104	$125,260	$130,791
13		2012	$176,648	$201,000	$265,720	$225,461	$235,494
14							

	A	B	C	D	E	F	G
4							
5			Jan	Feb	Mar	Apr	May
6		2011	$222,389	$224,524	$136,104	$125,260	$130,791
7		2012	$176,648	$201,000	$265,720	$225,461	$235,494
8							
9							
10			Raw Data				
11	Toggle for 2011 Data		Jan	Feb	Mar	Apr	May
12	TRUE	2011	$222,389	$224,524	$136,104	$125,260	$130,791
13		2012	$176,648	$201,000	$265,720	$225,461	$235,494
14							

Figure 12-11: When cell A12 reads True, 2011 data is displayed; when it reads False, the 2011 row shows only #N/A errors.

Finally, you create the chart that you saw earlier in this section (refer to Figure 12-8) using the staging table. Keep in mind that you can scale this to as many series as you like.

Figure 12-12 illustrates a chart that has multiple series whose visibility is controlled by check box controls. This allows you to make all but two series invisible so you can compare those two series unhindered. Then you can make another two visible, comparing those.

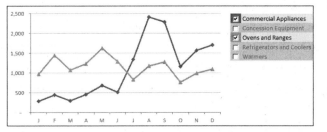

Figure 12-12: You can use check boxes to control how much data is shown in your chart at one time.

Using the Option Button Control

Option buttons allow users to toggle through several options one at a time. The idea is to have two or more option buttons in a group. Then selecting one option button automatically deselects the others. To add option buttons to your worksheet, follow these steps:

1. Click the Insert drop-down list under the Developer tab.

2. Select the option button Form control.

3. Click the location in your spreadsheet where you want to place your option button.

4. After you drop the control onto your spreadsheet, right-click the control and select Format Control.

5. Click the Control tab to see the configuration options, as shown in Figure 12-13.

6. First, select the state in which the option button should open.

   The default selection (Unchecked) typically works for most scenarios, so you rarely have to update this selection.

7. In the Cell Link box, enter the cell to which you want the option button to output its value. By default, an option button control outputs a number that corresponds to the order it was put onto the worksheet. For instance, the first option button you place on your worksheet outputs a number 1, the second outputs a number 2, the third outputs a number 3, and so on. Notice in Figure 12-13 that this particular control outputs to cell A1.

8. (Optional) You can check the 3-D property if you want the control to have a three-dimensional appearance.

9. Click OK to apply your changes.

10. To add another option button, simply copy the button you created and paste as many option buttons as you need. The nice thing about copying and pasting is that all the configurations you made to the original persist in all the copies.

Figure 12-13: Formatting the option button control.

To give your option button a meaningful label, right-click the control, select Edit Text, and then overwrite the existing text with your own.

Tip

Option button example: Showing many views through one chart

One of the ways you can use option buttons is to feed a single chart with different data, based on the option selected. Figure 12-14 illustrates an example of this. When each category is selected, the single chart is updated to show the data for that selection.

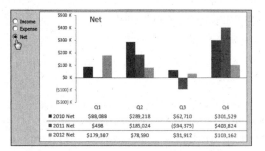

Figure 12-14: This chart is dynamically fed different data based on the selected option button.

Now, you could create three separate charts and show them all on your dashboard at the same time. However, using this technique as an alternative saves on valuable real estate by not having to show three separate charts. Plus, it's much easier to troubleshoot, format, and maintain one chart than three.

To create this example, you start with three raw datasets (as shown in Figure 12-15) that contain three categories of data; Income, Expense, and Net. Near the raw data, you reserve a cell where the option buttons output their values (Cell A8, in this example). This cell contains the ID of the option selected: 1, 2, or 3.

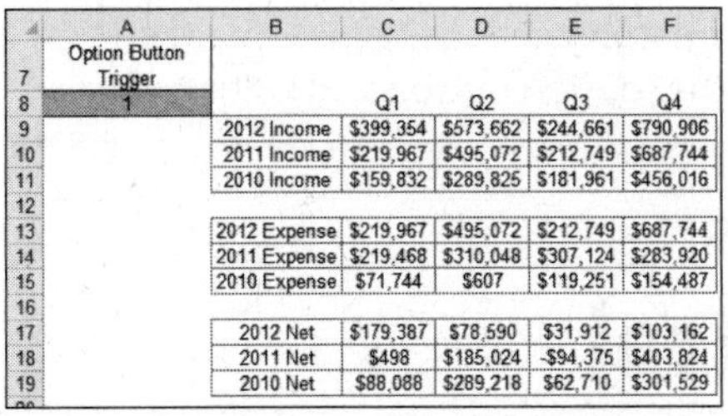

	A	B	C	D	E	F
7	Option Button Trigger					
8	1					
9			Q1	Q2	Q3	Q4
9		2012 Income	$399,354	$573,662	$244,661	$790,906
10		2011 Income	$219,967	$495,072	$212,749	$687,744
11		2010 Income	$159,832	$289,825	$181,961	$456,016
12						
13		2012 Expense	$219,967	$495,072	$212,749	$687,744
14		2011 Expense	$219,468	$310,048	$307,124	$283,920
15		2010 Expense	$71,744	$607	$119,251	$154,487
16						
17		2012 Net	$179,387	$78,590	$31,912	$103,162
18		2011 Net	$498	$185,024	-$94,375	$403,824
19		2010 Net	$88,088	$289,218	$62,710	$301,529

Figure 12-15: Start with the raw datasets and a cell where the option buttons can output their values.

You then create the analysis layer (the staging table) that consists of all formulas, as shown in Figure 12-16. The idea is that the chart reads from this staging table, allowing you to control what the chart sees. The first cell of the staging table contains the following formula:

```
=IF($A$8=1,B9,IF($A$8=2,B13,B17))
```

This formula tells Excel to check the value of cell A8 (the cell where the option buttons output their values). If the value of cell A8 is 1, which represents the value of the Income option, the formula returns the value in the Income dataset (cell B9). If the value of cell A8 is 2, which represents the value of the Expense option, the formula returns the value in the Expense dataset (cell B13). If the value of cell B1 is not 1 or 2, the value in cell B17 is returned.

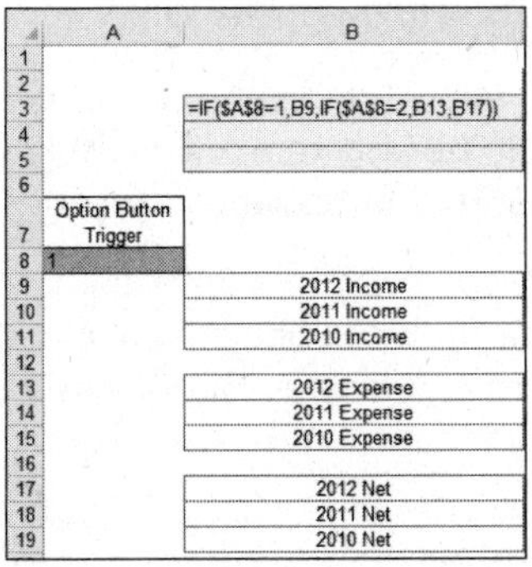

	A	B
1		
2		
3		=IF($A$8=1,B9,IF($A$8=2,B13,B17))
4		
5		
6		
7	Option Button Trigger	
8	1	
9		2012 Income
10		2011 Income
11		2010 Income
12		
13		2012 Expense
14		2011 Expense
15		2010 Expense
16		
17		2012 Net
18		2011 Net
19		2010 Net

Figure 12-16: Create a staging table and enter this formula in the first cell.

Tip

Notice that the formula shown in Figure 12-16 uses absolute references with cell A8. That is, the reference to cell A8 in the formula is prefixed with $ signs ($A$8). This ensures that the cell references in the formulas don't shift when they're copied down and across.

To test that the formula is working fine, you could change the value of cell A8 manually, from 1 to 3. When the formula works, you simply copy the formula across and down to fill the rest of the staging table.

When the setup is created, all that's left to do is create the chart using the staging table. Again, the major benefits you get from this type of setup are that any formatting changes can be made to one chart and it's easy to add another dataset by adding another option button and editing your formulas.

Using the Combo Box Control

The combo box control allows users to select from a list of predefined options from a drop-down list. The idea is that when an item from the combo box control is selected, some action is taken with that selection. To add a combo box to your worksheet, follow these steps:

1. Click the Insert drop-down list under the Developer tab.

2. Select the combo box Form control.

3. Click the location in your spreadsheet where you want to place your combo box.

4. After you drop the control onto your spreadsheet, right-click the control and select Format Control.

5. Click the Control tab to see the configuration options, as shown in Figure 12-17.

6. In the Input Range setting, identify the range that holds the predefined items you want to present as choices in the combo box.

7. In the Cell Link box, enter the cell to which you want the combo box to output its value.

   A combo box control outputs the index number of the selected item. This means that if the second item on the list is selected, the number 2 will be output. If the fifth item on the list is selected, the number 5 will be output. Notice in Figure 12-17 that this particular control outputs to cell E15.

8. In the Drop Down Lines box, enter the number of items you want shown at one time. You see in Figure 12-17 that this control is formatted to show 12 items at one time. This means when the combo box is expanded, the user sees 12 items.

9. (Optional) You can check the 3-D property if you want the control to have a three-dimensional appearance.

10. Click OK to apply your changes.

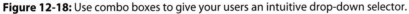

Figure 12-17: Formatting the combo box control.

Combo box example: Changing chart data with a drop-down selector

You can use combo box controls to give your users an intuitive way to select data via a drop-down selector. Figure 12-18 shows a thermometer chart controlled by the combo box above it. When a user selects the Southwest region, the chart responds by plotting the data for the selected region.

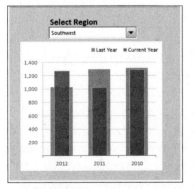

Figure 12-18: Use combo boxes to give your users an intuitive drop-down selector.

To create this example, you start with the raw dataset shown in Figure 12-19. This dataset contains the data for each region. Near the raw data, you reserve a cell where the combo box will output its value (Cell M7, in this example). This cell will catch the index number of the combo box entry selected.

	M	N	O	P	Q	R	S
5			Raw Data				
6	Trigger		Market	2012	2011	2010	2009
7	7		Canada	730	854	1911	1608
8			Midwest	952	1389	1113	1603
9			North	443	543	541	386
10			Northeast	1536	1760	1088	1737
11			South	1500	1600	1588	1000
12			Southeast	1257	1280	1734	1007
13			Southwest	1275	1024	1298	1312
14			West	1402	1045	1759	1075

Figure 12-19: Start with the raw dataset and a cell where the option buttons can output their values.

You then create the analysis layer (the staging table) that consists of all formulas, as shown in Figure 12-20. The idea is that the chart reads from this staging table, allowing you to control what the chart sees. The first cell of the staging table contains the following INDEX formula:

```
=INDEX(P7:P14,$M$7)
```

	L	M	N	O	P	Q
1					2012	2011
2				Current Year	=INDEX(P7:P14,$M$7)	=INDEX(Q7:Q14,$M$7)
3				Last Year	=Q2	=R2
4						
5				Raw Data		
6		Trigger		Market	2012	2011
7		7		Canada	730	854
8				Midwest	952	1389
9				North	443	543
10				Northeast	1536	1760
11				South	1500	1600
12				Southeast	1257	1280
13				Southwest	1275	1024
14				West	1402	1045

Figure 12-20: Create a staging table that uses the INDEX function to extract the appropriate data from the raw dataset.

The INDEX function converts an index number to a value that can be recognized. An INDEX function requires two arguments in order to work properly. The first argument is the range of the list you're working with. The second argument is the index number.

In this example, you're using the index number from the combo box (in cell M7) and extracting the value from the appropriate range (2012 data in P7:P14). Again, notice the use of the absolute $ signs. This ensures that the cell references in the formulas don't shift when they're copied down and across.

Take another look at Figure 12-20 to see what's happening. The INDEX formula in cell P2 points to the range that contains the 2012 data. It then captures the index number in cell M7 (which traps the output value of the combo box). The index number happens to be 7. So the formula in cell P2 will extract the 7th value from the 2012 data range.

When you copy the formula across, Excel adjusts the formula to extract the seventh value from each year's data range.

After your INDEX formulas are in place, you have a clean staging table that you can use to create your chart (see Figure 12-21).

L M N	O	P	Q	R	S
1		2012	2011	2010	2009
2	Current Year	1,275	1,024	1,298	1,312
3	Last Year	1,024	1,298	1,312	
4					
5	**Raw Data**				
6 Trigger	Market	2012	2011	2010	2009
7 [7]	Canada	730	854	1911	1608
8	Midwest	952	1389	1113	1603
9	North	443	543	541	386
10	Northeast	1536	1760	1088	1737
11	South	1500	1600	1588	1000
12	Southeast	1257	1280	1734	1007
13	Southwest	1275	1024	1298	1312
14	West	1402	1045	1759	1075

Figure 12-21: A clean staging table to use to create your chart.

Using the List Box Control

The list box control allows users to select from a list of predefined choices. The idea is that when an item from the list box control is selected, some action is taken with that selection. To add a list box to your worksheet, follow these steps:

1. Select the Insert drop-down list under the Developer tab.

2. Select the list box Form control.

3. Click the location in your spreadsheet where you want to place your list box.

4. After you drop the control onto your worksheet, right-click the control and select Format Control.

5. Click the Control tab to see the configuration options, as shown in Figure 12-22.

6. In the Input Range setting, identify the range that holds the predefined items you want to present as choices in the combo box.

    As you can see in Figure 12-22, this list box is filled with region selections.

7. In the Cell Link box, enter the cell where you want the list box to output its value.

    By default, a list box control outputs the index number of the selected item. This means that if the second item on the list is selected, the number 2 will be output. If the fifth item on the list is selected, the number 5 will be output. Notice in Figure 12-22 that this particular control outputs to cell P2. The Selection Type setting allows users to choose more than one selection in the list box. The choices here are Single, Multi, and Extend. Always leave this setting on Single, as Multi and Extend work only in the VBA environment.

8. (Optional) You can check the 3-D property if you want the control to have a 3-D appearance.

9. Click OK to apply your changes.

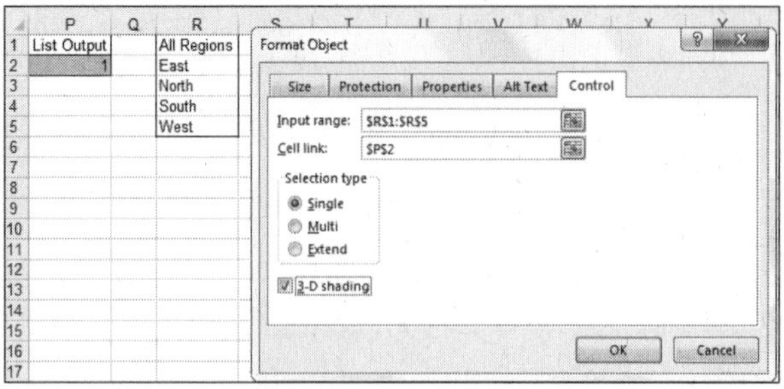

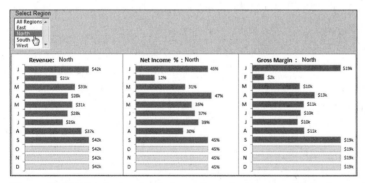

Figure 12-22: Formatting the list box control.

List box example: Controlling multiple charts with one selector

One of the more useful ways to use a list box is to control multiple charts with one selector. Figure 12-23 illustrates an example of this. As a region selection is made in the list box, all three charts are fed the data for that region, adjusting the charts to correspond with the selection made. Happily, all this is done without VBA code, just a handful of formulas and a list box.

Figure 12-23: This list box feeds the region selection to multiple charts, changing each chart to correspond with the selection made.

To create this example, you start with three raw datasets (as shown in Figure 12-24) that contain three categories of data: Revenues, Net Income %, and Gross Margin. Each dataset contains a separate line for each region (including one for All Regions).

	A	B	C	D	E	F	G	H	I	J	K	L	M
5													
6	Revenues	Jan	Feb	Mar	Apr	May	Jun	Jul	Aug	Sep	Oct	Nov	Dec
7	All Regions	98,741	54,621	96,555	109,625	87,936	84,637	81,339	97,281	98,741	98,741	98,741	98,741
8	East	27,474	22,674	35,472	36,292	31,491	27,672	23,853	25,284	27,474	27,474	27,474	27,474
9	North	41,767	20,806	32,633	28,023	31,090	27,873	24,656	36,984	41,767	41,767	41,767	41,767
10	South	18,911	1,125	17,020	34,196	12,989	18,368	23,747	22,087	18,911	18,911	18,911	18,911
11	West	10,590	10,016	11,430	11,115	12,367	10,724	9,082	12,926	10,590	10,590	10,590	10,590
12													
13	Net Income %	Jan	Feb	Mar	Apr	May	Jun	Jul	Aug	Sep	Oct	Nov	Dec
14	All Regions	49.9%	50.6%	48.7%	47.8%	41.4%	47%	52.8%	48.7%	49.9%	49.9%	49.9%	49.9%
15	East	63.1%	53.6%	55.8%	47.4%	41.5%	42%	42.5%	31.7%	63.1%	63.1%	63.1%	63.1%
16	North	45.3%	11.8%	31.0%	47.5%	35.2%	37%	39.1%	29.8%	45.3%	45.3%	45.3%	45.3%
17	South	31.2%	61.7%	41.8%	30.9%	9.0%	33%	56.9%	71.5%	31.2%	31.2%	31.2%	31.2%
18	West	60.1%	75.4%	66.1%	65.2%	79.8%	76%	72.7%	61.9%	60.1%	60.1%	60.1%	60.1%
19													
20	Gross Margin	Jan	Feb	Mar	Apr	May	Jun	Jul	Aug	Sep	Oct	Nov	Dec
21	All Regions	48,508	22,850	44,586	48,340	35,056	37,469	39,881	42,849	48,508	48,508	48,508	48,508
22	East	17,326	12,154	19,799	17,206	13,079	11,605	10,131	8,020	17,326	17,326	17,326	17,326
23	North	18,914	2,455	10,115	13,299	10,938	10,290	9,641	11,019	18,914	18,914	18,914	18,914
24	South	5,904	694	7,115	10,582	1,171	7,339	13,506	15,803	5,904	5,904	5,904	5,904
25	West	6,364	7,547	7,557	7,253	9,867	8,235	6,604	8,005	6,364	6,364	6,364	6,364

Figure 12-24: Start with the raw datasets that contain one line per region.

You then add a list box that outputs the index number of the selected item to cell P2 (see Figure 12-25).

Figure 12-25: Add a list box and note the cell where the output value will be placed.

Next, you create a staging table that will consist of all formulas. In this staging table, you use the Excel's CHOOSE function to select the correct value from the raw data tables based on the selected region.

Tip In Excel, the Choose function returns a value from a specified list of values based on a specified position number. For instance, the formula CHOOSE(3,"Red", "Yellow", "Green", "Blue") returns Green because Green is the third item in the list of values. The formula CHOOSE(1, "Red", "Yellow", "Green", "Blue") returns Red. See Chapter 11 to get a detailed look at the CHOOSE function.

As you can see in Figure 12-26, the CHOOSE formula retrieves the target position number from Cell P2 (the cell where the list box outputs the index number of the selected item) and then matches that position number to the list of cell references given. The cell references come directly from the raw data table.

In the example shown in Figure 12-26, the data that will be returned with this CHOOSE formula is 41767. Why? Because cell P2 contains the number 3, and the third cell reference within the CHOOSE formula is cell B9.

	A	B	O	P
1		J		List Output
2	Revenues	=CHOOSE($P$2,B7,B8,B9,B10,B11)		3
3	Net Income %			
4	Gross Margin			=INDEX(R1:R5,P2)
5				
6	Revenues	Jan		
7	All Regions	98741.4		
8	East	27473.82		
9	North	41767.27		
10	South	18910.81		
11	West	10589.5		

Figure 12-26: Use the CHOOSE function to capture the correct data corresponding to the selected region.

You entered the same type of CHOOSE formula into the Jan column and then copied it across (see Figure 12-27).

	A	B	C
1		J	F
2	Revenues	=CHOOSE($P$2,B7,B8,B9,B10,B11)	=CHOOSE($P$2,C7,C8,C9,C10,C11)
3	Net Income %	=CHOOSE($P$2,B14,B15,B16,B17,B18)	=CHOOSE($P$2,C14,C15,C16,C17,C18)
4	Gross Margin	=CHOOSE($P$2,B21,B22,B23,B24,B25)	=CHOOSE($P$2,C21,C22,C23,C24,C25)

Figure 12-27: Create similar CHOOSE formulas for each row/category of data and then copy the choose formulas across months.

To test that your formulas are working, change the value of cell P2 manually, entering **1**, **2**, **3**, **4**, or **5**. When the formulas work, all that's left to do is create the charts using the staging table.

Note

If Excel functions like CHOOSE or INDEX are a bit intimidating for you, don't worry. There are literally hundreds of ways to use various combinations of form controls and Excel functions to achieve interactive reporting. The examples given in this chapter are designed to give you a sense of how you can incorporate form controls into your dashboards and reports. There are no set rules on which form controls or Excel functions you need to use in your model.

Start with basic improvements to your dashboard, using controls and formulas you're comfortable with. Then gradually try to introduce some of the more complex controls and functions. With a little imagination and creativity, you can take the basics found in this chapter and customize your own dynamic dashboards.

Macro-Charged Reporting

In This Chapter

- Introducing macros
- Recording macros
- Setting up trusted locations for your macros
- Adding macros to your dashboards and reports

A *macro* is essentially a set of instructions or code that you create to tell Excel to execute any number of actions. In Excel, macros can be written or recorded. The key word here is *recorded*.

Recording a macro is like programming a phone number into your cell phone. You first manually dial and save a number. Then when you want, you can redial those numbers with the touch of a button. Just as on a cell phone, you can record your actions in Excel while you perform them. While you record, Excel gets busy in the background, translating your keystrokes and mouse clicks to written code (also known as *Visual Basic for Applications, VBA*). After a macro is recorded, you can play back those actions anytime you want.

In this chapter, you explore macros and discover how to simplify your life by using macros to automate recurring processes.

Why Use a Macro?

Macros can help you solve some common data-analysis problems.

> ➤ **Problem 1: Repetitive tasks.** As each new month rolls around, you have to *make the donuts* (that is, crank out those reports). You have to import that data. You have to update those pivot tables. You have to delete those columns, and so on. Wouldn't it be nice if you could fire up a macro and have those more redundant parts of your dashboard processes done automatically?

> ➤ **Problem 2: Human error.** When you do hand-to-hand combat with Excel, you're bound to make mistakes. When you're repeatedly applying formulas, sorting, and moving things around manually, there's always that risk of catastrophe. Add to that the looming deadlines

and constant requests for changes, and your error rate goes up. Why not calmly record a macro, ensure that everything is running correctly, and then forget it? The macro is sure to perform every action the same way every time you run it, reducing the chance for errors.

➤ **Problem 3: Awkward navigation.** Remember that you're creating these dashboards and reports for an audience that probably has a limited knowledge of Excel. If your reports are a bit too difficult to use and navigate, you'll slowly lose support for your cause. It's always help-ful to make your dashboard more user-friendly. Here are some ideas for macros that make things easier for everyone:

- A macro to format and print a worksheet or range of worksheets at the touch of a button

- Macros that navigate a multisheet worksheet with a navigation page or with a *go to* but-ton for each sheet in your workbook

- A macro that saves the open document in a specified location and then closes the appli-cation at the touch of a button.

Obviously, you can perform each of the preceding examples in Excel without the aid of a macro. However, your audience will appreciate the little touches that help make perusing your dashboard a bit more pleasant.

Recording Your First Macro

If you're starting off with dashboard automation, it's unlikely that you will be able to write the VBA code by hand. Without full knowledge of Excel's object model and syntax, writing the code needed would be impossible for most beginning users. This is where recording a macro comes in handy. You record the desired action and then run the macro each time you want that action to be performed.

On the Web | **To start creating your first macro, open the Chapter 13 Samples.xlsm file found in the sample files for this book. When the file is open, go to the Recording Your First Macro tab.**

To begin, you first need to unhide the Developer tab. The full macro toolset in Excel 2013 is found on the Developer tab, which is initially hidden. You have to explicitly tell Excel to make it visible. To enable the Developer tab, follow these steps:

1. Go to the Ribbon and select the File tab.

2. To open the Excel Options dialog box, click the Options button.

3. Click the Customize Ribbon button.

   In the list on the right, you see all the available tabs.

4. Select the Developer tab (see Figure 13-1).

5. Click OK.

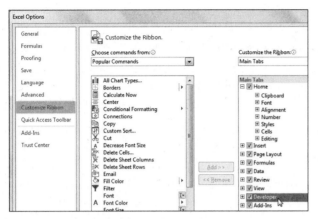

Figure 13-1: Enabling the Developer tab.

When you see the Developer tab on the Ribbon, you can select it and click the Record Macro command. This opens the Record Macro dialog box, as shown in Figure 13-2.

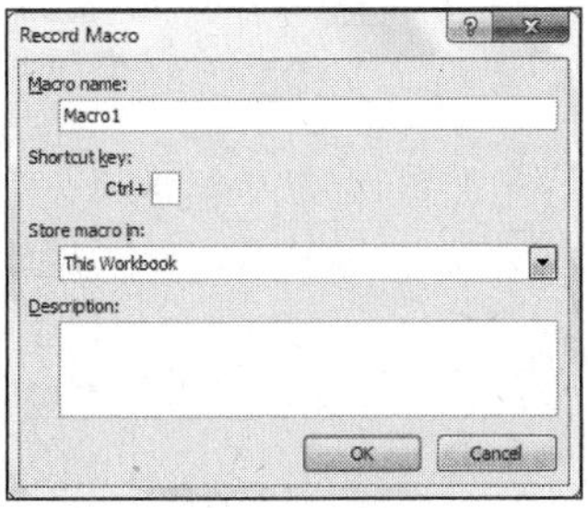

Figure 13-2: The Record Macro dialog box.

Here are the four fields in the Record Macro dialog box:

➤ **Macro Name:** Excel gives a default name to your macro, such as Macro1, but it's best practice to give your macro a name more descriptive of what it actually does. For example, you might name a macro that formats a generic table as AddDataBars.

➤ **Shortcut Key:** (Optional) Every macro needs an *event*, or something to happen, in order for it to run. This event can be a button press; a workbook opening; or, in this case, a keystroke combination. When you assign a shortcut key to your macro, entering that combination of keys triggers the macro to run. You don't need to enter a shortcut key to run the macro.

➤ **Store Macro In:** This Workbook is the default option. Storing your macro in This Workbook simply means that the macro is stored along with the active Excel file. The next time you open that particular workbook, the macro will be available. Similarly, if you send the workbook to another user, that user can run the macro as well (provided the macro security is properly set by your user — but more on that later).

➤ **Description:** (Optional) Useful if you have numerous macros in a spreadsheet or if you need to give a user a detailed description about what the macro does.

Follow these steps to start recording an action:

1. Enter the name in the Macro Name field.

   For this example, type **AddDataBars**.

2. Select This Workbook in the Store Macro In option (see Figure 13-3).

3. Click OK.

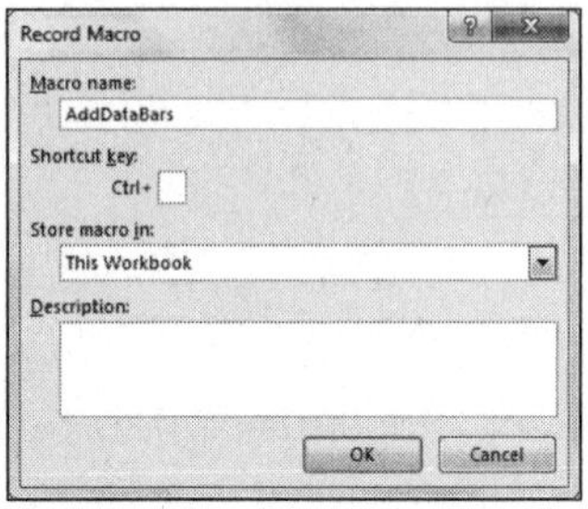

Figure 13-3: Start recording a new Macro called AddDataBars.

Excel is now recording your actions.

While Excel is recording, you can perform any actions you want. The following example records a macro to add data bars to a column of numbers.

1. Highlight cells C1:C21.

2. Go to the Home tab and select Conditional Formatting→New Rule.

   The New Formatting Rule dialog box opens.

3. In the New Formatting Rule dialog box, go to the Format Style drop-down menu and select Data Bar.

   The New Formatting Rule dialog box now shows a new set of options related to Data Bars.

4. Place a check in the Show Bar Only check box.

5. Click OK to apply your change.

6. Go to the Develop tab and click the Stop Recording command.

At this point, Excel stops recording. You now have a macro that replaces the data in C1:C21 with data bars.

Now, record a new macro to remove the data bars:

1. Go to the Developer tab and click the Record Macro command.

2. Enter **RemoveDataBars** in the Macro Name field and select This Workbook in the Store Macro In option (see Figure 13-4). Click OK.

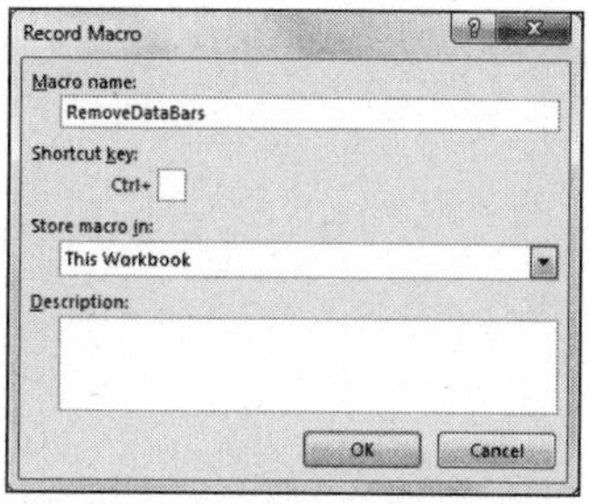

Figure 13-4: Start recording a new macro called RemoveDataBars.

3. Highlight cells C1:C21.

4. Go to the Home tab and select Conditional Formatting➜Clear Rules➜Clear Rules from Selected Cells.

5. Go to the Developer tab and click the Stop Recording command.

    Excel stops recording.

You now have a new macro that removes conditional formatting rules from cells C1:C21.

Running your macros

To see your macros in action, follow these steps:

1. Select the Macros command from the Developer tab.

    The dialog box in Figure 13-5 activates, allowing you to select the macro you want to run.

2. Select the AddDataBars macro.

3. Click the Run button.

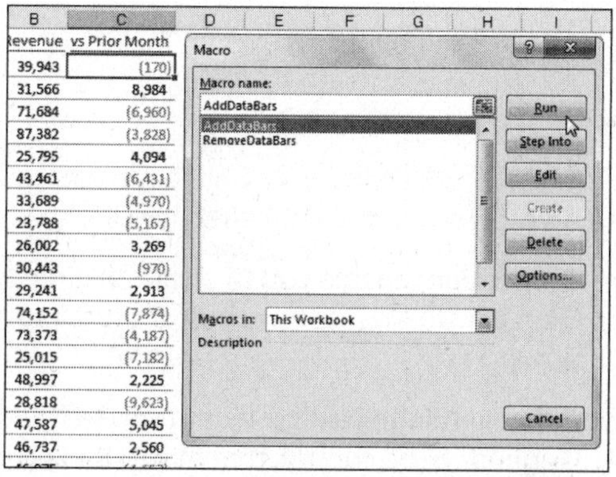

Figure 13-5: Use the Macro dialog box to select a macro and run it.

If all goes well, the AddDataBars macro plays back your actions to a T and applies the data bars as designed (see Figure 13-6).

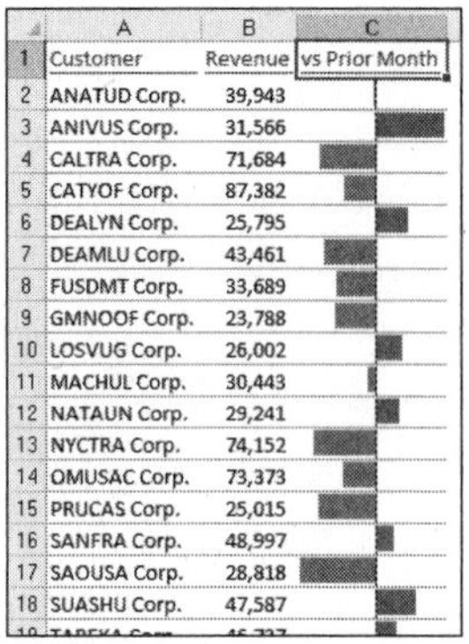

	A	B	C
1	Customer	Revenue	vs Prior Month
2	ANATUD Corp.	39,943	
3	ANIVUS Corp.	31,566	
4	CALTRA Corp.	71,684	
5	CATYOF Corp.	87,382	
6	DEALYN Corp.	25,795	
7	DEAMLU Corp.	43,461	
8	FUSDMT Corp.	33,689	
9	GMNOOF Corp.	23,788	
10	LOSVUG Corp.	26,002	
11	MACHUL Corp.	30,443	
12	NATAUN Corp.	29,241	
13	NYCTRA Corp.	74,152	
14	OMUSAC Corp.	73,373	
15	PRUCAS Corp.	25,015	
16	SANFRA Corp.	48,997	
17	SAOUSA Corp.	28,818	
18	SUASHU Corp.	47,587	

Figure 13-6: Your macro applied data bars automatically!

You can now call up the Macro dialog box again and test the RemoveDataBars macro shown in Figure 13-7.

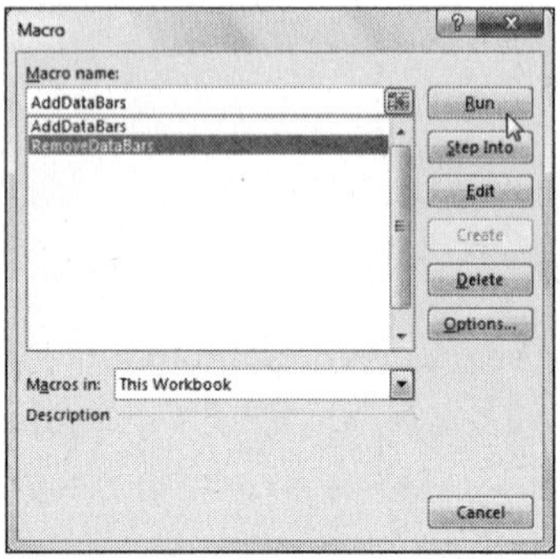

Figure 13-7: The RemoveDataBars macro will remove the applied data bars.

Assigning a macro to a button

When you create macros, you want to give your audience a clear and easy way to run each macro. A button, used directly in the dashboard or report, can provide a simple but effective UI.

Excel Form controls (refer to Chapter 12 for more information) enable you to create UI directly on your worksheets, simplifying work for your users. Form controls range from buttons (the most-commonly used control) to scroll bars and check boxes.

For a macro, you can place a Form control in a worksheet and then assign that macro to it — that is, a macro you've already recorded. When a macro is assigned to the control, that macro is executed, or *played*, each time the control is clicked.

Take a moment to create buttons for the two macros (AddDataBars and RemoveDataBars) you created earlier. Here's how:

1. Click the Insert drop-down list under the Developer tab.

2. Select the Button Form control (see Figure 13-8).

3. Click the location you want to place your button. When you drop the button control into your worksheet, the Assign Macro dialog box, shown in Figure 13-9, opens and asks you to assign a macro to this button.

4. Select the macro that you want to assign. In this case, you can select the AddDataBars macro and then click OK.

5. Repeat Steps 1 through 4 for the RemoveDataBars macro.

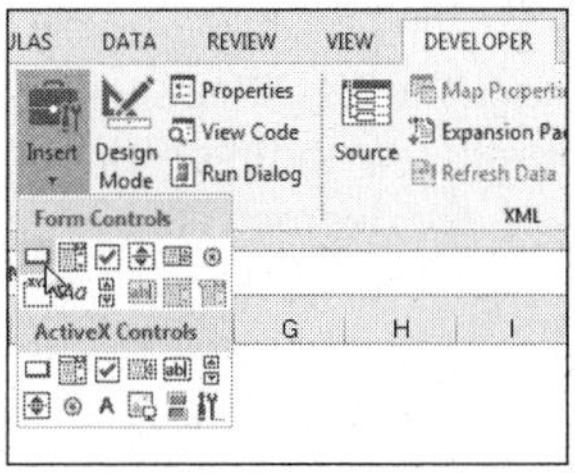

Figure 13-8: You can find the Form Controls in the Developer tab.

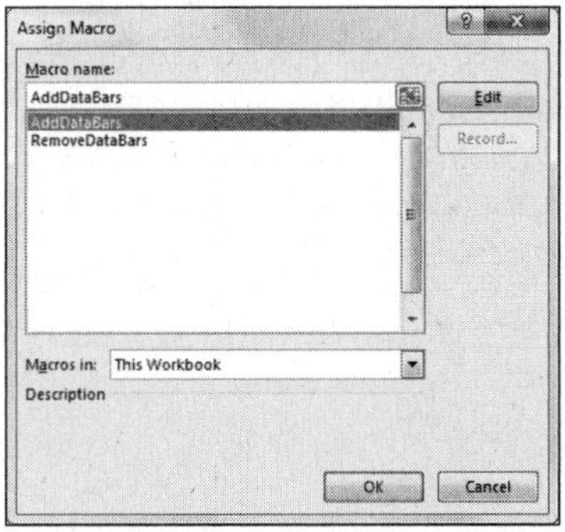

Figure 13-9: Assign a macro to the newly added button.

At this point, you have two buttons that run your macros. Keep in mind that all the controls in the Forms toolbar work the same way as the Command button — you assign a macro to run when the control is selected.

Tip

The buttons you create come with a default name, such as Button3. To rename your button, right-click the button and then select Edit Text.

> ## ▶ Form controls versus ActiveX controls
>
> Although the Form controls and ActiveX controls look similar, they're quite different:
>
> - Form controls are designed specifically for use on a worksheet
> - ActiveX controls are typically used on Excel UserForms.
>
> As a general rule, you want to use Form controls when working on a worksheet. Why? Form controls need less overhead, so they perform better, and configuring Form controls is far easier than configuring their ActiveX counterparts.

Enabling Macros in Excel 2013

With the release of Office 2013, Microsoft introduced significant changes to its Office security model. One of the most significant changes is the concept of Trusted Documents. Without getting into the technical minutia, a Trusted Document is essentially a workbook you have deemed safe by enabling macros.

Viewing the new Excel security message

If you open a workbook that contains macros in Excel 2013, you'll get a message in the form of a yellow bar under the Ribbon stating that Macros (active content) has, in effect, been disabled.

If you click Enable, the workbook automatically becomes a *Trusted Document*. This means you will no longer be prompted to enable the content as long as you open that file on your computer. The idea is that if you told Excel that you trust a particular workbook by enabling macros, it's highly likely that you'll enable macros each time you open it. Thus Excel remembers that you've enabled macros before and inhibits any further messages about macros (for that workbook).

This is great news for you and your clients. After enabling your macros just one time, they won't be annoyed by the constant messages about macros, and you won't have to worry that your macro-enabled dashboard will fall flat because macros have been disabled.

Setting up trusted locations

If the thought of any macro message coming up (even one time) unnerves you, you can set up a trusted location for your files. A *trusted location* is a directory that is deemed a safe zone where only trusted workbooks are placed. A trusted location allows you and your clients to run a macro-enabled workbook with no security restrictions as long as the workbook is in that location.

To set up a trusted location, follow these steps:

1. Select the Macro Security button on the Developer tab.

2. Click the Trusted Locations button.

   This opens the Trusted Locations menu (see Figure 13-10). You see all the directories that Excel considers trusted.

3. Click the Add New Location button.

4. Click Browse to find and specify the directory that will be considered a trusted location.

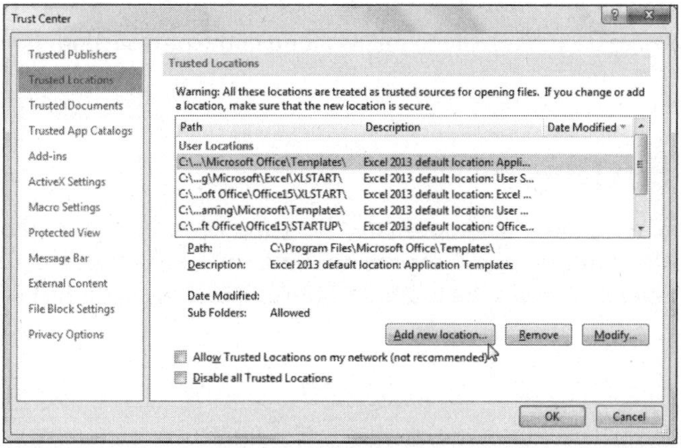

Figure 13-10: The Trusted Locations menu allows you to add directories that are considered trusted.

▶ Macro-enabled file extensions

Microsoft has created a separate file extension for workbooks that contain macros.

Excel 2007, 2010, and 2013 workbooks have the standard file extension `.xlsx`. Files with the `.xlsx` extension cannot contain macros. If your workbook contains macros and you then save that workbook as an `.xlsx` file, your macros are removed automatically. Of course, Excel warns you that macro content will be disabled when saving a workbook with macros as an `.xlsx` file.

If you want to retain the macros, you must save your file as an *Excel Macro-Enabled Workbook*. This gives your file an `.xlsm` extension. The idea is that all workbooks with an `.xlsx` file extension are automatically known to be safe, whereas you can recognize `.xlsm` files as a potential threat.

After you specify a trusted location, all Excel files opened from this location will have macros automatically enabled. The idea is to have your clients specify a trusted location and use your Excel files from there.

Excel Macro Examples

Covering the fundamentals of building and using macros is one thing. Coming up with good ways to incorporate them into your reporting processes is another. Take a moment to review a few examples of how you can implement macros in your dashboards and reports.

On the Web

Open the Chapter 13 `Samples.xlsm` **file to follow along in the next section.**

Building navigation buttons

The most common use of macros is navigation. Workbooks that have many worksheets or tabs can be frustrating to navigate. To help your audience, you can create some sort of switchboard, such as the one shown in Figure 13-11. When a user clicks the Example 1 button, he's taken to the Example 1 sheet.

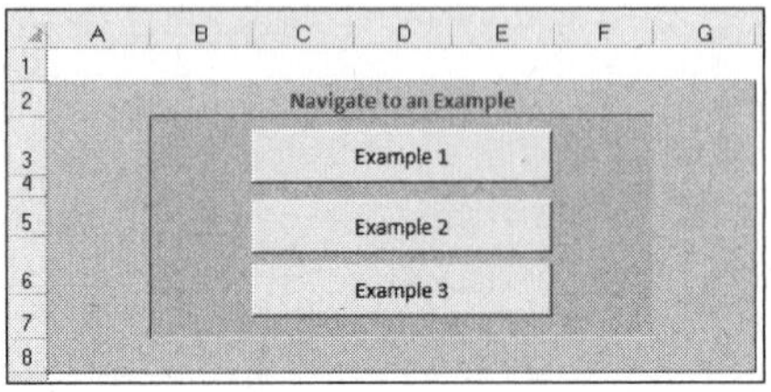

	A	B	C	D	E	F	G
1							
2				Navigate to an Example			
3				Example 1			
4							
5				Example 2			
6				Example 3			
7							
8							

Figure 13-11: Use macros to build buttons that help users navigate your reports.

Creating a macro to navigate to a sheet is quite simple.

1. Start at the sheet that will become your switchboard or starting point.

2. Start recording a macro.

3. While recording, click the destination sheet (the sheet this macro will navigate to).

4. After you click in the destination sheet, stop recording the macro.

5. Assign the macro to a button.

Tip

Excel has a built-in hyperlink feature, allowing you to convert the contents of a cell into a hyperlink that links to another location. That location can be a separate Excel workbook, a website, or even another tab in the current workbook. Although using a hyperlink may be easier than setting up a macro, you can't apply a hyperlink to Form controls (like buttons). Instead of a button, you use text to let users know where they'll go when they click the link.

Dynamically rearranging pivot table data

In the example illustrated in Figure 13-12, macros allow a user to change the perspective of the chart simply by selecting any one of the buttons shown.

Cross-Ref

For more information about pivot tables, see Chapter 14. For more information about pivot charts, see to Chapter 15.

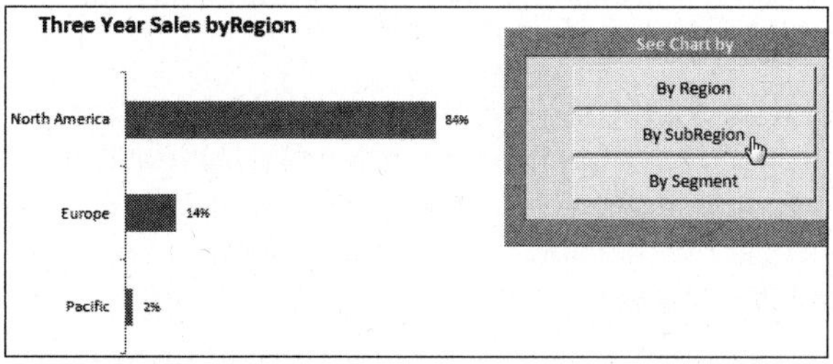

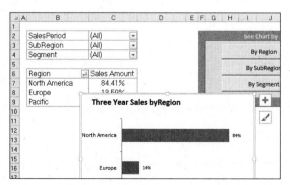

Figure 13-12: This report allows users to choose their perspective.

Figure 13-13 reveals that the chart is actually a pivot chart tied to a pivot table. The recorded macros assigned to each button are doing nothing more than rearranging the pivot table to slice the data using various pivot fields.

Figure 13-13: The macros behind these buttons rearrange the data fields in a pivot table.

Here are the high-level steps needed to create this type of setup:

1. Create your pivot table and a pivot chart.

2. Start recording a macro.

3. While recording, move a pivot field from one area of the pivot table to the other. When you're done, stop recording the macro.

4. Record another macro to move the data field back to its original position.

5. After both macros are set up, assign each one to a separate button.

You can fire your new macros in turn to see your pivot field dynamically move back and forth.

Offering one-touch reporting options

The last two examples demonstrate that you can record any action that you find of value. That is, if you think users would appreciate a certain feature being automated for them, why not record a macro to do so?

In Figure 13-14, notice that you can filter the pivot table for the top or bottom 20 customers. Because the steps to filter a pivot table for the top and bottom 20 have been recorded, anyone can get the benefit of this functionality without knowing how to do it themselves. Also, recording specific actions allows you to manage risk a bit. That is, you'll know that your users will interact with your reports in a method that has been developed and tested by you.

This not only saves them time and effort but it also allows users who don't know how to take these actions to benefit from them.

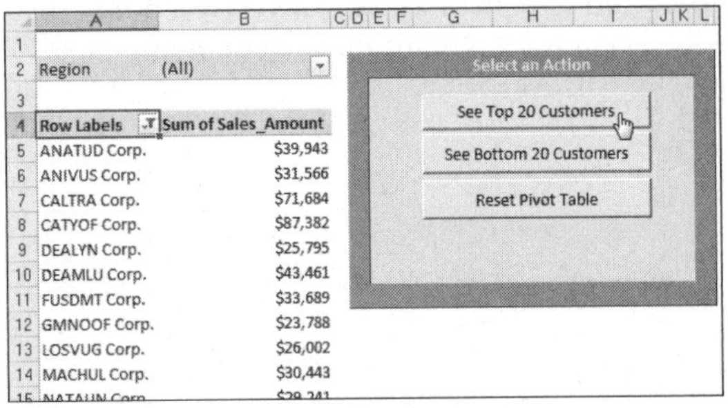

Figure 13-14: Offering prerecorded views saves time and effort and allows users who don't know how to use advanced features to benefit from them.

Tip   **Feel free to visit Chapter 14 for a refresher on how to create the top and bottom reports you see in Figure 13-14.**

Figure 13-15 demonstrates how you can give your audience a quick-and-easy way to see the same data on different charts. Don't laugh too quickly at the uselessness of this example. It's not uncommon to be asked to see the same data in different ways. Instead of taking up real estate, just record a macro that changes the Chart Type of the chart. Your clients will be able to switch views to their hearts' content.

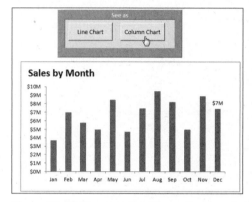

Figure 13-15: You can give your audience a choice in how they view data.

Pivot Table Driven Dashboards

Using Pivot Tables

In This Chapter

- Using pivot tables as your data model
- Creating and modifying a pivot table
- Customizing pivot table fields, formats, and functions
- Filtering data using Pivot Table views

In Chapter 11, we discuss using a data model as the foundation for your dashboards and reports. This data model helps you to organize your information into three logical layers: data, analysis, and presentation. As you discover in this chapter, pivot tables lend themselves nicely to this data model concept. With pivot tables, you can build data models that are easy to set up and that can then be updated with a simple press of a button. So you can spend less time maintaining your dashboards and reports and more time doing other things. No utility in Excel enables you to achieve a more efficient data model than a pivot table.

Introducing the Pivot Table

A pivot table is a tool that allows you to create an interactive view of your source data (commonly referred to as a *pivot table report*). A pivot table can help transform endless rows and columns of numbers into a meaningful presentation of data. You can easily create groupings of summary items — for example, combine Northern Region totals with Western Region totals, filter that data using a variety of views, and insert special formulas that perform new calculations.

Pivot tables get their namesake from your ability to interactively drag and drop fields within the pivot table to dynamically change (or pivot) the perspective, giving you an entirely new view using the same source data. You can then display subtotals and interactively drill down to any level of detail that you want. Note that the data itself doesn't change and is not connected to the pivot table. The reason a pivot table is so well suited to a dashboard is that you can quickly update the view of your pivot table by changing the source data that it points to. This allows you to set up both your analysis and presentation layers at one time. You can then simply press a button to update your presentation.

Anatomy of a pivot table

A pivot table is composed of four areas: Values, Row Labels, Column Labels, and Filters. The data you place in these areas defines both the use and presentation of the data in your pivot table. We now discuss the function of each of these four areas.

Values area

The Values area allows you to calculate and count the source data. In Figure 14-1, it is the large rectangular area below and to the right of the column and row headings. In this example, the Values area contains a sum of the values in the Sales Amount field.

The data fields that you drag and drop here are typically those that you want to measure — fields, such as the sum of revenue, a count of the units, or an average of the prices.

Region	(All)			
Sales Amount	Segment			
Market	Accessories	Bikes	Clothing	Components
Australia	23,974	1,351,873	43,232	203,791
Canada	119,303	11,714,700	383,022	2,246,255
Central	46,551	6,782,978	155,874	947,448
France	48,942	3,597,879	129,508	871,125
Germany	35,681	1,602,487	75,593	337,787
Northeast	51,246	5,690,285	163,442	1,051,702
Northwest	53,308	10,484,495	201,052	1,784,207
Southeast	45,736	6,737,556	165,689	959,337
Southwest	110,080	15,430,281	364,099	2,693,568
United Kingdom	43,180	3,435,134	120,225	712,588

Values Area

Figure 14-1: The Values area of a pivot table calculates and counts the data.

Row Labels area

The Row Labels area is shown in Figure 14-2. Dragging a data field into the Row Labels area displays the unique values from that field down the rows of the left side of the pivot table. The Row Labels area typically has at least one field, although it's possible to have no fields.

The types of data fields that you drop here include those that you want to group and categorize, such as products, names, and locations.

Column Labels area

The Column Labels area contains headings that stretch across the top of columns in the pivot table, as you can see in Figure 14-3. In this example, the Column Labels area contains the list of unique business segments.

Region	(All)		

Sales Amount	Segment			
Market	Accessories	Bikes	Clothing	Components
Australia	23,974	1,351,873	43,232	203,791
Canada	119,303	11,714,700	383,022	2,246,255
Central	46,551	6,782,978	155,874	947,448
France	48,942	3,597,879	129,508	871,125
Germany	35,681	1,602,487	75,593	337,787
Northeast	51,246	5,690,285	163,442	1,051,702
Northwest	53,308	10,484,495	201,052	1,784,207
Southeast	45,736	6,737,556	165,689	959,337
Southwest	110,080	15,430,281	364,099	2,693,568
United Kingdom	43,180	3,435,134	120,225	712,588

Row Area

Figure 14-2: The Row Labels area of a pivot table gives you a row-oriented perspective.

Column Area

Region	(All)		

Sales Amount	Segment			
Market	Accessories	Bikes	Clothing	Components
Australia	23,974	1,351,873	43,232	203,791
Canada	119,303	11,714,700	383,022	2,246,255
Central	46,551	6,782,978	155,874	947,448
France	48,942	3,597,879	129,508	871,125
Germany	35,681	1,602,487	75,593	337,787
Northeast	51,246	5,690,285	163,442	1,051,702
Northwest	53,308	10,484,495	201,052	1,784,207
Southeast	45,736	6,737,556	165,689	959,337
Southwest	110,080	15,430,281	364,099	2,693,568
United Kingdom	43,180	3,435,134	120,225	712,588

Figure 14-3: The Column Labels area of a pivot table gives you a column-oriented perspective.

Placing a data field into the Column Labels area displays the unique values from that field in a column-oriented perspective. The Column Labels area is ideal for creating a data matrix or showing trends over time.

Filter area

At the top of the pivot table, the Filter area is an optional set of one or more drop-down controls. In Figure 14-4, the Filter area contains the Region field, and the pivot table is set to show all regions.

Placing data fields into the Filter area allows you to change the views for the entire pivot table based on your selection. The types of data fields that you drop here include those that you want to isolate and focus on — for example, region, line of business, and employees.

Filter Area

Region	(All)

Sales Amount	Segment			
Market	Accessories	Bikes	Clothing	Components
Australia	23,974	1,351,873	43,232	203,791
Canada	119,303	11,714,700	383,022	2,246,255
Central	46,551	6,782,978	155,874	947,448
France	48,942	3,597,879	129,508	871,125
Germany	35,681	1,602,487	75,593	337,787
Northeast	51,246	5,690,285	163,442	1,051,702
Northwest	53,308	10,484,495	201,052	1,784,207
Southeast	45,736	6,737,556	165,689	959,337
Southwest	110,080	15,430,281	364,099	2,693,568
United Kingdom	43,180	3,435,134	120,225	712,588

Figure 14-4: The Filter area allows you to easily apply filters to your pivot table, focusing on specific data items.

Creating the basic pivot table

Now that you have a good understanding of the structure of a pivot table, follow these steps to create your first pivot table.

On the Web

You can find the example file for this chapter on this book's companion website at www.wiley.com/go/exceldr **in the workbook named Chapter 14 Samples.xlsx.**

1. In the Chapter 14 sample file, go to the tab called Sample Data and click any single cell inside the source data (the table you'll use to feed the pivot table).

2. Click the Insert tab on the Ribbon.

    Find the PivotTable icon, as shown in Figure 14-5.

3. From the drop-down list under the PivotTable icon, select PivotTable.

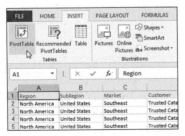

Figure 14-5: Start a pivot table by clicking the PivotTable icon found on the Insert tab.

This opens the Create PivotTable dialog box, as shown in Figure 14-6.

4. Specify the location of your source data.

5. Specify the worksheet where you want to put the pivot table.

In Figure 14-6, note that the default location for a new pivot table is New Worksheet. This means your pivot table will be placed in a new worksheet within the current workbook. To change this, select the Existing Worksheet option and specify the worksheet in which you want to place the pivot table.

Figure 14-6: The Create PivotTable dialog box.

6. Click OK.

At this point, you have an empty pivot table report on a new worksheet.

Laying out the pivot table

Next to the empty pivot table, you see the PivotTable Fields List dialog box, as shown in Figure 14-7.

You can add the fields you need into the pivot table by dragging and dropping the field names to one of the four areas found in the PivotTable Fields List — Filters, Columns, Rows, and Values.

Note **If clicking the pivot table doesn't activate the PivotTable Fields List dialog box, you can manually activate it by right-clicking anywhere inside the pivot table and selecting Show Field List. Alternatively, you can go to the Ribbon, click Option, and then select Field List in the Show group.**

Now before you start dropping fields into the various areas, ask yourself two questions: "What am I measuring?" and "How do I want to see it?" The answers to these questions will help guide you in determining which fields go where.

For your first pivot table example, you want to measure the dollar sales by market. This tells you that you need to work with the Sales Amount field and the Market field.

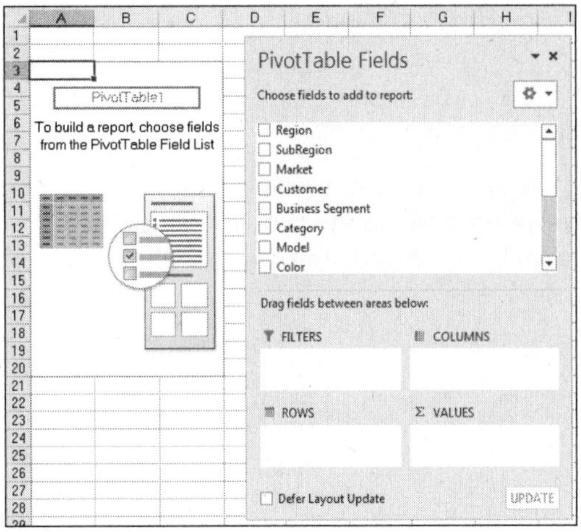

Figure 14-7: The PivotTable Fields List dialog box.

How do you want to view that? You want markets to go down the left side of the report and the sales amount to be calculated next to each market. You need to add the Market field to the Row Labels area and the Sales Amount field to the Values area.

1. In the fields list, select the Market field (see Figure 14-8).

   Now that you have regions in your pivot table, it's time to add the dollar sales.

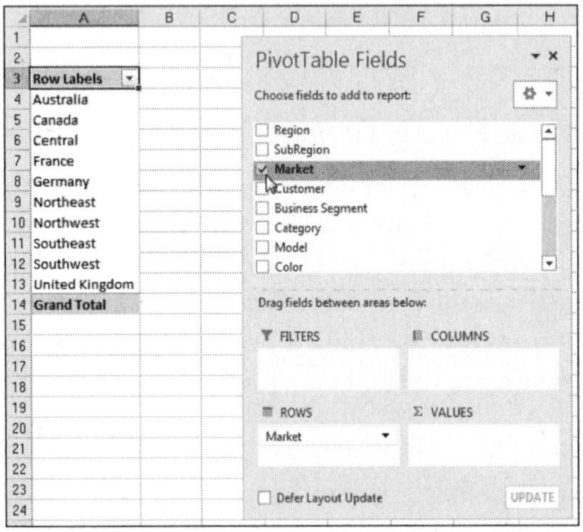

Figure 14-8: Select the Market field to add it to the fields selector list.

2. In the fields selector area, select the Sales Amount field (see Figure 14-9).

	A	B	C	D	E	F	G
1							
2							
3	**Row Labels**	**Sum of Sales Amount**					
4	Australia	1622869.422					
5	Canada	14463280.15					
6	Central	7932851.609					
7	France	4647454.207					
8	Germany	2051547.728					
9	Northeast	6956673.913					
10	Northwest	12523062.94					
11	Southeast	7908318.256					
12	Southwest	18598026.98					
13	United Kingdom	4311126.886					
14	**Grand Total**	**81015212.09**					

PivotTable Fields

Choose fields to add to report:

- ☐ SalesDate
- ☐ SalesPeriod
- ☐ ListPrice
- ☐ UnitPrice
- ☐ OrderQty
- ☑ Sales Amount

MORE TABLES...

Drag fields between areas below:

▼ FILTERS

▥ COLUMNS

▤ ROWS — Market

Σ VALUES — Sum of Sales Amount

☐ Defer Layout Update   UPDATE

Figure 14-9: Add the Sales Amount field.

Note

Placing a check next to any field that is non-numeric (text or date) automatically places that field into the Row Labels area of the pivot table. Placing a check next to any field that is numeric automatically places that field in the Values area of the pivot table.

One more thing: When you add new fields, you may find it difficult to see all the fields in the box for each area. You can expand the PivotTable Fields List dialog box by clicking and dragging the borders of the dialog box to avoid that problem.

As you can see, you have just analyzed the sales for each market in just nine steps! That's an amazing feat, considering you start with over 60,000 rows of data. With a little formatting, this modest pivot table can become the starting point for a dashboard or report.

Modifying the pivot table

Now here's the wonderful thing about pivot tables. For your data model, you can add as many analysis layers as possible by changing or rearranging the fields in your source data table. Say that you want to show the dollar sales each market earned by business segment. Because your pivot table already contains the Market and Sales Amount fields, all you have to add is the Business Segment field.

So simply click anywhere on your pivot table to reactivate the PivotTable Fields List dialog box and then select the Business Segment field. Figure 14-10 illustrates what your pivot table now looks like.

Note

If clicking the pivot table doesn't activate the PivotTable Fields List dialog box, you can manually activate it by right-clicking anywhere inside the pivot table and selecting Show Field List.

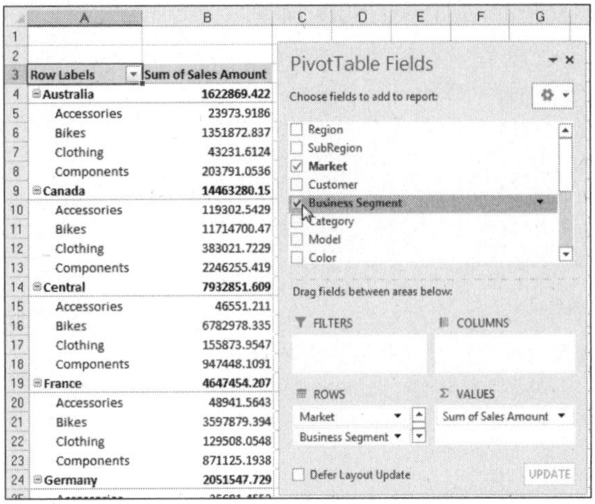

Figure 14-10: Adding a new analysis layer to your data model is as easy as selecting another field.

What if this layout doesn't work for you? Maybe you want to see business segments listed at the top of the pivot table results. No problem. Simply drag the Business Segment field from the Row Labels area to the Column Labels area. As you can see in Figure 14-11, this instantly restructures the pivot table to your specifications.

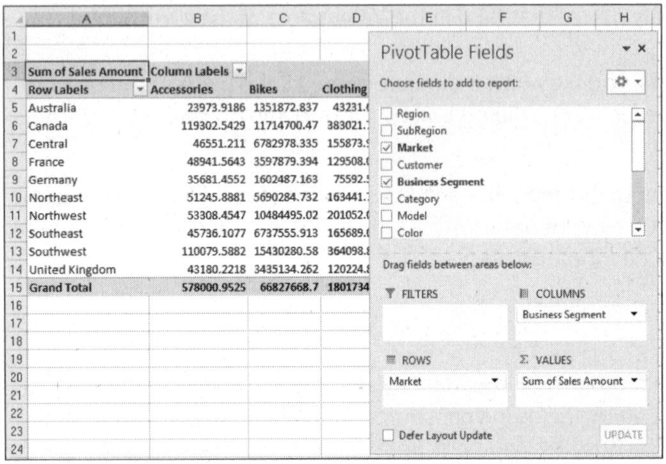

Figure 14-11: Your business segments are now column-oriented.

Changing the pivot table view

Often you're asked to produce reports for one particular region, market, product, and so on. Instead of working hours and hours building separate pivot tables for every possible scenario, you can leverage pivot tables to help create multiple views of the same data. For example, you can do so by creating a region filter in your pivot table.

Click anywhere on your pivot table to reactivate the PivotTable Fields List dialog box and then drag the Region field to the Filter area. This adds a drop-down control to your pivot table, as shown in Figure 14-12. You can then use this control to view one particular region at a time.

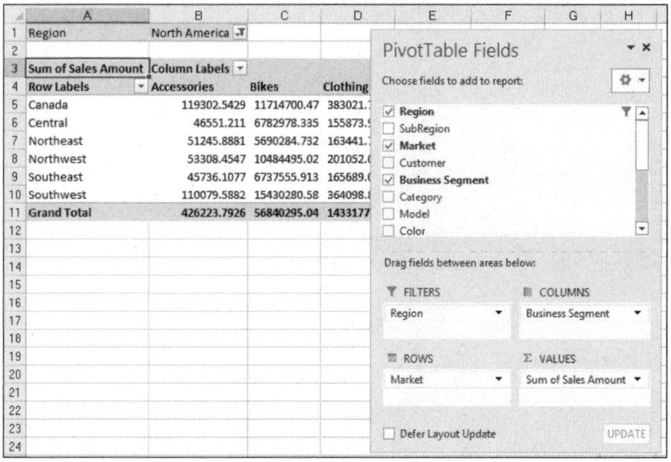

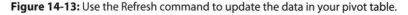

Figure 14-12: Add the Region field to view data for a specific geographic area.

Updating your pivot table

As time goes by, your data may change and grow with newly added rows and columns. You use the Refresh command to update your pivot table with these changes. To do so, simply right-click inside the pivot table and select Refresh, as demonstrated in Figure 14-13.

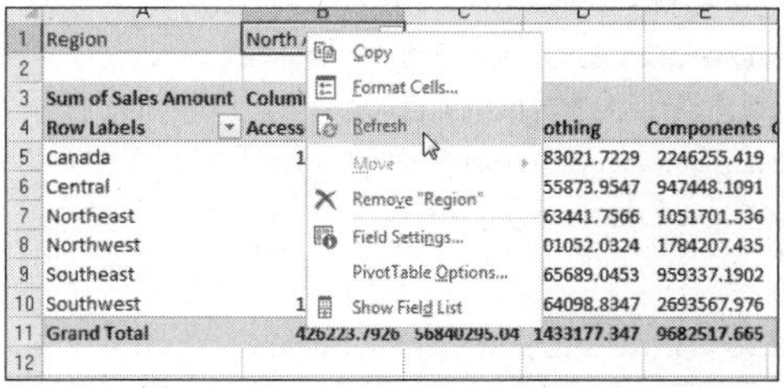

Figure 14-13: Use the Refresh command to update the data in your pivot table.

Sometimes, the source data that feeds your pivot table changes in structure. For example, you may want to add or delete rows or columns from your data table. These types of changes then affect the range of your data source, not just a few data items in the table.

In this case, a simple update of your pivot table data won't do. You have to update the range that is captured by the pivot table. Here's how:

1. Click anywhere inside your pivot table to activate the PivotTable Tools context tab in the Ribbon.

2. Click the Analyze tab.

3. Click the Change Data Source button, as demonstrated in Figure 14-14.

4. Change the range selection to include any new rows or columns (see Figure 14-15).

5. Click OK.

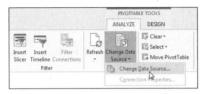

Figure 14-14: Changing the data range that feeds your pivot table.

Figure 14-15: Select the new range that feeds your pivot table.

▶ Pivot tables and worksheet bloat

It's important to understand that pivot tables do come with space and memory implications for your dashboards and reports. When you create a pivot table, Excel takes a snapshot of your source data and stores it in a pivot cache. A *pivot cache* is essentially a memory container that holds this snapshot of your data. Each pivot table that you create from a separate data source creates its own pivot cache, which increases your workbook's memory usage and file size. The increase in memory usage and file size depends on the size of the original data source that Excel duplicates to create the pivot cache.

Simple enough, right? Well, here's the rub: You often need to create separate pivot tables from the same data source in order to create two distinct analysis layers in your data model. If you create two pivot tables from the data source, Excel automatically creates a new pivot cache even though one may already exist for the same data source. This means that you're bloating your worksheet with redundant data each time you create a new pivot table using the same data source.

To work around this potential problem, you can use the copy and paste commands. That's right; simply copying a pivot table and pasting it somewhere else creates another pivot table, without duplicating the pivot cache. This enables you to create multiple pivot tables that use the same source data, with negligible increase in memory and file size.

Customizing Your Pivot Table

The pivot tables you create often need to be tweaked in order to get the look and feel that you're looking for. In this section, we cover some of the ways that you can customize your pivot tables to suit your dashboard's needs.

Changing the pivot table layout

Excel 2013 gives you a choice in the layout of your data in a pivot table. The three layouts, shown side by side in Figure 14-16, are the Compact Form, Outline Form, and Tabular Form. Although no layout stands out as being better than the others, most people prefer using the Tabular Form layout because it seems easiest to read, and it's the layout that most people who have seen pivot tables in the past are used to.

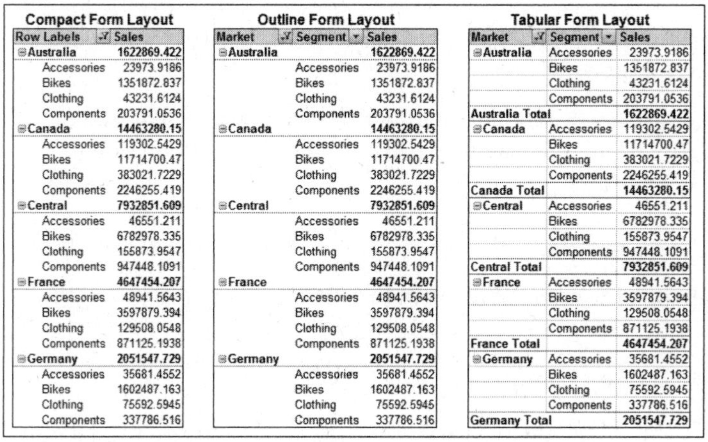

Compact Form Layout

Row Labels	Sales
Australia	**1622869.422**
Accessories	23973.9186
Bikes	1351872.837
Clothing	43231.6124
Components	203791.0536
Canada	**14463280.15**
Accessories	119302.5429
Bikes	11714700.47
Clothing	383021.7229
Components	2246255.419
Central	**7932851.609**
Accessories	46551.211
Bikes	6782978.335
Clothing	155873.9547
Components	947448.1091
France	**4647454.207**
Accessories	48941.5643
Bikes	3597879.394
Clothing	129508.0548
Components	871125.1938
Germany	**2051547.729**
Accessories	35681.4552
Bikes	1602487.163
Clothing	75592.5945
Components	337786.516

Outline Form Layout

Market	Segment	Sales
Australia		**1622869.422**
	Accessories	23973.9186
	Bikes	1351872.837
	Clothing	43231.6124
	Components	203791.0536
Canada		**14463280.15**
	Accessories	119302.5429
	Bikes	11714700.47
	Clothing	383021.7229
	Components	2246255.419
Central		**7932851.609**
	Accessories	46551.211
	Bikes	6782978.335
	Clothing	155873.9547
	Components	947448.1091
France		**4647454.207**
	Accessories	48941.5643
	Bikes	3597879.394
	Clothing	129508.0548
	Components	871125.1938
Germany		**2051547.729**
	Accessories	35681.4552
	Bikes	1602487.163
	Clothing	75592.5945
	Components	337786.516

Tabular Form Layout

Market	Segment	Sales
Australia	Accessories	23973.9186
	Bikes	1351872.837
	Clothing	43231.6124
	Components	203791.0536
Australia Total		**1622869.422**
Canada	Accessories	119302.5429
	Bikes	11714700.47
	Clothing	383021.7229
	Components	2246255.419
Canada Total		**14463280.15**
Central	Accessories	46551.211
	Bikes	6782978.335
	Clothing	155873.9547
	Components	947448.1091
Central Total		**7932851.609**
France	Accessories	48941.5643
	Bikes	3597879.394
	Clothing	129508.0548
	Components	871125.1938
France Total		**4647454.207**
Germany	Accessories	35681.4552
	Bikes	1602487.163
	Clothing	75592.5945
	Components	337786.516
Germany Total		**2051547.729**

Figure 14-16: The three layouts for a pivot table report.

The layout you choose not only affects the look and feel of your reporting mechanisms but also it may affect the way you build and interact with any dashboard models based on your pivot tables.

Changing the layout of a pivot table is easy. Follow these steps:

1. Click anywhere inside your pivot table to activate the PivotTable Tools context tab in the Ribbon.
2. Select the Design tab on the Ribbon.
3. Click the Report Layout icon and choose the layout you like (see Figure 14-17).

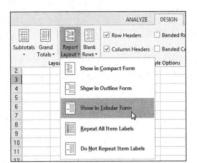

Figure 14-17: Changing the layout for your pivot table.

Renaming the fields

Notice that every field in your pivot table has a name. The fields in the row, column, and filter areas inherit their names from the data labels in your source data. For example, the fields in the Values area are given a name, such as Sum of Sales Amount.

Now, you might prefer the name Total Sales instead of the unattractive default name, like Sum of Sales Amount. In this situation, the ability to change your field name is handy. To change a field name, perform the following steps:

1. Right-click any value within the target field.

   For example, if you want to change the name of the field Sum of Sales Amount, you right-click any value under that field.

2. Select Value Field Settings (see Figure 14-18).

   This opens the Value Field Settings dialog box.

3. Type the new name in the Custom Name box (see Figure 14-19).

4. Click OK.

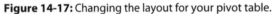

Figure 14-18: Right-click any value in the target field to select the Value Field Settings option.

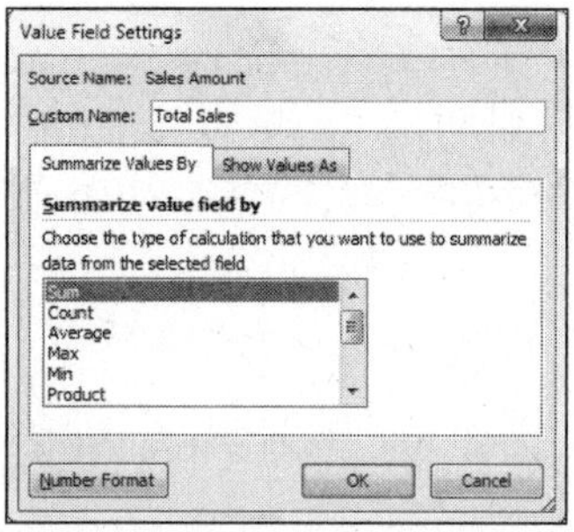

Figure 14-19: Use the Custom Name box to change the name.

Note

If you use the same name of the data label that you specified in your source data, you receive an error. In this example, if you try to rename the Sum of Sales Amount field as Sales Amount, you do get an error message. To get around this, you can add a space to the end of any field name. Excel considers Sales Amount (followed by a space) to be different from Sales Amount. This way, you can use the name that you want, and no one will notice any difference.

Formatting numbers

You can format numbers in a pivot table to fit your needs (such as currency, percent, or number). For example, you can control the numeric formatting of a field using the Value Field Settings dialog box. Here's how:

1. Right-click any value within the target field.

   For example, if you want to change the format of the values in the Sales Amount field, right-click any value under that field.

2. To display the Select Value Field Settings dialog box, select Value Field Settings.

3. To display the Format Cells dialog box, click Number Format.

4. Indicate the number format you desire, just as you normally would on your worksheet.

5. Click OK.

After you set a new format for a field, the applied formatting will persist even if you refresh or rearrange your pivot table.

Changing summary calculations

When you create your pivot table, Excel, by default, summarizes your data by either counting or summing the items. Instead of Sum or Count, you may want to choose other functions, such as Average, Min, Max, and so on. In all, 11 options are available, including:

- ➤ **Sum:** Adds all numeric data.

- ➤ **Count:** Counts all data items within a given field, including numeric-, text-, and date-formatted cells.

- ➤ **Average:** Calculates an average for the target data items.

- ➤ **Max:** Displays the largest value in the target data items.

- ➤ **Min:** Displays the smallest value in the target data items.

- ➤ **Product:** Multiplies all target data items together.

- ➤ **Count Nums:** Counts only the numeric cells in the target data items.

- ➤ **StdDevP and StdDev:** Calculates the standard deviation for the target data items. Use StdDevP if your data source contains the complete population. Use StdDev if your data source contains a sample of the population.

- ➤ **VarP and Var:** Calculates the statistical variance for the target data items. Use VarP if your data contains a complete population. If your data contains only a sampling of the complete population, use Var to estimate the variance.

To change the summary calculation for any given field, perform the following steps:

1. Right-click any value within the target field.

2. To display the Value Field Settings dialog box, select Value Field Settings.

3. Select the type of calculation you want to use from the list of calculations (see Figure 14-20).

4. Click OK.

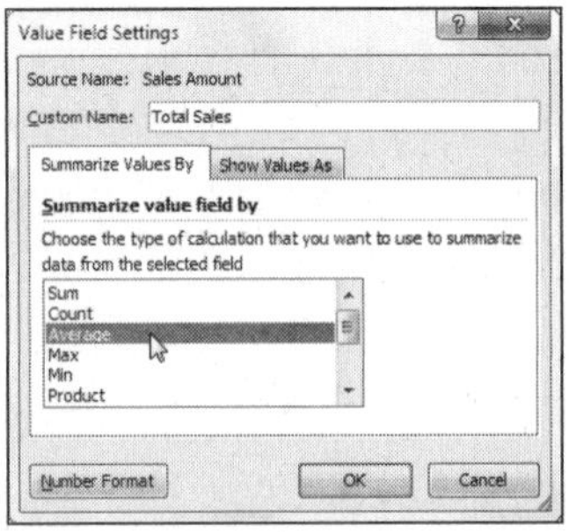

Figure 14-20: Change the type of calculation used for a field.

Note

Did you know that a single blank cell causes Excel to count instead of sum? That's right. If all the cells in a column contain numeric data, Excel chooses Sum. If just one cell is either blank or contains text, Excel chooses Count. Be sure to pay attention to the fields that you place into the Values area of the pivot table. If the field name starts with Count Of, Excel's counting the items in the field instead of summing the values.

Suppressing subtotals

Notice that each time you add a field to your pivot table, Excel adds a subtotal for that field. There may be, however, times when the inclusion of subtotals either doesn't make sense or just hinders a clear view of your pivot table report. For example, Figure 14-21 shows a pivot table where the subtotals inundate the report with totals that serve only to hide the real data you're trying to report.

	A	B	C	D	E
1	Region	SubRegion	Market	Business Segment	Sum of Sales Amount
2	North America	United States	Central	Accessories	46,551
3				Bikes	6,782,978
4				Clothing	155,874
5				Components	947,448
6			Central Total		7,932,852
7			Northeast	Accessories	51,246
8				Bikes	5,690,285
9				Clothing	163,442
10				Components	1,051,702
11			Northeast Total		6,956,674
12			Northwest	Accessories	53,308
13				Bikes	10,484,495
14				Clothing	201,052
15				Components	1,784,207
16			Northwest Total		12,523,063
17			Southeast	Accessories	45,736
18				Bikes	6,737,556
19				Clothing	165,689
20				Components	959,337
21			Southeast Total		7,908,318
22			Southwest	Accessories	110,080
23				Bikes	15,430,281
24				Clothing	364,099
25				Components	2,693,568
26			Southwest Total		18,598,027
27		United States Total			53,918,934
28	North America Total				53,918,934

Figure 14-21: Subtotals sometimes muddle the data you're trying to show.

Removing all subtotals at one time

You can remove all subtotals at once by performing these steps:

1. To activate the PivotTable Tools context tab on the Ribbon, click anywhere inside your pivot table.

2. Click the Design tab.

3. Select the Subtotals icon and select Do Not Show Subtotals (see Figure 14-22).

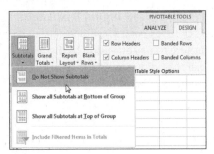

Figure 14-22: Use the Do Not Show Subtotals option to remove all subtotals at once.

As you can see in Figure 14-23, the same report without subtotals is much more pleasant to review.

	A	B	C	D	E
1	Region	SubRegion	Market	Business Segment	Sum of Sales Amount
2	North America	United States	Central	Accessories	46,551
3				Bikes	6,782,978
4				Clothing	155,874
5				Components	947,448
6			Northeast	Accessories	51,246
7				Bikes	5,690,285
8				Clothing	163,442
9				Components	1,051,702
10			Northwest	Accessories	53,308
11				Bikes	10,484,495
12				Clothing	201,052
13				Components	1,784,207
14			Southeast	Accessories	45,736
15				Bikes	6,737,556
16				Clothing	165,689
17				Components	959,337
18			Southwest	Accessories	110,080
19				Bikes	15,430,281
20				Clothing	364,099
21				Components	2,693,568
22	Grand Total				53,918,934

Figure 14-23: The same report without subtotals.

Removing the subtotals for only one field

Maybe you want to remove the subtotals for only one field? In such a case, you can perform the following steps:

1. Right-click any value within the target field.

2. To display the Field Settings dialog box, select Field Settings.

3. Select None under the Subtotals options (see Figure 14-24).

4. Click OK.

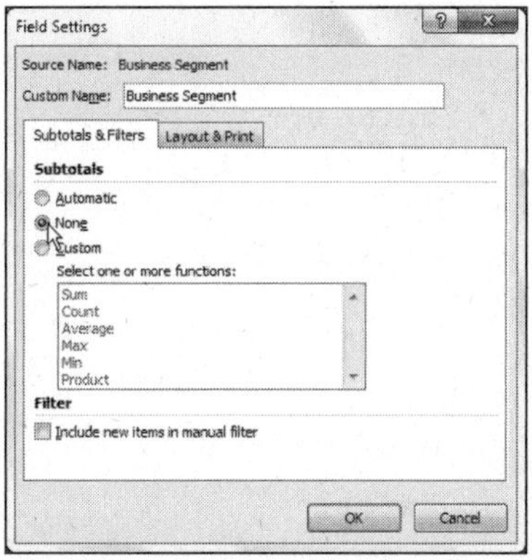

Figure 14-24: Select the None option to remove subtotals for one field.

Removing grand totals

You may want to remove the Grand Totals field from your pivot table.

1. Right-click anywhere on your pivot table.

2. To display the Options dialog box, select PivotTable Options.

3. Click the Totals & Filters tab.

4. Deselect Show Grand Totals for Rows.

5. Deselect Show Grand Totals for Columns.

6. Click the OK button to confirm your change.

Hiding and showing data items

A pivot table summarizes and displays all the information in your source data. There may, however, be situations when you want to inhibit certain data items from being included in your pivot table summary. In these situations, you can choose to hide a data item.

In terms of pivot tables, hiding doesn't just mean preventing the data item from displaying on the dashboard; hiding a data item also prevents it from being factored into the summary calculations.

The pivot table in Figure 14-25 shows sales amounts for all Business Segments by Market. In this example, however, you want to show totals without taking sales from the Bikes segment into consideration. In other words, you want to hide the Bikes segment.

	A	B	C
1	Market	Business Segment	Sum of Sales Amount
2	Australia	Accessories	$23,974
3		Bikes	$1,351,873
4		Clothing	$43,232
5		Components	$203,791
6	Australia Total		$1,622,869
7	Canada	Accessories	$119,303
8		Bikes	$11,714,700
9		Clothing	$383,022
10		Components	$2,246,255
11	Canada Total		$14,463,280
12	Central	Accessories	$46,551
13		Bikes	$6,782,978
14		Clothing	$155,874
15		Components	$947,448
16	Central Total		$7,932,852
17	France	Accessories	$48,942

Figure 14-25: You want to remove Bikes from this analysis.

To hide the Bikes Business Segment, in the Business Segment drop-down list, deselect Bikes (see Figure 14-26).

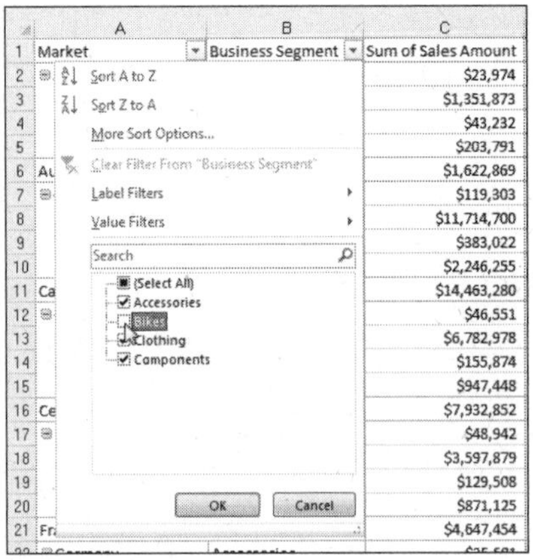

Figure 14-26: Removing the check from the Bike items hides the Bikes segment.

After clicking OK, the pivot table instantly recalculates, leaving out the Bikes segment. As you can see in Figure 14-27, the Market total sales now reflect the sales without Bikes.

Also note in Figure 14-27 that the filter icon next to Business Segment gives you a visual indicator that a filter is being applied.

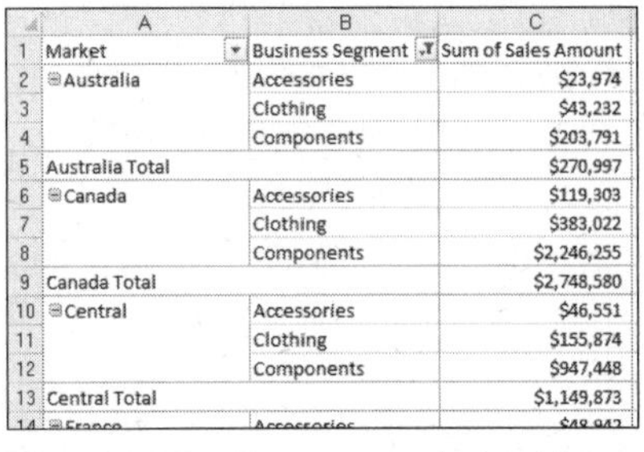

	A	B	C
1	Market	Business Segment	Sum of Sales Amount
2	Australia	Accessories	$23,974
3		Clothing	$43,232
4		Components	$203,791
5	Australia Total		$270,997
6	Canada	Accessories	$119,303
7		Clothing	$383,022
8		Components	$2,246,255
9	Canada Total		$2,748,580
10	Central	Accessories	$46,551
11		Clothing	$155,874
12		Components	$947,448
13	Central Total		$1,149,873
14	France	Accessories	$48,942

Figure 14-27: Segment analysis without the Bikes segment.

You can just as quickly reinstate all hidden data items for the field. Simply click the Business Segment drop-down list and choose Select All (see Figure 14-28).

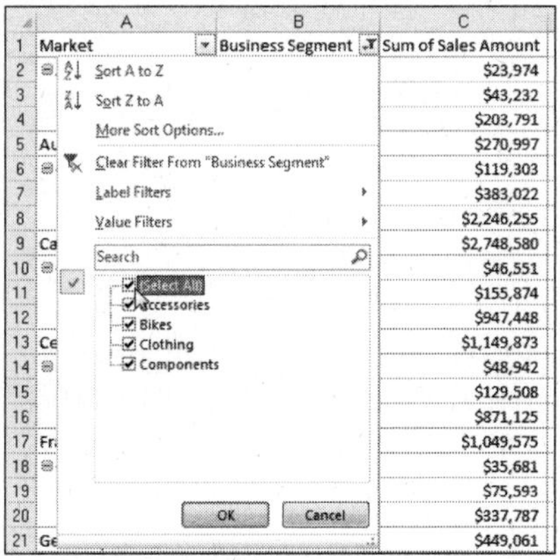

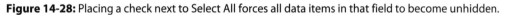

Figure 14-28: Placing a check next to Select All forces all data items in that field to become unhidden.

Hiding or showing items without data

By default, your pivot table shows only data items that have data. This may cause unintended problems for your data.

Look at Figure 14-29, which shows a pivot table with the SalesPeriod field in the Row Labels area and the Region field in the Filter area. Note that the Region field is set to (All), and every sales period appears in the report.

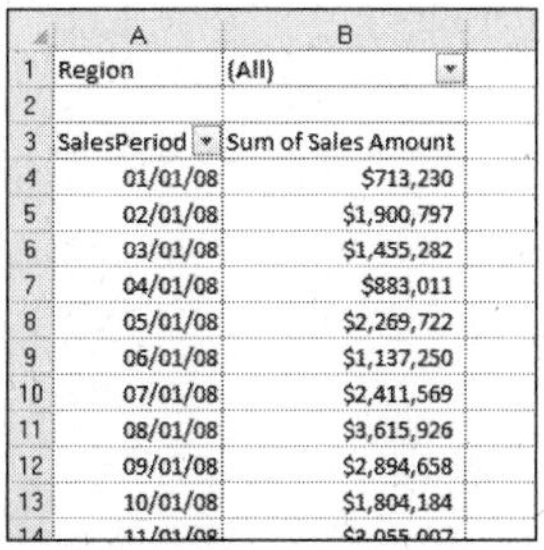

Region	(All)
SalesPeriod	Sum of Sales Amount
01/01/08	$713,230
02/01/08	$1,900,797
03/01/08	$1,455,282
04/01/08	$883,011
05/01/08	$2,269,722
06/01/08	$1,137,250
07/01/08	$2,411,569
08/01/08	$3,615,926
09/01/08	$2,894,658
10/01/08	$1,804,184

Figure 14-29: All sales periods are showing.

If you display only Europe in the filter area, only a portion of all the sales periods now show (see Figure 14-30).

	A	B
1	Region	Europe
2		
3	SalesPeriod	Sum of Sales Amount
4	07/01/08	$180,241
5	08/01/08	$448,373
6	09/01/08	$373,122
7	10/01/08	$119,384
8	11/01/08	$330,026
9	12/01/08	$254,011
10	01/01/09	$71,313
11	02/01/09	$264,487
12	03/01/09	$177,006
13	04/01/09	$105,153
14	05/01/09	$200,692

Figure 14-30: Filtering for the Europe region causes some of the sales periods to not display.

But displaying only those items with data could cause trouble if we plan on using this pivot table as the source for your charts or other dashboard components. With that in mind, it isn't ideal if half the year disappears each time a customer selects Europe.

Here's how you can prevent Excel from hiding pivot items without data:

1. Right-click any value within the target field.

   In this example, the target field is the SalesPeriod field.

2. To display the Field Settings dialog box, select Field Settings.

3. Click the Layout & Print tab in the Field Settings dialog box.

4. Select Show Items with No Data (see Figure 14-31).

5. Click OK.

Figure 14-31: Select the Show Items with No Data option to display all data items.

As you can see in Figure 14-32, after you select the Show Items with No Data option, all the sales periods appear whether the selected region had sales that period or not.

	A	B
1	Region	Europe
2		
3	SalesPeriod	Sum of Sales Amount
4	01/01/08	
5	02/01/08	
6	03/01/08	
7	04/01/08	
8	05/01/08	
9	06/01/08	
10	07/01/08	$180,241
11	08/01/08	$448,373
12	09/01/08	$373,122
13	10/01/08	$119,384
14	11/01/08	$330,026

Figure 14-32: All sales periods display even if there is no data.

Now that you're confident that the structure of the pivot table is locked, you can use it as the source for all charts and other components in your dashboard.

Tip

When you show items with no data, you will see plenty of empty cells. Excel gives you the option of replacing empty cells with a value of your own (such as 0 or n/a). This will give your customers a clear indication that there is truly no data for the items that show empty. To replace empty cells with your own value, right-click your pivot table and select PivotTable Options. In the PivotTable Options dialog box, you see a For Empty Cells Show setting. Simply enter the value you want to show instead of empty cells.

Sorting your pivot table

By default, items in each pivot field are sorted in ascending sequence based on the item name. Excel gives you the freedom to change the sort order of the items in your pivot table.

Like many actions that you can perform in Excel, lots of different ways exist to sort data within a pivot table. The easiest way, and the way that we use the most, is to apply the sort directly in the pivot table. Here's how:

1. Right-click any value within the target field (the field you need to sort).

   In the example shown in Figure 14-33, you want to sort by Sales Amount.

2. Select Sort and then select the sort direction.

4	Bib-Shorts	$168,003	
5	Bike Racks	$200,077	Copy
6	Bottles and Cages	$7,555	Format Cells...
7	Bottom Brackets	$51,826	Number Format...
8	Brakes	$66,062	Refresh
9	Caps	$31,824	
10	Chains	$9,386	Sort ▸ Sort Smallest to Largest
11	Cleaners	$11,300	Remove "Sum of Sales Amount" / Sort Largest to Smallest
12	Cranksets	$204,065	Summarize Values By ▸ More Sort Options...
13	Derailleurs	$70,263	Show Values As ▸
14	Forks	$77,969	
15	Gloves	$211,942	Show Details
16	Handlebars	$170,657	Value Field Settings...

Figure 14-33: Applying a sort to a pivot table field.

The changes take effect immediately and persist while you work with your pivot table.

Examples of Filtering Your Data

At this point in your exploration of pivot tables, you know enough to start creating your own pivot table and specifying unique views. In this section, we share a few ways we like to view the data. Although you could specify these views by hand, using the pivot table feature saves you hours of work and allows you to more easily update and maintain your information.

Producing top and bottom views

You'll often find that people are interested in the top and bottom measurement of things — for example, the top 50 customers, the bottom 5 sales reps, the top 10 products. Although you may think this is because they have the attention span of a four-year-old, there's a more logical reason for focusing on the outliers.

Effective dashboards and reports are often about showing actionable data. If you, as a manager, know which accounts are the bottom ten revenue-generating accounts, you could apply your effort and resources in building up those accounts. Because you most likely wouldn't have the resources to focus on all accounts, viewing a manageable subset of accounts would be more useful.

Luckily, pivot tables make it easy to filter your data for the top five, the bottom ten, or any conceivable combination of top or bottom records. Here's an example.

Imagine that in your company, the Accessories Business Segment is a high-margin business — you make the most profit for each dollar of sales in the Accessories segment. To increase sales, your manager wants to focus on the 50 customers who spend the least amount of money on Accessories. He obviously wants to spend his time and resources on getting those customers to buy more accessories. Here's what to do:

1. Build a pivot table with Business Segment in the Filter area, Customer in the Row Labels area, and Sales Amount in the Values area (see Figure 14-34). For cosmetic value, change the layout to Tabular Form.

	A	B
1	Business Segment	(All)
2		
3	Customer	Sum of Sales Amount
4	A Bike Store	$85,177
5	A Great Bicycle Company	$9,055
6	A Typical Bike Shop	$83,457
7	Acceptable Sales & Service	$1,258
8	Accessories Network	$2,216
9	Acclaimed Bicycle Company	$7,682
10	Ace Bicycle Supply	$3,749
11	Action Bicycle Specialists	$328,503
12	Active Cycling	$1,805
13	Active Life Toys	$200,013
14	Active Systems	$643
15	Active Transport Inc.	$88,246
16	Activity Center	$42,804
17	Advanced Bike Components	$363,131
18	Aerobic Exercise Company	$2,677
19	Affordable Sports Equipment	$311,446
20	All Cycle Shop	$2,020

Figure 14-34: Build this pivot table to start.

2. Right-click any customer name in the Customer field, select Filter, and then select Top 10 (see Figure 14-35).

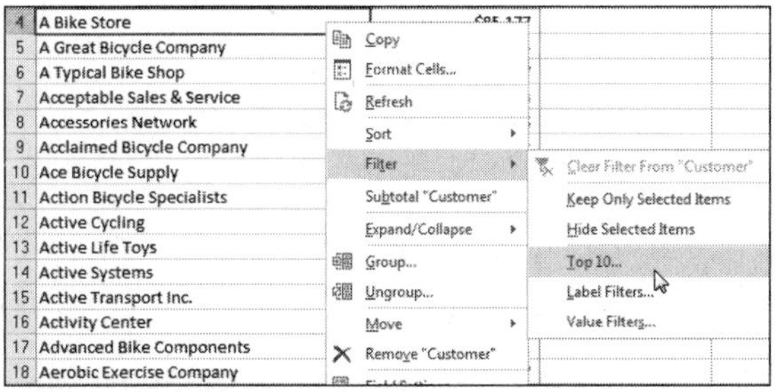

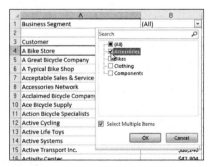

Figure 14-35: Select the Top 10 filter option.

3. In the Top 10 Filter dialog box (see Figure 14-36), define the view you're looking for.

In this example, you want the Bottom 50 Items (Customers), as defined by the Sum of Sales Amount field.

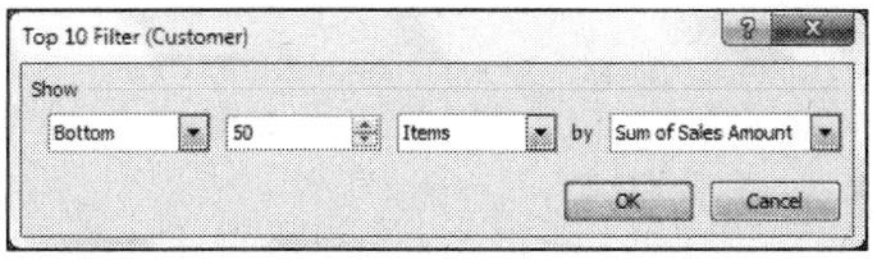

Figure 14-36: Specify the filter you want to apply.

4. Click OK.

5. In the Filter area, click the drop-down list for the Business Segment field and select Accessories (see Figure 14-37).

Figure 14-37: Filter your pivot table report to show Accessories.

At this point, you have exactly what you need — the 50 customers who spend the least amount of money on accessories. You can go a step further and format the report a bit by sorting on the Sum of Sales Amount and applying a currency format to the numbers (see Figure 14-38).

	A	B
1	Business Segment	Accessories
2		
3	Customer	Sum of Sales Amount
4	Running and Cycling Gear	$21
5	Local Sales and Rental	$21
6	Futuristic Bikes	$21
7	Instruments and Parts Company	$21
8	New Bikes Company	$20
9	Daring Rides	$20
10	Non-Slip Pedal Company	$20
11	Extended Tours	$20
12	Traditional Department Stores	$20
13	Blue Bicycle Company	$20
14	Noiseless Gear Company	$20

Figure 14-38: Your final report.

Note that because you built this view using a pivot table, you can now filter according to any new field. For example, you can add the Market field to the Filter area to get the 50 United Kingdom customers who spend the least amount of money on accessories. This, my friends, is the power of using pivot tables for the basis of your dashboards and reports. Continue to play around with the Top 10 filter option to see what kind of reports you can come up with (see Figure 14-39).

	A	B
1	Business Segment	Accessories
2	SubRegion	United Kingdom
3		
4	Customer	Sum of Sales Amount
5	Vigorous Sports Store	$3
6	Closest Bicycle Store	$3
7	Exclusive Bicycle Mart	$15
8	Extended Tours	$20
9	Instruments and Parts Company	$21
10	Tachometers and Accessories	$23
11	Metropolitan Bicycle Supply	$26
12	Number One Bike Co.	$30
13	Nearby Cycle Shop	$36
14	Metro Metals Co.	$46
15	Cycles Wholesaler & Mfg.	$376
16	Cycling Goods	$433
17	Exceptional Cycle Services	$758
18	Channel Outlet	$918
19	Express Bike Services	$1,718
20	Downhill Bicycle Specialists	$1,915
21	Uttermost Bike Shop	$3,807
22	Bulk Discount Store	$4,067
23	Commerce Bicycle Specialists	$4,436
24	Action Bicycle Specialists	$4,861
25	Exhibition Showroom	$5,723
26	Riding Cycles	$6,459
27	Prosperous Tours	$7,487

Figure 14-39: You can easily adapt this report to produce any combination of views.

Note

You may notice that in Figure 14-39, the bottom 50 view is showing only 23 records. This is because there are fewer than 50 customers in the United Kingdom market that have accessories sales. Because I asked for the bottom 50, Excel shows up to 50 accounts; but fewer if there are fewer than 50. If there's a tie for any rank in the bottom 50, Excel shows you all the tied records.

You can remove the applied filters in your pivot tables by taking these actions:

1. Click anywhere inside your pivot table to activate the PivotTable Tools context tab in the Ribbon.
2. Click the Analyze tab.
3. Select the Clear icon and select Clear Filters, as shown in Figure 14-40.

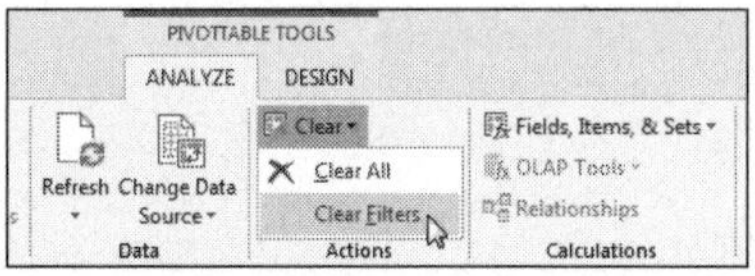

Figure 14-40: Select Clear Filters to remove the applied filters in a field.

Creating views by month, quarter, and year

Raw transactional data is rarely aggregated by month, quarter, or year for you. This type of data is often captured by the day. However, people often want reports by month or quarters instead of detail by day. Fortunately, pivot tables make it easy to group date fields into various time dimensions. Here's how:

1. Build a pivot table with Sales Date in the Row Labels area and Sales Amount in the Values area, similar to the one in Figure 14-41.

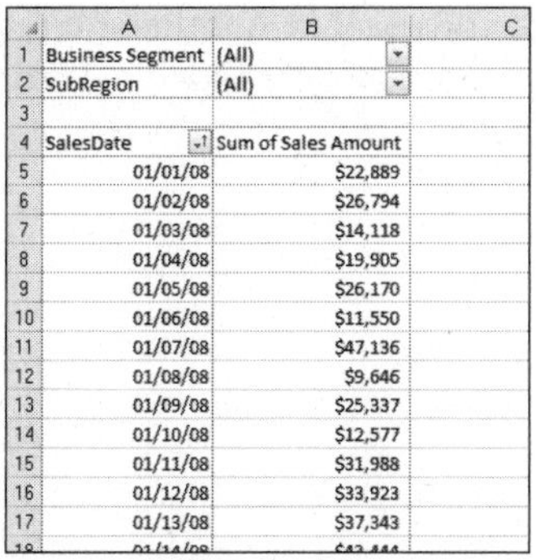

	A	B	C
1	Business Segment	(All)	
2	SubRegion	(All)	
3			
4	SalesDate	Sum of Sales Amount	
5	01/01/08	$22,889	
6	01/02/08	$26,794	
7	01/03/08	$14,118	
8	01/04/08	$19,905	
9	01/05/08	$26,170	
10	01/06/08	$11,550	
11	01/07/08	$47,136	
12	01/08/08	$9,646	
13	01/09/08	$25,337	
14	01/10/08	$12,577	
15	01/11/08	$31,988	
16	01/12/08	$33,923	
17	01/13/08	$37,343	

Figure 14-41: Build this pivot table to start.

2. Right-click any date and select Group, as shown in Figure 14-42.

   The Grouping dialog box appears, as shown in Figure 14-43.

3. Select the time dimensions that you want.

   In this example, you can select Months, Quarters, and Years.

4. Click OK.

Figure 14-42: Select the Group option.

Figure 14-43: Select the time dimensions that suit your needs.

Here are several interesting things to note about the resulting pivot table. First, notice that Quarters and Years have been added to your field list. Keep in mind that your source data hasn't changed to include these new fields; instead, these fields are now part of your pivot table. Another interesting thing to note is that, by default, the Years and Quarters fields are automatically added next to the original date field in the pivot table layout, as shown in Figure 14-44.

	A	B	C	D
1	Business Segment	(All)		
2	SubRegion	(All)		
3				
4	Years	Quarters	SalesDate	Sum of Sales Amount
5	⊞ 2008	⊞ Qtr1	Jan	$713,230
6			Feb	$1,682,318
7			Mar	$1,673,760
8		⊞ Qtr2	Apr	$872,568
9			May	$2,280,165
10			Jun	$1,102,021
11		⊞ Qtr3	Jul	$2,446,798
12			Aug	$3,615,926
13			Sep	$2,826,440
14		⊞ Qtr4	Oct	$1,872,402
15			Nov	$2,939,785
16			Dec	$2,303,436
17	⊞ 2009	⊞ Qtr1	Jan	$1,318,597
18			Feb	$2,166,151
19			Mar	$1,784,231
20		⊞ Qtr2	Apr	$1,829,387

Figure 14-44: Your pivot table is now grouped by Years and Quarters.

After your date field is grouped, you can use each added time grouping just as you would any other field in your pivot table. For instance, in Figure 14-45, I moved the Years and Quarters fields to the Column area and filtered on 2011.

	A	B	C	D	E	F
1	Business Segment	(All)				
2	SubRegion	(All)				
3						
4	Sum of Sales Amount	Years	Quarters			
5		⊟2010				Grand Total
6	Market	Qtr1	Qtr2	Qtr3	Qtr4	
7	Australia	$340,522	$236,578	$170,142		$747,242
8	Canada	$1,024,564	$1,114,589	$884,516	$886,391	$3,910,059
9	Central	$626,424	$481,199	$565,002	$608,210	$2,280,836
10	France	$597,773	$680,722	$101,901		$1,380,396
11	Germany	$406,367	$399,498	$100,772		$906,637
12	Northeast	$475,563	$508,589	$288,912	$353,648	$1,626,712
13	Northwest	$1,166,061	$1,162,232	$931,871	$1,072,927	$4,333,091
14	Southeast	$500,399	$532,449	$719,666	$872,692	$2,625,207
15	Southwest	$1,441,357	$1,457,835	$1,069,882	$1,109,502	$5,078,576
16	United Kingdom	$542,587	$511,905	$225,600		$1,280,092
17	Grand Total	$7,121,616	$7,085,597	$5,058,264	$4,903,371	$24,168,848

Figure 14-45: You can use your newly created time dimensions just like a normal pivot field.

Creating a percent distribution view

A *percent distribution* (or percent contribution) view allows you to see how much of the total is made up of a specific data item. This view is useful when you're trying to measure the general impact of a particular item.

The pivot table, as shown in Figure 14-46, gives you a view into the percent of sales that comes from each business segment. Here, you can tell that bikes make up 81 percent of Canada's sales, whereas only 77 percent of France's sales come from bikes.

	A	B	C	D	E	F
4	Sum of Sales Amount	Business 5				
5	Market	Accessories	Bikes	Clothing	Components	Grand Total
6	Australia	1.48%	83.30%	2.66%	12.56%	100.00%
7	Canada	0.82%	81.00%	2.65%	15.53%	100.00%
8	Central	0.59%	85.50%	1.96%	11.94%	100.00%
9	France	1.05%	77.42%	2.79%	18.74%	100.00%
10	Germany	1.74%	78.11%	3.68%	16.46%	100.00%
11	Northeast				15.12%	100.00%
12	Northwest					
13	Southeast					
14	Southwest					
15	United Kingdom					
16	Grand Total					
17						
18						
19						
20						

Context menu:
- Copy
- Format Cells...
- Number Format...
- Refresh
- Sort ▶
- Remove "Sum of Sales Amount"
- Summarize Values By ▶
- Show Values As ▶

Submenu:
- No Calculation
- % of Grand Total
- % of Column Total
- ✓ % of Row Total
- % Of...
- % of Parent Row Total
- % of Parent Column Total
- % of Parent Total...

Figure 14-46: This view shows percent of total for the row.

You'll also notice in Figure 14-46 that this view was created by selecting the % of Row Total option in the Value Field Settings dialog box. Here are the steps to create this type of view:

1. **Right-click any value within the target field.**

   For example, if you want to change the settings for the Sales Amount field, right-click any value under that field.

2. **Select Show Values As.**

3. **Select % of Row Total.**

The pivot table in Figure 14-47 gives you a view into the percent of sales that comes from each market. Here, you have the same type of view, but this time, you use the % of Column Total option.

Sum of Sales Amount	Business Se				
Market	Accessories	Bikes	Clothing	Components	Grand Total
Australia	4.15%	2.02%	2.40%	1.73%	2.00%
Canada	20.64%	17.53%	21.26%	19.02%	17.85%
Central	8.05%	10.15%	8.65%	8.02%	9.79%
France	8.47%				5.74%
Germany	6.17%				2.53%
Northeast	8.87%				8.59%
Northwest	9.22%				
Southeast	7.91%				
Southwest	19.04%				
United Kingdom	7.47%				
Grand Total	100.00%				

Context menu items: Copy, Format Cells..., Number Format..., Refresh, Sort, Remove "Sum of Sales Amount", Summarize Values By, Show Values As, Show Details

Show Values As submenu: No Calculation, % of Grand Total, ✓ % of Column Total, % of Row Total, % Of..., % of Parent Row Total, % of Parent Column Total, % of Parent Total

Figure 14-47: This view shows percent of total for the column.

Again, remember that because you built these views in a pivot table, you have the flexibility to slice the data by region, bring in new fields, rearrange data, and most importantly, refresh this view when new data comes in.

Creating a YTD totals view

Sometimes, it's useful to capture a running totals view to analyze the movement of numbers on a year-to-date (YTD) basis. Figure 14-48 illustrates a pivot table that shows a running total of revenue by month for each year. In this view, you can see where the YTD sales stand at any given month in each year. For example, you can see that in August 2010 revenues were about a million dollars lower than the same point in 2009.

SubRegion	(All)		
Sum of Sales Amount	Years		
SalesDate	2008	2009	2010
Jan	$713,230	$1,318,597	$1,670,606
Feb	$2,395,549	$3,484,749	$4,192,484
Mar	$4,069,309	$5,268,979	$7,121,616
Apr	$4,941,877	$7,098,366	$9,290,064
May	$7,222,042	$10,020,068	$12,670,668
Jun	$8,324,063	$11,952,318	$14,207,214
Jul	$10,770,861	$14,741,281	$16,588,415
Aug	$14,386,786	$19,055,823	$18,128,489
Sep	$17,213,226	$23,036,113	$19,265,477
Oct	$19,085,628	$25,506,056	$20,139,655
Nov	$22,025,413	$28,833,967	$22,408,366
Dec	$24,328,849	$32,517,515	$24,168,848
Grand Total			

Value Field Settings dialog:
Source Name: Sales Amount
Custom Name: Sum of Sales Amount
Summarize Values By | Show Values As
Show values as
Running Total In
Base field: SalesDate, SalesPeriod, ListPrice, UnitPrice, OrderQty, Sales Amount
Base item:
Number Format | OK

Figure 14-48: This view shows a running total of sales for each month.

Note

In the sample data for this chapter, you don't see Months and Years. You have to create them by grouping the SalesDate field. Feel free to review the "Creating views by month, quarter, and year" section earlier in this chapter to find out how.

To create this type of view, follow these steps:

1. Right-click any value within the target field.

   For example, if you want to change the settings for the Sales Amount field, right-click any value under that field.

2. Select Value Field Settings.

   The Value Field Settings dialog box appears.

3. Click the Show Values As tab.

4. Select Running Total In from the drop-down list.

5. In the Base Field list, select the field that you want the running totals to be calculated against.

   In most cases, this will be a time series such as, in this example, the SalesDate field.

6. Click OK.

Creating a month-over-month variance view

Another commonly requested view is a month-over-month variance. How did this month's sales compare to last month's sales? The best way to create these types of views is to show the raw number and the percent variance together.

In that light, you can start creating this view by building a pivot table similar to the one shown in Figure 14-49. Notice that you bring in the Sales Amount field twice. One of these remains untouched, showing the raw data. The other is changed to show the month-over-month variance.

	A	B	C
1			
2	SubRegion	(All)	
3			
4		Values	
5	SalesDate	Sum of Sales Amount	Sum of Sales Amount2
6	Jan	$3,702,433	$3,702,433
7	Feb	$6,370,348	$6,370,348
8	Mar	$6,387,124	$6,387,124
9	Apr	$4,870,403	$4,870,403
10	May	$8,582,470	$8,582,470
11	Jun	$4,570,817	$4,570,817
12	Jul	$7,616,962	$7,616,962
13	Aug	$9,470,541	$9,470,541
14	Sep	$7,943,719	$7,943,719
15	Oct	$5,216,523	$5,216,523
16	Nov	$8,536,406	$8,536,406
17	Dec	$7,747,467	$7,747,467
18	Grand Total	$81,015,212	$81,015,212

Figure 14-49: Build a pivot table that contains the Sum of Sales Amount twice.

Figure 14-50 illustrates the settings that convert the second Sum of Sales Amount field into a month-over-month variance calculation.

2	SubRegion	(All)	
3			
4		Values	
5	SalesDate	Sum of Sales Amount	Sum of Sales Amount2
6	Jan	$3,702,433	
7	Feb	$6,370,348	72.06%
8	Mar	$6,387,124	0.26%
9	Apr	$4,870,403	-23.75%
10	May	$8,582,470	76.22%
11	Jun	$4,570,817	-46.74%
12	Jul	$7,616,962	66.64%
13	Aug	$9,470,541	24.33%
14	Sep	$7,943,719	-16.12%
15	Oct	$5,216,523	-34.33%
16	Nov	$8,536,406	63.64%
17	Dec	$7,747,467	-9.24%
18	Grand Total	$81,015,212	
19			
20			
21			

Value Field Settings dialog box:

Source Name: Sales Amount
Custom Name: Sum of Sales Amount2

Summarize Values By | Show Values As

Show values as
% Difference From

Base field:
Customer
Business Segment
Category
Model
Color
SalesDate
SalesPeriod
ListPrice
UnitPrice

Base item:
(previous)
(next)
Jan
Feb
Mar
Apr
May
Jun
Jul

Number Format | OK | Cancel

Figure 14-50: Configure the second Sum of Sales Amount field to show month-over-month variance.

As you can see, after applying these settings, the pivot table gives you a nice view of raw sales dollars and the variance over last month. You can obviously change the field names (see the "Renaming the fields" section earlier in this chapter) to reflect the appropriate labels for each column.

Note In the sample data for this chapter, you don't see Months and Years. You have to create them by grouping the SalesDate field. Feel free to review the section, "Creating views by month, quarter, and year," earlier in this chapter to find out how.

To create the view in Figure 14-50, follow these steps:

1. Right-click any value within the target field.

   In this case, the target field is the second Sum of Sales Amount field.

2. Select Value Field Settings.

   The Value Field Settings dialog box appears.

3. Click the Show Values As tab.

4. Select % Difference From in the drop-down list.

5. In the Base Field list, select the field that you want the running totals to be calculated against.

   In most cases, this is a time series like, in this example, the SalesDate field.

6. In the Base Item list, select the item you want to compare against when calculating the percent variance. In this example, you want to calculate each month's variance to the previous month. Therefore, select the (previous) item.

Using Pivot Charts

A *pivot chart* is a graphical representation of a data summary displayed in a pivot table. A pivot chart is always based on a pivot table. Excel lets you create a pivot table and a pivot chart at the same time, but you can't create a pivot chart without a pivot table.

If you're familiar with creating charts in Excel, you'll have no problem creating and customizing pivot charts. Most of Excel's charting features are available in a pivot chart. But as you'll see, pivot charts are actually a completely different animal.

Cross-Ref

The discussion here assumes that you're familiar with the inner workings of pivot tables, which is covered in Chapter 14. Feel free to refer to Chapter 14 if you need a refresher on pivot tables.

Getting Started with Pivot Charts

When you create a standard chart from data that isn't in a pivot table, you feed the chart a range made up of individual cells holding individual pieces of data. Each cell is an individual object with its own piece of data, so your chart treats each cell as an individual data point, charting each one separately.

However, the data in your pivot table is part of a larger object. The pieces of data you see inside your pivot table aren't individual pieces of data that occupy individual cells. Rather, they are items inside a larger pivot table object that is occupying space on your worksheet.

When you create a chart from your pivot table, you're not feeding it individual pieces of data inside individual cells; you're feeding it the entire pivot table layout. Thus your pivot chart can interactively add, remove, filter, and refresh data fields inside the chart just like your pivot table. The result of all this action is a graphical representation of the data you see in your pivot table.

Cross-Ref

If you're new to Excel charts, we highly recommend you first read through Part II of this book.

Creating a pivot chart

To see how to create a pivot chart, look at the pivot table in Figure 15-1. This pivot table provides a simple view of revenue by market. In the Business Segment field in the report filter area, you can parse out revenue by line of business.

	A	B
1	Business_Segment	(All)
2		
3	**Market**	**Sum of Sales_Amount**
4	BUFFALO	$450,478
5	CALIFORNIA	$2,254,735
6	CANADA	$776,245
7	CHARLOTTE	$890,522
8	DALLAS	$467,089
9	DENVER	$645,583
10	FLORIDA	$1,450,392
11	KANSASCITY	$574,899
12	MICHIGAN	$678,705
13	NEWORLEANS	$333,454
14	NEWYORK	$873,581
15	PHOENIX	$570,255
16	SEATTLE	$179,827
17	TULSA	$628,405
18	**Grand Total**	**$10,774,172**

Figure 15-1: This basic pivot table shows revenue by market and allows for filtering by line of business.

To start the process, place your cursor anywhere in the pivot table, go to the Ribbon, and click the Insert tab. Find the Charts group, where you can choose the chart type you want to use for your pivot chart. For this example, click the Column Chart icon and select the first 2-D column chart, as demonstrated in Figure 15-2. A chart appears, as shown in Figure 15-3.

Notice that pivot charts are now, by default, placed on the same sheet as the source pivot table. If you long for the days when pivot charts were located on their own chart sheet, you are in luck. All you have to do is place your cursor in your pivot table and then press F11 on your keyboard, and a pivot chart is created on its own sheet.

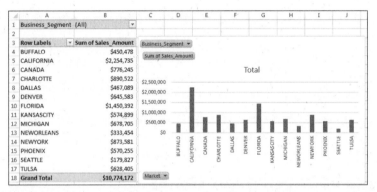

Figure 15-2: Select the chart type you want to use.

Figure 15-3: Excel creates your pivot chart on the same sheet as your pivot table.

You can easily change the location of your pivot charts by simply right-clicking on the chart (outside the plot area) and selecting Move Chart. This activates the Move Chart dialog box, where you can specify the new location.

Tip

In Figure 15-3, notice the pivot field buttons on the pivot chart — the gray buttons with drop-down arrows. Using these pivot field buttons, you can rearrange the chart and apply filters to the underlying pivot table.

If you aren't too keen on showing the pivot field buttons directly on your pivot charts, you can remove them by clicking on the chart and selecting the Analyze tab. On the Analyze tab, you can use the Field Buttons drop-down button to hide some or all of the pivot field buttons.

You now have a chart that is a visual representation of your pivot table. Moreover, because the pivot chart is tied to the underlying pivot table, changing the pivot table in any way changes the chart. For example, as Figure 15-4 illustrates, adding the Region field to the pivot table adds a region dimension to your chart.

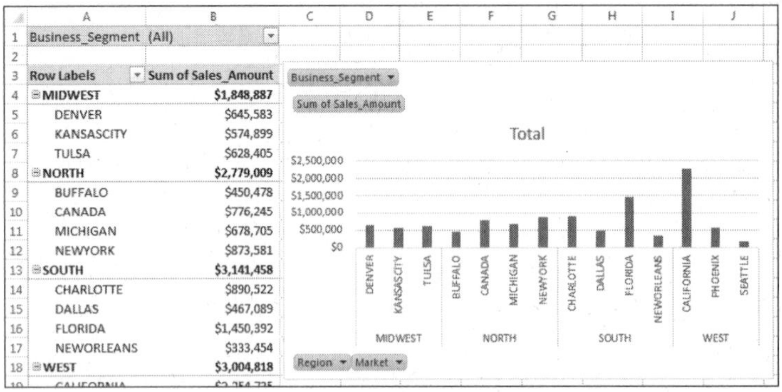

Figure 15-4: Your pivot chart displays the same fields your underlying pivot table displays.

In addition, selecting a Business Segment from the Page field filter filters both the pivot table and the pivot chart. All this behavior occurs because pivot charts use the same pivot cache and pivot layout as their corresponding pivot tables. Thus, if you add or remove data from your data source and refresh your pivot table, your pivot chart updates to reflect the changes.

Take a moment to think about the possibilities. You can essentially create a fairly robust interactive reporting tool on the power of one pivot table and one pivot chart; no programming is necessary.

Understanding the link between pivot charts and pivot tables

The primary rule to remember is that your pivot chart is merely an extension of your pivot table. If you refresh, move a field, add a field, remove a field, hide a data item, show a data item, or apply a filter, your pivot chart reflects your changes.

One common mistake people make when using pivot charts is assuming that Excel will place the values in the column area of the pivot table in the *x*-axis of the pivot chart.

For instance, the pivot table in Figure 15-5 is in a format that's easy to read and comprehend. The structure chosen shows Sales Periods in the column area and the Region in the row area. This structure works fine in the pivot table view.

	A	B	C	D	E	F	G
1	Business_Segment	(All)					
2							
3	Sum of Sales_Amount	Column Labels					
4	Row Labels	P01	P02	P03	P04	P05	P06	P0
5	MIDWEST	$109,498	$207,329	$101,861	$155,431	$159,298	$149,426	$1
6	NORTH	$180,772	$260,507	$183,151	$214,665	$235,369	$221,791	$1
7	SOUTH	$198,415	$334,189	$189,493	$255,558	$283,012	$249,258	$1
8	WEST	$193,180	$314,891	$183,106	$239,843	$248,124	$248,456	$1
9	Grand Total	$681,865	$1,116,916	$657,611	$865,498	$925,802	$868,930	$6

Figure 15-5: The placement of your data fields may work for a pivot table, but not for a pivot chart.

Suppose you decide to create a pivot chart from this pivot table. You would instinctively expect to see fiscal periods across the *x*-axis and lines of business along the *y*-axis. However, as you can see in Figure 15-6, your pivot chart comes out with Region in the *x*-axis and Sales Period in the *y*-axis.

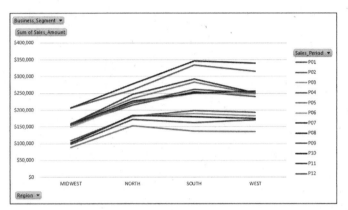

Figure 15-6: Creating a pivot chart from your nicely structured pivot table doesn't yield the results you expected.

So why doesn't the structure in your pivot table translate to a clean pivot chart? The answer has to do with the way pivot charts handle the different areas of your pivot table.

In a pivot chart, both the *x*-axis and the *y*-axis correspond to a specific area in your pivot table.

➤ The *y*-axis of your pivot chart corresponds to the column area in your pivot table.

➤ The *x*-axis of your pivot chart corresponds to the row area in your pivot.

Given this new information, look at the pivot table in Figure 15-5 again. This structure says that the Sales_Period field will be treated as the *y*-axis because it is in the column area. Meanwhile, the Region field will be treated as the *x*-axis because it is in the row area.

Now suppose you rearrange the pivot table to show fiscal periods in the row area and lines of business in the column area, as shown in Figure 15-7. This format makes reading more difficult in a pivot table view, but it gives your pivot chart the effect you want (see Figure 15-8).

	A	B	C	D	E	F
1	Business_Segment	(All)				
2						
3	Sum of Sales_Amount	Column Labels				
4	Row Labels	MIDWEST	NORTH	SOUTH	WEST	Grand Total
5	P01	$109,498	$180,772	$198,415	$193,180	$681,865
6	P02	$207,329	$260,507	$334,189	$314,891	$1,116,916
7	P03	$101,861	$183,151	$189,493	$183,106	$657,611
8	P04	$155,431	$214,665	$255,558	$239,843	$865,498
9	P05	$159,298	$235,369	$283,012	$248,124	$925,802
10	P06	$149,426	$221,791	$249,258	$248,456	$868,930
11	P07	$101,809	$184,350	$180,146	$174,282	$640,587
12	P08	$207,278	$277,905	$345,842	$339,236	$1,170,262
13	P09	$98,129	$172,271	$163,153	$171,000	$604,552
14	P10	$156,974	$227,469	$251,042	$255,769	$891,253
15	P11	$159,130	$246,435	$293,184	$250,855	$949,605
16	P12	$154,276	$221,242	$261,113	$251,034	$887,665
17	P13	$88,448	$153,083	$137,053	$135,041	$513,625
18	Grand Total	$1,848,887	$2,779,009	$3,141,458	$3,004,818	$10,774,172

Figure 15-7: Moving fiscal periods to the row area allows your pivot chart to accurately plot the data.

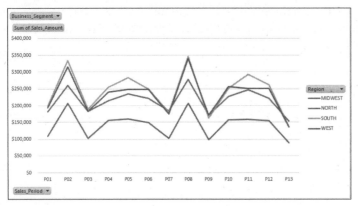

Figure 15-8: With the new arrangement in your pivot table, you get a pivot chart that makes sense.

Limitations of pivot charts

Overall, the look and feel of pivot charts in Excel 2013 is similar to the look and feel of standard charts, making them much more of a viable reporting option. However, a few limitations persist in this version of Excel.

➤ You cannot use XY (scatter) charts, bubble charts, or stock charts when creating a pivot chart.

➤ Applied trend lines are often lost when adding or removing fields in the underlying pivot table.

➤ The chart titles in the pivot chart cannot be resized.

Tip

Although you cannot resize the chart titles in a pivot chart, making the font bigger or smaller indirectly resizes the chart title.

Using conditional formatting with pivot tables

In Excel 2007, Microsoft introduced a robust set of conditional formatting visualizations, including data bars, color scales, and icon sets. These new visualizations allow users to build dashboard-style reporting that goes far beyond the traditional red, yellow, and green designations. What's more, conditional formatting was extended to integrate with pivot tables, which means that conditional formatting is now applied to a pivot table's structure, not just the cells it occupies.

In this section, you find out how to leverage the magic combination of pivot tables and conditional formatting to create interactive visualizations that serve as an alternative to pivot charts.

To start the first example, create the pivot table shown in Figure 15-9.

	A	B	C
1			
2	**Market**	**Sum of Sales_Amount**	**Sum of Sales_Amount2**
3	BUFFALO	$450,478	450,478
4	CALIFORNIA	$2,254,735	2,254,735
5	CANADA	$776,245	776,245
6	CHARLOTTE	$890,522	890,522
7	DALLAS	$467,089	467,089
8	DENVER	$645,583	645,583
9	FLORIDA	$1,450,392	1,450,392
10	KANSASCITY	$574,899	574,899
11	MICHIGAN	$678,705	678,705
12	NEWORLEANS	$333,454	333,454
13	NEWYORK	$873,581	873,581
14	PHOENIX	$570,255	570,255
15	SEATTLE	$179,827	179,827
16	TULSA	$628,405	628,405
17	**Grand Total**	**$10,774,172**	**10,774,172**

Figure 15-9: Create this pivot table.

Suppose you want to create a report that allows your managers to see the performance of each sales period graphically. You could build a pivot chart, but you decide to use conditional formatting. In this example, go the easy route and quickly apply some data bars:

1. Select all the Sum of Sales_Amount2 values in the values area.

2. Click the Home tab and select Conditional Formatting➔Data Bars as shown in Figure 15-10.

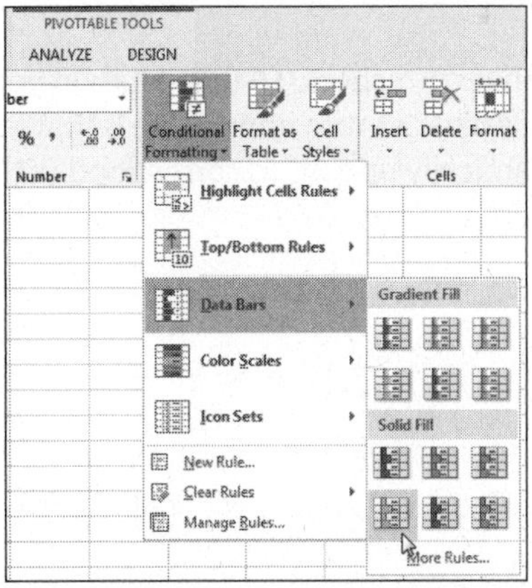

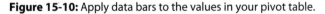

Figure 15-10: Apply data bars to the values in your pivot table.

You immediately see data bars in your pivot table under the values in the Sum of Sales_Amount2 field. Notice that the Data Bars coexist with the data values. To get a clean visualization, you want to show only the Data Bars by following these steps:

1. Go to the Home tab, click the Conditional Formatting button, and select Manage Rules.

   The Rules Manager dialog box appears.

2. Select the Data Bar rule you just created and then select Edit Rule.

   The Edit Formatting Rule dialog box appears.

3. Click the Show Bar Only option (see Figure 15-11).

Figure 15-11: Click the Show Bar Only option to get a clean view of just the data bars.

As you can see in Figure 15-12, you now have a set of bars that correspond to the values in your pivot table. This visualization looks like a sideway chart, doesn't it? What's more impressive is that as you filter the markets in the report filter area, the data bars dynamically update to correspond with the data for the selected market.

	A	B	C
1			
2	Market	Sum of Sales_Amount	Sum of Sales_Amount2
3	BUFFALO	$450,478	
4	CALIFORNIA	$2,254,735	
5	CANADA	$776,245	
6	CHARLOTTE	$890,522	
7	DALLAS	$467,089	
8	DENVER	$645,583	
9	FLORIDA	$1,450,392	
10	KANSASCITY	$574,899	
11	MICHIGAN	$678,705	
12	NEWORLEANS	$333,454	
13	NEWYORK	$873,581	
14	PHOENIX	$570,255	
15	SEATTLE	$179,827	
16	TULSA	$628,405	
17	Grand Total	$10,774,172	10,774,172

Figure 15-12: You have applied conditional data bars with just three easy clicks!

Excel 2013 has a handful of preprogrammed scenarios that can be leveraged when you want to spend less time configuring your conditional formatting and more time analyzing your data. For example, to create the data bars you've just employed, Excel uses a predefined algorithm that takes the largest and smallest values in the selected range and calculates the condition levels for each bar.

Other examples of preprogrammed scenarios include

Top Nth Items

Top Nth %

Bottom Nth Items

Bottom Nth %

Above Average

Below Average

To remove the applied conditional formatting, place your cursor in the pivot table and then select Home➔Conditional Formatting➔Clear Rules➔Clear Rules from This PivotTable.

Customizing conditional formatting

You are by no means limited to preprogrammed scenarios. You can create your own custom conditions. To see what we mean, create the pivot table shown in Figure 15-13.

	A	B	C	D
1	Product_Description	(All)		
2				
3	**Market**	Sales_Amount	Contracted Hours	Dollars Per Hour
4	BUFFALO	$450,478	6,864	$65.63
5	CALIFORNIA	$2,254,735	33,014	$68.30
6	CANADA	$776,245	12,103	$64.14
7	CHARLOTTE	$890,522	14,525	$61.31
8	DALLAS	$467,089	6,393	$73.06
9	DENVER	$645,583	8,641	$74.71
10	FLORIDA	$1,450,392	22,640	$64.06
11	KANSASCITY	$574,899	8,547	$67.26
12	MICHIGAN	$678,705	10,744	$63.17
13	NEWORLEANS	$333,454	5,057	$65.94
14	NEWYORK	$873,581	14,213	$61.46
15	PHOENIX	$570,255	10,167	$56.09
16	SEATTLE	$179,827	2,889	$62.25
17	TULSA	$628,405	9,583	$65.57
18	Grand Total	$10,774,172	165,380	$65.15

Figure 15-13: This pivot shows Sales_Amount, Contracted_Hours, and a calculated field that calculates Dollars per Hour.

Here you want to evaluate the relationship between total revenue and dollars per hour. The idea is that some strategically applied conditional formatting helps identify opportunities for improvement. Follow these steps:

1. Place your cursor in the Sales_Amount column.

2. Click the Home tab and select Conditional Formatting.

3. Select New Rule.

   The New Formatting Rule dialog box appears, as shown in Figure 15-14.

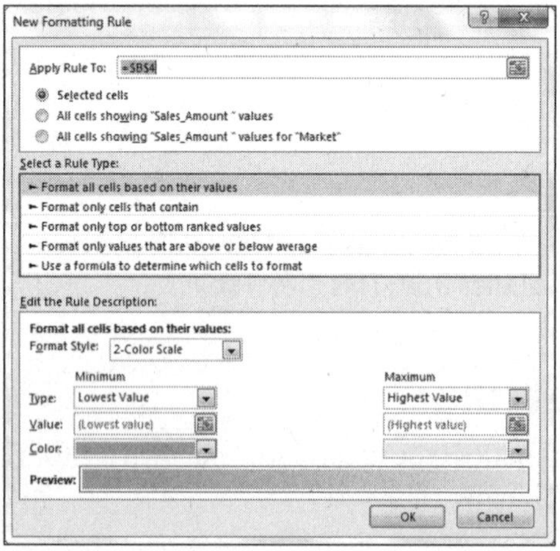

Figure 15-14: The New Formatting Rule dialog box.

The objective in this dialog box is to identify the cells where the conditional formatting will be applied, specify the rule type to use, and define the details of the conditional formatting.

1. Identify the cells where your conditional formatting will be applied.

   You have three choices:

   ● Selected Cells: This selection applies conditional formatting to only the selected cells.

   ● All cells showing Sales_Amount values: This selection applies conditional formatting to all values in the Sales_Amount column, including all subtotals and grand totals. This selection is ideal for use in analyses in which you're using averages, percentages, or other calculations where a single conditional formatting rule makes sense for all levels of analysis.

   ● All cells showing Sales_Amount values for Market: This selection applies conditional formatting to all values in the Sales_Amount column at the Market level only (excludes subtotals and grand totals). This selection is ideal for use in analyses where you're using calculations that make sense only within the context of the level being measured.

Note

The words *Sales_Amount* and *Market* are not permanent fixtures of the New Formatting Rule dialog box. These words change to reflect the fields in your pivot table. *Sales_ Amount* is used because your cursor is in that column. *Market* is used because the active data items in the pivot table are in the Market field.

In this example, the third selection (All cells showing Sales_Amount values for Market) makes the most sense, so click that radio button, as demonstrated in Figure 15-15.

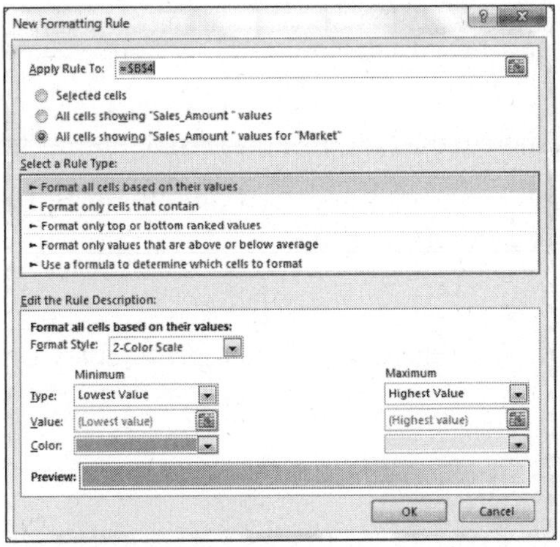

Figure 15-15: Click the radio button next to All cells showing "Sales_Amount" values for "Market".

2. In the Select a Rule Type section, you need to specify the rule type you want to use for the conditional format.

You can select one of five rule types:

- Format All Cells Based on Their Values: This selection allows you to apply conditional formatting based on some comparison of the actual values of the selected range. That is, the values in the selected range are measured against each other. This selection is ideal when you want to identify general anomalies in your dataset.

- Format Only Cells That Contain: This selection allows you to apply conditional formatting to those cells that meet specific criteria you define. Keep in mind that the values in your range aren't measured against each other when you use this rule type. This selection is useful when you're comparing your values against a predefined benchmark.

- Format Only Top or Bottom Ranked Values: This selection allows you to apply conditional formatting to those cells that are ranked in the top or bottom nth number or percent of all the values in the range.

- Format Only Values That Are Above or Below the Average: This selection allows you to apply conditional formatting to those values that are mathematically above or below the average of all values in the selected range.

- Use a Formula to Determine Which Cells to Format: This selection allows you to specify your own formula and evaluate each value in the selected range against that formula. If the values evaluate as true, the conditional formatting is applied. This selection comes in handy when you're applying conditions based on the results of an advanced formula or mathematical operation.

Data bars, color scales, and icon sets can be used only when the selected cells are formatted based on their values. This means that if you want to use data bars, color scales, and icon sets, you must select the Format All Cells Based on Their Values rule type.

In this scenario, you want to identify problem areas using icon sets; therefore, you want to format the cells based on their values.

3. Define the details of the conditional formatting in the Edit the Rule Description section.

   Again, you want to identify problem areas using the slick new icon sets offered by Excel 2013. Select Icon Sets from the Format Style drop-down menu.

4. Select a style appropriate to your analysis.

   The style selected in Figure 15-16 is ideal for situations in which your pivot tables cannot always be viewed in color.

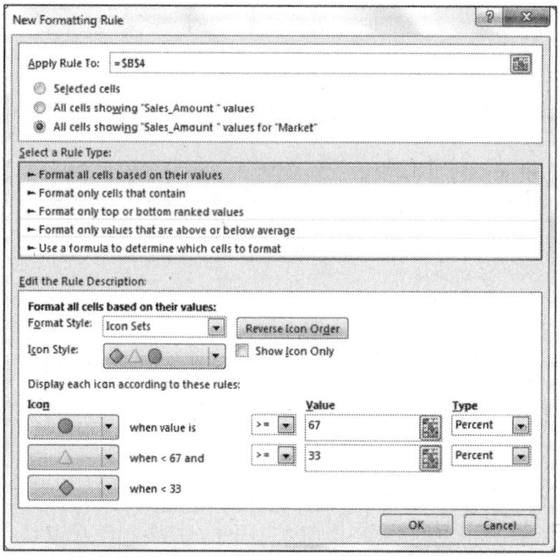

Figure 15-16: Select Icon Sets from the Format Style drop-down menu.

With this configuration, Excel applies the sign icons based on the percentile bands >=67, >=33, and <33. Keep in mind that the actual percentile bands can be changed based on your needs. In this scenario, the default percentile bands are sufficient.

5. Click OK to apply the conditional formatting.

As you can see in Figure 15-17, you now have icons that allow you to quickly determine where each market falls in relation to other markets as it pertains to revenue.

	A	B	C	D
1	Product_Description (All)			
2				
3	Market	Sales_Amount	Contracted Hours	Dollars Per Hour
4	BUFFALO	◆ $450,478	6,864	$65.63
5	CALIFORNIA	● $2,254,735	33,014	$68.30
6	CANADA	◆ $776,245	12,103	$64.14
7	CHARLOTTE	▲ $890,522	14,525	$61.31
8	DALLAS	◆ $467,089	6,393	$73.06
9	DENVER	◆ $645,583	8,641	$74.71
10	FLORIDA	▲ $1,450,392	22,640	$64.06
11	KANSASCITY	◆ $574,899	8,547	$67.26
12	MICHIGAN	◆ $678,705	10,744	$63.17
13	NEWORLEANS	◆ $333,454	5,057	$65.94
14	NEWYORK	▲ $873,581	14,213	$61.46
15	PHOENIX	◆ $570,255	10,167	$56.09
16	SEATTLE	◆ $179,827	2,889	$62.25
17	TULSA	◆ $628,405	9,583	$65.57
18	Grand Total	$10,774,172	165,380	$65.15

Figure 15-17: You have applied your first custom conditional formatting!

6. Apply the same conditional formatting to the Dollars per Hour field.

When you are done, your pivot table should look similar to the one shown in Figure 15-18.

	A	B	C	D
1	Product_Description (All)			
2				
3	Market	Sales_Amount	Contracted Hours	Dollars Per Hour
4	BUFFALO	◆ $450,478	6,864 ▲	$65.63
5	CALIFORNIA	● $2,254,735	33,014 ▲	$68.30
6	CANADA	◆ $776,245	12,103 ▲	$64.14
7	CHARLOTTE	▲ $890,522	14,525 ◆	$61.31
8	DALLAS	◆ $467,089	6,393 ●	$73.06
9	DENVER	◆ $645,583	8,641 ●	$74.71
10	FLORIDA	▲ $1,450,392	22,640 ▲	$64.06
11	KANSASCITY	◆ $574,899	8,547 ▲	$67.26
12	MICHIGAN	◆ $678,705	10,744 ▲	$63.17
13	NEWORLEANS	◆ $333,454	5,057 ▲	$65.94
14	NEWYORK	▲ $873,581	14,213 ◆	$61.46
15	PHOENIX	◆ $570,255	10,167 ◆	$56.09
16	SEATTLE	◆ $179,827	2,889 ◆	$62.25
17	TULSA	◆ $628,405	9,583 ▲	$65.57
18	Grand Total	$10,774,172	165,380	$65.15

Figure 15-18: You have successfully created an interactive visualization.

Take a moment to analyze what you have here. With this view, a manager can analyze the relationship between total revenue and dollars per hour. For example, the Dallas market manager can see that he is in the bottom percentile for revenue but in the top percentile for dollars per hour. With this information, he immediately sees that his dollars per hour rates may be too high for his market. Conversely, the New York market manager can see that she is in the top percentile for revenue but in the bottom percentile for dollars per hour. This tells her that her dollars-per-hour rates may be too low for her market.

And all this is driven by a pivot table and some conditional formatting!

Alternatives to Pivot Charts

There are generally two reasons why you need an alternative to using pivot charts: You don't want the overhead that comes with a pivot chart, and you want to avoid some of the formatting limitations of pivot charts.

In fact, sometimes you may create a pivot table simply to summarize and shape your data in preparation for charting. In these situations, you don't plan on keeping your source data, and you definitely don't want a pivot cache taking up memory and file space.

In the example in Figure 15-19, you can see a pivot table that summarizes revenue by quarter for each product.

	A	B	C	D	E	F
1						
2	Sum of Sales_Amount	Invoice_Date				
3	Product_Description	Qtr1	Qtr2	Qtr3	Qtr4	Grand Total
4	Cleaning & Housekeeping Services	$257,218	$290,074	$297,251	$294,049	$1,138,593
5	Facility Maintenance and Repair	$563,799	$621,715	$600,810	$574,834	$2,361,158
6	Fleet Maintenance	$612,496	$691,440	$674,592	$649,269	$2,627,798
7	Green Plants and Foliage Care	$293,194	$325,276	$329,787	$328,527	$1,276,783
8	Landscaping/Grounds Care	$288,797	$310,670	$303,086	$288,363	$1,190,915
9	Predictive Maintenance/Preventative Maintenance	$533,127	$567,391	$552,380	$526,027	$2,178,925
10	Grand Total	$2,548,631	$2,806,566	$2,757,906	$2,661,069	$10,774,172

Figure 15-19: This pivot table was created to summarize and chart revenue by quarter for each product.

The idea here is that you create this pivot table only to summarize and shape your data for charting. You don't want to keep the source data, nor do you want to keep the pivot table with all its overhead. The problem is that if you try to create a chart using the data in the pivot table, you inevitably create a pivot chart, which means you have all the overhead of the pivot table looming in the background. Of course, this could be problematic if you don't want to share your source data with end users or you don't want to inundate them unnecessarily with large files.

The good news is that with a few simple techniques, you can create a chart from a pivot table, but not end up with a pivot chart.

Disconnecting charts from pivot tables

Sometimes you want to chart the data in your pivot table, but don't need the chart to remain connected to the pivot table. Maybe you want to e-mail just the chart to someone without the pivot table. Maybe you need a quick one-time chart and don't need to keep the connection to the pivot table. Whatever the case, you can use any of these three alternative techniques for creating charts that are disconnected from pivot tables.

Create a standard chart from current pivot table values

After you've created and structured your pivot table appropriately, select the entire pivot table and copy it. Then under the Insert tab, select Paste Values, as shown in Figure 15-20.

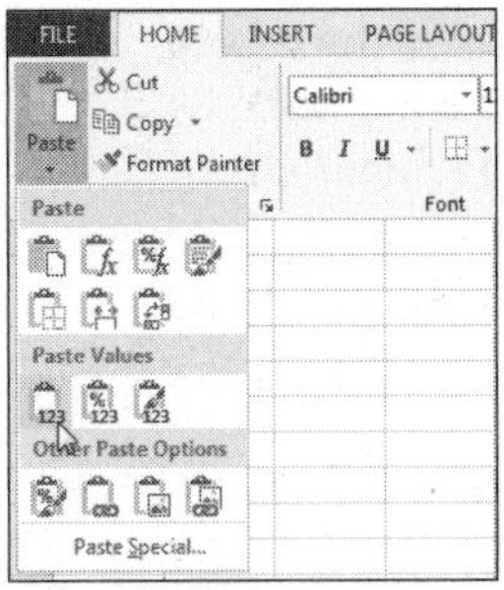

Figure 15-20: The Paste Values functionality is useful when you want to create hard-coded values from pivot tables.

This action essentially deletes your pivot table, leaving you with the last values that were displayed in the pivot table. These values can subsequently be used to create a standard chart.

This technique disables the dynamic functionality of your pivot chart. That is, your pivot chart becomes a standard chart that cannot be interactively filtered or refreshed.

Delete the underlying pivot table

If you've already created your pivot chart, you can turn it into a standard chart by simply deleting the underlying pivot table. To do so, select the entire pivot table and press Delete on the keyboard.

With this method, you are left with none of the values that made up the source data for the chart. In other words, if anyone asks for the data that feeds the chart, you will not have it.

Tip
If you ever find that you have a chart but the data source isn't available, activate the chart's data table. The data table lets you see the data values that feed each series in the chart. See Chapter 7 to learn how to add the data table to a chart.

Create a picture of the pivot chart

A picture of your pivot chart freezes all of the text and numbers without any other information. In addition to very small file sizes, you get the added benefit of controlling what your clients get to see.

To use this method, follow these steps:

1. Copy the pivot chart by right-clicking on the chart (outside the plot area) and selecting Copy.

2. Open a new workbook.

3. Right-click anywhere in the new workbook and select Paste Special; then select the picture format you prefer.

   A picture of your pivot chart is then placed in the new workbook.

Caution

If you have pivot field buttons on your chart, they will also show up in the copied picture, which may confuse your audience about why the buttons don't work. Be sure to hide all pivot field buttons before copying a pivot chart as a picture. You can remove them by clicking your chart and then selecting the Analyze tab. On the Analyze tab, use the Field Buttons drop-down button to hide all of the pivot field buttons.

Create standalone charts that are connected to your pivot table

To retain key functionality in your pivot table, such as report filters and top ten ranking, you can link a standard chart to your pivot table without creating a pivot chart.

In the example in Figure 15-21, a pivot table shows the top ten markets by contracted hours along with their total revenue. Notice that the report filter area allows you to filter by business segment so you can see the top ten markets segment.

⏴	A	B	C
1	Business_Segment (All)		
2			
3	**Market** ⏷	**Contracted Hours**	**Sales_Amount**
4	CALIFORNIA	33,014	$2,254,735
5	FLORIDA	22,640	$1,450,392
6	CHARLOTTE	14,525	$890,522
7	NEWYORK	14,213	$873,581
8	CANADA	12,103	$776,245
9	MICHIGAN	10,744	$678,705
10	PHOENIX	10,167	$570,255
11	TULSA	9,583	$628,405
12	DENVER	8,641	$645,583
13	KANSASCITY	8,547	$574,899
14	**Grand Total**	**144,177**	**$9,343,323**

Figure 15-21: This pivot table allows you to filter by business segment to see the top ten markets by total contracted hours and revenue.

Suppose you want to turn this view into an XY scatter chart to be able to point out the relationship between the contracted hours and revenues. You need to keep the capability to filter out ten records by model number; however, you also want the ability to create XY.

A pivot chart is definitely out because you can't build pivot charts with certain chart types (such as XY scatter charts). The preceding techniques are also out because those methods disable the interactivity you need. So what's the solution? Use the cells around the pivot table to link back to the data you need and then chart those cells. That is, you can build a mini dataset that feeds your standard chart.

This dataset links back to the data items in your pivot table, so when your pivot table changes, your dataset changes. Follow these steps to create a standalone chart that is connected to your pivot table:

1. Click in a cell next to your pivot table (see Figure 15-22) and reference the first data item you want plotted on your chart.

	A	B	C	D	E
1	Business_Segment (All)				
2					
3	**Market**	Contracted Hours	Sales_Amount		
4	CALIFORNIA	33,014	$2,254,735		=B4
5	FLORIDA	22,640	$1,450,392		
6	CHARLOTTE	14,525	$890,522		
7	NEWYORK	14,213	$873,581		
8	CANADA	12,103	$776,245		
9	MICHIGAN	10,744	$678,705		
10	PHOENIX	10,167	$570,255		
11	TULSA	9,583	$628,405		
12	DENVER	8,641	$645,583		
13	KANSASCITY	8,547	$574,899		
14	**Grand Total**	**144,177**	**$9,343,323**		

Figure 15-22: Start your linked dataset by referencing the first data item you need to capture.

2. Copy the formula you just entered and paste it down and across to create your complete dataset.

At this point, you have a dataset that looks similar to the one in Figure 15-23.

	A	B	C	D	E	F
1	Business_Segment (All)					
2						
3	**Market**	Contracted Hours	Sales_Amount		Contracted Hours	Sales_Amount
4	CALIFORNIA	33,014	$2,254,735		33,014	2,254,735
5	FLORIDA	22,640	$1,450,392		22,640	1,450,392
6	CHARLOTTE	14,525	$890,522		14,525	890,522
7	NEWYORK	14,213	$873,581		14,213	873,581
8	CANADA	12,103	$776,245		12,103	776,245
9	MICHIGAN	10,744	$678,705		10,744	678,705
10	PHOENIX	10,167	$570,255		10,167	570,255
11	TULSA	9,583	$628,405		9,583	628,405
12	DENVER	8,641	$645,583		8,641	645,583
13	KANSASCITY	8,547	$574,899		8,547	574,899
14	**Grand Total**	**144,177**	**$9,343,323**			

Figure 15-23: Copy the formula and paste it down and across to create your complete dataset.

3. After your linked dataset is complete, use it to create a standard chart.

In this example, you create an XY scatter chart with this data, which you can't do with a pivot chart.

Figure 15-24 demonstrates how this solution offers the best of both worlds:

➤ You kept the ability to filter out a particular business segment using the Page field.

➤ You have all the formatting freedom of a standard chart without any of the issues related to using a pivot chart.

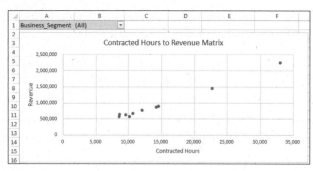

Figure 15-24: This solution provides the functionality of your pivot table without the formatting limitations of a pivot chart.

Adding Interactivity with Slicers

Slicers allow you to filter your pivot table, similar to the way Filter fields filter a pivot table. The difference is that slicers offer a user-friendly interface, enabling you to better manage the filter state of your pivot table reports. Happily, Microsoft has added another dimension to slicers with the introduction of Timeline slicers. Timeline slicers are designed to work specifically with date-based filtering.

In this chapter, you explore slicers and their potential to add an attractive as well as interactive user interface to your dashboards and reports.

Understanding Slicers

If you've worked your way through Chapter 14, you know that pivot tables allow for interactive filtering using Filter fields. Filter fields are the drop-down lists you can include at the top of your pivot table, allowing users to interactively filter for specific data items. As useful as Filter fields are, they've always had a couple of drawbacks:

➤ Filter fields are not cascading filters. They don't work together to limit selections when needed.

For example, look at Figure 16-1. You can see that the Region filter is set to the North region. However, the Market filter still allows you to select markets that are clearly not in the North region (California, for example). Because the Market filter is not in any way limited based on the Region Filter field, you have the annoying possibility of selecting a market that could yield no data because it isn't in the North region.

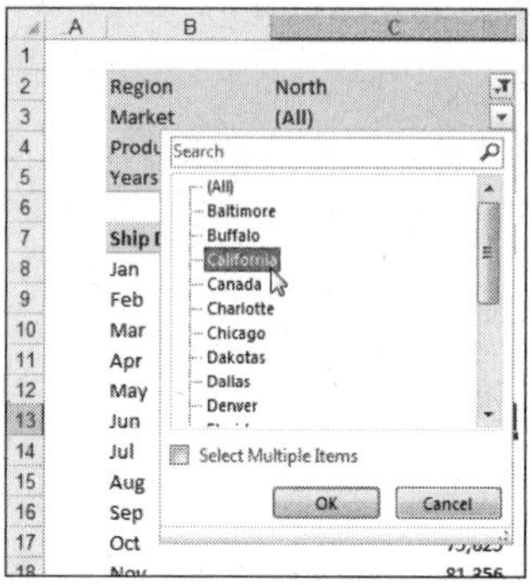

Figure 16-1: Default pivot table Filter fields don't work together to limit filter selections.

➤ Filter fields don't provide an easy way to tell what exactly is being filtered when you select multiple items.

Figure 16-2 shows an example of this. As you can see, the Region filter has been limited to three regions: Midwest, North, and Northeast. However, notice that the Region filter value shows (Multiple Items). By default, Filter fields will show (Multiple Items) when you select more than one item. The only way to tell what has been selected is to click the drop-down. You can imagine the confusion on a printed version of this report, when there is no way to click down to see which data items make up the numbers on the page.

Figure 16-2: Filter fields show "(Multiple Items)" when multiple selections are made.

By contrast, slicers don't have these issues. Slicers respond to one another. As illustrated in Figure 16-3, the Market slicer visibly highlights the relevant markets when the North region is selected. The rest of the markets are muted, signaling that they're not part of the North region.

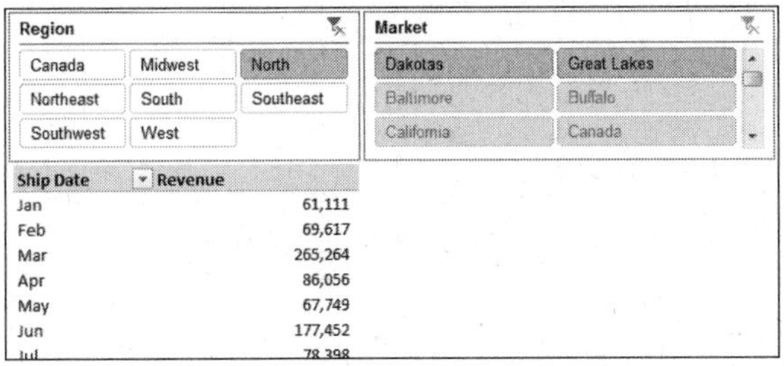

Region				Market		
Canada	Midwest	North		Dakotas	Great Lakes	
Northeast	South	Southeast		Baltimore	Buffalo	
Southwest	West			California	Canada	

Ship Date	Revenue
Jan	61,111
Feb	69,617
Mar	265,264
Apr	86,056
May	67,749
Jun	177,452
Jul	78,398

Figure 16-3: Slicers work together to show you relevant data items based on your selection.

When selecting multiple items in a slicer, you can easily see that multiple items have been chosen. In Figure 16-4, the pivot table is filtered by the Midwest, North, and Northeast regions. No more (Multiple Items).

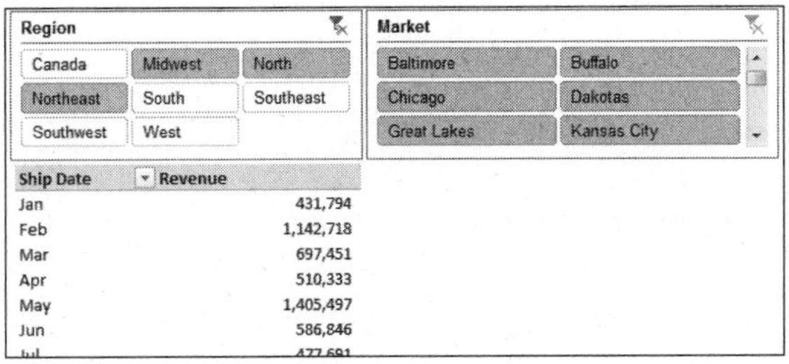

Region				Market		
Canada	Midwest	North		Baltimore	Buffalo	
Northeast	South	Southeast		Chicago	Dakotas	
Southwest	West			Great Lakes	Kansas City	

Ship Date	Revenue
Jan	431,794
Feb	1,142,718
Mar	697,451
Apr	510,333
May	1,405,497
Jun	586,846
Jul	477,691

Figure 16-4: Slicers do a better job at displaying multiple item selections.

Creating a Standard Slicer

It's time to create your first slicer. Follow these steps:

1. Place your cursor anywhere inside your pivot table; then go to the Ribbon and select the Analyze tab.

2. Click the Insert Slicer icon (see Figure 16-5).

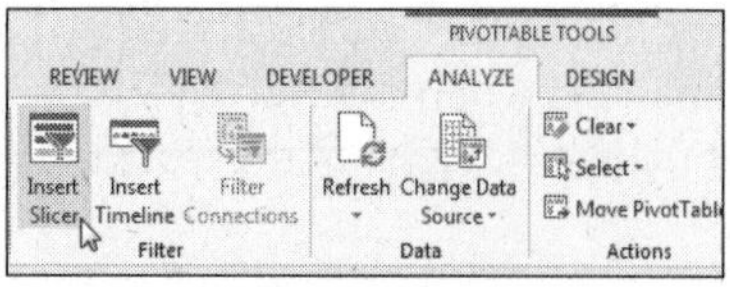

Figure 16-5: Inserting a slicer.

The Insert Slicers dialog box appears.

3. Click the filter values to filter your pivot table (see Figure 16-6).

The idea is to select the dimensions you want to filter. In this example, the Region and Market slicers will be created.

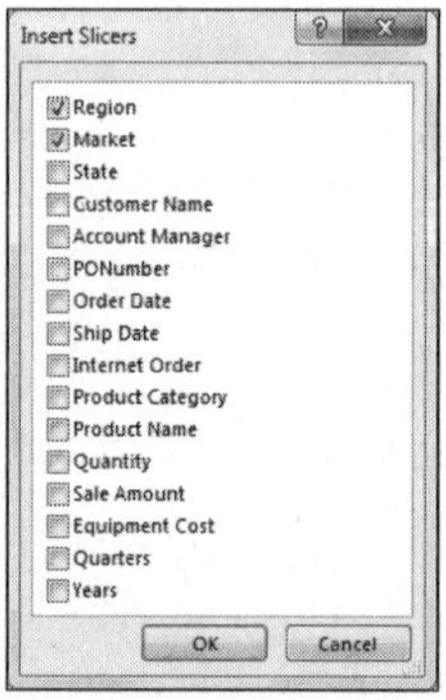

Figure 16-6: Select the dimensions for which you want slicers created.

As you can see in Figure 16-7, clicking Midwest in the Region slicer not only filters your pivot table, but also the Market slicer responds by highlighting the markets that belong to the Midwest region.

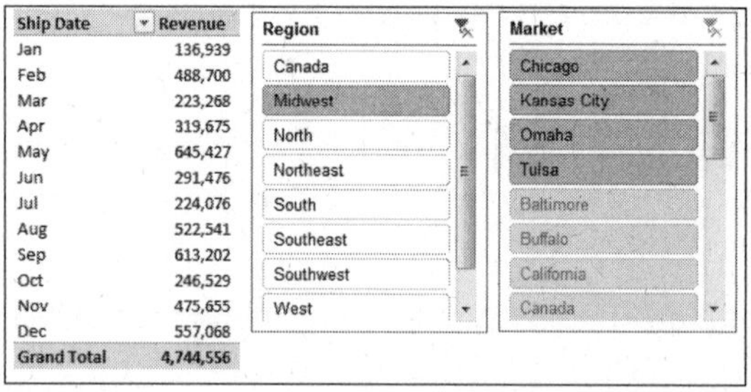

Figure 16-7: Select the dimensions you want filtered using slicers.

You can also select multiple values by holding the Ctrl key while selecting the needed filters. As illustrated in Figure 16-8, you press Ctrl while selecting Baltimore, California, Charlotte, and Chicago, which highlights the selected markets in the Market slicer and their associated regions in the Region slicer.

Ship Date	Revenue	Region		Market	
Jan	767,777	Midwest		Baltimore	
Feb	1,181,050	Northeast		Buffalo	
Mar	1,443,527	Southeast		California	
Apr	1,207,014			Canada	
May	1,536,345	West			
Jun	1,520,544	Canada		Charlotte	
Jul	1,905,681	North		Chicago	
Aug	2,579,320				
Sep	2,817,887	South		Dakotas	
Oct	1,518,105	Southwest		Dallas	
Nov	2,115,237				
Dec	2,562,649				
Grand Total	**21,155,134**				

Figure 16-8: The fact that you can visually see the current filter state gives slicers a unique advantage over the Filter field.

To clear the filtering on a slicer, simply click the Clear Filter icon on the target slicer (shown in Figure 16-9).

Region		Market	
Midwest		Baltimore	
Northeast		Buffalo	
Southeast		California	
West		Canada	
Canada		Charlotte	
North		Chicago	
South		Dakotas	
Southwest		Dallas	

Figure 16-9: Clearing the filters on a slicer.

Formatting slicers

When using slicers in a dashboard environment, you must do a bit of formatting to make your slicers match the theme and layout of your dashboard. The following subsections describe a few common formatting adjustments you can make to slicers.

Size and placement

A slicer behaves like a standard Excel shape object in that you can move it around and adjust its size by clicking on it and dragging its position points (see Figure 16-10).

Region	
Midwest	
Northeast	
Southeast	
West	

Ship Date	Revenue
Jan	767,777
Feb	1,181,050
Mar	1,443,527

Figure 16-10: Adjust the slicer size and placement by dragging its position points.

You can also right-click the slicer and select Size and Properties, which accesses the Format Slicer pane illustrated in Figure 16-11. Here you can adjust the size of the slicer, how the slicer behaves when cells are shifted, and whether the slicer will be shown when the worksheet is printed.

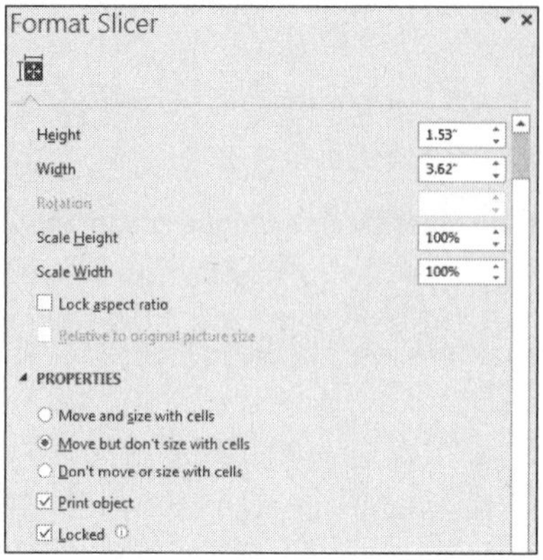

Figure 16-11: The Format Slicer pane offers more control over how the slicer behaves in relation to the worksheet it's on.

Data item columns

By default, all slicers are created with one column of data items. You change this by right-clicking the slicer and selecting Size and Properties. This accesses the Format Slicer pane. Under the Position and Layout section, you specify the number of columns. Adjusting the number to 2 (as demonstrated in Figure 16-12) forces the data times to be displayed in two columns. Adjusting the number to 3 forces the data items to display in three columns, and so on.

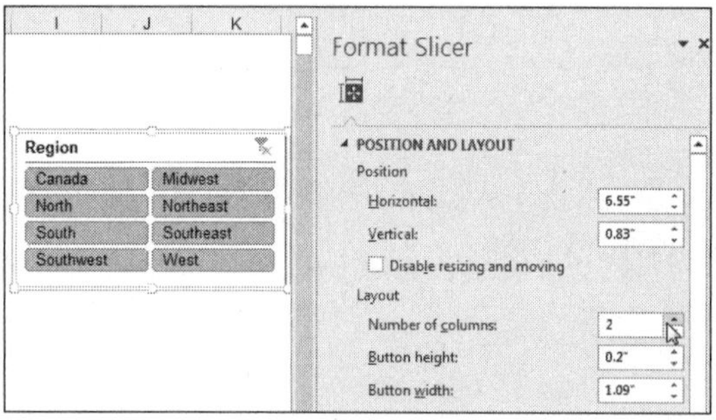

Figure 16-12: Adjust the Number of Columns property to display the slicer data items in more than one column.

Color and style

You can quickly change the color and style of your slicer. Click it; then select a style from the Slicer Style gallery on the Slicer Tools' Options tab (see Figure 16-13). The default styles available will suit the majority of your dashboards.

If you want more control over the color and style of your slicer, click the New Slicer Style button at the lower-left corner of the Slicer Style gallery shown in Figure 16-13. A dialog box appears where you can apply detailed formatting for each component part of the slicer.

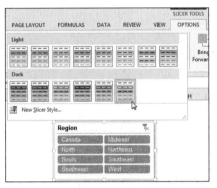

Figure 16-13: Use the Slicer Style gallery to apply a default style or create your own.

Other slicer settings

Right-clicking your slicer and selecting Slicer Settings activates the Slicer Settings dialog box shown in Figure 16-14. With this dialog box, you can control the look of your slicer's header, how your slicer is sorted, and how filtered items are handled.

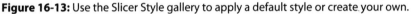

Figure 16-14: The Slicer Settings dialog box.

With minimal effort, you can integrate your slicers nicely into your dashboard layout. Figure 16-15, illustrates two slicers and a pivot chart working together as a cohesive dashboard component.

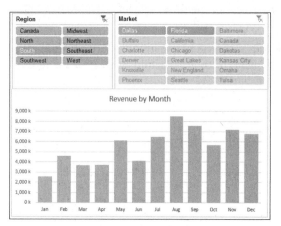

Figure 16-15: With a little formatting, slicers can be made to adopt the look and feel of your overall dashboard.

Controlling multiple pivot tables

Another advantage you gain with slicers is that each slicer can be tied to more than one pivot table. That is to say, any filter you apply to your slicer can be applied to multiple pivot tables.

To connect your slicer to more than one pivot table, simply right-click the slicer and select Report Connections. This activates the Report Connections dialog box shown in Figure 16-16. Place a check next to any pivot table that you want to filter using the current slicer.

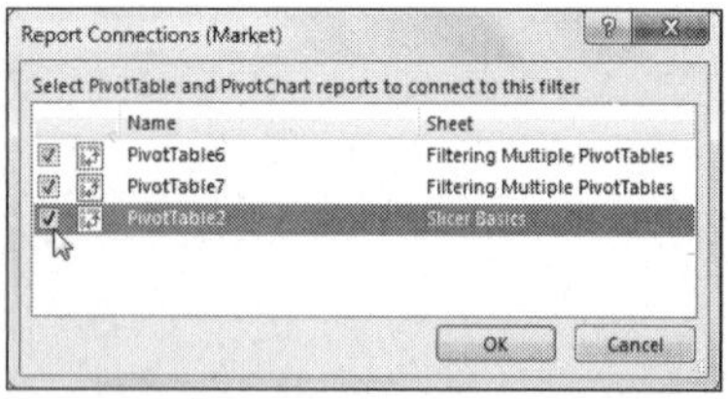

Figure 16-16: Choose the pivot tables that will be filtered by this slicer.

At this point, any filter you apply to the slicer will be applied to all the connected pivot tables. Controlling the filter state of multiple pivot tables is a powerful feature, especially in dashboards that run on multiple pivot tables.

Creating a Timeline Slicer

The Timeline slicer is new in Excel 2013. The Timeline slicer is similar to a standard slicer: You filter a pivot table using a visual selection mechanism instead of the old Filter fields. The difference is that the Timeline slicer is designed to work exclusively with date fields, providing an excellent visual method to filter and group the dates in your pivot table.

To create a Timeline slicer, your pivot table must contain a field where *all* the data is formatted as a date. It's not enough to have a column of data that contains a few dates. All the values in your date field must be a valid date and be formatted as such.

To create a Timeline slicer, follow these steps:

1. Place your cursor anywhere inside your pivot table; then go up to the Ribbon and select the Analyze tab.

2. Click the Timeline Slicer icon (see Figure 16-17).

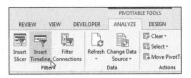

Figure 16-17: Inserting a Timeline slicer.

The Insert Timelines dialog box, shown in Figure 16-18, activates, showing you all the available date fields in the chosen pivot table.

3. Select the date fields for which you want to create the timeline.

Figure 16-18: Select the date fields for which you want slicers created.

After your Timeline slicer is created, you can filter the data in your pivot table and pivot chart, using this dynamic data selection mechanism. Figure 16-19 demonstrates how selecting Mar, Apr, and May in the Timeline slicer automatically filters the pivot chart.

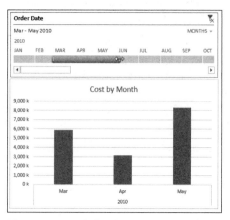

Figure 16-19: Click a date selection to filter your pivot table or pivot chart.

Figure 16-20 illustrates how you can expand the slicer range with the mouse to include a wider range of dates in your filtered numbers.

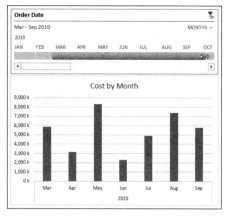

Figure 16-20: You can expand the range on the Timeline slicer to include more data in the filtered numbers.

Want to quickly filter your pivot table by quarters? Well, that's easy with a Timeline slicer. Simply click the time period drop-down menu and select Quarters. As you can see in Figure 16-21, you also have the option of switching to Years or Days, if needed.

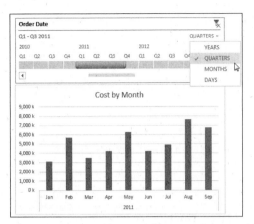

Figure 16-21: Quickly switch between Quarters, Years, Months, and Days.

Note

Timeline slicers apply filters based on standard calendar years. In other words, Q1 means Jan, Feb, and Mar. However, if your fiscal year starts in October, your Q1 is made up of Oct, Nov, and Dec. So the quarter slicers may not be as useful for your organization. Currently you can't force a slicer to adjust to your own custom fiscal year.

Note

Timeline slicers are not backward-compatible, meaning they are usable only in Excel 2013. If you open a workbook with Timeline slicers in Excel 2010 or previous versions, the Timeline slicers will be disabled.

Using Slicers as Form Controls

In Chapter 12, you discovered how to add interactivity to a dashboard using data modeling techniques and Form controls. Although the techniques in that chapter are powerful, the one drawback is that Excel Form controls are starting to look a bit dated, especially when paired with the modern-looking charts that come with Excel 2013.

One clever way to alleviate this problem is to highjack the slicer feature for use as a proxy Form control of sorts. Figure 16-22 demonstrates this option with a chart that responds to the slicer on the left. When you click Income, the chart fills with income data. When you click Expense, the chart fills with expense data. Keep in mind that the chart is no way connected to a pivot table.

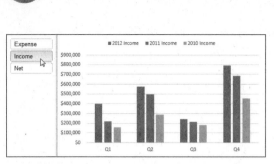

Figure 16-22: You can highjack pivot slicers and use them as more attractive Form controls for models not built on pivot tables.

> **Cross-Ref**
>
> If you skipped Chapter 12, you may want to visit it now in order to better understand the data modeling and setup demonstrated in this example.

To build this basic model, follow these steps:

1. Create a simple table that holds the names you want for your controls, along with some index numbering. In this case, the table contains three rows under a field called Metric.

   Each row contains a metric name and index number for each metric (Income, Expense, and Net).

2. Using this simple table, create a pivot table (see Figure 16-23).

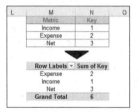

Figure 16-23: Create a simple table that holds the names for your controls along with some index numbering; then using that table, create a pivot table.

3. Place your cursor anywhere inside the newly created pivot table, select the Analyze tab, and then click the Insert Slicer icon. In the Insert Slicer dialog box, create a slicer for the Metric field.

   At this point, you have a slicer with the three metric names.

4. Right-click the slicer and choose Slicer Settings to activate the Slicer Settings dialog box.

5. In the Slicer Settings dialog box, uncheck the Display Header option (see Figure 16-24).

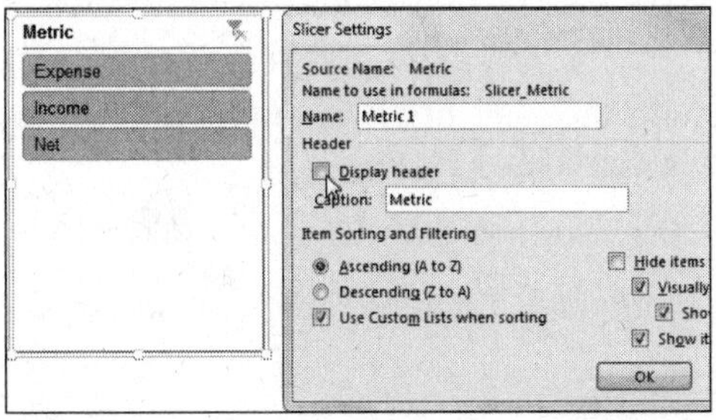

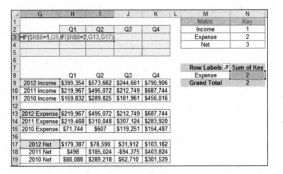

Figure 16-24: Create a slicer for the Metric field and remove the header.

Each time the Metric slicer is clicked, the associated pivot table is filtered to show only the selected metric.

Figure 16-25 demonstrates that this action also filters the index number for that metric. The filtered index number always shows up in the same cell (N8 in this case). So this cell can now be used as a trigger cell for VLOOKUP formulas, INDEX formulas, and If statements.

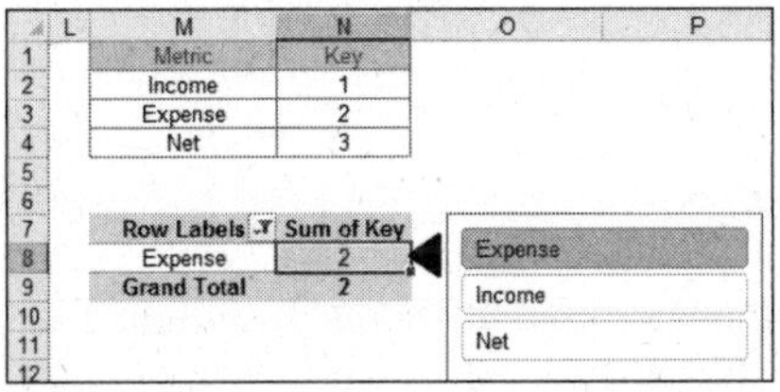

Figure 16-25: Clicking an item in the slicer filters out the correct index number for the selected metric.

6. Use the slicer-fed trigger cell (N8) to drive the formulas in your staging area, as demonstrated in Figure 16-26.

Figure 16-26: Use the filtered trigger cell to drive the formulas in your staging area.

This formula tells Excel to check the value of cell N8:

- If the value of cell N8 is 1, which represents the value of the Income option, the formula returns the value in the Income dataset (cell G9).

- If the value of cell N8 is 2, which represents the value of the Expense option, the formula returns the value in the Expense dataset (cell G13).

- If the value of cell N8 is neither 1 nor 2, the value in the Net dataset (cell G17) is returned.

7. Copy the formula down and across to build out the full staging table (see Figure 16-27).

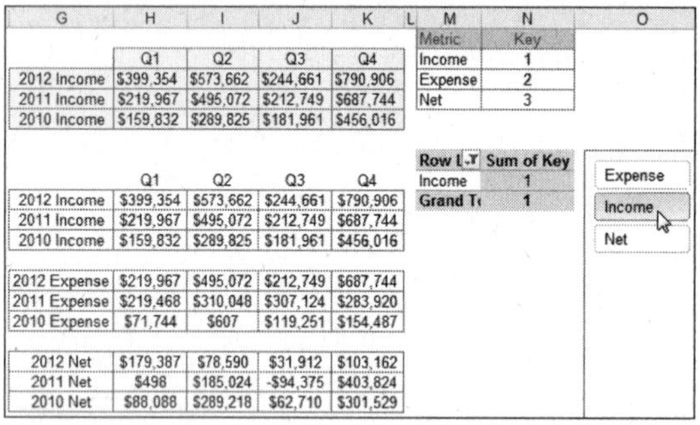

Figure 16-27: The final staging table fed via the slicer.

8. Create a chart using the staging table as the source.

With this simple technique, you can provide your customers with an attractive interactive menu that more effectively adheres to the look and feel of their dashboards.

Using the Internal Data Model and Power View

In This Chapter

- Understanding the internal Data Model
- Starting a Power View dashboard
- Creating and working with Power View charts
- Visualizing data on a Power View map

Excel 2013 introduces a new feature called Power View. Power View is essentially an interactive canvas that allows you to display charts, tables, maps, and slicers in one dashboard window. The components in the Power View window are inherently linked so that they all work together and respond to any filtering or slicing you apply while using the dashboard. Select a region in one chart, and the other components in the Power View dashboard automatically respond to show you data for only that region.

This powerful feature runs on the new internal Data Model found in Excel 2013. The internal Data Model is an in-memory analytics engine that allows you to store disparate data sources in a kind of OLAP cube within Excel. OLAP is a category of data warehousing that allows you to mine and analyze vast amounts of data with ease and efficiency.

This chapter shows you how to combine the internal Data Model and Power View to create powerful interactive dashboards.

Note

Sadly, Microsoft has made Power View available only with Office 2013 Professional Plus or the Office 365 Small Business Premium subscription service. You won't even see the options for Power View if you don't have one of these versions of Office 2013. However, the internal Data Model discussed in this chapter is happily available in all versions of Excel 2013. This feature is powerful enough on its own as you will see in the following section.

Understanding the Internal Data Model

Excel 2013 introduces a new in-memory analytics engine called the internal Data Model. Every workbook has one internal Data Model that allows you to work with analyze disparate data sources like never before.

The idea behind the Data Model is simple. Let's say you have two tables — a Customers table and an Orders table. The Orders table has basic information about invoices (Customer Number, Invoice Date, and Revenue). The Customers table has basic information like Customer Number, Customer Name, and State.

If you want to analyze revenue by state, you must join the two tables and aggregate the Revenue field in the Orders table by the State field in the Customers table.

In the past, you would have to go through a series of gyrations involving VLOOKUPs, SUMIFs, or other formulas. With the new Excel 2103 data model, however, you can simply tell Excel how the two tables are related (in this case, they both have a customer number) and then pull them into the internal Data Model. The Excel Data Model will then build an internal analytical database based on that customer number relationship and expose the data through a pivot table. With the pivot table, you can create the aggregation by state with a few clicks of the mouse.

Building out your first data model

Imagine that you have the Transactions table you see in Figure 17-1. On another worksheet, you have a Generators table (see Figure 17-2) that contains location information about each generator.

	A	B	C	D	E
1	GENERATOR_ID	WASTE_CODE	GENERATOR_SIZE	ON_SITE_MANAGEMENT	GENERATED_QTY
2	RID001201508	W205	MEDIUM	N	2,392
3	RID001201508	W205	MEDIUM	N	2,392
4	RID001201508	W219	MEDIUM	N	1,020
5	RID001201508	W206	MEDIUM	N	1,587
6	RID001201508	W200	MEDIUM	N	4,795
7	RID980914550	W219	MEDIUM	N	6,800
8	RIR000508416	W203	MEDIUM	N	1,845
9	SC0000029843	W211	LARGE	N	3,895

Figure 17-1: This table shows transactions by generator number.

	A	B	C	D	E
1	GENERATOR_ID	GENERATOR_NAME	GEN_CITY	GEN_STATE	GEN_ZIP
2	AK1210022157	USARMY FT RICH	ANCHORAGE	AK	99505
3	AK1570028646	USAF EIELSON A	EIELSON AFB	AK	99702
4	AK3210022155	US ARMY FT GRE	DELTA JUNCTION	AK	99737
5	AK4170024323	FORMER U. S. N	ADAK	AK	99546
6	AK6210022426	US ARMY FT WA	FT WAINWRIGH	AK	99703
7	AK8570028649	USAF ELMENDO	ANCHORAGE	AK	99506
8	AK8690360492	USDHS CG BSU K	KETCHIKAN	AK	99901
9	AK9570028705	USAF EARECKSO	SHEMYA ISLAND	AK	98736
10	AK9690330742	USDHS CG BASE	KODIAK	AK	99619

Figure 17-2: This table provides location information on each generator.

On the Web

You can find the example file for this chapter on this book's companion website at www.wiley.com/go/exceldr **in the workbook named Chapter 17 Samples.xlsx.**

The first step in building your data model is to convert your separate data ranges to named Excel Tables. Converting a range to a table ensures that the internal Data Model will recognize it as an actual data source.

Convert your data ranges to Tables

For each data range you want to import into the internal Data Model, follow these steps:

1. Click anywhere in the Transactions data table and press Ctrl+T on your keyboard.

   The Create Table dialog box opens, as shown in Figure 17-3.

2. Ensure that the range for the table is correct and click OK.

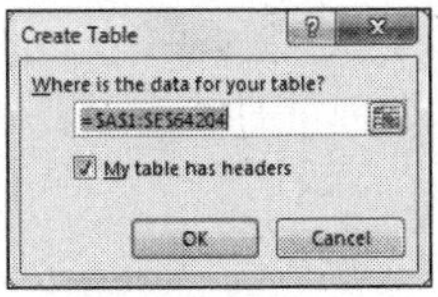

Figure 17-3: Convert your first data range into an Excel Table.

Click inside your Excel Table, and you will see a Table Tools Design tab on the Ribbon. Note that if you create multiple tables in a worksheet, the Table Tools Design tab will apply to the Excel Table you have selected.

3. Click the Table Tools Design tab and enter a friendly name for your table in the Table Name box (see Figure 17-4).

   This step ensures that you will be able to recognize the table when adding it to the internal Data Model.

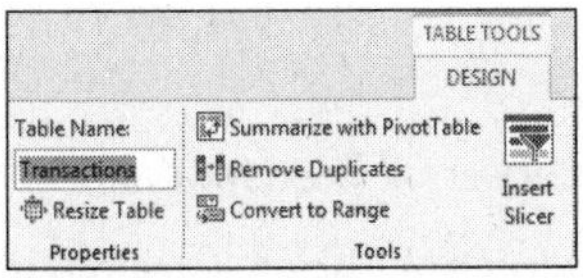

Figure 17-4: Give your newly created Excel Table a friendly name.

In this scenario, you use the same steps to convert your Generators range to an Excel Table.

Add your Tables to the internal Data Model

Each 2013 workbook has an internal Data Model that (by default) is exposed as a connection called ThisWorkbookDataModel when you add data sources to it. You can add your newly created Tables to the internal Data Model using the Workbook Connections dialog box. Follow these steps:

1. Go to the Ribbon, click the Data tab, and select Connections.

2. In the Workbook Connections dialog box, click the drop-down arrow beside the Add button and select Add to the Data Model (see Figure 17-5).

Figure 17-5: Open the Workbook Connections dialog box and select Add to the Data Model.

The Existing Connections dialog box opens, as shown in Figure 17-6.

3. Click the Tables tab, choose the table you want to add, and click OK.

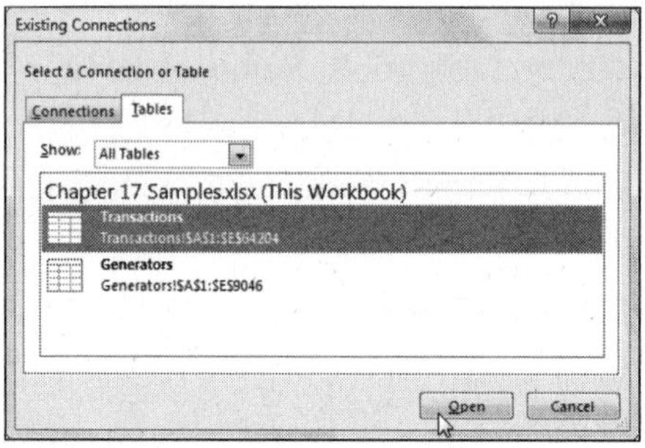

Figure 17-6: Choose a table to add and click OK.

4. Repeat Steps 2 and 3 for each Table you want to add to the internal Data Model.

After adding all your tables, the Workbook Connections dialog box shows a connection called ThisWorkbookDataModel, listing all the data sources associated with it.

As you can see in Figure 17-7, you now have your two tables in the internal Data Model.

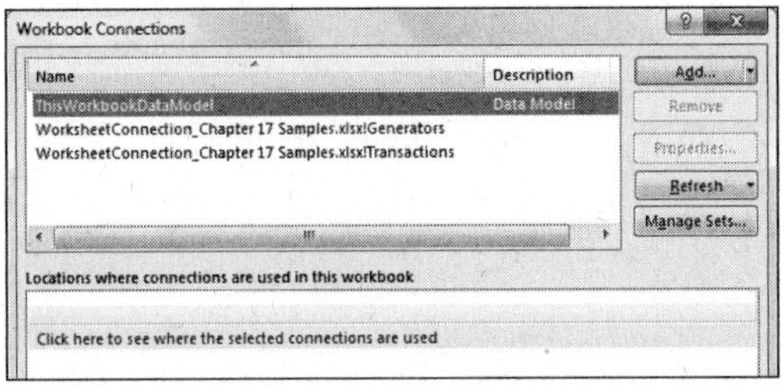

Figure 17-7: The internal Data Model now contains the Transactions and Generators tables.

Note Any changes made to your tables (such as adding records, deleting records, and adding columns) are automatically captured in the internal Data Model. No need to perform a refresh action.

Build relationships for the Tables in the internal Data Model

Although your data now exists in the internal Data Model, Excel doesn't inherently know how your tables relate to one another. For example, your two tables have a column called Generator_ID (refer to Figures 17-1 and 17-2). This column is the key that connects the two tables, allowing you to match transactions with customer location.

You need to explicitly define this relationship before Excel recognizes how to handle the data in the Data Model. Follow these steps:

1. Go to the Ribbon, click the Data tab, and select Relationships.

   The Manage Relationships dialog box opens.

2. Click the New button.

   The Create Relationship dialog box opens, as shown in Figure 17-8.

3. Select the tables and fields that define the relationship.

   In Figure 17-8, note that the Transactions table has a Generator_ID field; it's related to the Generators table via the Generator_ID field.

4. Click OK to confirm the relationship.

   You are returned to the Manage Relationships dialog box (see Figure 17-9). Here you can add any additional relationships you may need. Notice that you can also delete and edit relationships in this dialog box.

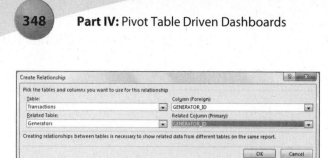

Figure 17-8: Create the relationships between your tables, defining each table and the associated fields.

Figure 17-9: Use the Manage Relationships dialog box to add, delete, and edit relationships.

Note

In Figure 17-8, at the lower right, notice the Related Column (Primary) drop-down field. The term *Primary* means that the internal Data Model will use this field from the associated table as the primary key. Every relationship must have a field you designate as the primary key. Primary key fields are necessary in the Data Model to prevent aggregation errors and duplications. Thus the Excel Data model must impose some strict rules around the primary key. You cannot have duplicates or null values in a field being used as the primary key. So the Generators table (shown in Figure 17-8) must have all unique values in its Generator_ID field, with no blanks or null values. This is the only way Excel can ensure data integrity when joining multiple tables.

Using your Data Model in a pivot table

After you fill your internal Data Model, you can start using it. Later, in the "Creating a Power View Dashboard" section, you find out how to leverage it with Power View. First, explore how to leverage the Data Model in pivot tables to analyze the data within. To create a pivot table from the internal Data Model, follow these steps:

1. Click the Insert tab and select PivotTable to start a pivot table.

2. In the Create PivotTable dialog box, select Use an External Data Source and click the Choose Connection button (see Figure 17-10).

    The Existing Connections dialog box opens, as shown in Figure 17-11.

3. Click the Tables tab and choose Tables in Workbook Data Model. Click Open to confirm.

    You return to the Create PivotTable dialog box.

4. Click OK to finalize the pivot table.

Figure 17-10: Start a pivot table and opt to choose an external connection.

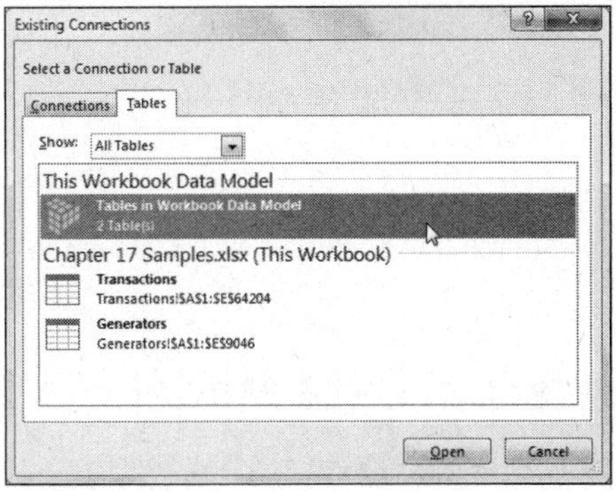

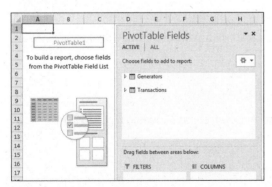

Figure 17-11: Select the Tables in Workbook Data Model option to use the internal Data Model as the source for your pivot table.

After you create the pivot table, you'll see that the Pivot Field list shows each table in the internal Data Model (similar to Figure 17-12).

Figure 17-12: Pivot tables that use the internal Data Model as the source will show all the tables within the Data Model in the pivot field list.

With a Data Model–driven pivot table, you can merge disparate data sources into one analytical engine. Figure 17-13 demonstrates how you can build a view using data fields from the different tables in the Data Model.

	A	B	C	D	E	F	G	H
1	Row Labels	Sum of GENERATED_QTY						
2	⊟AK	667,520						
3	LARGE	31,484						
4	MEDIUM	96,253						
5	SMALL	63,459						
6	X-LARGE	476,324						
7	⊟AL	284,223,180						
8	LARGE	4,259,542						
9	MEDIUM	1,515,179						
10	SMALL	126,393						
11	X-LARGE	278,322,066						
12	⊟AR	487,933,057						
13	LARGE	1,948,005						
14	MEDIUM	1,487,490						
15	SMALL	59,609						
16	X-LARGE	484,437,952						
17	⊟AZ	18,667,891						
18	LARGE	2,043,549						
19	MEDIUM	865,941						
20	SMALL	67,751						
21	X-LARGE	15,690,649						
22	⊟CA	794,473,621						

PivotTable Fields ▾ ×

ACTIVE | ALL

Choose fields to add to report: ⚙ ▾

▲ 🎛 Generators
☑ GEN_STATE
☐ GEN_ZIP

▲ 🎛 Transactions
☐ GENERATOR_ID
☐ WASTE_CODE
☑ GENERATOR_SIZE

Drag fields between areas below:

▼ FILTERS   ▥ COLUMNS

▥ ROWS   Σ VALUES
GEN_STATE ▾   Sum of GENERATED_... ▾
GENERATOR_SIZE ▾

Figure 17-13: With a Data Model–driven pivot table, you can analyze data using the fields for each table in the Data Model.

Using external data sources in your internal Data Model

The internal Data Model isn't limited to using only data that already exists in your Excel workbooks. You can fill your Data Model with all kinds of external data sources. In Chapter 18, you dive into using external data sources in your dashboarding models. Now, though, take a look at how to bring external data sources into the Data Model.

Say that you have an Access database that contains a normalized set of tables. You want to analyze the data in that database in Excel. You decide to use the new internal Data Model to present the data you need through a pivot table.

On the Web   **You can find the Facility Services Access database on this book's companion website at** `www.wiley.com/go/exceldr.`

To use external tables in your Data Model, follow these steps.

1. On the Data tab of the Ribbon, select the From Access icon, as shown in Figure 17-14.

FILE	HOME	INSERT	PAGE LAYOUT	FORMULAS	**DATA**

From Access | From Web | From Text | From Other Sources ▾ | Existing Connections | Refresh All ▾ | 🔗 Connections / 🔲 Properties / 🔲 Edit Links | A↓ / Z↓

Get External Data   Connections

Figure 17-14: Click the From Access button to get data from your Access database.

2. Browse to your target Access database and open it.

   The Select Data dialog box opens.

3. In the Select Data dialog box, place a check next to Enable Selection of Multiple Tables (see Figure 17-15).

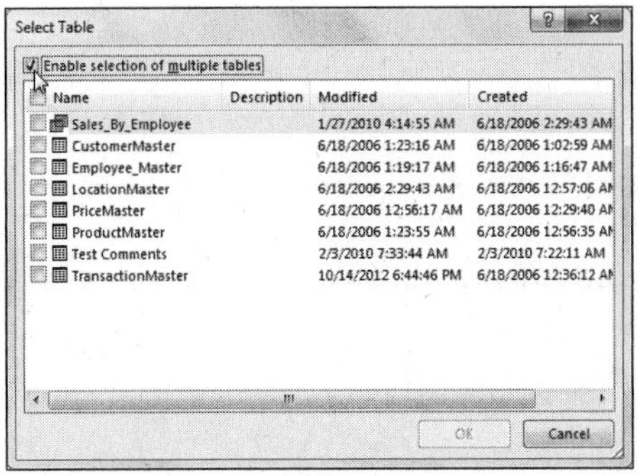

Figure 17-15: Enable the selection of multiple tables.

4. Place a check next to each table you want to bring into the internal Data Model, as demonstrated in Figure 17-16.

5. Click OK.

   The Import Data dialog box opens, as shown in Figure 17-17.

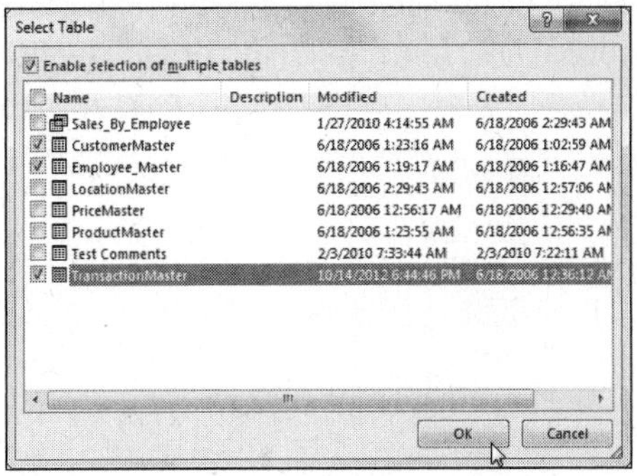

Figure 17-16: Place a check next to each table you want to import to the internal Data Model; then click OK.

6. In the Import Data dialog box, click the Properties drop-down arrow and remove the check next to Import Relationships Between Tables.

   This ensures that Excel doesn't error out because of misinterpretations about how the tables are related. In other words, you want to create relationships yourself.

Figure 17-17: Remove the check next to Import Relationships Between Tables.

7. In the Import Data dialog box, choose PivotTable Report and click OK to create the base pivot.

8. Go to the Ribbon, click the Data tab, and choose Relationships.

   The Manage Relationships dialog box opens, as shown in Figure 17-18.

9. Create the needed relationships and then click the Close button.

Note

As mentioned earlier in this chapter (in the section called "Build Relationships for the Tables in the Internal Data Model"), when creating the relationships for your Data Model, you will need to remain aware of which table you designate in the Related Column (Primary) drop-down field on the Manage Relationships dialog box. The table you use in this field cannot have duplicates or null values in a field being used as the primary key. So in this scenario, you will not be able to designate the TransactionMaster table in this field, as it contains transactional line items that may contain duplicates.

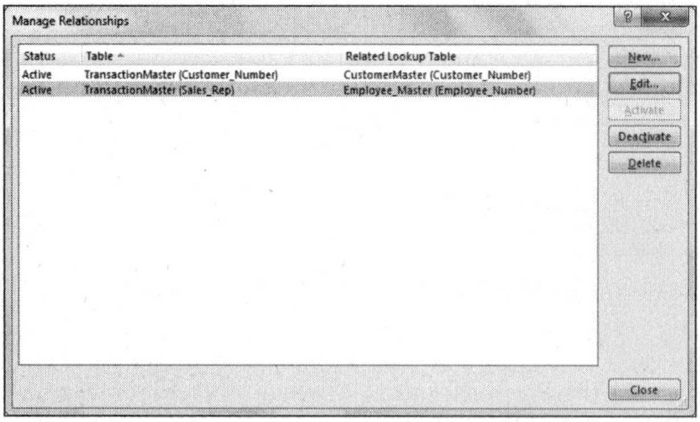

Figure 17-18: Create the needed relationships for the tables you just imported.

If all went well, you should end with a pivot table similar to the one illustrated in Figure 17-19. In just a few clicks, you created a powerful platform to build and maintain pivot table analysis based on data in an Access database!

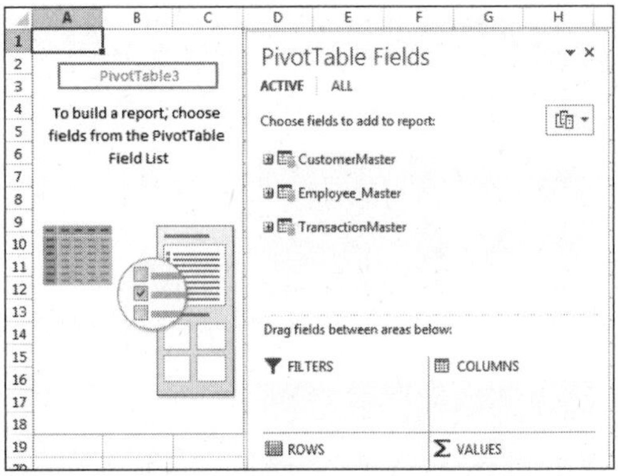

Figure 17-19: You're ready to build your pivot table analysis based on multiple external data tables.

Creating a Power View Dashboard

After you have data in your internal Data Model, you can create a Power View dashboard from that Data Model. Just go to the Ribbon, click the Insert tab, and click Power View. Excel takes a moment to create a new worksheet called Power ViewX, where *X* represents a number that will make the sheet name unique (for example, Power View1).

This new worksheet has the three main sections shown in Figure 17-20: Canvas, Filter Pane, and Field List.

The canvas contains the charts, tables, and maps you add to your dashboard. The filter pane contains the data filters you define. You use the field list to add and configure the data for your dashboard.

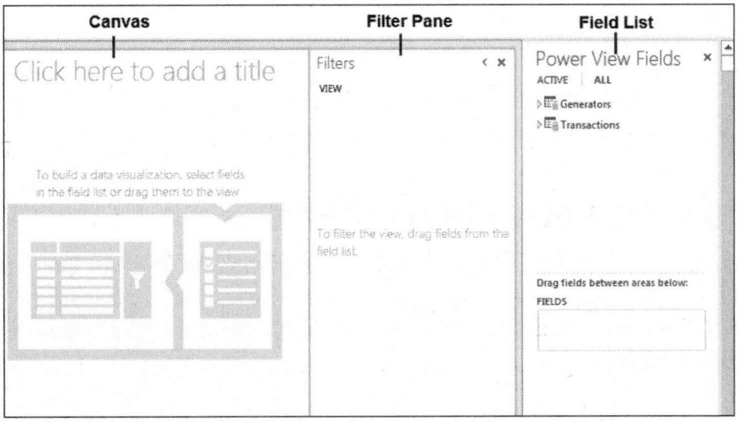

Figure 17-20: The three main sections of a Power View worksheet.

You build up your Power View dashboard by dragging the fields from the field list to the respective sections. For example, dragging the Generator_Size field to the filter pane creates a list of filterable items (see Figure 17-21) that can be checked and unchecked. The filter pane has a few icons that help you work with the filters. These icons enable you to expand or collapse the entire filter pane, clear applied filters, call up advanced filter options, or delete the filter.

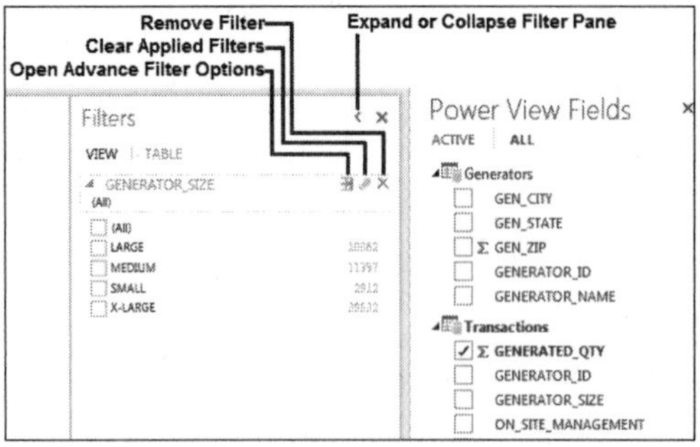

Figure 17-21: The filter pane has a few icons that help you work with the filters.

To add data to the canvas, use the field list to drag the needed data fields to the FIELDS drop zone. In Figure 17-22, you can see that the Waste_Code field and the Generated_Qty field have been moved to the FIELDS drop zone. This results in a new table of data on the canvas.

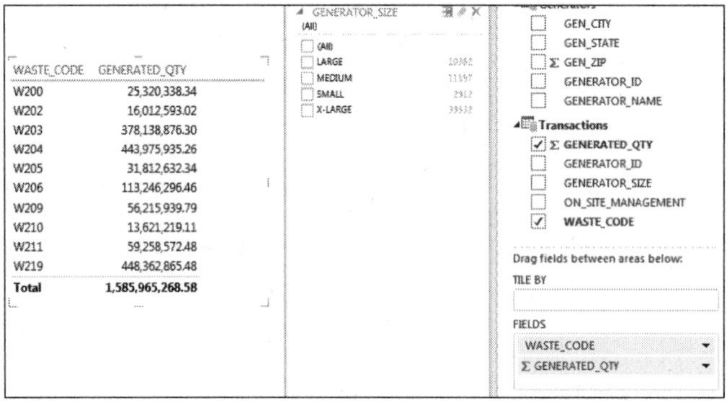

Figure 17-22: Use the field list to drag data fields to the FIELDS drop zone, resulting in a table on the canvas.

Creating and working with Power View charts

All data in Power View starts off as a table, as shown in Figure 17-22. Again, dragging fields to the FIELDS drop zone creates these tables. After you have a data table on the canvas, you can transform it into a chart by clicking it, selecting the Design tab, and choosing a chart type. Figure 17-23 demonstrates the selection of a Clustered Bar chart.

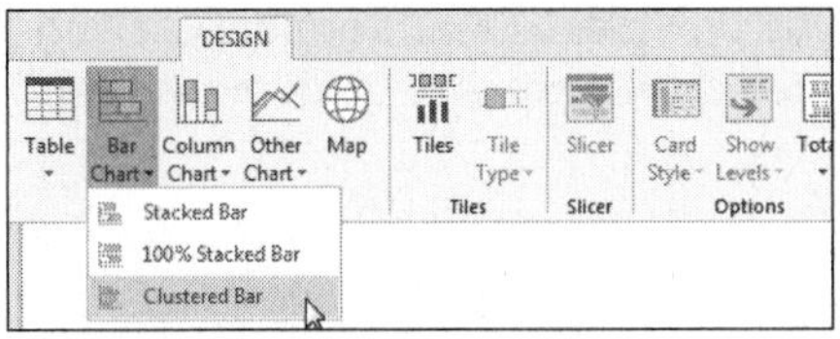

Figure 17-23: Transform data tables in the canvas by selecting the table and choosing a chart type on the Design tab.

In Figure 17-24, note that after the data is converted to a chart, new drop zones appear in the field list. These new drop zones are used to configure to the look and utility of the chart.

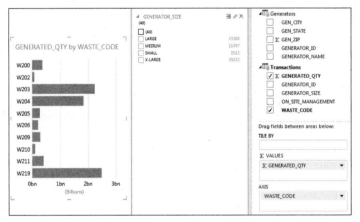

Figure 17-24: When your table is transformed into a chart, new drop zones appear in the field list.

When you click a Power View chart, a context menu appears above the chart. With this menu, you can sort the chart series, filter the chart, and expand/collapse the chart to full screen (see Figure 17-25).

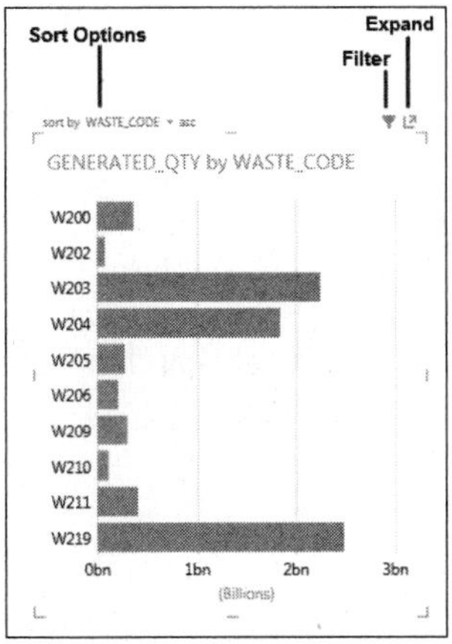

Figure 17-25: Clicking a Power View chart activates a context menu for that chart.

When you select a chart in the Power View canvas, the filter pane provides a CHART option. Clicking that link allows you to see and apply custom filters to the selected chart. Figure 17-26 demonstrates filtering by the Generated_Qty field using a nifty slider.

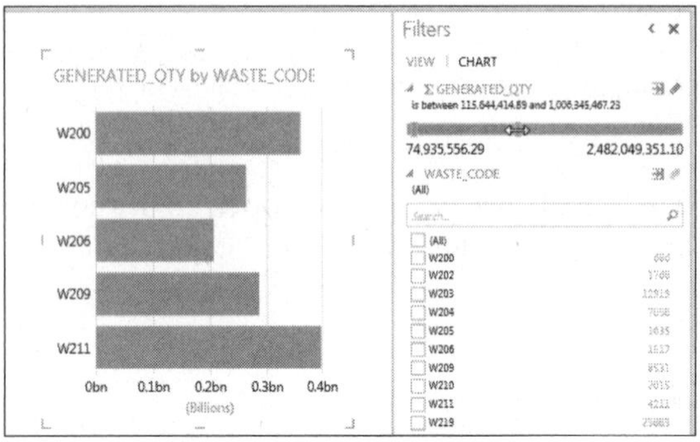

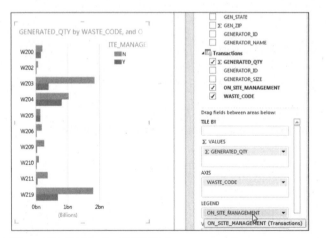

Figure 17-26: You can use the filter pane to apply chart-specific custom filters.

You can slice your chart series by dragging a new data field into the LEGEND drop zone. In the example shown in Figure 17-27, the On_Site_Management field is placed in the LEGEND drop zone; as a result, the original chart is sliced by the data items in the newly placed field.

Figure 17-27: Use the LEGEND drop zone to slice your chart series.

Alternatively, you can use the VERTICAL MULTIPLES or the HORIZONTAL MULTIPLES drop zone to turn your original chart into a panel of charts. Figure 17-28 illustrates how your original chart has been replicated to show a separate chart for each data item in the On_Site_Management field.

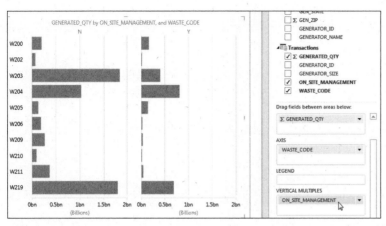

Figure 17-28: Dragging the On_Site_Management field to the VERTICAL MULTIPLES drop zone creates a panel of charts.

Another neat trick is to add drill-down capabilities to a chart, which you do by dragging a new data field to the AXIS drop zone. Figure 17-29 shows the Gen_State field dragged to the AXIS drop zone. Initially, it will seem as though nothing happened. But in the background, Power View has layered in the newly selected field as a new category axis.

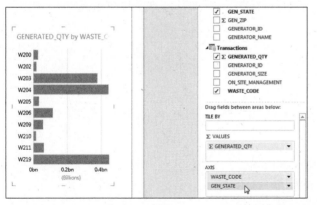

Figure 17-29: Dragging a new field to the AXIS drop zone creates a drill-down effect.

After you add your new field to the AXIS drop zone, double-click any data point in the chart. The chart automatically drills into the next level. In this case, because you added Gen_State (generator state) to the AXIS drop zone, the chart drills down to show the breakdown by state for the data point that you double-clicked (see Figure 17-30). Note the arrow icon that allows you to drill back up.

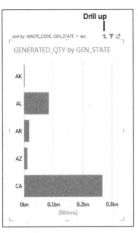

Figure 17-30: With multiple data fields in the AXIS drop zone, you can drill into the next layer of data and then drill back up using the arrow icon.

You can create as many charts as you want to your Power View canvas. And as mentioned at the beginning of this chapter, all components in the Power View window are automatically linked so that they respond to one another. For instance, Figure 17-31 shows two charts on the same Power View canvas. Clicking the pie slice for Arkansas (AR) dynamically recolors the bar chart so that it highlights the portion of the bar that's made up by the Arkansas data — all without any extra work from you!

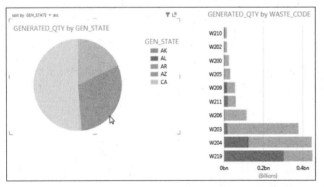

Figure 17-31: Charts in a Power View dashboard automatically respond to one another.

Visualizing data in a Power View map

The latest buzz in the dashboarding world is location intelligence: visualizing data on a map to quickly compare performance by location. Since Excel 2003, we haven't had a good way of building map-based visualizations without convoluted workarounds. Excel 2013 changes all that with the introduction of Power View maps.

To add a map to your Power View dashboard, follow these steps:

1. Start with some location data in the Power View canvas.

   Figure 17-32 illustrates some Zip Code data from your Data Model.

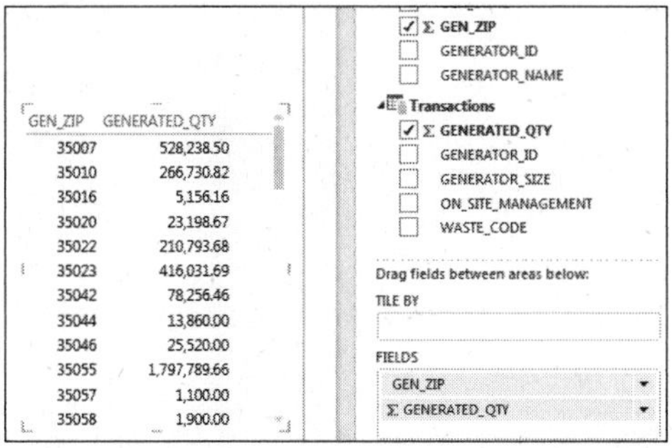

Figure 17-32: Add location data to your Power View canvas.

2. With your location data selected, click the Design tab.

3. Choose Map from the Switch Visualization group (see Figure 17-33).

Figure 17-33: Choose to show the data as a Map.

After a moment of gyrating, Excel generates a Bing map.

As you can see in Figure 17-34, the initial map will often be fairly useless. How Excel decides to initially handle your data is a bit of a black box and varies from data set to data set. You typically need to make some adjustments to get the view you need.

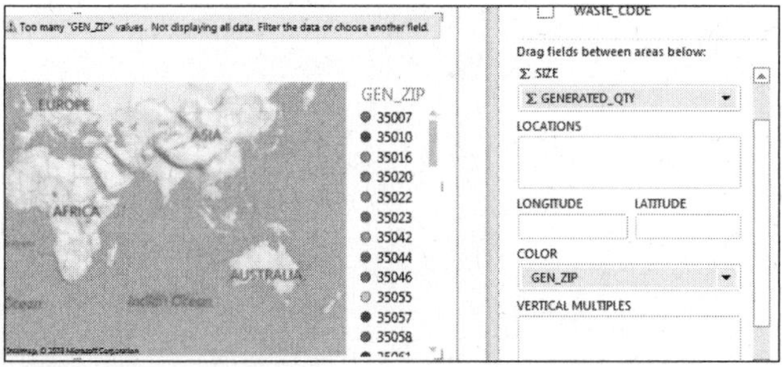

Figure 17-34: Excel generates an initial Bing map.

After you create your map, try moving your location field to the different drop zones in the field list. The drop zone you end up on will vary according to how you want to see your data. In this example (see Figure 17-35), moving the Gen_Zip field to the LOCATIONS drop zone fixes your map and creates a nice view of your data by Zip Code.

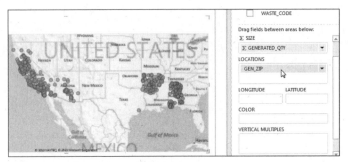

Figure 17-35: Moving the Gen_Zip field to the LOCATIONS drop zone creates a nice view by Zip Code.

You have limited control over how your map looks. With your map selected, you can go to the Layout tab and customize the map title, legend, data labels, and map background (see Figure 17-36).

Figure 17-36: The Layout tab provides a limited set of options for customizing your Power View map.

The map is fully interactive, allowing you to zoom and move around using the buttons at the top-right corner of the map, as illustrated in Figure 17-37.

Figure 17-37: You can interactively zoom and move around on the map.

You can use the COLOR drop zone to add an extra layer of analysis to your map. For instance, Figure 17-38 demonstrates how adding the Waste_Code field to the COLOR drop zone differentiates each plotted location based on waste code.

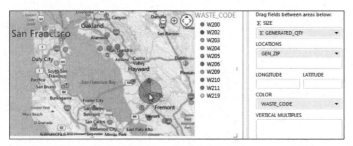

Figure 17-38: Add data fields to the COLOR drop zone to add an extra layer of analysis to your map.

Changing the look of your Power View dashboard

Excel grants you limited control over how your Power View dashboard looks. On the Power View tab (see Figure 17-39), you see a Themes group. Here you can set the overall font, background, and theme for your Power View dashboard.

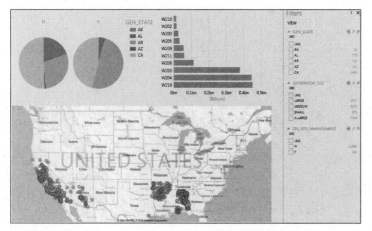

Figure 17-39: Changing the theme of your Power View dashboard.

The theme you choose changes the colors for your charts, backgrounds, filters, tables, and plotted map points. The Bing map will not change to match your theme. Figure 17-40 illustrates a full Power View dashboard with an applied theme.

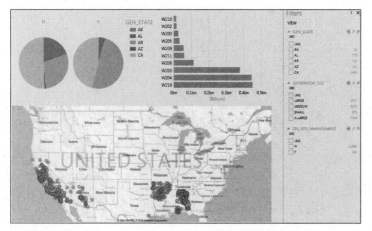

Figure 17-40: A completed Power View dashboard with an applied theme.

Working with the Outside World

Integrating External Data into Excel Reporting

In This Chapter

- Importing data from Microsoft Access databases

- Importing data from SQL Server databases

- Running SQL Server stored procedures from Excel

- Creating dynamic connections with VBA

- Creating a data model with multiple external data tables

Wouldn't it be wonderful if all the data you come across could be neatly packed into one easy-to-use Excel table? The reality is that sometimes the data you need comes from external data sources. External data is exactly what it sounds like: data that isn't located in the Excel workbook in which you're operating. Some examples of external data sources are text files, Access tables, SQL Server tables, and even other Excel workbooks.

This chapter explores some efficient ways to get external data into your Excel data models. Before jumping in, however, your humble authors want to throw out one disclaimer. There are numerous ways to get data into Excel. In fact, between the functionality found in the UI and the VBA/code techniques, there are too many techniques to focus on in one chapter. So for this endeavor, you focus on a handful of techniques that can be implemented in most situations and don't come with a lot of pitfalls and gotchas.

Importing Data from Microsoft Access

Microsoft Access is used in many organizations to manage a series of tables that interact with each other, such as a Customers table, an Orders table, and an Invoices table. Managing data in Access provides the benefit of a relational database where you can ensure data integrity, prevent redundancy, and easily generate datasets via queries.

Excel 2013 offers several methods for getting your Access data into your Excel data model.

The drag-and-drop method

For simplicity, you just can't beat the drag-and-drop method. You can simultaneously open an empty Excel workbook and an Access database from which you want to import a table or query. When both are open, resize each application's window so that they're both fully visible on your screen.

Hover the mouse over the Access table or query you want to copy into Excel. Now click the table and drag it to the blank worksheet in Excel (see Figure 18-1).

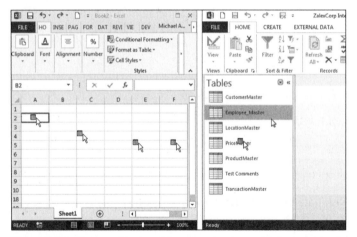

Figure 18-1: Copy an Access table using the drag-and-drop method.

The drag-and-drop method comes in handy when you're doing a quick one-time analysis where you need a specific set of data in Excel. However, the method isn't so useful for the following:

➤ You expect this step to occur routinely, as a part of a repeated analysis or report.

➤ You expect the users of your Excel presentation to get or update the data via this method.

➤ It's not possible or convenient for you to simply open up Access every time you need the information.

In the preceding scenarios, it's much better to use another technique.

The Microsoft Access Export Wizard

Access has an Export Wizard, and it's relatively simple to use.

1. With your Access database open, click your target table or query to select it.

2. On the External Data tab on the Ribbon, select the Excel icon under the Export group.

   The wizard that you see in Figure 18-2 opens.

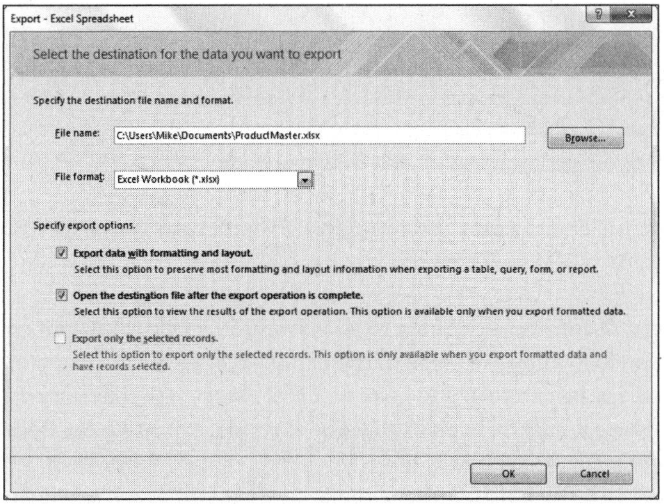

Figure 18-2: Export data to Excel using the Excel Export Wizard.

As you can see in Figure 18-2, you can specify certain options in the Excel Export Wizard. You can specify the file location, the file type, and some format preservation options.

3. In the Excel Export Wizard, select Export Data with Formatting and Layout; then select Open the Destination File After the Export Operation Is Complete.

4. Click OK.

   Excel opens to show you the exported data.

In Access, the last page in the Export Wizard (Figure 18-3) asks if you want to save your export steps. Saving your export steps can be useful if you expect to frequently send that particular query or table to Excel.

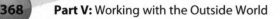

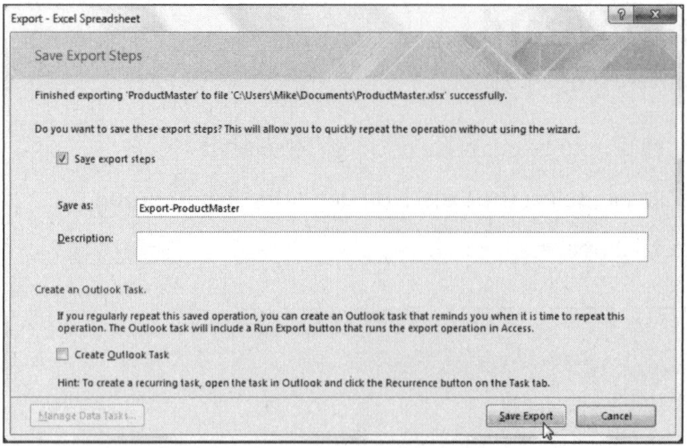

Figure 18-3: Use the Save Export Steps option if you export your data frequently.

The benefit to this method is that, unlike dragging and dropping, the ability to save export steps allows you to automate your exports by using Access macros.

> **Caution**
>
> You may export your Access table or query to an existing Excel file instead of creating a new file. But note the following: the name of the exported object is the name of the table or query in Access. Be careful if you have an Excel object with that same name in your workbook because it may be overwritten. For example, exporting the PriceMaster table to an Excel worksheet that already has a worksheet named PriceMaster will cause the worksheet to be overwritten. Also, make sure the workbook to which you're exporting is closed. If you try to export to an open workbook, you will likely receive an error in Access.

The Get External Data icon

The option to pull data from Access has been available in Excel for many versions; it was just buried several layers deep in somewhat cryptic menu titles. This made getting Access data into Excel seem like a mysterious and tenuous proposition for many Excel analysts. With the introduction of the Ribbon in Excel 2007, Microsoft put the Get External Data group of commands right on the Ribbon under the Data tab, making it easier to import data from Access and other external data sources.

Excel allows you to establish an updatable data connection between Excel and Access. To see the power of this technique, walk through these steps:

1. Open a new Excel workbook and select the Data tab on the Ribbon.

2. In the Get External Data group, select the From Access icon.

The Select Data Source dialog box opens (see Figure 18-4). If the database from which you want to import data is local, browse to the file's location and select it. If your target Access database resides on a network drive at another location, you will need to have the proper authorization and access in order to select it.

3. Navigate to your sample database and click Open.

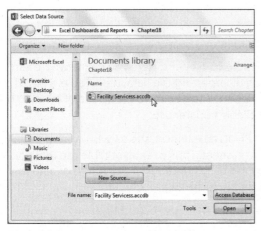

Figure 18-4: Choose your source database.

In some environments, a series of Data Link Properties dialog boxes open, asking for credentials (that is, username and password). Most Access databases don't require logon credentials, but if your database does require a username and password, type them in the Data Link Properties dialog box.

4. Click OK.

The Select Table dialog box (see Figure 18-5) opens. This dialog box lists all the available tables and queries in the selected database.

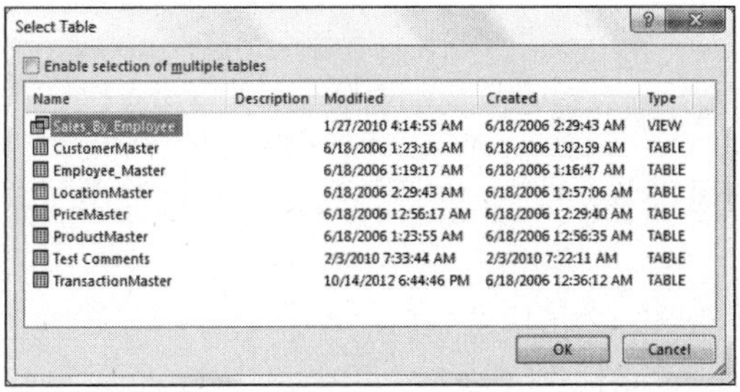

Figure 18-5: Select the Access object you want to import.

Tip

The Select Table dialog box in Figure 18-5 contains a column called Type. There are two types of Access objects you can work with: View and Table. View indicates that the dataset listed is an Access query, and Table indicates that the dataset is an Access table. In this example, Sales_By_Employee is actually an Access query. This means that you import the results of the query. This is true interaction at work; Access does all the back-end data management and aggregation, and Excel handles the analysis and presentation!

5. Select your target table or query and click OK.

   The Import Data dialog box shown in Figure 18-6 opens. Here you define where and how to import the table. You have the option of importing the data into a Table, a PivotTable Report, or a PivotChart and PivotTable Report. You also have the option of creating only the connection, making the connection available for later use.

   Note that if you choose PivotChart and PivotTable Report, the data is saved to a pivot cache without writing the actual data to the worksheet. Thus your pivot table can function as normal without you having to import potentially hundreds of thousands of data rows twice (once for the pivot cache and once for the spreadsheet).

6. Select Table as the output view and define cell A1 as the output location (see Figure 18-6).

7. Click OK.

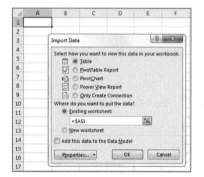

Figure 18-6: Choosing how and where to view your Access data.

Your reward for all the work will be a table similar to the one shown in Figure 18-7, which contains the imported data from your Access database.

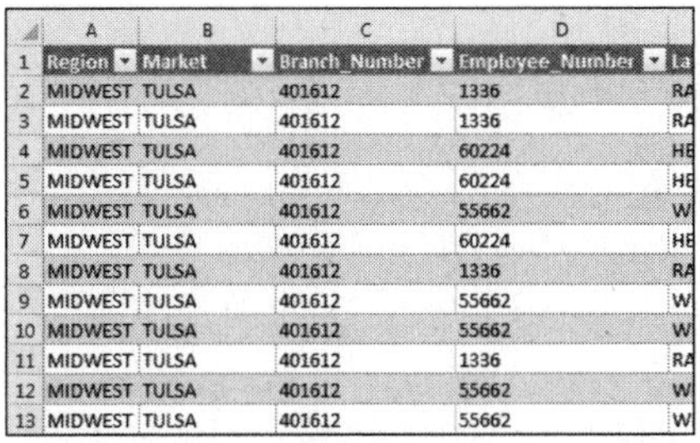

	A	B	C	D	
1	Region	Market	Branch_Number	Employee_Number	La
2	MIDWEST	TULSA	401612	1336	RA
3	MIDWEST	TULSA	401612	1336	RA
4	MIDWEST	TULSA	401612	60224	HE
5	MIDWEST	TULSA	401612	60224	HE
6	MIDWEST	TULSA	401612	55662	W
7	MIDWEST	TULSA	401612	60224	HE
8	MIDWEST	TULSA	401612	1336	RA
9	MIDWEST	TULSA	401612	55662	W
10	MIDWEST	TULSA	401612	55662	W
11	MIDWEST	TULSA	401612	1336	RA
12	MIDWEST	TULSA	401612	55662	W
13	MIDWEST	TULSA	401612	55662	W

Figure 18-7: Your imported Access data.

The incredibly powerful thing about importing data this way is that it's refreshable. That's right. If you import data from Access using this technique, Excel creates a table that you can update by right-clicking it and selecting Refresh from the pop-up menu, as shown in Figure 18-8. When you update your imported data, Excel reconnects to your Access database and imports the data again. As long as a connection to your database is available, you can refresh with a mere click of the mouse.

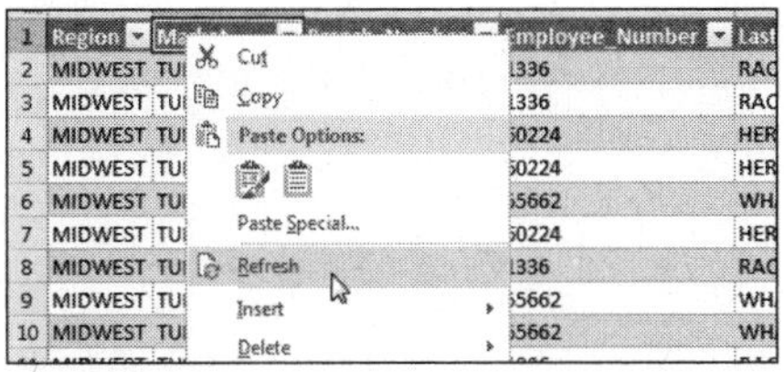

Figure 18-8: As long as a connection to your database is available, you can update your table with the latest data.

Again, a major advantage to using the Get External Data group is that you can establish a refreshable data connection between Excel and Access. In most cases, you can set up the connection one time and then just update the data connection when needed. You can even record an Excel macro to update the data on some trigger or event, which is ideal for automating the transfer of data from Access.

▶ Managing external data properties

When you import external data into a table, you can control a few adjustable properties via the Properties dialog box. You can get to the properties of a particular external data table by clicking the target table and selecting the Properties icon under the Data tab.

This activates the External Data Properties dialog box. The properties found in this dialog box allow you to further customize your query tables to suit your needs. Take a moment to familiarize yourself with some of the useful options in this dialog box.

- **Include Row Numbers:** This property is deselected by default. Selecting this property creates a dummy column that contains row numbers. The first column of your dataset will be this row number column upon refresh.

- **Adjust Column Width:** This property is selected by default, telling Excel to adjust the column widths each time the data is refreshed. Deselecting this option will cause the column widths to remain the same.

- **Preserve Column/Sort/Filter/Layout:** If this property is selected, the order of the columns and rows of the Excel range remains unchanged. This way, you can rearrange and sort the columns and rows of the external data in your worksheet without worrying about blowing away your formatting each time you refresh. Deselecting this property will make the Excel range look like the query.

- **Preserve Cell Formatting:** This property is selected by default, telling Excel to keep the applied cell formatting when you refresh.

- **Insert Cells for New Data, Delete Unused Cells:** This is the default setting for data range changes. When data rows decrease, you may have errors in adjacent cells that reference your external range. The cells these formulas referenced are deleted, so you will get an #VALUE error in your formula cells.

- **Insert Entire Rows for New Data, Clear Unused Cells:** When the unused cells are cleared instead of deleted, the formula may no longer return an error. Instead, it continues to reference cells from the original range — even though some of them are blank now. This could still give you erroneous results.

- **Overwrite Cells for New Data, Clear Unused Cells:** The third option should be the same as option two when rows decrease as unused cells are cleared.

Importing Data from SQL Server

In the spirit of collaboration, Excel 2013 vastly improves your ability to connect to transactional databases such as SQL Server. With the connection functionality found in Excel, creating a connected table or pivot table from SQL Server data is as easy as ever.

Start on the Data tab and follow these steps:

1. Select From Other Sources to see the drop-down menu shown Figure 18-9; then select From SQL Server.

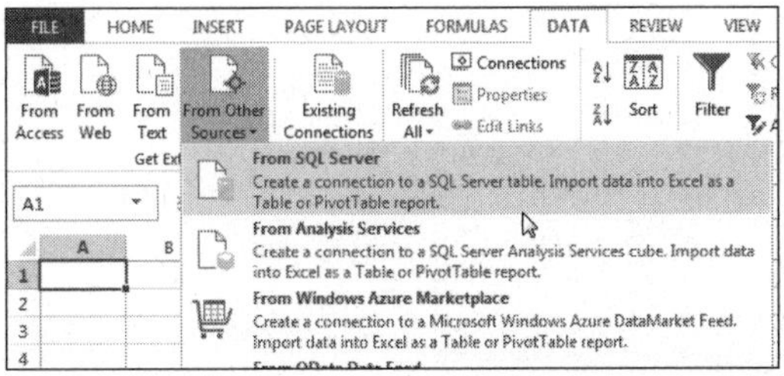

Figure 18-9: Select From SQL Server from the drop-down menu.

Selecting this option activates the Data Connection Wizard, as shown in Figure 18-10. The idea here is that you configure your connection settings so Excel can establish a link to the server.

2. Provide Excel with some authentication information.

As you can see in Figure 18-10, you enter the name of your server as well as your username and password. If you're typically authenticated via Windows authentication, you simply select the Use Windows Authentication option.

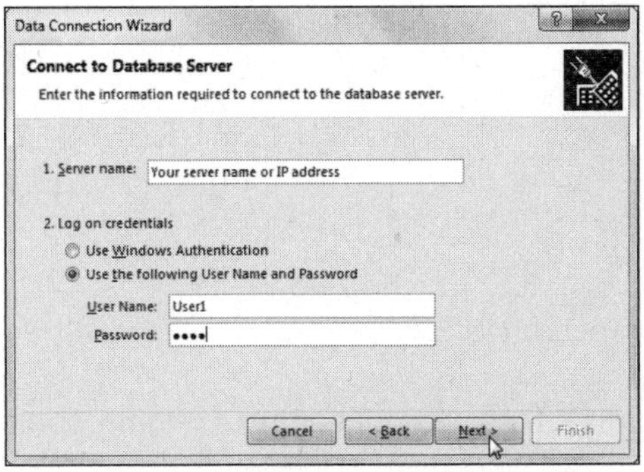

Figure 18-10: Enter your authentication information and click Next.

3. Select the database with which you're working from a drop-down menu containing all available databases on the specified server.

As you can see in Figure 18-11, a database called AdventureWorks2012 is selected in the drop-down box. Selecting this database causes all the tables and views in it be shown in the list of objects below the drop-down menu.

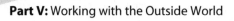

4. Choose the table or view you want to analyze and then click Next.

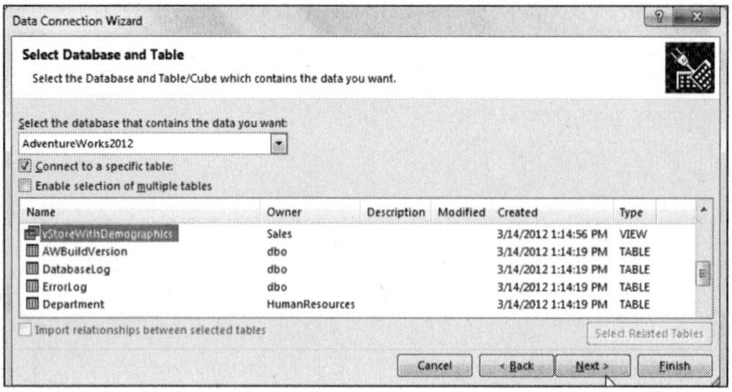

Figure 18-11: Specify your database and then choose the table or view you want to analyze.

5. In the screen that appears in the wizard, enter descriptive information about the connection you've just created (see Figure 18-12).

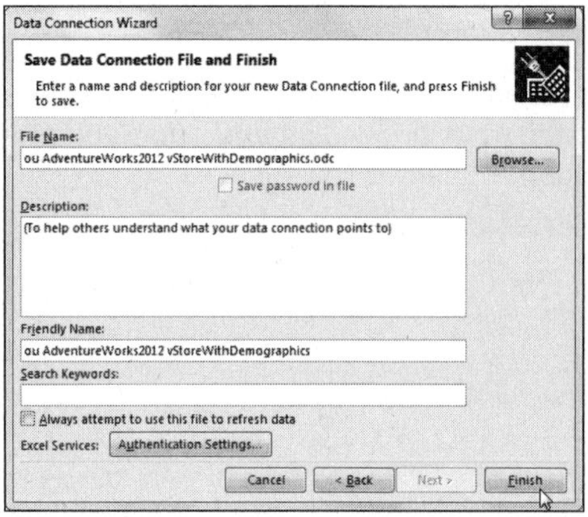

Figure 18-12: Enter descriptive information for your connection.

This information is optional. If you bypass this screen without editing anything, your connection will work fine.

The fields that you use most often are

- **File Name:** In the File Name input box, you can change the filename of the `.odc` (Office Data Connection) file generated to store the configuration information for the link you just created.

- **Save Password in File:** Under the File Name input box, you have the option of saving the password for your external data in the file itself (via the Save Password in File check box). Placing a check in this check box actually enters your password in the file. This password is not encrypted, so anyone interested enough could potentially get the password for your data source simply by viewing your file with a text editor.

- **Description:** In the Description field, you can enter a plain description of what this particular data connection does.

- **Friendly Name:** The Friendly Name field allows you to specify your own name for the external source. You typically enter a name that is descriptive and easy to read.

6. When you are satisfied with your descriptive edits, click Finish to finalize your connection settings.

   You immediately see the Import Data dialog box where you can choose how to import your data. As you can see in Figure 18-13, this data will be shown in a pivot table.

Figure 18-13: Choosing how and where to view your SQL Server data.

When the connection is finalized, we can start building our pivot table.

Passing Your Own SQL Statements to External Databases

If you're proficient at writing your own SQL queries, you can use the connection properties to write your own SQL statements. This gives you more control over the data you pull into your Excel model and allows you to perform advanced actions like running SQL Server stored procedures.

Manually editing SQL statements

After you're connected to your external database, you can go to the Data tab on the Ribbon and select Connections. This activates the Workbook Connections dialog box illustrated in Figure 18-14. Choose the connection you want to edit and then click the Properties button.

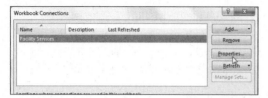

Figure 18-14: Click the Properties button for the connection you want to change.

The Connection Properties dialog box opens. Here you can click the Definition tab (see Figure 18-15). Change the Command Type property to SQL and then enter your SQL statement.

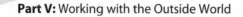

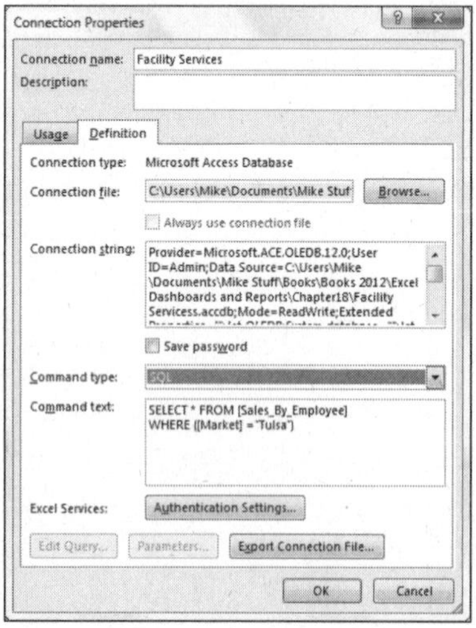

Figure 18-15: On the Definition tab, select the SQL command type and enter your SQL Statement.

Running stored procedures from Excel

If you're connecting to an SQL Server database, you can use your own SQL Statement to fire a stored procedure. The SQL Statement demonstrated in Figure 18-16 executes the SP_MarketSummary stored procedure.

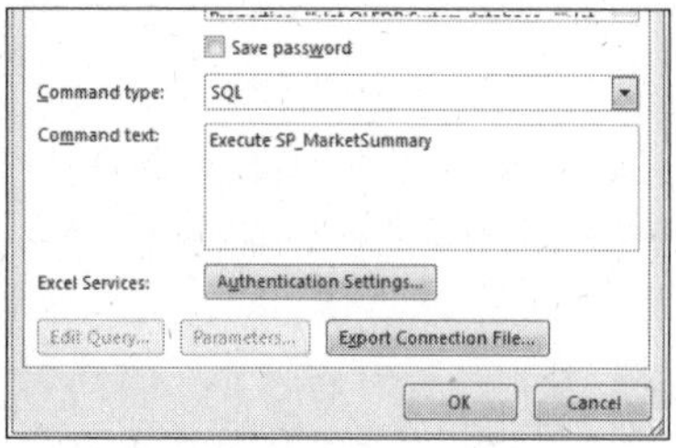

Figure 18-16: Running an SQL Server stored procedure from Excel.

Some stored procedures require parameters (criteria inputs) to run successfully. If your stored procedures require parameters to run, you can simply include them in your SQL statement. Figure 18-17 illustrates this by running a stored procedure with two parameters:

➤ A parameter that passes the required market name

➤ A parameter that passes the required quarter

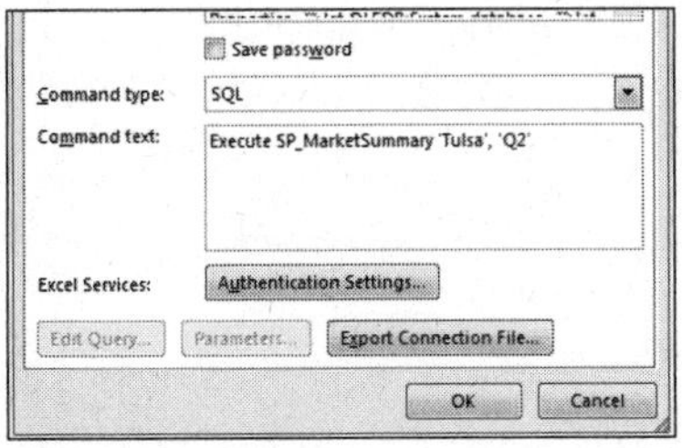

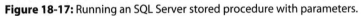

Figure 18-17: Running an SQL Server stored procedure with parameters.

Using VBA to create dynamic connections

You may have noticed that the preceding examples hard-coded the criteria in the SQL statements. For example, in Figure 18-17, Tulsa is specified directly in the SQL statement WHERE clause. This obviously would cause the data being returned to always be data for Tulsa.

But what if you want to select a market and have the SQL statement dynamically change to respond to your selection? Well, you can use a bit of VBA to change the SQL statement on the fly. Follow these steps:

1. Designate a cell in your worksheet that will catch the dynamic selection for your criteria.

   For example, in Figure 18-18, cell C2 is where users can select a market. You typically give users a way to select criteria with either a combo box or a Data Validation list.

Figure 18-18: Designate a cell to trap the criteria selection.

2. Click the Connections button on the Data tab to open the Workbook Connections dialog box.

   Note the name for the connection you want to dynamically change. In Figure 18-19, the connection name is Facility Services.

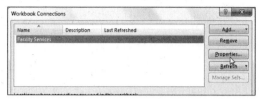

Figure 18-19: Take note of the connection name (Facility Services, in this example).

3. Close the Workbook Connections dialog box and press Alt+F11 on your keyboard.

   The Visual Basic Editor opens.

4. Select Insert→Module from menu bar.

5. Enter the following code in the newly created module:

```
Sub RefreshQuery()

ActiveWorkbook.Connections("Facility Services").OLEDBConnection.
  CommandText = _
"SELECT * FROM [Sales_By_Employee] WHERE [Market] = '" & _
  Range("C2").Value & "'"

ActiveWorkbook.Connections("Facility Services").Refresh

End Sub
```

This code creates a new macro called RefreshQuery. The RefreshQuery macro points to the correct connection (Facility Services) and specifies the Command Text for that connection.

The Command Text is essentially the SQL Statement you want the connection to run when triggered. In this example, the Command Text selects from the [Sales_By_Employee] table and sets the criteria for the [Market] field to the value in cell C2. The code then refreshes the Facility Services connection.

6. Close the Visual Basic Editor and place a new command button on your worksheet.

   To do so, click on the Developer tab, select the Insert drop-down button, and add a Button Form control.

Cross-Ref

Refer to Chapter 12 for a detailed overview on using Form controls in your dashboards and reports.

7. Assign the newly created RefreshQuery macro to the command button, as shown in Figure 18-20.

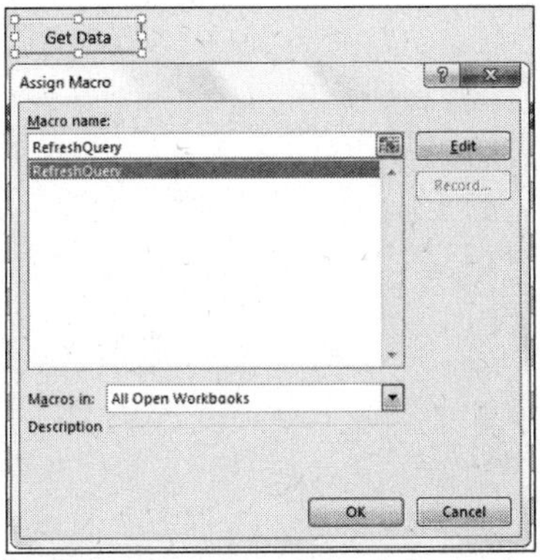

Figure 18-20: Add a command button and assign your newly created RefreshQuery macro.

If all goes smoothly, you'll have a nifty mechanism that allows dynamic extraction of data from your external database based on the criteria you specified (see Figure 18-21).

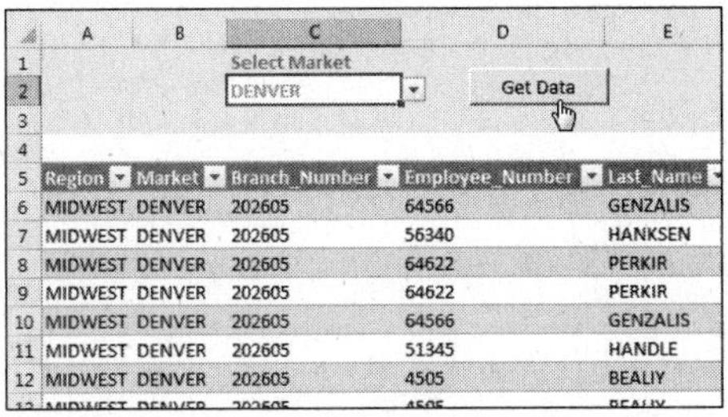

Region	Market	Branch_Number	Employee_Number	Last_Name
MIDWEST	DENVER	202605	64566	GENZALIS
MIDWEST	DENVER	202605	56340	HANKSEN
MIDWEST	DENVER	202605	64622	PERKIR
MIDWEST	DENVER	202605	64622	PERKIR
MIDWEST	DENVER	202605	64566	GENZALIS
MIDWEST	DENVER	202605	51345	HANDLE
MIDWEST	DENVER	202605	4505	BEALIY

Figure 18-21: You now have an easy-to-use mechanism to pull external data for a specified market.

Sharing Your Work with the Outside World

In This Chapter

- Controlling access to your dashboards and reports
- Displaying your Excel dashboards in PowerPoint
- Saving your dashboards and reports to a PDF file
- Saving your dashboards to the web

The focus of this chapter is preparing your dashboard for life outside your PC. Here, we discuss the various methods of protecting your work from accidental and purposeful meddling and discover how you can distribute your dashboards via PowerPoint and PDF files.

Securing Your Dashboards and Reports

Before distributing any Excel-based work, always consider protecting your file by using the security capabilities native to Excel. Although none of Excel's protection methods is hacker-proof, they do serve to protect the formulas, data structures, and other objects that make your dashboard tick.

Securing access to the entire workbook

Perhaps the best way to protect your Excel file is to use Excel's protection options for file sharing. These options enable you to apply security at the workbook level, requiring a password to view or make changes to the file. This method is by far the easiest to apply and manage because there's no need to protect each worksheet one at a time. You can apply a blanket protection to guard against unauthorized access and edits. Take a moment to review the file-sharing options, which are as follows:

➤ Forcing read-only access to a file until a password is given

➤ Requiring a password to open an Excel file

➤ Removing workbook-level protection

The next few sections discuss these options in detail.

Permitting read-only access unless a password is given

You can force your workbook to go into read-only mode until the user types the password. This way, you can keep your file safe from unauthorized changes yet still allow authorized users to edit the file.

Here are the steps to force read-only mode:

1. With your file open, click the File tab.

2. To open the Save As dialog box, select Save As and then double-click the Computer icon.

3. In the Save As dialog box, click the Tools button and select General Options (see Figure 19-1).

   The General Options dialog box appears.

4. Type an appropriate password in the Password to Modify input box (see Figure 19-2) and click OK.

5. Excel asks you to reenter your password, so reenter your chosen password.

6. Save your file to a new name.

   At this point, your file is password protected from unauthorized changes. If you were to open your file, you'd see something similar to Figure 19-3. Failing to type the correct password causes the file to go into read-only mode.

File name:	Book1.xlsx	
Save as type:	Excel Workbook (*.xlsx)	
Authors: Mike Alexander		Tags: Add a tag
	Save Thumbnail	

ide Folders   Tools ▾   Save   Cancel
                Map Network Drive...
                Web Options...
                General Options...
                Compress Pictures...

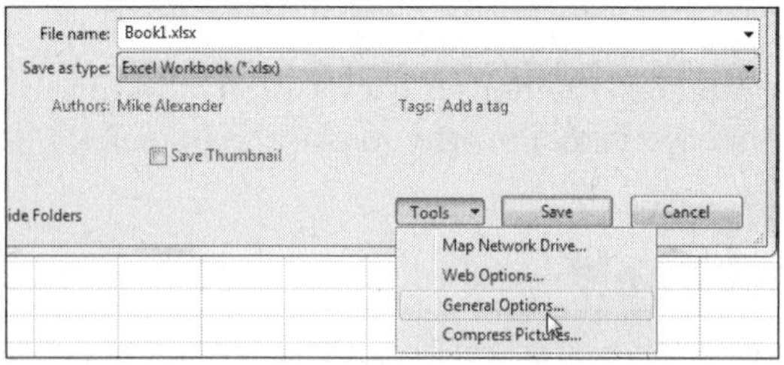

Figure 19-1: The File Sharing options are well hidden away in the Save As dialog box under General Options.

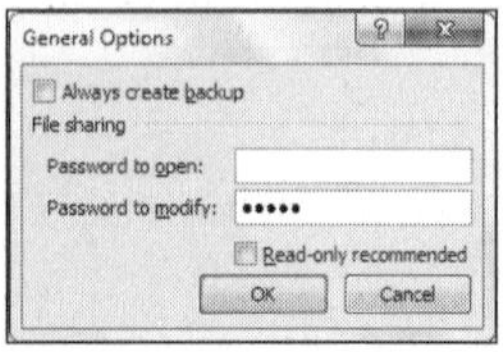

General Options
☐ Always create backup
File sharing
Password to open:
Password to modify: •••••
☐ Read-only recommended
OK   Cancel

Figure 19-2: Type the password needed to modify the file.

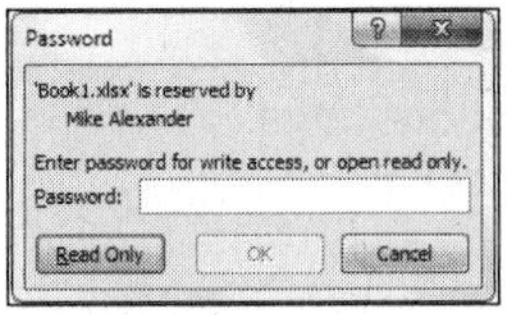

Figure 19-3: A password is now needed to make changes to the file.

Tip

Note that Excel passwords are case-sensitive, so make sure Caps Lock on your keyboard is in the off position when entering your password.

Requiring a password to open an Excel file

You may have instances where your Excel dashboards are so sensitive only certain users are authorized to see them. In these cases, you can require your workbook to receive a password to open it. Here are the steps to set up a password for the file:

1. With your file open, click the File tab.

2. To open the Save As dialog box, select Save As and then double-click the Computer icon.

3. In the Save As dialog box, click the Tools button and select General Options (refer to Figure 19-1).

   The General Options dialog box opens.

4. Type an appropriate password in the Password to Open text box (as shown in Figure 19-4) and click OK.

5. Excel asks you to reenter your password.

6. Save your file to a new name.

   At this point, your file is password protected from unauthorized viewing.

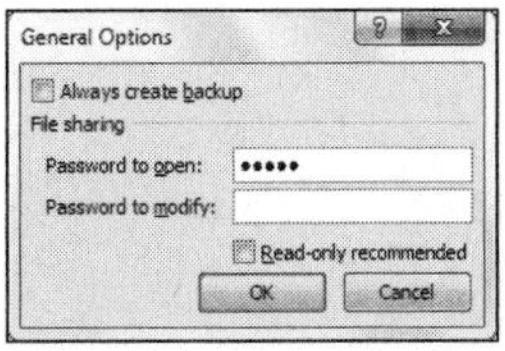

Figure 19-4: Type the password needed to modify the file.

Removing workbook-level protection

Removing workbook-level protection is as easy as clearing the passwords from the General Options dialog box. Here's how you do it:

1. With your file open, click the File tab.

2. To open the Save As dialog box, select Save As.

3. In the Save As dialog box, click the Tools button and select General Options (refer to Figure 19-1).

   The General Options dialog box opens.

4. Clear the Password to Open input box as well as the Password to Modify input box and click OK.

5. Save your file.

Tip

When you select the Read-Only Recommended check box in the General Options dialog box (refer to Figure 19-4), you get a cute but useless message recommending read-only access upon opening the file. This message is only a recommendation and doesn't prevent anyone from opening the file as read/write.

Limiting access to specific worksheet ranges

You may find that you need to lock specific worksheet ranges, preventing users from taking certain actions. For example, you may not want users to break your data model by inserting or deleting columns and rows. You can prevent this by locking those columns and rows.

Unlocking editable ranges

By default, all cells in a worksheet are set to be locked when you apply worksheet-level protection. The cells on that worksheet can't be altered in any way. That being said, you may find you need certain cells or ranges to be editable even in a locked state, like the example shown in Figure 19-5.

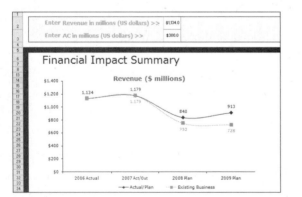

Figure 19-5: Though this sheet is protected, users can enter 2006 data into the input cells provided.

Before you protect your worksheet, you can unlock the cell or range of cells that you want users to be able to edit. (The next section shows you how to protect your entire worksheet.) Here's how to do it:

1. Select the cells you need to unlock.

2. Right-click and select Format Cells.

3. On the Protection tab, as shown in Figure 19-6, deselect the Locked check box.

4. Click OK to apply the change.

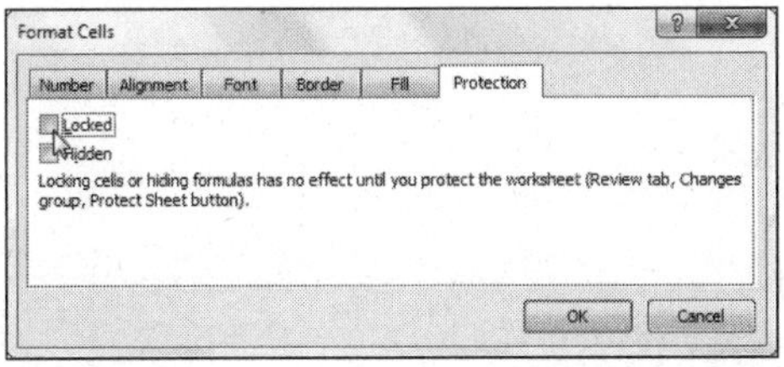

Figure 19-6: To ensure that a cell remains unlocked when the worksheet is protected, deselect the Locked check box.

Applying worksheet protection

After you've selectively unlocked the necessary cells, you can begin to apply worksheet protection. Just follow these steps:

1. To open the Protect Sheet dialog box, click the Protect Sheet icon on the Review tab of the Ribbon (see Figure 19-7).

2. Type a password in the text box (see Figure 19-8) and then click OK.

   This is the password that removes worksheet protection. Note that because you can apply and remove worksheet protection without a password, specifying one is optional.

3. In the list box (see Figure 19-8), select which elements users can change after you protect the worksheet.

   When a check box is cleared for a particular action, Excel prevents users from taking that action.

4. If you provided a password, reenter the password.

5. Click OK to apply the worksheet protection.

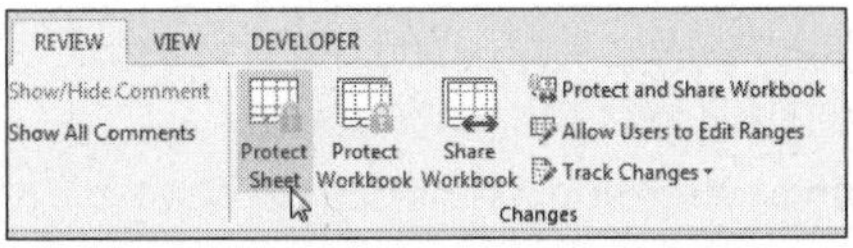

Figure 19-7: Select Protect Sheet in the Review tab.

Figure 19-8: Specify a password that removes worksheet protection.

▶ Protect sheet elements and actions

Take a moment to familiarize yourself with the some of the other actions you can limit when protecting a worksheet (refer to Figure 19-8). They are as follows:

- **Select Locked Cells:** Allows or prevents the selection of locked cells.

- **Select Unlocked Cells:** Allows or prevents the selection of unlocked cells.

- **Format Cells:** Allows or prevents the formatting of cells.

- **Format Columns:** Allows or prevents the use of column formatting commands, including changing column width or hiding columns.

- **Format Rows:** Allows or prevents the use of row formatting commands, including changing row height or hiding rows.

- **Insert Columns:** Allows or prevents the inserting of columns.

- **Insert Rows:** Allows or prevents the inserting of rows.

- **Insert Hyperlinks:** Allows or prevents the inserting of hyperlinks.

- **Delete Columns:** Allows or prevents the deleting of columns. Note that if Delete Columns is protected and Insert Columns is not protected, you can technically insert columns you can't delete.

- **Delete Rows:** Allows or prevents the deleting of rows. Note that if Delete Rows is protected and Insert Rows is not protected, you can technically insert columns you can't delete.

- **Sort:** Allows or prevents the use of Sort commands. Note that this doesn't apply to locked ranges. Users can't sort ranges that contain locked cells on a protected worksheet, regardless of this setting.

- **Use AutoFilter:** Allows or prevents use of Excel's AutoFilter functionality. Users can't create or remove AutoFiltered ranges on a protected worksheet, regardless of this setting.

- **Use PivotTable Reports:** Allows or prevents the modifying, refreshing, or formatting pivot tables found on the protected sheet.

- **Edit Objects:** Allows or prevents the formatting and altering of shapes, charts, text boxes, controls, or other graphics objects.

- **Edit Scenarios:** Allows or prevents the viewing of scenarios.

Removing worksheet protection

Just follow these steps to remove any worksheet protection you may have applied:

1. Click the Unprotect Sheet icon on the Review tab.

2. If you specified a password while protecting the worksheet, Excel asks you for that password (see Figure 19-9). Type the password and click OK to immediately remove protection.

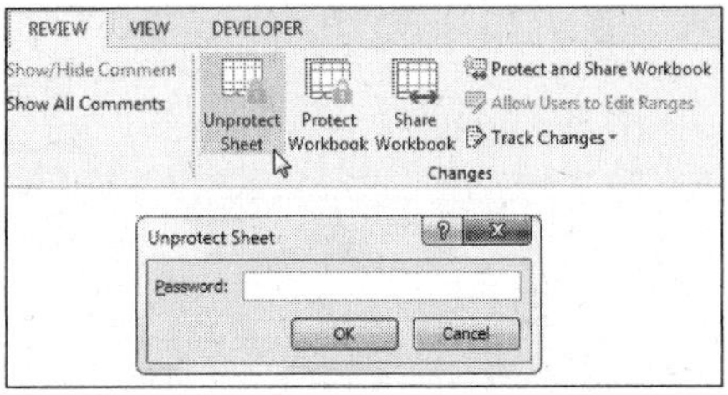

Figure 19-9: The Unprotect Sheet icon removes worksheet protection.

Protecting the workbook structure

If you look under the Review tab in the Ribbon, you see the Protect Workbook icon next to the Protect Sheet icon. Protecting the workbook enables you to prevent users from taking any action that affects the structure of your workbook, such as adding/deleting worksheets, hiding/unhiding worksheets, and naming or moving worksheets. Just follow these steps to protect a workbook:

1. To open the Protect Structure and Windows dialog box, click the Protect Workbook icon on the Review tab of the Ribbon, as shown in Figure 19-10.

2. Choose which elements you want to protect: workbook structure, windows, or both. When a check box is cleared for a particular action, Excel prevents users from taking that action.

3. If you provided a password, reenter the password.

4. Click OK to apply the worksheet protection.

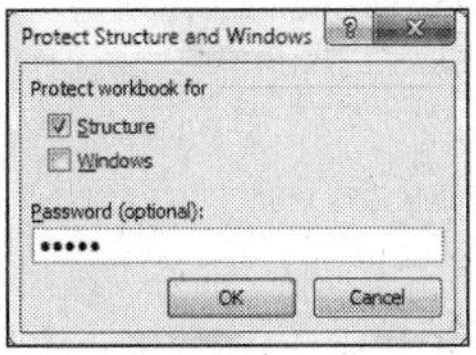

Figure 19-10: The Protect Structure and Windows dialog box.

Selecting Structure prevents users from doing the following:

➤ Viewing worksheets that you've hidden

➤ Moving, deleting, hiding, or changing the names of worksheets

➤ Inserting new worksheets or chart sheets

➤ Moving or copying worksheets to another workbook

➤ Displaying the source data for a cell in a pivot table Values area or displaying pivot table Filter pages on separate worksheets

➤ Creating a scenario summary report

➤ Using an Analysis ToolPak utility that requires results to be placed on a new worksheet

➤ Recording new macros

Choosing Windows prevents users from changing, moving, or sizing the workbook windows while the workbook is opened.

Linking Your Excel Dashboards to PowerPoint

You may find that your organization heavily favors PowerPoint presentations for periodic updates. Several methods exist for linking your Excel dashboards to a PowerPoint presentation. For current purposes, we focus on the method that is most conducive to presenting frequently updated dashboards and reports in PowerPoint — creating a *dynamic link*. A dynamic link allows your PowerPoint presentation to automatically pick up changes that you make to data in your Excel worksheet.

Tip

This technique of linking Excel charts to PowerPoint is ideal if you aren't proficient at building charts in PowerPoint. Build the chart in Excel and then create a link for the chart in PowerPoint.

Creating the link between Excel and PowerPoint

When you create a link to a range in Excel, PowerPoint stores the location information to your source field and then displays a representation of the linked data. The net effect is that when the data in your source file changes, PowerPoint updates its representation of the data to reflect the changes.

On the Web

You can find the example Chapter 19 Samples.xlsx file for this chapter on this book's companion website at `www.wiley.com/go/exceldr`.

To test this concept of linking to an Excel range, follow these steps:

1. Open the Chapter 19 Samples.xlsx file.

2. Click the chart to select it and press Ctrl+C on your keyboard to copy the chart.

3. Open a new PowerPoint presentation and place your cursor at the location that you want to display the linked table.

4. On the Home tab in PowerPoint, choose Paste➜Paste Special, as shown in Figure 19-11.

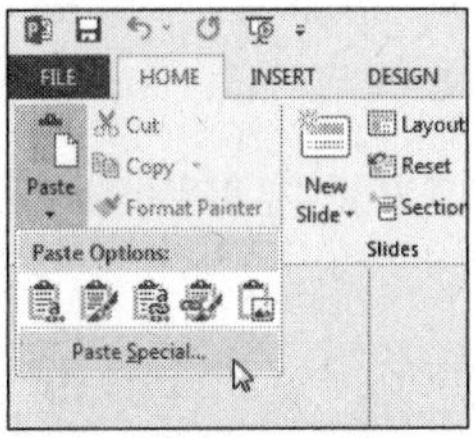

Figure 19-11: Select Paste Special from the Home tab in PowerPoint.

The Paste Special dialog box appears (see Figure 19-12).

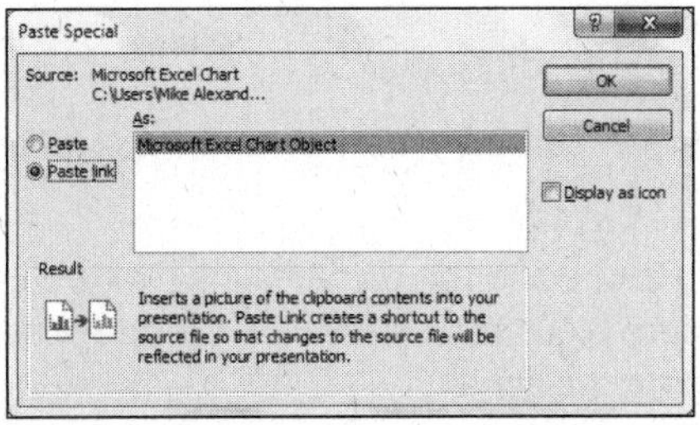

Figure 19-12: Be sure to select Paste Link and set the link as an Excel Chart Object.

5. Select the Paste Link radio button and choose Microsoft Excel Chart Object from the list of document types.

6. Click OK to apply the link.

Your chart on your PowerPoint presentation now links back to your Excel worksheet (see Figure 19-13).

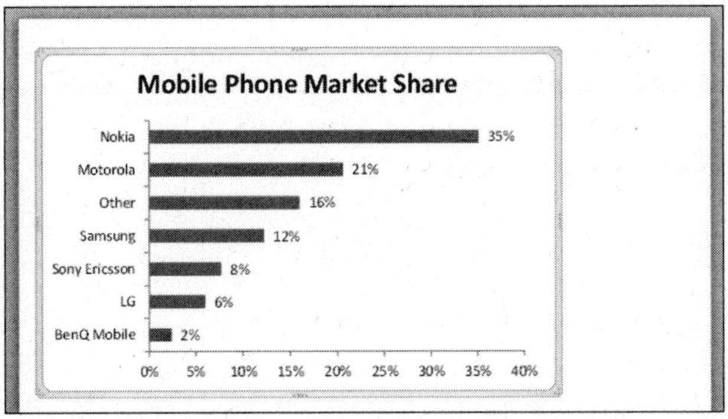

Figure 19-13: Your Excel chart is now linked into your new PowerPoint presentation.

Tip

If you're copying multiple charts, select the range of cells that contains the charts and press Ctrl+C to copy. This way, you're copying everything in that range of cells — charts and all.

Manually updating links to capture updates

The nifty thing about dynamic links is that they can be updated, enabling you to capture any new data in your Excel worksheets without re-creating the links. To see how this works, follow these steps:

1. Go back to your Excel file (from the example in the previous section) and change the values for Samsung and Nokia, as shown in Figure 19-14.

   Note the chart has changed.

2. Return to PowerPoint, right-click the chart link in your presentation and choose Update Link, as demonstrated in Figure 19-15.

   You see that your linked chart automatically captures the changes.

3. Save and close both your Excel file and your PowerPoint presentation and then open only your newly created PowerPoint presentation.

   Now you see the message shown in Figure 19-16. Clicking the Update Links button updates all links in the PowerPoint presentation. Each time you open any PowerPoint presentation with links, it asks you whether you want to update the links.

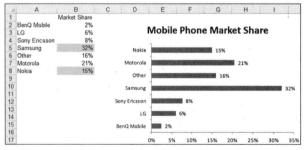

Figure 19-14: With a linked chart, you can make changes to the raw data without worrying about re-exporting the data into PowerPoint.

Figure 19-15: You can manually update links.

Figure 19-16: PowerPoint, by default, asks if you want to update all links in the presentation.

Automatically updating links

Having PowerPoint ask you whether you want to update the links each and every time you open your presentation quickly gets annoying. You can avoid this message by specifying that PowerPoint automatically updates your dynamic links upon opening the presentation file. Here's how:

1. In PowerPoint, click the File tab to get to the Backstage View.

2. In the Info Pane, go to the lower-right corner of the screen and select Edit Links to Files, as shown in Figure 19-17.

   The Links dialog box opens (see Figure 19-18).

3. Click each of your links and select the Automatic radio button.

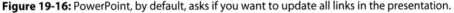

Figure 19-17: Open the dialog box to manage your links.

Figure 19-18: Setting the selected links to update automatically.

When your links are set to update automatically, PowerPoint automatically synchronizes with your Excel worksheet file and ensures that all your updates are displayed.

> **Tip**
>
> **To select multiple links in the Links dialog box, press the Ctrl key on your keyboard while you select your links.**

Distributing Your Dashboards via a PDF

Starting with Excel 2010, Microsoft has made it possible to convert your Excel worksheets to a PDF document. A PDF is the standard document-sharing format developed by Adobe.

Although it may not seem intuitive to distribute your dashboards with PDF files, some distinct advantages make PDF an attractive distribution tool.

➤ There are many advantages to publishing a Balanced Scorecard in PDF.

➤ Distributing your reports and dashboards as a PDF file allows you to share your final product without sharing all the formulas and back-end plumbing that comes with the workbook.

➤ Dashboards display in PDF files with full fidelity, meaning they display consistently on any computer and screen resolution.

➤ PDF files can be used to produce high-quality prints.

➤ Anyone using the free Adobe Reader can post comments and sticky notes on the distributed PDF files.

➤ Unlike Excel Security, the security in a PDF is generally better, allowing for multiple levels of security, including public-key encryption and certificates.

To convert your workbook to a PDF, follow these simple steps:

1. Click the File tab and then choose the Export command.

2. In the Export pane, select Create PDF/XPS Document (see Figure 19-19).

3. The Publish as PDF or XPS dialog box opens. Click the Options button, as demonstrated in Figure 19-20.

4. In the Options dialog box (illustrated in Figure 19-21), you can specify what you want to print. You have the option of printing the entire workbook, specific pages, or a range that you've selected.

5. Click OK to confirm your selections.

6. Click Save.

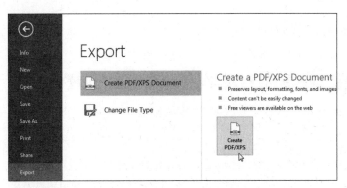

Figure 19-19: In Excel 2013, you can natively save as PDF.

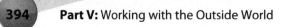

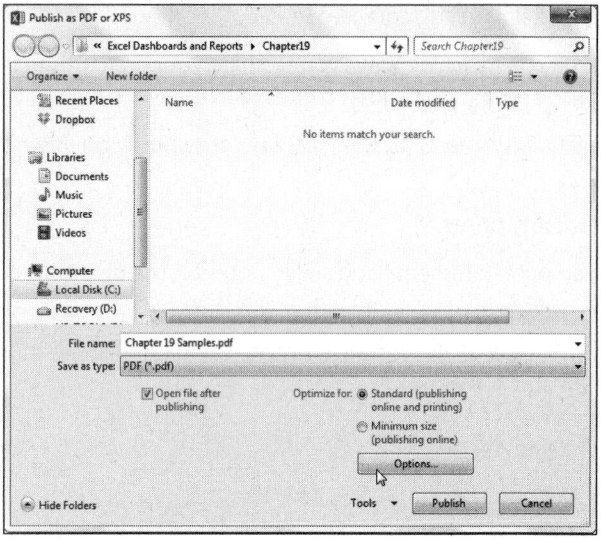

Figure 19-20: Select a location for your PDF; then click the Options button.

Figure 19-21: Excel allows you to define what gets sent to PDF.

Distributing Your Dashboards to SkyDrive

SkyDrive is Microsoft's answer to Google Spreadsheets. You can think of it as a Microsoft Office platform in the cloud, allowing you to save, view, and edit your Office documents on the web.

When you publish your Excel dashboards or reports to SkyDrive, you can

➤ View and edit your workbooks from any browser, even if the computer you're using doesn't have Excel installed.

➤ Provide a platform where two or more people can collaborate on and edit the same Excel file at the same time.

➤ Share only specific sheets from your workbook by hiding sheets you don't want the public to see. When a sheet in a published workbook is hidden, the browser doesn't even recognize its existence, so there is no way for the sheet to be unhidden or hacked into.

➤ Offer up web-based interactive reports and dashboards that can be sorted and filtered.

To publish a workbook to SkyDrive, follow these steps:

1. Click the File tab on the Ribbon, click the Save As command, and choose SkyDrive, as demonstrated in Figure 19-22.

    The SkyDrive pane allows you to sign in to your SkyDrive account.

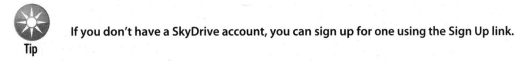

Tip   **If you don't have a SkyDrive account, you can sign up for one using the Sign Up link.**

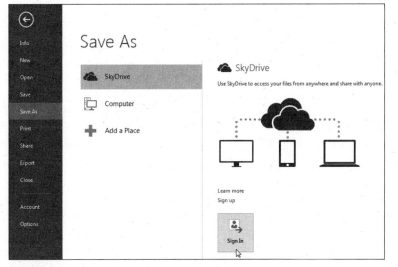

Figure 19-22: Go to the SkyDrive pane.

2. Sign in to your SkyDrive account.

    After signing in, the Save As dialog box in Figure 19-23 appears.

3. Click Browser View Options to select which components of your workbook will be viewable to the public.

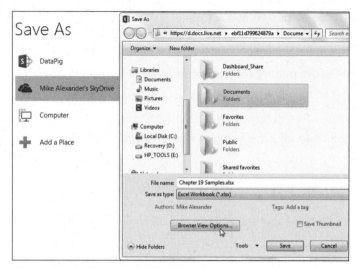

Figure 19-23: Click Browser View Options.

The Browser View Options dialog box allows you to control what the public is able to see and manipulate in your workbook.

4. Click the Show tab (illustrated in Figure 19-24).

Here, you can check and uncheck the Sheets and other Excel objects. Removing the check next to any sheet or object prevents it from being viewable through the browser. Again, this is a fantastic way to share your dashboard interfaces without exposing the back-end calculations and data model.

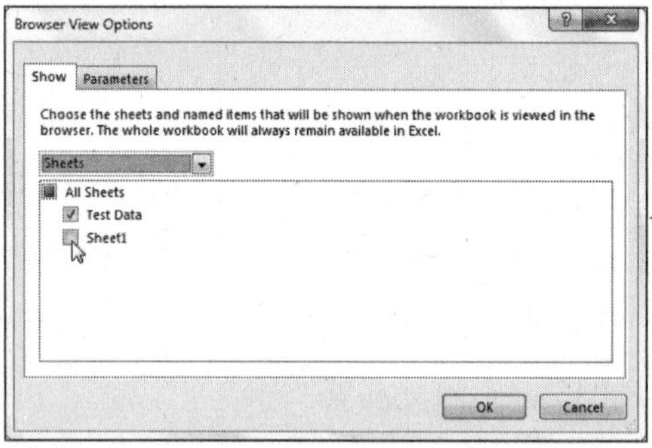

Figure 19-24: You have full control over which sheets and objects are available to the public when publishing to the web.

5. After you confirm your browser view options, save the file into your Documents folder.

At this point, you can sign in to Live.com and navigate to your SkyDrive documents to see your newly published file.

There are several ways to share your newly published workbook:

➤ Copy the web link from the browser address bar and e-mail that to your cohorts.

➤ Click the File tab in the web version of your file, choose Share (as shown in Figure 19-25), and then click the Share with People command to send an e-mail to anyone you specify.

➤ Use the Embed command on the same Share pane to generate HTML code to embed your workbook into a web page or blog.

Figure 19-25: Sharing options in an Excel web document.

Limitations when publishing to the web

It's important to understand that workbooks that run on the web are running in an Excel Web App that is quite different from the Excel client application you have on your PC. The Excel Web App has limitations on the features it can render in the web browser. Some limitations exist because of security issues, whereas others exist simply because Microsoft hasn't had time to evolve the Excel Web App to include the broad set of features that come with standard Excel.

In any case, the Excel Web App has some limitations:

➤ Data Validation doesn't work on the web. This feature is simply ignored when you publish your workbook to the web.

➤ No form of VBA, including macros, will run in the Excel Web App. Your VBA procedures simply will not transfer with the workbook.

➤ Worksheet protection will not work on the web. Instead, you will need to plan for and use the Browser View Options demonstrated earlier in Figure 19-23.

➤ Links to external workbooks will no longer work after publishing to the web.

➤ You can use any pivot tables with full fidelity on the web, but you cannot create any new pivot tables while your workbook is on the web. You will need to create pivot tables in the Excel client on your PC before publishing on the web.

Index

Symbols and Numerics

More great Excel guides from Mr. Spreadsheet!

Need to know more about Excel? John Walkenbach has it covered.